Citrix XenServer 6.0 Administration Essential Guide

Deploy and manage XenServer in your enterprise
to create, integrate, manage, and automate a virtual
datacenter quickly and easily

Daniele Tosatto

[PACKT] enterprise

PUBLISHING

professional expertise distilled

BIRMINGHAM - MUMBAI

Citrix XenServer 6.0 Administration Essential Guide

First published: June 2012

Production Reference: 1180612

Published by Packt Publishing Ltd.
Livery Place
35 Livery Street
Birmingham B3 2PB, UK.

ISBN 978-1-84968-616-7

www.packtpub.com

Cover Image by Mark Holland (MJH767@bham.ac.uk)

Credits

Author
Daniele Tosatto

Reviewers
Esther Barthel, M.Sc.
Ferdinand Feenstra
Juan Perez
Todd Pigram

Acquisition Editor
Rashmi Phadnis

Lead Technical Editor
Dayan Hyames

Technical Editors
Joyslita D'Souza
Veronica Fernandes

Project Coordinator
Sai Gamare

Proofreader
Katherine Tarr

Indexer
Rekha Nair

Graphics
Valentina D'silva
Manu Joseph

Production Coordinators
Aparna Bhagat
Prachali Bhiwandkar

Cover Work
Aparna Bhagat

About the Author

Daniele Tosatto is a highly experienced Senior Systems Engineer based in Venice, Italy. He is a Microsoft Certified IT Professional, Microsoft Certified Technology Specialist, Microsoft Certified Systems Engineer, and Citrix Certified Administrator and has been working in ICT since 2000 as a System Administrator. In 2008 he started working for one of the Italian Citrix Platinum Partners. He has delivered many IT projects based on Microsoft and Citrix technologies for enterprises located in Italy and Europe. He is focused on Active Directory, server virtualization, application virtualization, and delivery and IT infrastructure management. He maintains a blog at `http://www.danieletosatto.com`.

I'd like to thank my family, my girlfriend Valentina, and all the guys at Packt Publishing for the support and patience during the writing of my first book.

About the Reviewers

Esther Barthel, after finishing her Master of Science in Computer Science, started working as a Web Application Developer. With a very broad interest in IT technologies, she shifted her interests and broadened her technical knowledge with System, Database, and Network Administration consultancy. When she discovered Citrix MetaFrame XP, she found a product that combined server, application, and user technologies and allowed her to specialize in Server Based Computing solutions. Nowadays she works on different virtualization projects as a Citrix Architect and RES Software Specialist implementing and designing new Citrix and RES Software environments.

She likes to share her knowledge with the Citrix community by posting blogs on her own website http://www.virtues.it and by using her Twitter handle @virtues_it.

She was asked by her colleague Sjaak Laan to review his book *IT Infrastructure Architecture* (ISBN: 9781447881285) and by Packt Publishing to review *Citrix XenServer 6.0 Administration Essential Guide* (ISBN: 9781849686167)—a new way to share her knowledge with an even bigger community.

Ferdinand Feenstra is a Citrix Architect and senior specialist in Microsoft environments. He has experience in many complex environments with different customers in different functions.

His experience is categorized in building and designing of Citrix environments, implementations, migrations, projects, and advice.

He has a blog, named www.CitrixGuru.net and is located in the Netherlands.

Juan Perez has been in the IT field for 12 years. He has always strived to be a solution-based resource. Where a challenge is sometimes an obstacle for others, he sees it as an opportunity to make things happen, learn, and grow his skill set. His career began in technical support, working with software issues and helping end users get through their challenges via phone support. This is where he thrived and learned a lot about how to take problem situations and break them down to workable and successful experiences. This allowed him to work his way up to secondary level support where only the harder issues were escalated to him and his team. This also started him on training others and learning how to document and validate solutions to problems, a skill that has been used even now. His simplistic approach to problems is what he believes is the key to his success.

His career has not been like most in IT. He has worked for just a few companies, but in that time he has been able to learn a broad range of technologies. He worked for Decore-ative Specialties in the city of Monrovia, a family owned cabinet door manufacturer, which is one of the largest and most prominent companies in that industry. He started out as a PC Technician and worked his way up to Senior Network Administrator. Going from small day-to-day tasks to fully supporting, designing, and maintaining the company infrastructure. He learned from many talented people there who had years of experience—a great resource for a young up and coming IT professional.

He is currently working for Stearns Lending, a fast growing company that has put the challenge on the IT team to help them grow to a world class company. Stearns is fully equipped with Citrix Xenapp, XenDesktop, and XenServer. Since being introduced to Citrix, he has learned the basics, and moved on to completely managing multiple XenServer environments. He also moved virtual servers off from other Hypervisor platform to XenServer. His goal and interest is to be the best Citrix resource possible to Stearns and others. He is working on getting certified for Citrix and who knows, if the doors open, to work for Citrix and be a fully fledged Citrix Pro.

This is the first book that he has worked on. It was a great experience and he hopes to be able to contribute to, if not write a book himself one day.

I would like to thank Mrs. Sprague, my high school AP English teacher who encouraged me to write even when I didn't want to, my family and friends who encourage me to keep growing, and my wife and kids who inspire me. Thanks to Packt Publishing for giving me the opportunity to be a part of this book. I look forward to future works and someday publishing my own book.

Todd Pigram is currently a Solutions Architect for a system integrator, designing solutions around Citrix and other technologies based on customer needs. Prior to this, he was an Enterprise Systems Engineer at a large healthcare organization in the Cleveland area. At this organization, he was part of a team of five engineers that designed, implemented, and supported two Citrix farms totaling 400 servers with 16,000 CCUs. He has been working with Citrix products since 1999.

www.PacktPub.com

Support files, eBooks, discount offers and more

You might want to visit www.PacktPub.com for support files and downloads related to your book.

Did you know that Packt offers eBook versions of every book published, with PDF and ePub files available? You can upgrade to the eBook version at www.PacktPub.com and as a print book customer, you are entitled to a discount on the eBook copy. Get in touch with us at service@packtpub.com for more details.

At www.PacktPub.com, you can also read a collection of free technical articles, sign up for a range of free newsletters and receive exclusive discounts and offers on Packt books and eBooks.

http://PacktLib.PacktPub.com

Do you need instant solutions to your IT questions? PacktLib is Packt's online digital book library. Here, you can access, read and search across Packt's entire library of books.

Why Subscribe?

- Fully searchable across every book published by Packt
- Copy and paste, print and bookmark content
- On demand and accessible via web browser

Free Access for Packt account holders

If you have an account with Packt at www.PacktPub.com, you can use this to access PacktLib today and view nine entirely free books. Simply use your login credentials for immediate access.

Instant Updates on New Packt Books

Get notified! Find out when new books are published by following @PacktEnterprise on Twitter, or the *Packt Enterprise* Facebook page.

Table of Contents

Preface

Citrix XenServer is a complete, managed server virtualization platform built on the Xen hypervisor. You can use XenServer for virtualizing Microsoft Windows and Linux servers easily and efficiently.

XenServer is the enterprise-ready, cloud-proven virtualization platform that contains all the capabilities required to create and manage a virtual infrastructure.

XenServer is available in four different editions. Starting from the free edition, you will be able to set up a virtual infrastructure with live migration, snapshots, and management features.

This book will take you through deploying XenServer in your enterprise and teach you how to create and maintain your datacenter. The book contains practical examples covering typical tasks related to virtual infrastructure management.

The book starts by providing an overview of the XenServer platform and Resource Pool concepts. Next, it covers user authentication and storage repositories management. The book then dives deep into topics such as virtual machine creation and management, management of XenServer memory and networking, snapshots, and High Availability features and monitoring.

What this book covers

Chapter 1, Introducing XenServer Resource Pools, begins with an overview of the XenServer history, Resources Pools overview, and requirements. Also, we will run through the process of Resource Pool creation and management.

Chapter 2, Managing User Authentication, covers user authentication management and Microsoft Active Directory integration. In this chapter, we will discover the Role Based Access Control feature and how to use it to assign roles and permissions to users in order to define different levels of administration.

Chapter 3, Managing Storage Repositories, introduces you to storage management. This chapter covers concepts regarding storage technologies and protocols and emphasizes the process of creating different types of storage repositories in XenServer.

Chapter 4, Creating Virtual Machines, gives you an overview of the virtual machine creation process. It also shows you how to install XenServer Tools, a set of paravirtualized drivers used to provide the best performance in your virtual machines.

Chapter 5, Managing Virtual Machines, covers typical tasks related to virtual machine management. We will see how to import and export a virtual machine, clone existing virtual machines, and create a custom template for deploying pre-configured servers. Also, the chapter highlights the process for converting a physical machine to a virtual machine.

Chapter 6, Managing XenServer and Virtual Machine Memory, enables the user to configure XenServer memory in order to provide best performance for virtual machines. The chapter also describes the Dynamic Memory Control feature and how to use this feature to dynamically allocate memory to virtual machines.

Chapter 7, Managing XenServer Networking, covers networking concepts and explains how to configure networking in XenServer. In the chapter, we will discover the Distributed vSwitch Controller that can be used to control the flow and performance of traffic sent to and from a virtual machine.

Chapter 8, Managing High Availability and Snapshots, shows how to configure the High Availability feature in order to ensure your virtual machines are always available and have an optimal level of service within a resource pool. In the chapter, you will discover the Snapshots feature that you can use to record a point-in-time state of a virtual machine, useful when you need to test an application update.

Chapter 9, Protecting and Monitoring XenServer, explains the aspects of backing up and monitoring a XenServer environment. The chapter also highlights the usage of VM Protection policies to have scheduled backups of virtual machines and introduces you to the Workload Balancing component, used for automating the virtual environment and monitoring performance.

Appendix A, Supported Guest Operating Systems and Virtual Machine Templates, gives you a quick reference of the supported guest operating systems and an overview of the virtual machine templates XenServer provides by default.

Appendix B, Applying Updates and Hotfixes, covers the process of installing updates and hotfixes on the XenServer virtual environment.

What you need for this book

You will need one of the following operating systems:

- Windows 7
- Windows XP
- Windows Vista
- Windows Server 2003
- Windows Server 2008
- Windows Server 2008 R2

You will need the following software:

- Citrix XenCenter 6.0
- Citrix XenServer 6.0
- Microsoft .NET Framework 3.5 (Required to run XenCenter)

For updated XenServer requirements, see the XenServer Installation Guide available at `http://support.citrix.com/article/CTX130421`.

Who this book is for

If you are new to or you have a basic understanding of XenServer and you want to embrace the virtualization world, this book is for you.

The book assumes that you have a basic understanding of XenServer administration, but you need not have working experience with XenServer.

IT Consultants who want to approach XenServer as a virtualization platform will also find this book useful.

Conventions

In this book, you will find a number of styles of text that distinguish between different kinds of information. Here are some examples of these styles, and an explanation of their meaning.

Code words in text are shown as follows: "Run the `xe pool-join` command on the new server to join the pool."

Any command-line input or output is written as follows:

```
xe host-disable uuid=<host_uuid>
xe host-evacuate uuid=<host_uuid>
```

New terms and **important words** are shown in bold. Words that you see on the screen, in menus or dialog boxes for example, appear in the text like this: "Enter your details in the activation form, and then click on **Submit**."

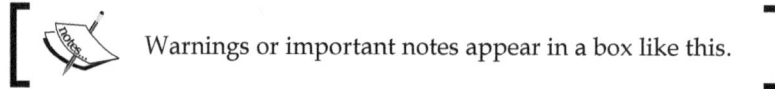

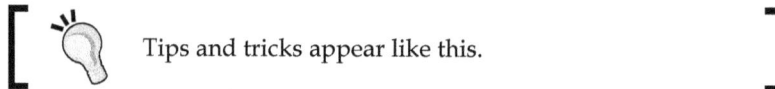

> Warnings or important notes appear in a box like this.

> Tips and tricks appear like this.

Reader feedback

Feedback from our readers is always welcome. Let us know what you think about this book — what you liked or may have disliked. Reader feedback is important for us to develop titles that you really get the most out of.

To send us general feedback, simply send an e-mail to feedback@packtpub.com, and mention the book title through the subject of your message.

If there is a topic that you have expertise in and you are interested in either writing or contributing to a book, see our author guide on www.packtpub.com/authors.

Customer support

Now that you are the proud owner of a Packt book, we have a number of things to help you to get the most from your purchase.

Downloading the example code

You can download the example code files for all Packt books you have purchased from your account at http://www.packtpub.com. If you purchased this book elsewhere, you can visit http://www.packtpub.com/support and register to have the files e-mailed directly to you.

Errata

Although we have taken every care to ensure the accuracy of our content, mistakes do happen. If you find a mistake in one of our books—maybe a mistake in the text or the code—we would be grateful if you would report this to us. By doing so, you can save other readers from frustration and help us improve subsequent versions of this book. If you find any errata, please report them by visiting http://www.packtpub. com/support, selecting your book, clicking on the **errata submission form** link, and entering the details of your errata. Once your errata are verified, your submission will be accepted and the errata will be uploaded to our website, or added to any list of existing errata, under the Errata section of that title.

Piracy

Piracy of copyright material on the Internet is an ongoing problem across all media. At Packt, we take the protection of our copyright and licenses very seriously. If you come across any illegal copies of our works, in any form, on the Internet, please provide us with the location address or website name immediately so that we can pursue a remedy.

Please contact us at copyright@packtpub.com with a link to the suspected pirated material.

We appreciate your help in protecting our authors, and our ability to bring you valuable content.

Questions

You can contact us at questions@packtpub.com if you are having a problem with any aspect of the book, and we will do our best to address it.

1
Introducing XenServer Resource Pools

Xen originated as a research project at the University of Cambridge, led by Ian Pratt, senior lecturer at Cambridge and founder of XenSource, Inc. The first public release of Xen occurred in 2003. Citrix Systems acquired XenSource, Inc in October 2007 and subsequently renamed XenSource's products under the Citrix brand "XenServer".

On 21 October 2009, Citrix further announced their, now commercial, applications of XenServer would be fully open source and made freely available to the public under the name Xen Cloud Platform (XCP).

Although Citrix acquired XenSource, Xen is developed and maintained by the community as free software, licensed under the GNU General Public License (GPLv2).

Citrix XenServer 6.0 is the last release of the Citrix server virtualization platform. The XenServer package contains all you need to create and manage a deployment of virtual x86 and x64 computers running on Xen®, the open source paravirtualizing hypervisor with near-native performance.

XenServer runs directly on server hardware without requiring an underlying operating system, which results in an efficient and scalable system. XenServer works by abstracting elements from the physical machine (such as hard drives, resources, and ports) and allocating them to the virtual machines running on it.

In Xen systems the hypervisor is the lowest and most privileged software layer. This layer supports one or more guest operating systems that are run on the physical CPUs. The first guest operating system, called in Xen terminology Control Domain (dom0) is executed automatically when the hypervisor boots and receives special management privileges and direct access to all physical hardware. The Control Domain is a secure privileged Virtual Machine that runs the XenServer management toolstack. Besides providing XenServer management functions, the Control Domain also runs the driver stack that provides user-created virtual machines access to physical devices.

A virtual machine (VM) is a computer composed entirely of software that can run its own operating system and applications as if it were a physical computer. A VM behaves exactly like a physical computer and contains its own virtual (software-based) CPU, RAM, hard disk, and network interface card (NIC). XenServer is available in four editions:

- **Citrix XenServer (Free)**: Proven virtualization platform that delivers uncompromised performance, scale, and flexibility at no cost

- **Citrix XenServer Advanced Edition**: Key high availability and advanced management tools that take virtual infrastructure to the next level

- **Citrix XenServer Enterprise Edition**: Essential integration and optimization capabilities for production deployments of virtual machines

- **Citrix XenServer Platinum Edition**: Advanced automation and cloud computing features for enterprise-wide virtual environments

You can find more information about features included in each edition at `http://www.citrix.com/English/ps2/products/subfeature.asp?contentID=2300456`.

> You can download XenServer `http://www.citrix.com/English/ss/downloads/results.asp?productID=683148`.

In this chapter we will cover the following topics:

- XenServer resource pool overview and requirements

- XenServer resource pool creation

- Creating an heterogeneous XenServer resource pool

- Designating a new Pool Master host

- Removing a XenServer Host from a resource pool

- Preparing a Pool of XenServer Hosts for Maintenance

- Licensing XenServer hosts

XenServer resource pool overview

A Citrix XenServer pool is a group of XenServer hosts and allows you to view multiple servers as a single resource, enabling flexible deployment of virtual machines based on the resource needs and business priorities.

A pool is comprised of multiple XenServer hosts bound together as a single managed entity. When combined with shared storage, virtual machines (VMs) can be started on any XenServer host in the pool that has sufficient available resources such as CPU or memory, and then dynamically moved between hosts while running, using the "XenMotion" feature with minimal downtime. If an individual XenServer host suffers a hardware failure, you can restart the failed VM(s) on another host in the same pool.

If the High Availability (HA) feature (only available to XenServer Advanced Edition or higher) is enabled, VMs are automatically moved to another host in the event of a host failure.

XenServer resource pool requirements

A pool always has at least one physical host, known as the "pool master", that provides a single point of contact for all of the servers in the pool, known as "slaves", managing communication to other members of the pool as necessary.

If the pool master is shut down or unavailable, you will not able to connect to the pool until the master is online again or until you nominate one of the other members as the new pool master for the pool. Virtual machines that are started at the time the pool master became unavailable continue running. Note that every member of a resource pool contains all the information necessary to take on the role of master, if you need to replace a pool master.

> If the pool's master fails, automatic master reselection will only take place if High Availability is enabled. You can learn about High Availability in *Chapter 8, Managing High Availability and Snapshots*.

A resource pool is a *homogeneous* aggregate of one or more XenServer hosts, up to a maximum of 16. What is the definition of homogeneous?

A XenServer pool is homogeneous when:

- The CPUs on the server joining the pool are the same (in terms of vendor, model, and features) as the CPUs on servers already in the pool

- The server joining the pool is running the same version of XenServer software, at the same patch level, as servers already in the pool

- When you join a host to a pool, remember also that XenServer will enforce additional constraints, in particular:
    - It is not a member of an existing resource pool
    - It has no shared storage configured
    - There are no running or suspended Virtual Machines on the XenServer host you are joining to the pool
    - There are no active operations on the VMs in progress such as restart or shutdown

- When you want to join a new host remember to check the following:
    - Clock of the host joining the pool is synchronized to the same time as the pool master (for example, by using NTP)
    - Its primary management interface is not bonded (you can configure this once the host has successfully joined the pool)
    - Its management IP address is static (either configured on the host itself or by using an appropriate configuration on your DHCP server)

> The requirement for a XenServer host to have a static IP address to be part of a resource pool also applies to servers providing shared NFS or iSCSI storage for the pool.

Why have we introduced the concept *homogeneous*? Because In XenServer 6.0, you can also create a *heterogeneous* pool. A pool is heterogeneous when you join disparate hosts together.

XenServer 6.0 makes it possible to create a heterogeneous pool by leveraging technologies in recent Intel (FlexMigration) and AMD (Extended Migration) CPUs that provide CPU "masking" or "leveling". These features allow a CPU to be configured to appear as providing a different make, model, or functionality than it actually does. CPU masking enables you to create pools of hosts with disparate CPUs and permits you to use the XenMotion feature safely.

Using XenServer to mask the CPU features of a new server, so that it will match the features of the existing servers in a pool, requires the following:

- The CPUs of the server joining the pool must be of the same vendor (that is, AMD, Intel) as the CPUs on servers already in the pool
- The CPUs of the server joining the pool must support either Intel FlexMigration or AMD Enhanced Migration

- The features of the older CPUs must be a subset of the features of the CPUs of the server joining the pool
- The server joining the pool is running the same version of the XenServer software, with the same hotfixes installed, as servers already in the pool

> Heterogeneous resource pool creation is only available to XenServer Advanced editions and above.

Creating a XenServer resource pool

After we have introduced the resource pool concept and requirements, we can start discussing how to create a resource pool in XenServer.

Resource pools can be created using either the XenCenter management console or the xe command-line interface (CLI). When you join a new host to a resource pool, the joining host synchronizes its local database with the pool-wide one, hosted and managed by the pool master, and inherits some settings from the pool:

- VM, local, and remote storage configuration is added to the pool-wide database.
- The joining host inherits existing shared storage repositories in the pool and appropriate PBD (Physical Block Devices) records are created, so that the new host can access existing shared storage automatically.
- Networking information is partially inherited by the joining host: The structural details of NICs, VLANs, and bonded interfaces are all inherited, but policy information is not. This policy information, which must be re-configured, includes:
  - The IP addresses of management NICs, which are preserved from the original configuration.
  - The location of the primary management interface, which remains the same as the original configuration. For example, if the other pool hosts have their primary management interfaces on a bonded interface, then the joining host must be explicitly migrated to the bond once it has joined.
  - Dedicated storage NICs, which must be re-assigned to the joining host from XenCenter or the CLI, and the PBDs re-plugged to route the traffic accordingly.

Concepts related to storage and networking will be discussed in *Chapter 2, Managing User Authentication*, and *Chapter 5, Managing Virtual Machines*.

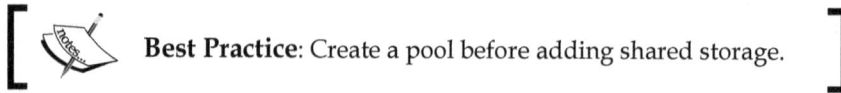

> **Best Practice**: Create a pool before adding shared storage.

Now, we are ready to create a XenServer resource pool. Two hosts will be part of this pool, xenserver1 and xenserver2.

Host xenserver1 is configured with IP address 192.168.0.1 and host xenserver2 is configured with IP address 192.168.0.2.

We will configure the resource pool using XenCenter and CLI.

Usually XenCenter is a faster and user-friendly method for doing this task, so we will create the resource pool using XenCenter first:

1. Start XenCenter:

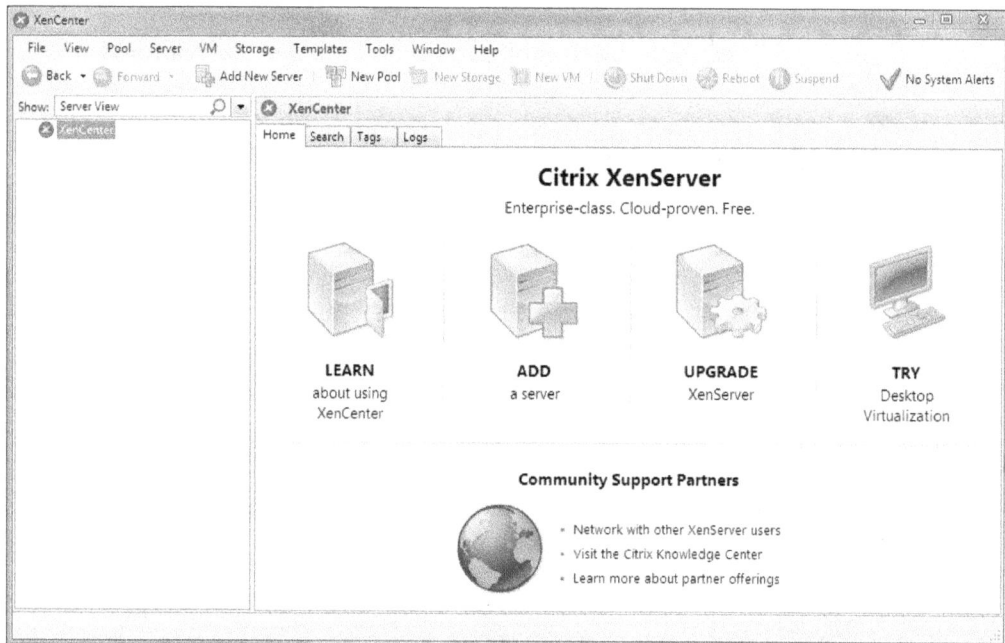

2. Click on **Server | Add** to add the xenserver1 host to the console.

3. Type the IP address of xenserver1 and password for the user root.

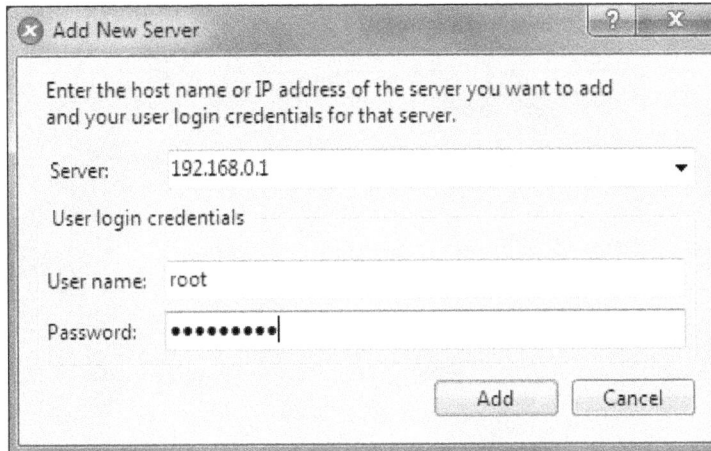

The first time you add a new host, the **Save and Restore Connection State** dialog box appears. This enables you to set your preferences for storing your host connection information and automatically restoring server connections.

4. Now, the xenserver1 host is visible on the XenCenter console:

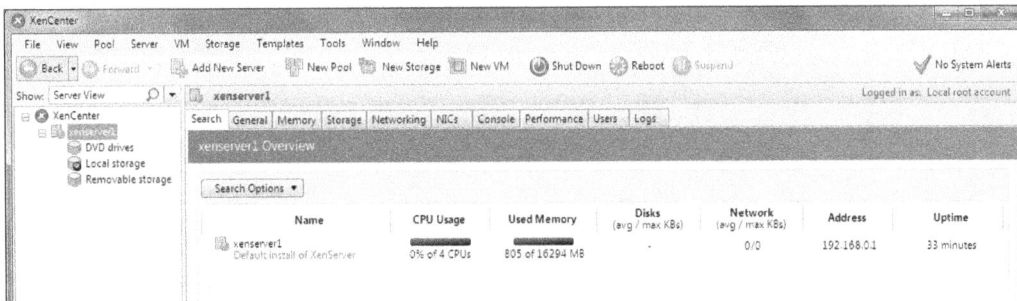

5. Repeat the previous steps to add the xenserver2 host.
6. Click on **Pool | New Pool**.

7. Type a name for the pool and, optionally, a description. Select the master and click on the servers that will be joined. In this example, we named the pool `XenPool` and the master `xenserver1`.

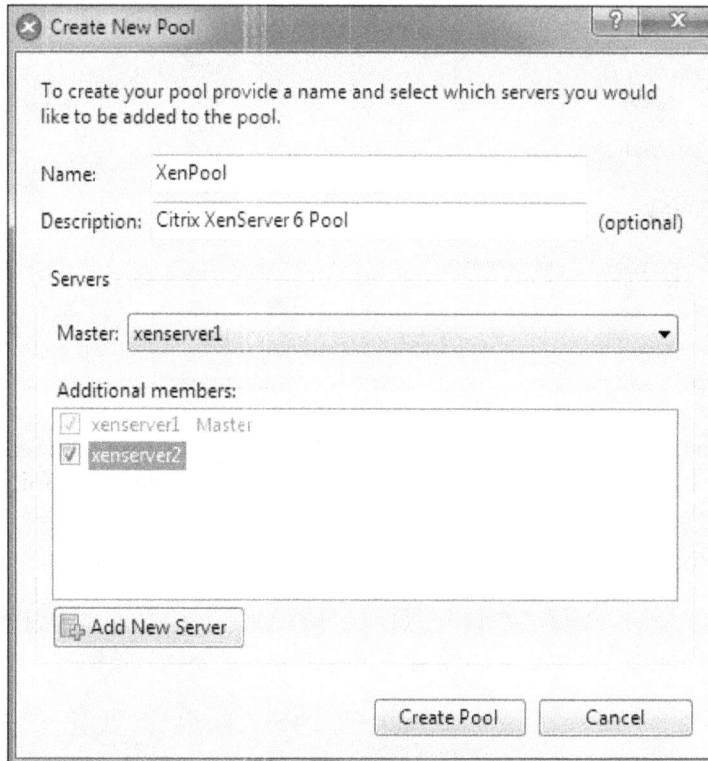

8. Click on **Create Pool**. The new pool will be created and configured:

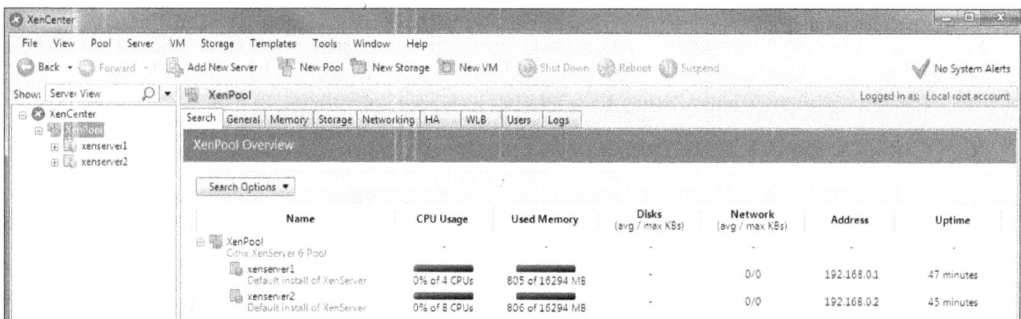

If you want to check if a XenServer host is the pool master for a pool, look at the **Pool Master** property available on the **General** tab of the host in XenCenter. If the value is **Yes** in the **Pool Master** property the host is acting as the pool master for the pool. Also, when you connect to a XenServer pool, the first host displayed is the pool master. For example, if `xenserver2` is the pool master of the pool, `xenserver2` will be displayed first in XenCenter.

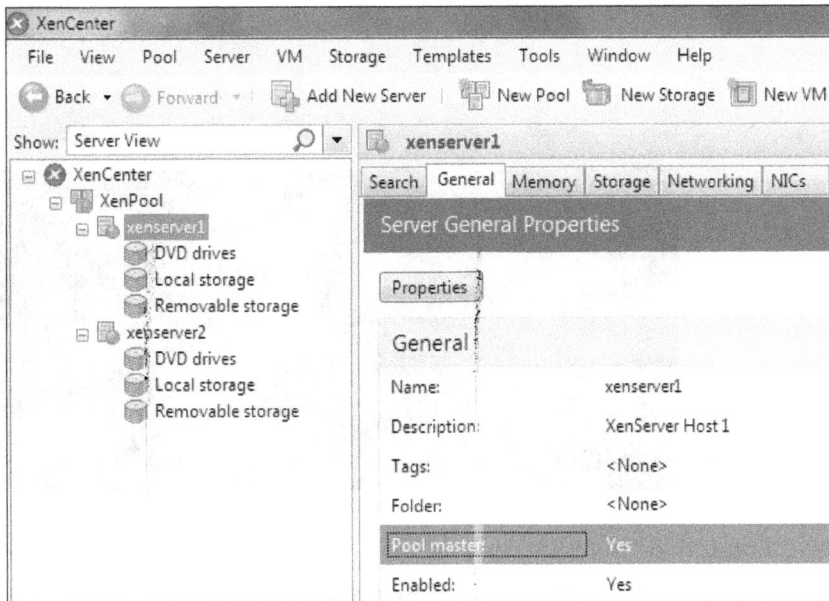

Now it is time to discover how to designate a pool master using the xe command-line interface. You can open the xe CLI from XenCenter by clicking on the **Console** tab or from a computer with XenCenter installed executing the `xe.exe` command from the path `C:\Program Files\Citrix\XenCenter`:

```
xe -s <server> -u <username> -pw <password> [-p <port>]
<command> <arguments>
```

where:

- The *server* parameter is used to specify the hostname or IP address
- The *username* and *password* parameters are used to specify credentials for logging in
- An optional *port* parameter can be used to specify the agent port on the remote XenServer Host (defaults to 443)

- The *command* parameter is the `xenserver` command you want to execute
- The *arguments* parameter is the argument related to the `xenserver` command you want to execute

In the following example, we use the xe CLI from XenCenter:

1. From XenCenter, select `xenserver1` and click on the **Console** tab:

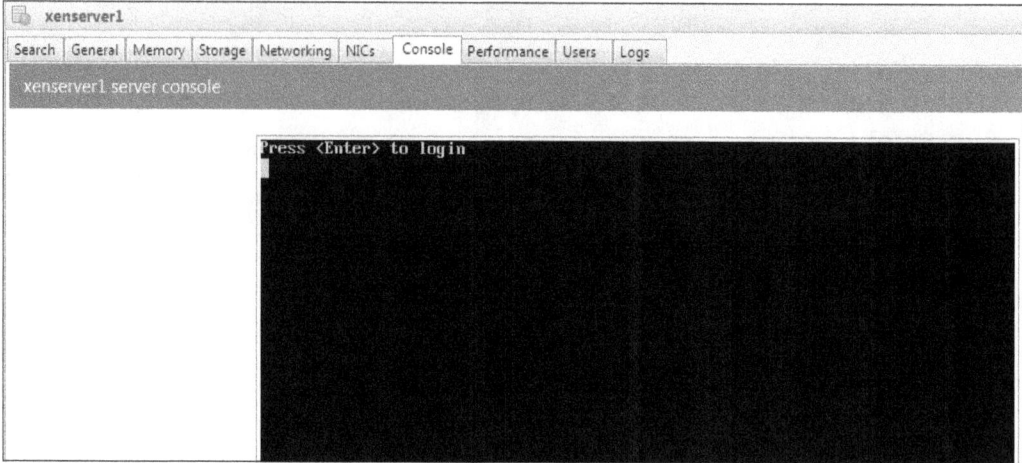

2. Press **Enter** to log in to the console.
3. XenServer hosts belong to an unnamed pool by default. To create your first resource pool, rename the existing nameless pool using the following command:

```
xe pool-param-set name-label=<"New Pool"> uuid=<pool_uuid>
```

where `name-label` is the name to assign to the pool and `uuid` is the the unique identifier/object reference for the pool. To find the UUID for the pool, press the **Tab** key on your keyboard.

4. We will run following command to create the pool named `XenPool`:

```
xe pool-param-set name-label="XenPool"
uuid=8eaa281f-c7ae-20d3-f37d-00e8596e4bc4
```

5. Now we have to join the `xenserver2` host to the pool. To do this, we will open the console on `xenserver2` and execute the following command:

   ```
   xe pool-join master-address=<host1> master-
   username=<administrator_username>
   master-password=<password>
   ```

   where `master-address` is the fully-qualified domain name or IP address of the pool master, `master-username` is the name of the master's administrator (`root`), and `master-password` must be the administrator password set when the XenServer host acting as master was installed.

6. We will run the following command to join `xenserver2` to the `XenPool`:

   ```
   xe pool-join master-address=192.168.0.1 master-username=root
   master-password=xenserver
   ```

7. Host xenserver2 will join the pool, as shown in the following screenshots:

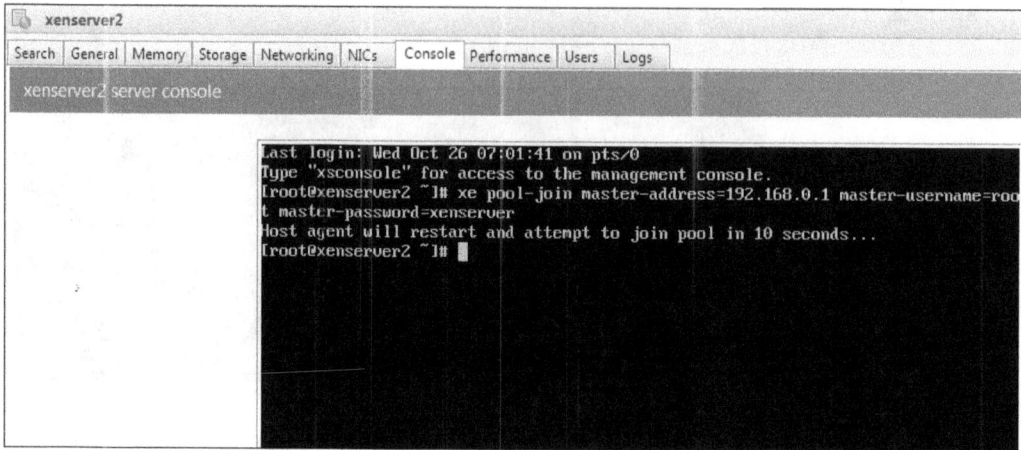

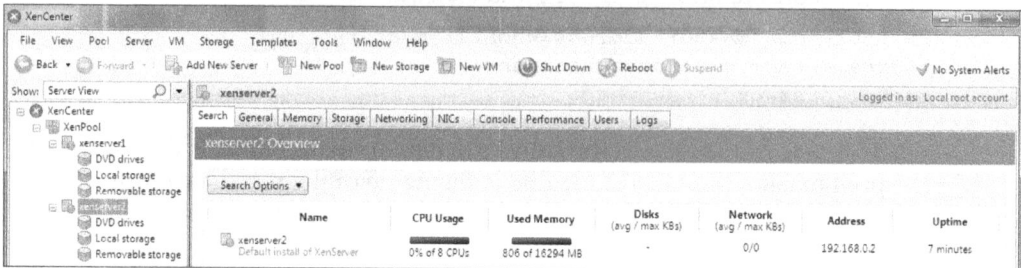

> You can use a program such as "PuTTY" to connect to
> XenServer hosts and execute console commands. You can
> download it from http://www.chiark.greenend.org.
> uk/~sgtatham/putty/download.html.

In the real world, virtual infrastructure grows according to the needs of the
enterprise. It is often difficult to acquire multiple servers with the exact same
CPUs and so minor variations are permitted. If you have a XenServer host in
your environment with a different CPU you can join it to the pool by forcing the
operation using the following xe command:

```
xe pool-join master-address=<host1>
master-username=<administrator_username>
master-password=<password> --force
```

where:

- `master-address` is the fully-qualified domain name or IP address of the pool master
- `master-username` is the name of the master's administrator (root)
- `master-password` is the administrator password set when the XenServer host acting as master was installed

Creating a heterogeneous XenServer resource pool

Creating heterogeneous resource pools is most easily done with XenCenter. XenCenter will automatically suggest using CPU masking whenever possible.

To add a heterogeneous XenServer host to a resource pool using the xe CLI use the following procedure:

1. Find the CPU features of the Pool Master by running the following command:

    ```
    xe host-get-cpu-features
    ```

2. On the new server, run the `xe host-set-cpu-features` command and copy and paste the Pool Master's features into the features parameter. For example:

```
xe host-set-cpu-features features= <pool_master's_cpu_features>
```

```
xe host-set-cpu-features features=17bae3ff-
bfebfbff-00000001-28100800
```

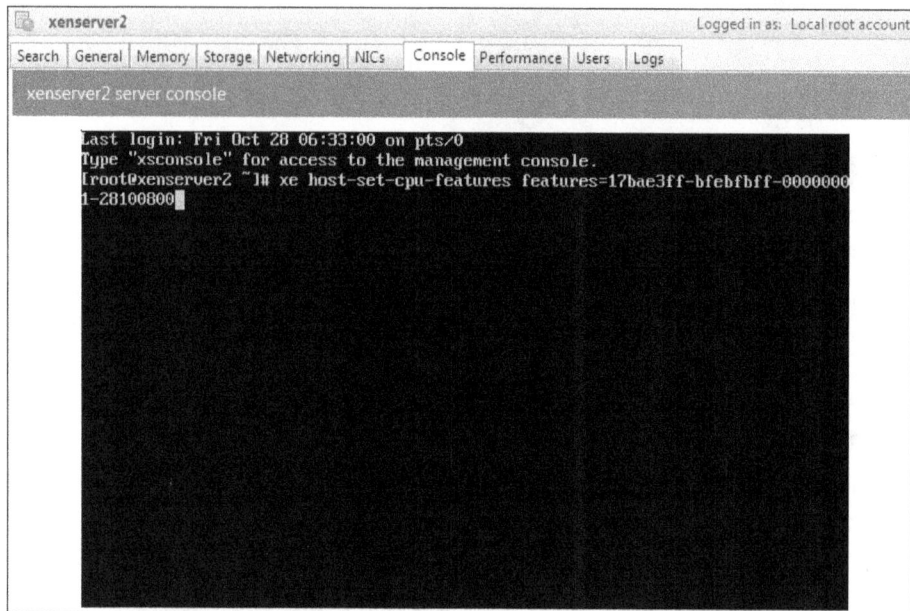

3. Restart the new server.

4. Run the `xe pool-join` command on the new server to join the pool.

5. To return a server with masked CPU features back to its normal capabilities, run the following command:

```
xe host-reset-cpu-features
```

> To display a list of all properties of the CPUs in a host, run the `xe host-cpu-info` command.

Designating a new pool master host

It can be useful to learn how to designate a new master host for our pool XenPool. Designating a new pool master is an important task that a XenServer administrator should know.

The first thing to remember is that you can only do it using CLI.

In the next example, we designate the xenserver2 host as the new pool master:

1. Open a console on any host of the pool.

2. Identify the UUID of the host that will be the new master executing the command:

   ```
   xe host-list
   ```

3. Execute the following command to designate the new master:

   ```
   xe pool-designate-new-master host-uuid=<host-uuid>
   ```

   where host-uuid is the value you have found in the previous step.

4. We will run the following command to designate xenserver2 the new master for the XenPool:

   ```
   xe pool-designate-new-master host-uuid=8791cc9e-e1e0-43f0-9104-d608bb033b9b
   ```

> After the designation process is completed, XenServer resets the internal stack in order to apply the new configuration to the pool.

Removing a XenServer host from a resource pool

You may have the need to remove a XenServer host from a resource pool because that host is no longer available or because you decide to retire it.

When a XenServer host is removed (ejected) from a pool, the machine is rebooted, reinitialized, and left in a state equivalent to that after a fresh installation. It is important not to eject a XenServer host from a pool if there is important data on the local disks, because all of the data will be erased upon ejection from the pool.

Note: Before removing a XenServer host from a pool, ensure that you shut down all the VMs running on that host. You may see a warning stating that the host cannot be removed.

> You cannot remove the host acting as pool master from a resource pool. First, designate another host as master.

You can remove a host using XenCenter or CLI.

You have decided to substitute your host xenserver2 with a new server so to complete this task you will have to remove it from the pool named XenPool:

1. Open **XenCenter** and select host xenserver2. Right-click and select **Remove server from Pool** as shown in the following screenshot:

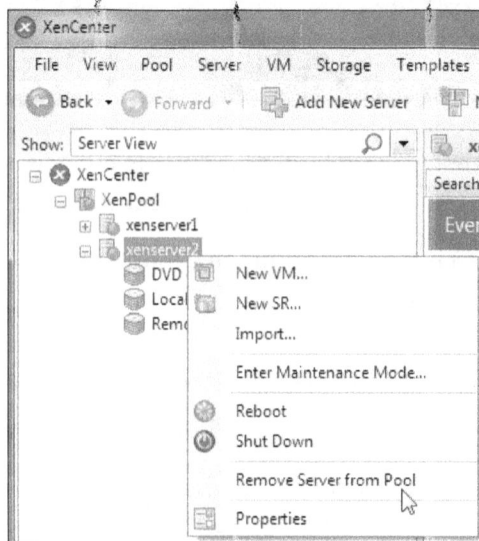

2. A warning will be displayed informing you that the operation will erase all the data. Click on **Yes**.

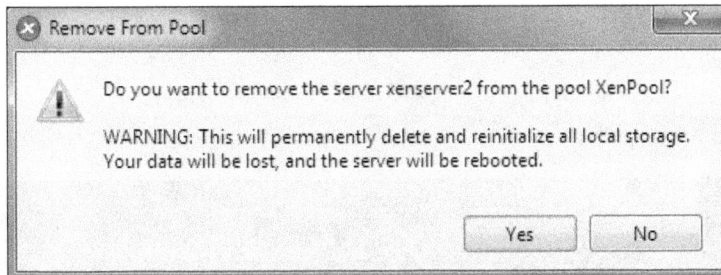

3. The server will be removed from the pool and will be restarted.

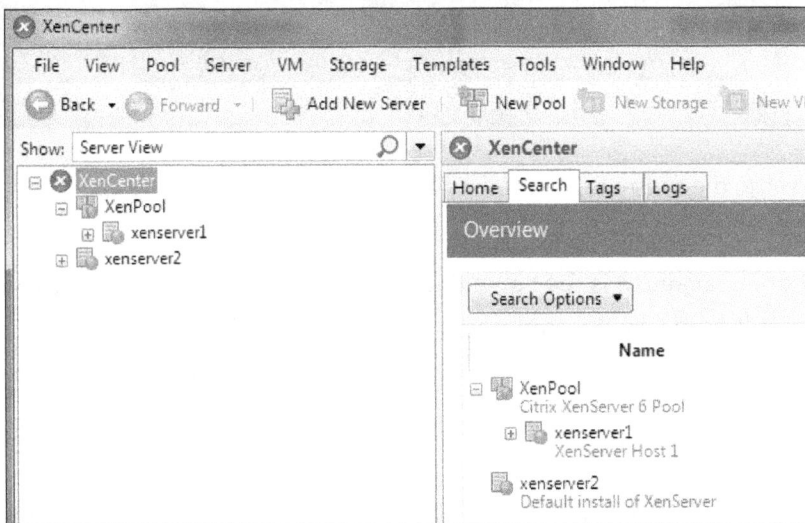

4. To perform the same task using the CLI, follow this procedure:

5. Open a console on any host of the pool.

5. Identify the UUID of the host that you have to eject by executing the following command:

```
xe host-list
```

6. Execute the following command to start the removal process:

```
xe pool-eject host-uuid=<host_uuid>
```

where host-uuid is the value that you have found in the previous step.

8. We will run following command to remove xenserver2 from the XenPool:

```
xe pool-eject host-uuid=8791cc9e-e1e0-43f0-9104-d608bb033b9b
```

9. Type yes to continue. The host will be ejected and left in a freshly-installed state.

Preparing a XenServer host for maintenance

You may need to take a managed server offline for a number of reasons, such as a rolling upgrade of virtualization software, adding or testing connectivity to a new network, diagnosing an underlying hardware issue, or adding connectivity to a new storage system. In XenCenter, you can take a server offline temporarily by placing it into **Maintenance Mode**.

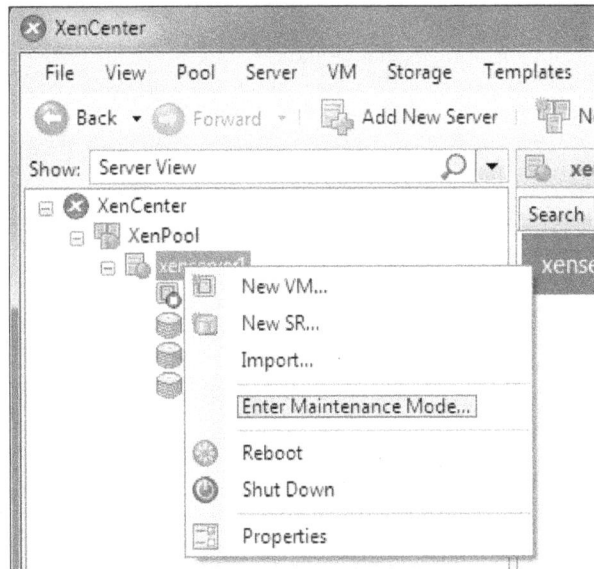

If the server is in a resource pool, when you place it into **Maintenance Mode**, all running VMs will be automatically migrated from it to another server in the same pool. If the server is the pool master, a new master will also be selected for the pool.

While a server is in Maintenance Mode you cannot create or start any VMs on it.

When all running VMs have been successfully migrated off the server, the server's status is changed to 🔲 and set to **Disabled**.

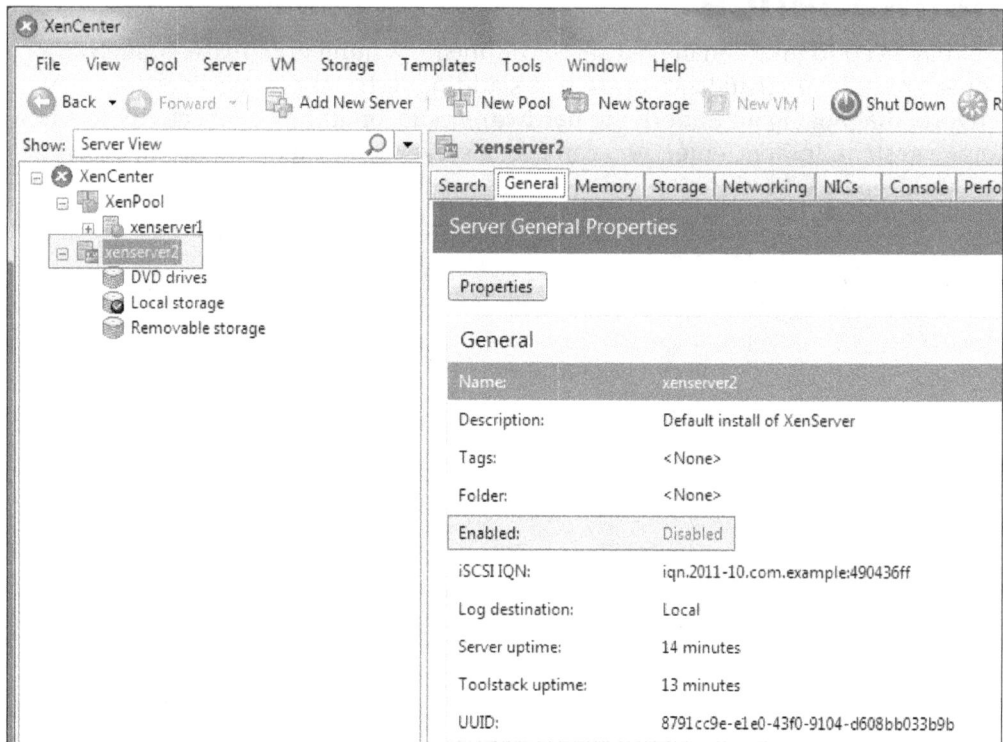

To take a server out of **Maintenance Mode**, select the server and then click on **Exit Maintenance Mode** in the shortcut menu, as shown in the following screenshot:

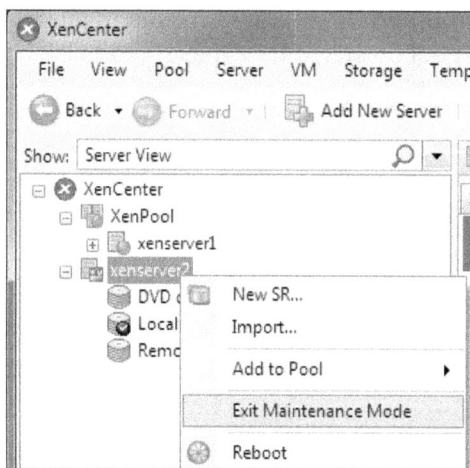

To prepare a XenServer host in a pool for maintenance operations using the CLI use the following procedure:

1. Open a console on any host of the pool.

2. Identify the UUID of the host you want to place in Maintenance Mode:

   ```
   xe host-list
   ```

3. Execute the following commands to start the removal process:

   ```
   xe host-disable uuid=<host_uuid>
   ```

   ```
   xe host-evacuate uuid=<host_uuid>
   ```

   where the host-uuid parameter is the value you have found in the previous step.

   This will disable the XenServer host and then migrate any running VMs to other XenServer hosts in the pool.

4. Once the maintenance operation is completed, enable the XenServer host by executing the following command:

```
xe host-enable
```

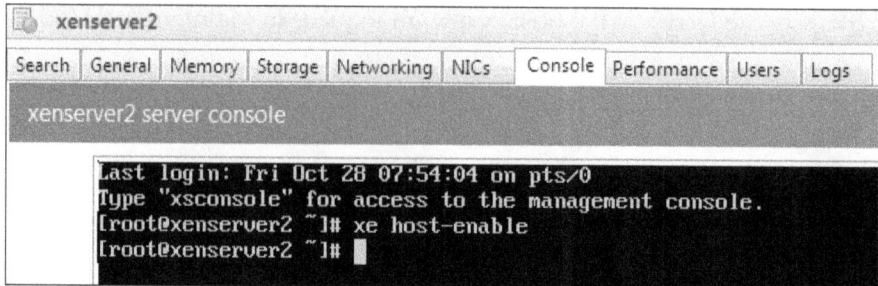

Licensing XenServer

XenServer is available in four editions but you can move towards virtualization (if you have not yet done this in your enterprise) with just the free edition. It can be used without time limits and restrictions. Citrix requires you only to activate the product within 30 days after you have installed it and then renew the free license on an annual basis.

Activating a free edition

To activate the free edition, follow this procedure:

1. Request an activation key from Citrix using XenCenter.

2. Click on the **Tools** menu and select **License Manager**.

3. Select one or more hosts that you wish to activate. Click on **Activate Free XenServer** and then select **Request Activation Key**, as shown in the following screenshot:

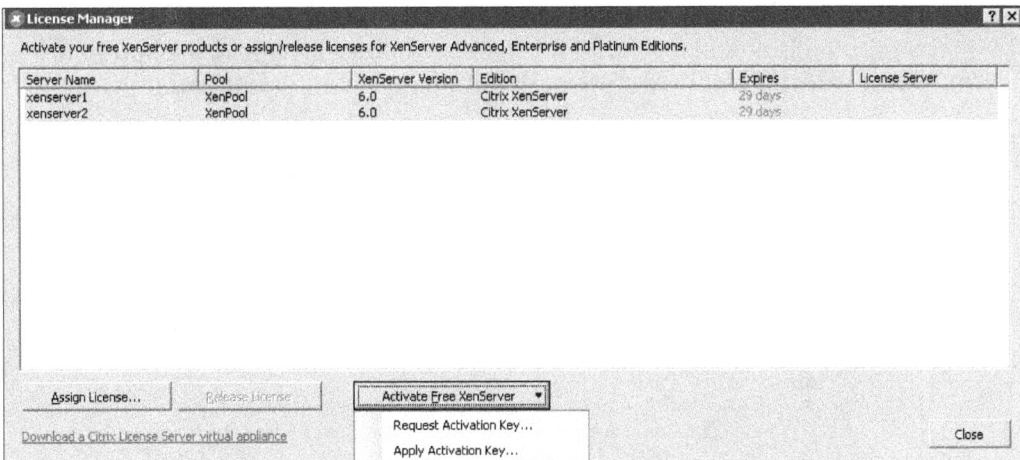

4. XenCenter opens a web browser and takes you to the Citrix XenServer Activation page as shown in the following screenshot:

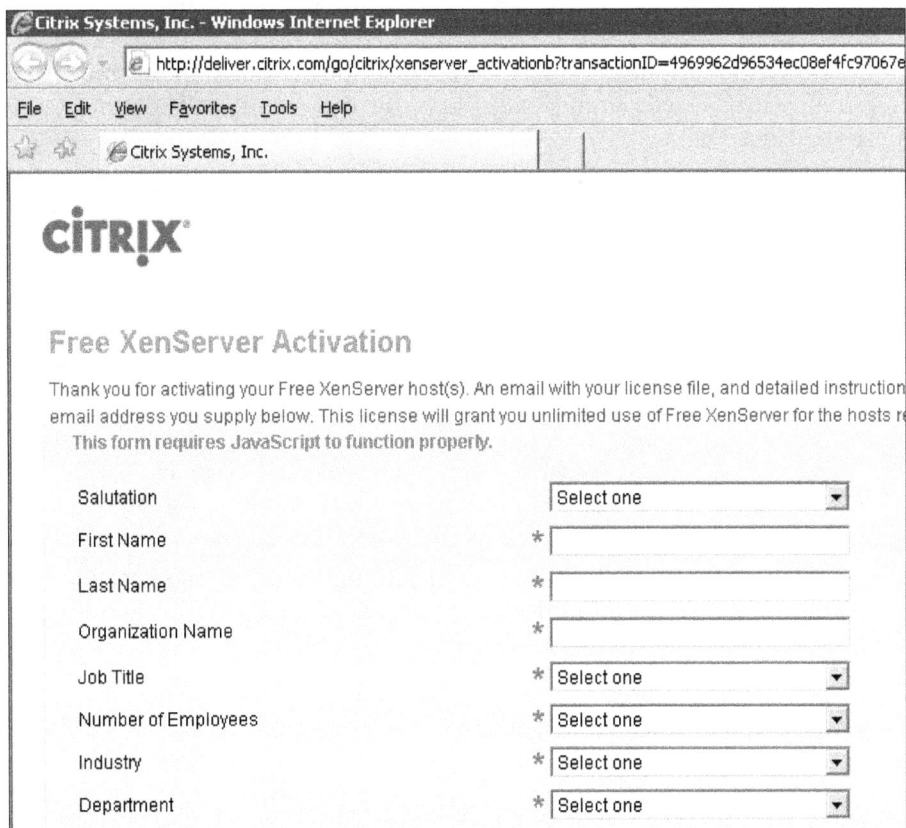

If XenCenter is unable to connect to the activation page (because the Internet connection is down, for example), then XenCenter gives you the option to save a `.txt` file locally with the activation request information.

> You can upload the `.txt` file to `https://activate.vmd.citrix.com` at a later date.

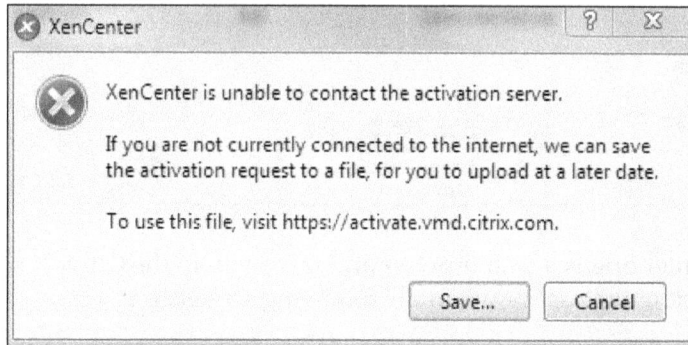

> **XenCenter**
>
> XenCenter is unable to contact the activation server.
>
> If you are not currently connected to the internet, we can save the activation request to a file, for you to upload at a later date.
>
> To use this file, visit https://activate.vmd.citrix.com.
>
> Save...   Cancel

1. Enter your details in the activation form, and then click on **Submit**. An e-mail with the activation key (`.xslic` file extension) will be sent to you shortly afterwards.

2. Save the attached activation key to a known location on the computer running XenCenter or xe CLI.

3. Apply the activation key to your XenServer host using XenCenter or xe CLI.

To apply an activation key using XenCenter:

1. Click on the **Tools** menu and select **License Manager**.

> You can also launch the XenCenter License Manager by double-clicking the activation key file in Windows Explorer.

2. Select the host you wish activate (you can only activate one host at a time). Click on **Activate Free XenServer**, and then select **Apply Activation Key** as shown in the following screenshot:

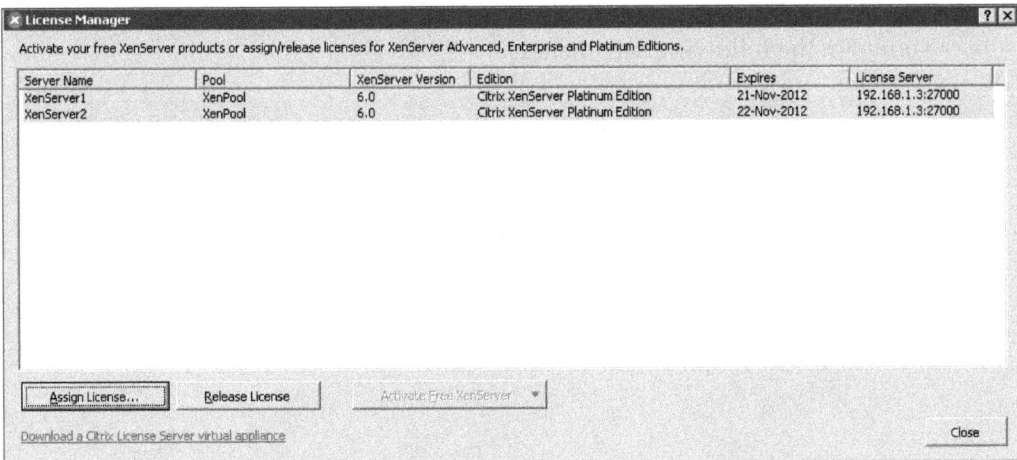

3. Browse to and select the activation key file, and select **Open** as shown in the following screenshot:

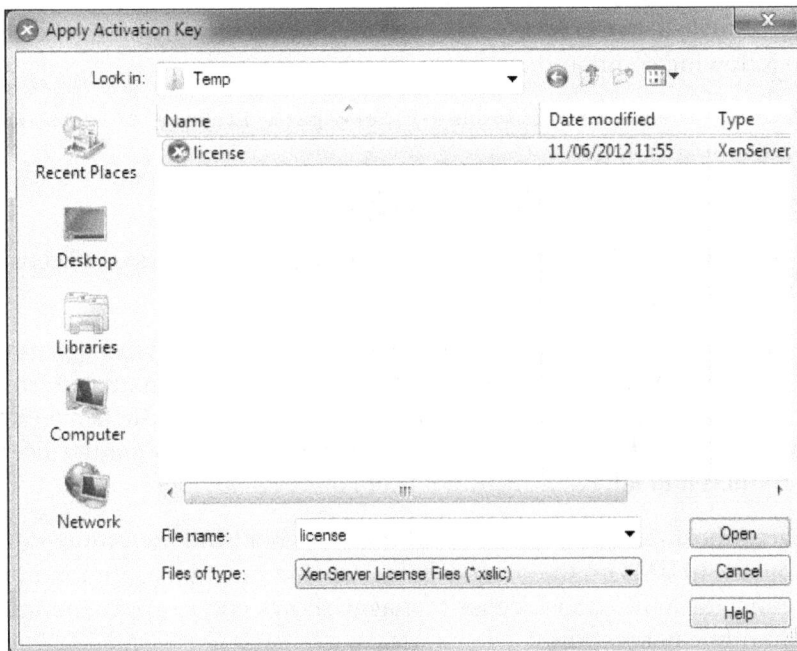

4. The information shown in the XenCenter License Manager will be updated as shown in the following screenshot:

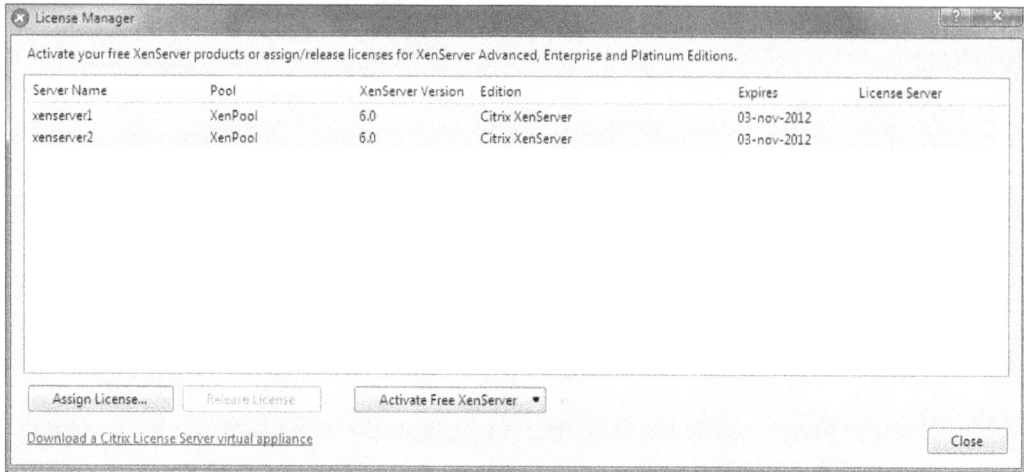

5. To install an activation key using xe CLI, open a console on the host and run the following command:

```
xe host-license-add [license-file=<<path/license_filename>>]
```

Activating a non-free edition

XenServer Advanced, Enterprise, and Platinum editions use the same licensing model as other Citrix products.

XenServer Advanced editions and higher require a license for each XenServer host you use. All XenServer editions licenses must be added to and managed from a Citrix Licensing Server. If you are familiar with other Citrix products, you know this is the standard approach for licensing them. Citrix License Server stores licenses for all Citrix products and allocates them per users or devices.

Each XenServer host requires a license, but this does not limit the number of users that may connect to VMs on that host. While licensing must be configured for each XenServer host, the XenCenter License Manager allows you to apply the same settings to multiple hosts at once.

To license XenServer Advanced editions and higher:

1. Install the Citrix License Server and console on a Microsoft Windows Server machine.

> XenServer 6.0 requires Citrix Licensing 11.6.1 or higher. Refer to Citrix license server documentation for setup available at `http://support.citrix.com/proddocs/topic/technologies/lic-library-node-wrapper.html`.

2. Obtain your XenServer license files and load them onto the Citrix License Server.

3. Configure licensing for each XenServer host using XenCenter or xe CLI.

To configure licensing for XenServer hosts using XenCenter:

1. Click on **Tools** menu | **License Manager**.

2. Select one or more host(s) that you wish to assign a license to. Click on **Assign License**.

3. The **Apply License** dialog box opens.

4. In the **Apply License** dialog box, choose the XenServer license edition and then enter the Citrix Licensing Server details. 27000 is the port that the licensing server uses by default for communication with Citrix products. If you changed the default port on the licensing server, enter the new number in the **Port number** box as shown in the following screenshot:

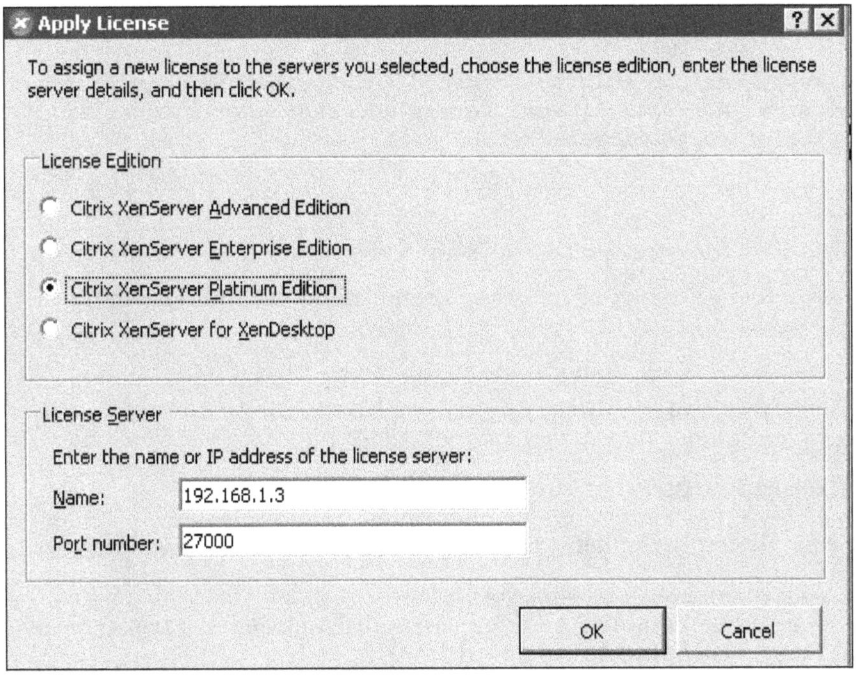

XenCenter contacts the specified license server and checks out a license for the specified host(s). The information shown in the XenCenter License Manager will be updated.

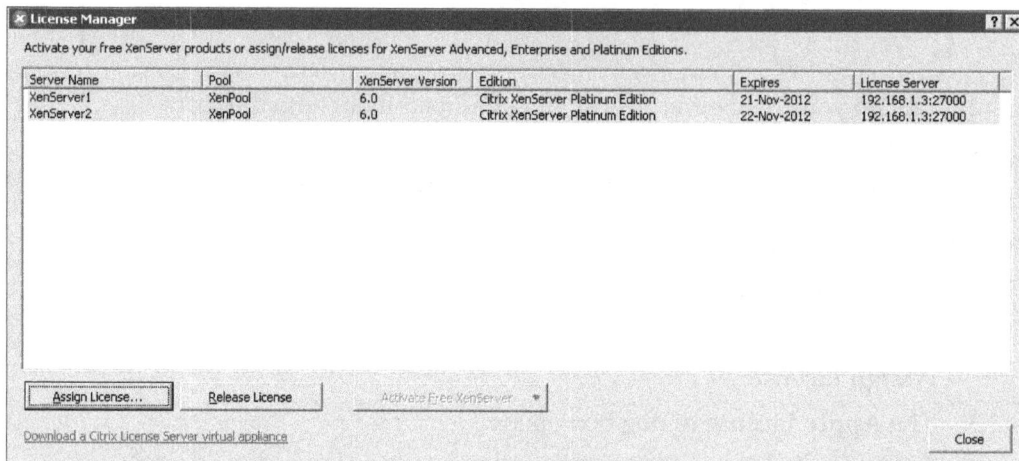

Server Name	Pool	XenServer Version	Edition	Expires	License Server
XenServer1	XenPool	6.0	Citrix XenServer Platinum Edition	21-Nov-2012	192.168.1.3:27000
XenServer2	XenPool	6.0	Citrix XenServer Platinum Edition	22-Nov-2012	192.168.1.3:27000

To release a license (to set a licensed host to the free XenServer edition) from the **License Manager**, select a host, and then click on **Release License**.

You can use the CLI to configure licensing for XenServer hosts as well.

To assign a license, execute the following command:

```
xe host-apply-edition edition=advanced|enterprise|platinum|enterprise-xd
license-server-address=<license_server_address> host-uuid=<uuid_of_host>
license-server-port=<license_server_port>
```

where:

- The edition parameter is the edition of XenServer you have bought
- The license-server-address parameter is the IP address of the license server
- The host-uuid parameter is the unique identifier/object reference of the XenServer host
- The license-server-port parameter is the port number you have set on the license server configuration

We will run following command to assign a Platinum license to xenserver1:

```
xe host-apply-edition edition=platinum
license-server-address=192.168.1.3 host-uuid=bdced52b-2228-4fb4-b02e-
211f9aef1db6 license-server-port=27000
```

You only need to supply the license server IP address and port number parameters the first time you assign a license. The values are stored and used automatically if you do not specify the license server parameters in the future.

If no host UUID is specified, the license will be applied to the host that you are running the command on.

Summary

In this chapter we have learned resource pool concepts and requirements. Specifically:

- Homogeneous and heterogeneous resource pool concepts
- Creating a resource pool using XenCenter and xe CLI
- Removing a XenServer host from a pool
- Preparing a XenServer host for maintenance mode
- Designating a new pool master host
- Licensing a XenServer host

Knowing the commands and operations for managing the pool master and resource pool is the first step to successfully managing virtualization infrastructure based on Citrix XenServer.

In the next chapter we will discuss how to manage user authentication.

2
Managing User Authentication

In the first chapter, we discussed XenServer resource pools, their concepts, requirements and how to manage them.

As you have learned, a Citrix XenServer pool is composed of multiple XenServer host installations, bound together as a single managed entity. It allows you to view multiple servers and their connected shared storage as a single unified resource, enabling flexible deployment of virtual machines based on the resource needs and business priorities.

In this chapter, we will discover how to manage user authentication and how to control access to your XenServer infrastructure. We will cover the following topics:

- User management overview
- Authenticating users with Active Directory
- Role Based Access Control overview
- Roles and permissions
- Assigning roles to users and groups

User management overview

Defining users, groups, roles, and permissions allows you to control who has access to your XenServer hosts and pools and what actions they can perform. XenServer supports Microsoft Active Directory as a directory and authentication service in order to add new users to your virtual infrastructure.

The XenServer setup creates by default a special user account during the installation. This account is the local super user (LSU) and is known by the term `root`. It is authenticated locally by the XenServer host. It is used for system administration and has full rights over the pool and the hosts.

What can you do if you cannot log in to the XenServer infrastructure in the case of Active Directory unavailability? You will agree that this could be a painful situation and the answer is that using LSU, you can always access the XenServer physical servers, log in, and manage them through the xe command line interface (CLI).

You can create additional users by adding their Active Directory accounts through either the XenCenter's **User** tab or the CLI.

All editions of XenServer can add user accounts from Active Directory. However, only XenServer Enterprise and Platinum editions let you assign these Active Directory accounts different levels of permissions through the Role Based Access Control (RBAC) feature. We will discover this feature later in this chapter. The permissions assigned to users when you first add their accounts varies according to your version of XenServer:

- **XenServer free and advanced editions**: When you create new users, they are granted full access to the pool. So all users will have the pool administrator role.

- **XenServer Enterprise and Platinum editions**: When you create new users, no access is assigned to them. As a result, these accounts do not have any access to the XenServer pool until you assign them a role.

Authenticating users with Active Directory

We have understood that if you want to have multiple user accounts and manage different levels of access for these users on a server or a pool, you must use Active Directory. This lets XenServer users log in to a pool using their Windows domain credentials. Before discovering how to enable Active Directory authentication, we have to introduce some concepts regarding authentication.

Access is controlled by the use of **subjects**. A subject in XenServer maps to an **entity** on your Active Directory server. This entity can be either a user or a group belonging to your Active Directory domain. When external authentication is enabled, the credentials used to create a session are first checked against the local root credentials (in case your directory server is unavailable) and then against the subject list. To permit access, you must create a subject entry for the person or group you wish to grant access to. This can be done using XenCenter or the xe CLI. We will discover how to enable Active Directory integration later in this chapter.

XenServer xe CLI uses a slightly different terminology to refer to Active Directory and user account features. This is shown in the following table:

XenCenter terminology	XenServer CLI terminology
Users	Subjects
Add Users	Add Subjects

This difference can create confusion, so we refer to user and groups using the word "subject".

Understanding Active Directory authentication

XenServer supports use of Active Directory based on Windows 2003 or later.

XenServer lets you use Active Directory accounts for XenServer user accounts. To do so, it passes Active Directory credentials to the Active Directory domain controller.

When added to XenServer, Active Directory users and groups become XenServer subjects. When a subject is registered with XenServer, users/groups are authenticated with Active Directory on login and do not need to qualify their username with a domain name (for example, DOMAIN\UserName or UserName@domain.com). You need to qualify an Active Directory user account with its domain name only when the user account belongs to a trusted Active Directory domain. For example, your XenServer environment is joined to the Active Directory domain domain1.local and you try to log in using a user belonging to Active Directory domain domain2.local.

> By default, XenCenter always attempts to log users in to Active Directory domain controllers using the domain to which it is currently joined. So remember that when a pool is joined to a domain, only users in that domain (or a trusted domain) can connect to the pool.

It is important to remember the following:

- XenServer hostnames should be unique throughout the XenServer deployment.

- XenServer labels the computer account in Active Directory using its hostname. Therefore, if two XenServer hosts have the same hostname and are joined to the same Windows domain, the second XenServer will overwrite the AD computer account of the first XenServer, regardless of whether they are in the same or in different pools, causing the AD authentication on the first XenServer to stop working.

- It is possible to use the same hostname in two XenServer hosts, as long as they join different AD domains and when they are members of different resource pools.

- The XenServer hosts can be in different time zones, as it is the UTC time that is compared. Mixed-authentication pools are not supported. You cannot have a pool where some hosts are configured to use Active Directory and some are not. The only communication protocol used by XenServer to communicate with Active Directory is Kerberos. Other protocols such as NTLM are not supported.

- For external authentication using Active Directory to be successful, it is important that the clocks on your XenServer hosts are synchronized with those on your Active Directory server. Use the same NTP servers for the XenServer pool and the Active Directory domain controllers to have the clocks synchronized.

> Host names must consist solely of no more than 63 alphanumeric characters, and must not be purely numeric.

Once you have Active Directory authentication enabled, if you add a new server to that pool, you are prompted to configure Active Directory on the server joining the pool. When you are prompted for credentials on the joining server, enter the Active Directory credentials with sufficient privileges to add servers to that domain.

In order to give XenServer access to the Active Directory domain controllers, make sure that the following TCP\UDP ports are open on your firewall:

Network Port	Protocol
53 UDP/TCP	DNS
88 UDP/TCP	Kerberos
123 UDP	NTP

Network Port	Protocol
137 UDP	NetBIOS
139 TCP	SMB
389 UDP/TCP	LDAP
445 TCP	SMB over TCP
464 UDP/TCP	Machine password changes
3268 TCP	Global Catalog Search

Enabling Active Directory authentication on a pool

Active Directory authentication can be configured using either XenCenter or the xe CLI. Now we discover how to configure authentication using XenCenter:

1. In the **Resources** pane, select the pool or server for which you want to grant somebody permissions.

2. Click on the **Users** tab.

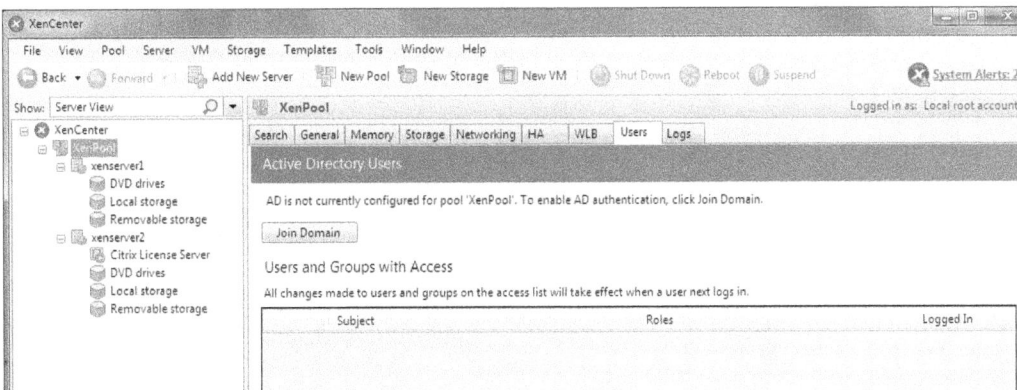

3. Click on **Join Domain**.

4. Enter the Active Directory credentials with sufficient privileges to add servers to the domain you want to join. The domain to be joined must be specified as a fully qualified domain name (FQDN). In this example, we use domain name `lab.local`, as shown in the following screenshot:

5. At the end, your XenServer pool will be joined to Active Directory.

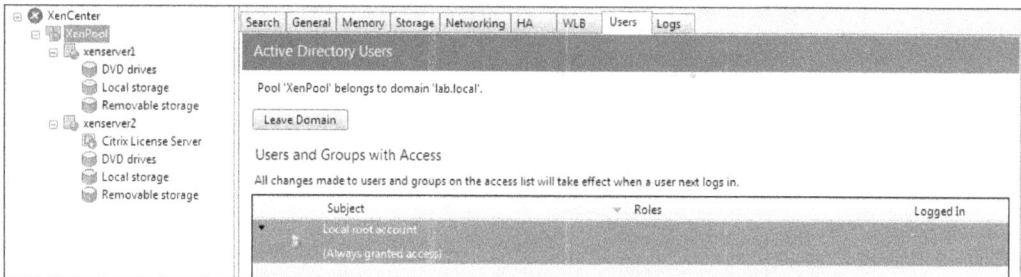

If you prefer to use xe CLI execute the following command on the pool master server:

```
xe pool-enable-external-auth auth-type=AD
service-name=<fully-qualified-domain> config:user=<username>
config:pass=<password>
```

In our example, we will run the following command to join the `lab.local` Active Directory domain:

```
xe pool-enable-external-auth auth-type=AD service-name=lab.local
config:user=Administrator config:pass=password
```

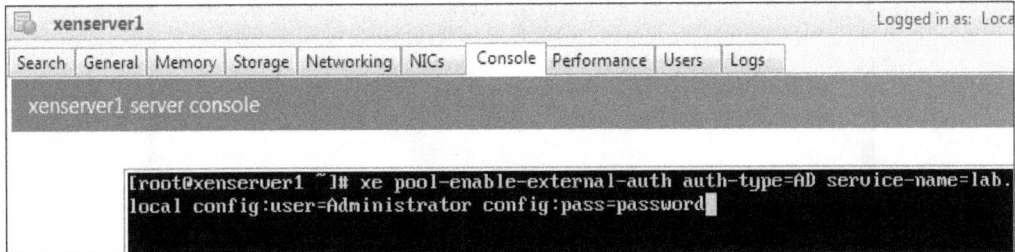

The user you specify needs to have **Add/remove computer objects or workstations** Active Directory privilege, which is the default for domain administrators in a Windows domain.

After you have joined the Active Directory domain, you can find XenServer host computer accounts in the Active Directory container `Computers`. You can create a new Organizational Unit in your domain and dedicate it to placing and storing XenServer hosts computer accounts.

> **Best practice**: External authentication is a per-host property. Citrix advises that you enable and disable this on a per-pool basis.

Disabling Active Directory Authentication

In some conditions, you might need to disable AD authentication. For example, when you have to join a new Active Directory domain. In this case, you have to leave the current domain and then join the new domain.

To leave a domain, you have to disable AD authentication using XenCenter or xe CLI. Using XenCenter, follow this procedure:

1. In the **Resources** pane, select the pool or server that you want to disconnect from its Active Directory domain.

2. Click on **Leave Domain** and select **Yes** to continue.

3. Enter Active Directory credentials with sufficient privileges to disable servers in the domain you want to leave.

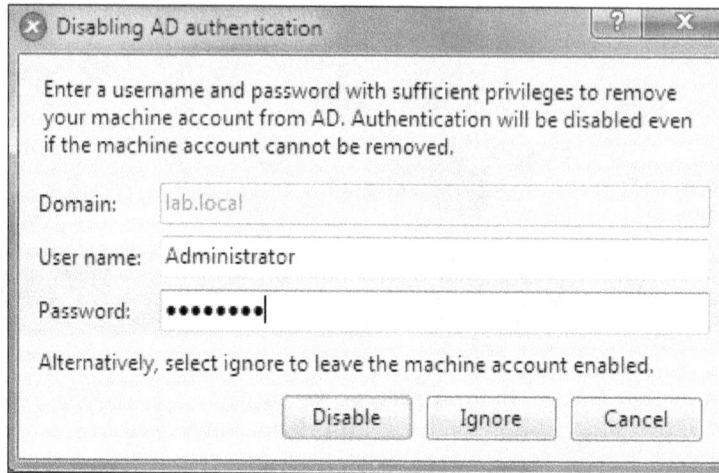

4. Decide whether to disable the computer accounts in the Active Directory server, and then click one of the following:

   ○ **Disable**: Removes the pool or server from the domain and disables the computer account for the server or pool master in the Active Directory database.

   ○ **Ignore**: Select this option if you did not fill in the username/password or you do not know an account with sufficient privileges to remove the server or pool master's computer account from the Active Directory database. (This option removes the pool or server from the domain, but leaves the computer account for the server or pool master in the Active Directory.)

> When you leave the domain any users who are authenticated to the pool or server with Active Directory credentials are disconnected.

Using CLI, execute the following command:

```
xe pool-disable-external-auth
```

User authentication

To allow a user access to your XenServer host, you must add a subject for that user or a group that they are in.

> **Best Practice**: When you have to assign security permissions to users, the best solution is to create a security group in your Active Directory domain, add users to this group, and at the end grant rights and\or permissions to this group. This approach reduces your management effort because it is simpler to add or remove users from a group than to manage each user's permissions in XenServer. Also, when you want to assign the Pool Administrator role to a group, remember that the number of users in the Active Directory group must not exceed 500.

To allow a user access to XenServer using XenCenter follow this procedure:

1. In the **Users** tab, click on **Add**, as shown in the following screenshot:

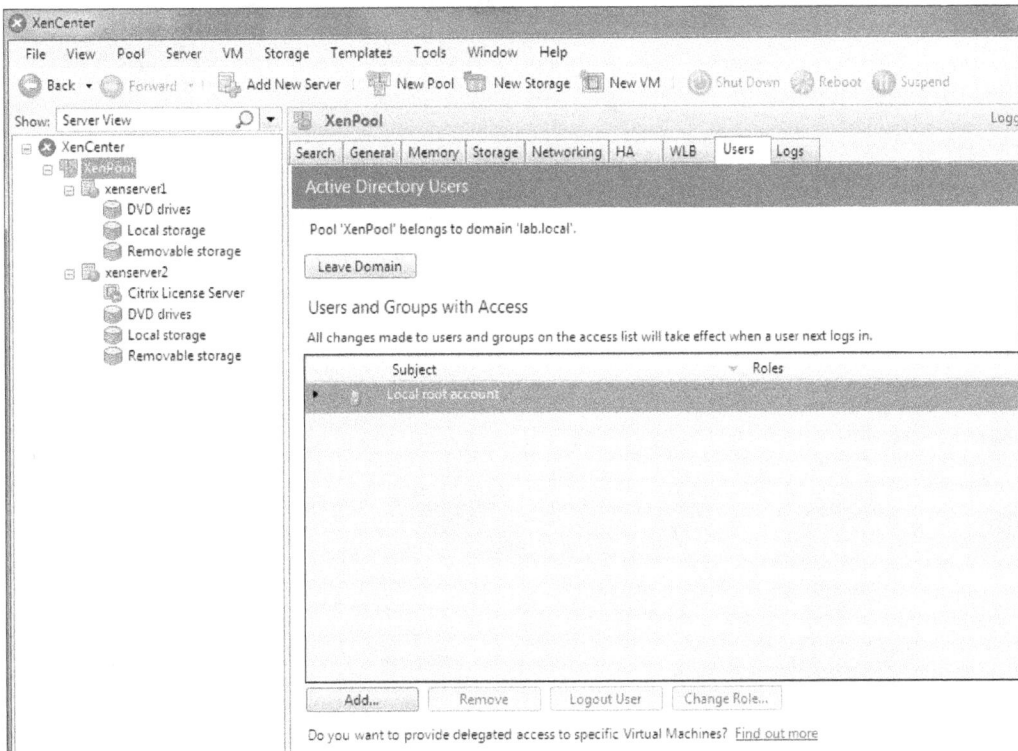

2. In the **Add Users** dialog box, enter one or more user or group names. Separate multiple names by commas. To specify a user in a different, trusted domain (other than the one currently joined), supply the domain name with the username (for example, `other_domain\jsmith`) or enter a fully qualified domain name (FQDN) (for example, `jsmith@other_domain.com`).

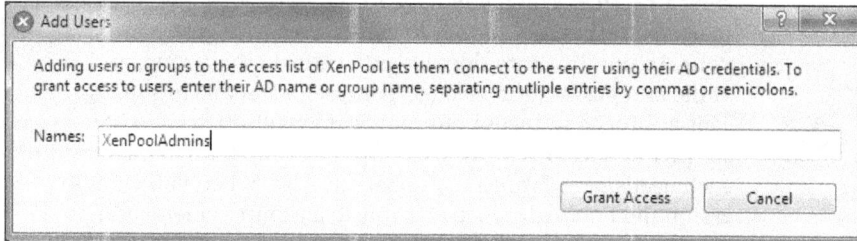

In this example, we add the `XenPoolAdmins` Active Directory Security Group in the `lab.local` domain.

3. Click on **Grant Access**.

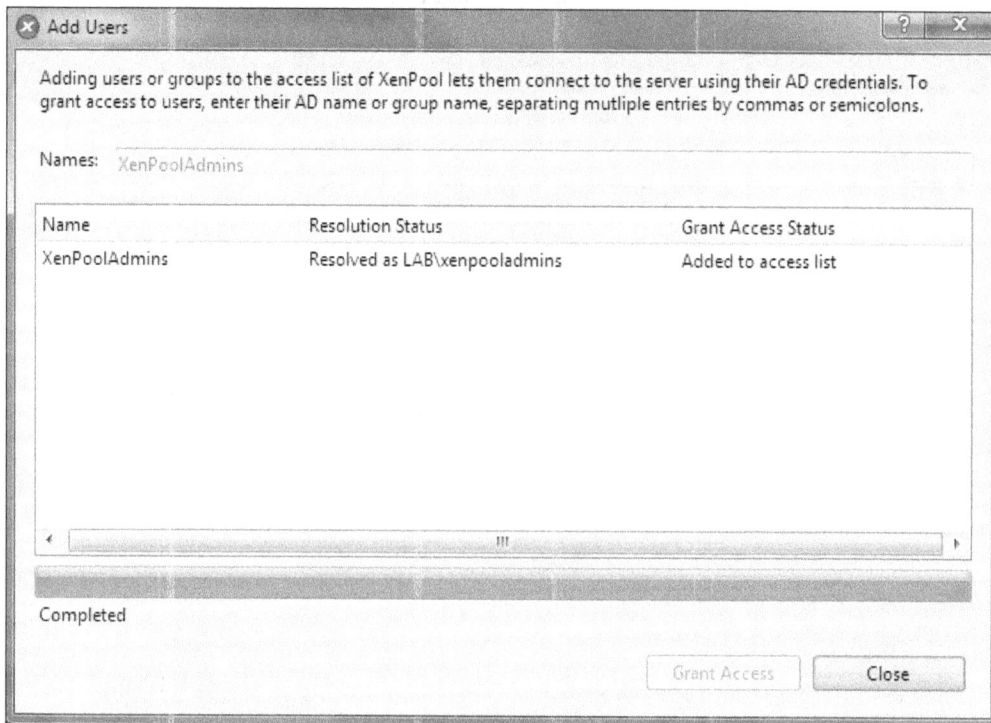

> If you have XenServer Enterprise or higher, you have to assign roles to users and groups you have added. In other editions (Free and Advanced), XenServer assigns the Pool Admin role by default. Also note that any user accounts created in the previous XenServer version are assigned the role of Pool Admin for backwards compatibility reasons.

In this example, we are using XenServer Platinum so XenPoolAdmins is added as a XenServer user and no role is assigned to it. We will discover how to manage roles for users in XenServer later in this chapter.

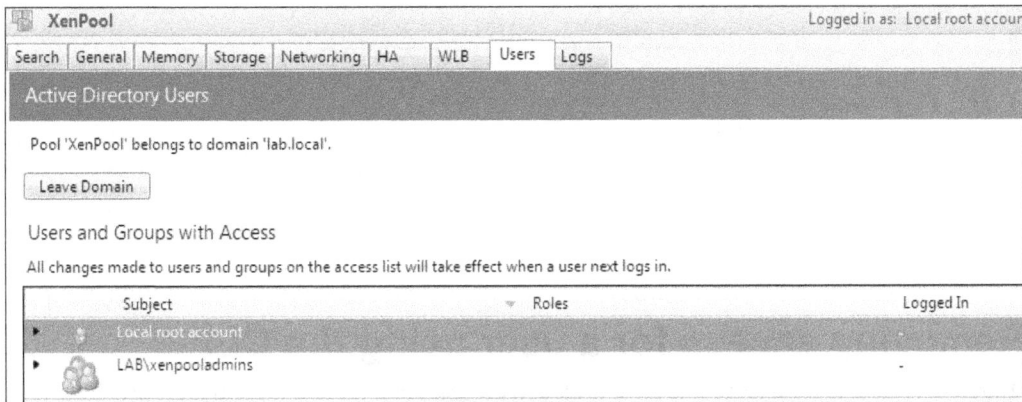

Using xe CLI, execute the following command to add an AD subject to XenServer:

```
xe subject-add subject-name=<entity name>
```

The entity name should be the name of the user or group to which you want to grant access. For example, for adding user Xen John Rab (Active Directory account name is xen.jrab) use the following command:

```
xe subject-add subject-name=xen.jrab
```

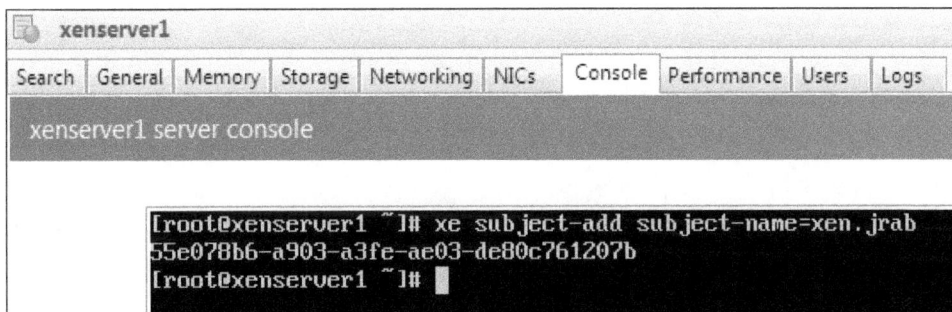

We have added the user Xen John Rab to XenServer, as seen in the following screenshot:

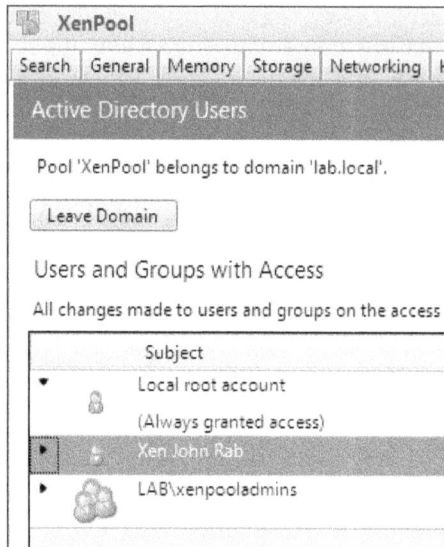

Removing access for a user using the CLI

In some cases, you have to remove a user from XenServer. For example, the user leaves the company so your Human Resources department asks you to revoke access for this user.

This task is easy to accomplish in XenCenter. Follow the given steps:

1. In the **Users** tab, select the user you want to remove.

2. Click on **Remove** and select **Yes** to continue, as shown in the following screenshot:

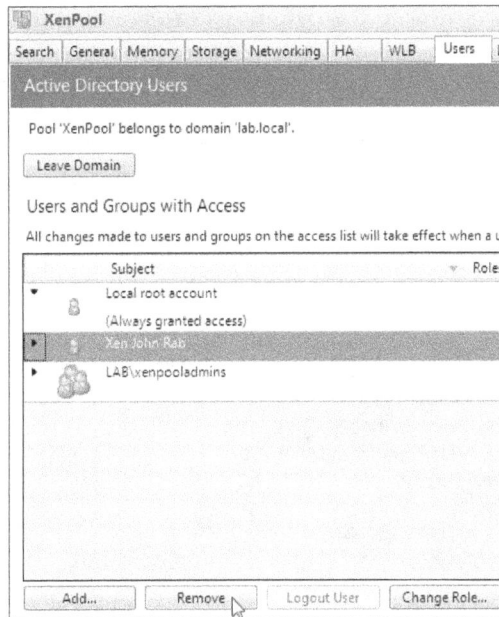

Using xe CLI, this task is a little more time consuming because you have to identify the subject identifier for the subject you wish to revoke access to first and then remove this user.

To identify the subject, execute the following command:

```
xe subject-list
```

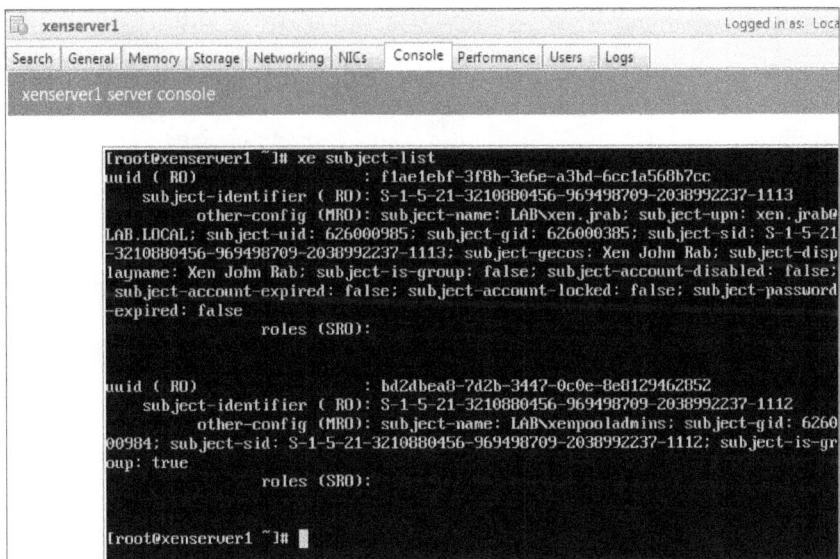

You may wish to apply a filter to the list, for example to get the subject identifier for the user named Xen John Rab in the LAB domain, you could use the following command:

```
xe subject-list other-config:subject-name='LAB\xen.jrab'
```

```
[root@xenserver1 ~]# xe subject-list other-config:subject-name='LAB\xen.jrab'
uuid ( RO)                : f1ae1ebf-3f8b-3e6e-a3bd-6cc1a568b7cc
    subject-identifier ( RO): S-1-5-21-3210880456-969498709-2038992237-1113
        other-config (MRO): subject-name: LAB\xen.jrab; subject-upn: xen.jrab@
LAB.LOCAL; subject-uid: 626000985; subject-gid: 626000385; subject-sid: S-1-5-21
-3210880456-969498709-2038992237-1113; subject-gecos: Xen John Rab; subject-disp
layname: Xen John Rab; subject-is-group: false; subject-account-disabled: false;
 subject-account-expired: false; subject-account-locked: false; subject-password
-expired: false
            roles (SRO):
```

Take a note of the subject-identifier value; in this example it is the following:

```
uuid ( RO)                      : f1ae1ebf-3f8b-3e6e-a3bd-6cc1a568b7cc
```

Remove the user by using the subject-remove command, passing in the subject identifier you have found in the previous step:

```
xe subject-remove subject-uuid=<subject-uuid>
```

In our example, we will execute the following command:

```
xe subject-remove subject-uuid=f1ae1ebf-3f8b-3e6e-a3bd-6cc1a568b7cc
```

```
Last login: Thu Nov 17 05:13:56 on pts/0
Type "xsconsole" for access to the management console.
[root@xenserver1 ~]# xe subject-remove subject-uuid=f1ae1ebf-3f8b-3e6e-a3bd-6cc1
a568b7cc
```

Role Based Access Control overview

In the section related to user management we have introduced the Role Based Access Control (RBAC) feature. Now it is time to discover it in detail.

RBAC allows you to assign roles and permissions to users in order to control who has access to your XenServer pool and what actions they can perform. Using RBAC, you can map a user or a group of users that can access your XenServer pool to defined roles. Each role has some associated permissions that give to the user or the group of users the ability to perform certain operations.

RBAC allows you to easily restrict which operations different groups of users can perform, thus reducing the probability of an accident by an inexperienced user.

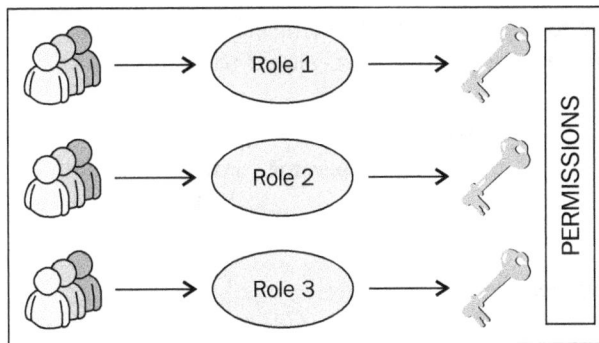

Note that you must enable Active Directory authentication in order to take advantage of RBAC. So you must join the pool to the domain and add Active Directory accounts before you can assign roles.

> The full RBAC feature is only available in Citrix XenServer Enterprise Edition or higher.

Roles and Permissions

XenServer is shipped with the following six pre-established roles:

- **Pool Administrator (Pool Admin)**: Like LSU, this role grants you rights to perform all operations on XenServer pools and hosts
- **Pool Operator (Pool Operator)**: This role can do everything on XenServer pools and hosts apart from adding/removing users and modifying their roles

- **Virtual Machine Power Administrator (VM Power Admin)**: This role grants you rights to create and manage virtual machines in the pool
- **Virtual Machine Administrator (VM Admin)**: This role is similar to a VM Power Admin but does not grant you the right to migrate VMs or perform snapshots
- **Virtual Machine Operator (VM Operator)**: This role grants you the right to perform start/stop/reset operations
- **Read-only (Read Only)**: This role grants you the right to view resource pool and performance data

Definitions of RBAC Roles and Permissions

After roles, it is time to discover which permissions are available for each role. The following tables summarize permissions related to roles:

Permissions	Pool Admin	Pool Operator	VM Power Admin	VM Admin	VM Operator	Read Only
Assign/modify roles	X					
Log in to (physical) server consoles (through SSH and XenCenter)	X					
Server backup/restore	X					
Import/export OVF/OVA packages; import disk images	X					
Log out active user connections	X	X				
Create and dismiss alerts	X	X				
Cancel task of any user	X	X				
Pool management	X	X				
VM advanced operations	X	X	X			
VM create/destroy operations	X	X	X	X		
VM change CD media	X	X	X	X	X	
VM change power state	X	X	X	X	X	
View VM consoles	X	X	X	X	X	

Permissions	Pool Admin	Pool Operator	VM Power Admin	VM Admin	VM Operator	Read Only
XenCenter view mgmt ops	X	X	X	X	X	
Cancel own tasks	X	X	X	X	X	X
Read audit logs	X	X	X	X	X	X
Configure, Initialize, Enable, Disable WLB	X	X				
Apply WLB Optimization Recommendations	X	X				
Modify WLB Report Subscriptions	X	X				
Accept WLB Placement Recommendations	X	X	X			
Display WLB Configuration	X	X	X	X	X	X
Generate WLB Reports	X	X	X	X	X	X
Connect to pool and read all pool metadata	X	X	X	X	X	X

The following table provides additional details about permissions:

Permission	Allows Assignee To	Comments
Assign/modify roles	Add and remove users	This permission lets the user grant himself or herself any permission or perform any task.
	Add and remove roles from users	
	Enable and disable Active Directory integration (being joined to the domain)	Warning: This role lets the user disable the Active Directory integration and all subjects added from Active Directory.
Log in to server consoles	Server console access through ssh	Warning: With access to a root shell, the assignee could arbitrarily reconfigure the entire system, including RBAC.
	Server console access through XenCenter	

Permission	Allows Assignee To	Comments
Server backup/ restore	Back up and restore servers	The ability to restore a backup lets the assignee revert RBAC configuration changes.
VM create/destroy operations	Back up and restore pool metadata	
Import/export OVF/ OVA packages; import disk images	Import OVF and OVA packages	
	Import disk images	
	Export VMs as OVF/OVA packages	
Log out active user connections	Ability to disconnect logged in users	
Create/dismiss alerts		Warning: A user with this permission can dismiss alerts for the entire pool.
		Note: The ability to view alerts is part of the Connect to Pool and read all pool metadata permission.
Cancel task of any user	Cancel any user's running task	This permission lets the user request XenServer cancel an in-progress task initiated by any user.

Permission	Allows Assignee To	Comments
Pool management	Emergency master address Emergency recover slaves Designate new master Manage pool and server certificates Patching Set server properties Configure server logging Enable and disable servers Shut down, reboot, and power-on servers System status reports Apply license Live migration of all other VMs on a server to another server, due to either WLB, Maintenance Mode, or HA Configure server management interfaces Disable server management Delete crashdumps Add, edit, and remove networks Add, edit, and remove PBDs/PIFs/VLANs/Bonds/SRs	This permission includes all the actions required to maintain a pool. Note: If the management interface is not functioning, no logins can authenticate except local root logins.

Permission	Allows Assignee To	Comments
VM advanced operations	Adjust VM memory (through Dynamic Memory Control) Create a VM snapshot with memory, take VM snapshots, and rollback VMs Migrate VMs Start VMs, including specifying physical server Resume VMs	This permission provides the assignee with enough privileges to start a VM on a different server if they are not satisfied with the server XenServer selected.
VM create/destroy operations	Install and delete VMs Clone/copy VMs Add, remove, and configure virtual disk/CD devices Add, remove, and configure virtual network devices Import/export XVA files VM configuration change	
VM change CD media	Eject current CD Insert new CD	
VM change power state	Start VMs (automatic placement) Shut down VMs Reboot VMs Suspend VMs Resume VMs (automatic placement)	This permission does not include start_on, resume_on, and migrate, which are part of the VM advanced operations permission.

Permission	Allows Assignee To	Comments
View VM consoles	See and interact with VM consoles	This permission does not let the user view server consoles.
Configure, Initialize, Enable, Disable WLB	Configure WLB Initialize WLB and change WLB servers Enable WLB Disable WLB	When a user's role does not have this permission, this functionality is not visible.
Apply WLB Optimization Recommendations	Apply any optimization recommendations that appear in the **WLB** tab.	
Modify WLB Report Subscriptions	Change the WLB report generated or its recipient	
Accept WLB Placement Recommendations	Select one of the servers Workload Balancing recommends for placement ("star" recommendations)	
Display WLB Configuration	View **WLB** settings for a pool as shown on the **WLB** tab	
Generate WLB Reports	View and run WLB reports, including the Pool Audit Trail report	
XenCenter view management operations	Create and modify global XenCenter folders Create and modify global XenCenter custom fields Create and modify global XenCenter searches	Folders, custom fields, and searches are shared between all users accessing the pool.
Cancel own tasks	Lets a user cancel their own tasks	

Permission	Allows Assignee To	Comments
Read audit log	Download the XenServer audit log	
Connect to pool and read all pool metadata	Log in to pool	
	View pool metadata	
	View historical performance data	
	View logged in users	
	View users and roles	
	View tasks	
	View messages	
	Register for and receive events	

Calculating RBAC roles

After we have introduced roles and permissions, we have to discover how XenServer calculates roles for a user or group.

Here you can find the workflow related to the application of roles:

1. User logs in and his credentials are authenticated in Active Directory. During authentication, Active Directory also determines if the subject belongs to any other containing groups in Active Directory.

2. XenServer then verifies which roles have been assigned to the subject and to any Active Directory groups of which it is a member.

3. XenServer applies the highest level of permissions to the subject. Because subjects can be members of multiple Active Directory groups, they will inherit all of the permissions of the associated roles.

In the following figure you can find an example of roles assigned to a user:

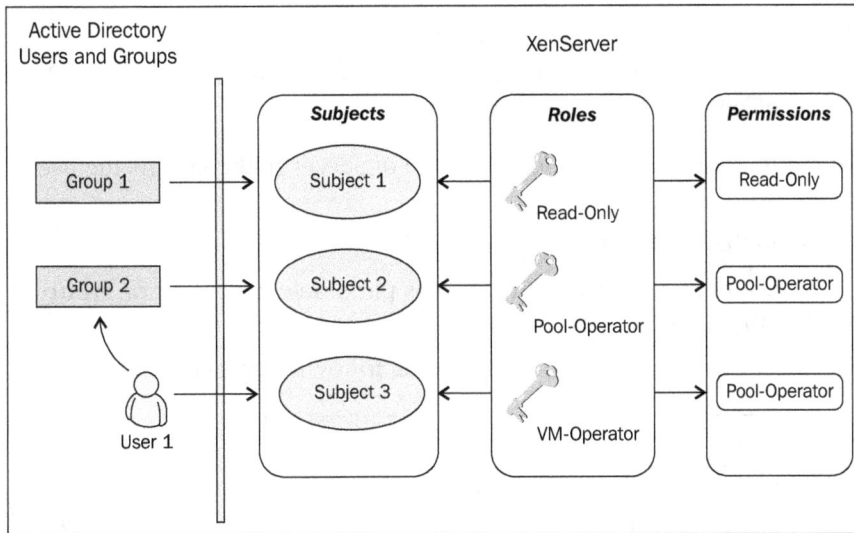

Subject 2 (Group 2) is the Pool Operator and **User 1** is a member of **Group 2**. When **Subject 3 (User 1)** tries to log in, he or she inherits both **Subject 3 (VM Operator)** and **Group 2 (Pool Operator)** roles. Since the Pool Operator role is higher, the resulting role for **Subject 3 (User 1)** is Pool Operator and not VM Operator.

Assigning roles to users and groups

All XenServer users must have an RBAC role. We have discovered that when new users are added in the XenServer free and advanced editions, they are automatically assigned the Pool Administrator role. If you have the Enterprise or higher edition, you must assign roles to newly added accounts separately, because XenServer does not assign account roles automatically in these editions.

You can assign a user a different role by one of the following methods:

- Change the role assigned to the user in the **Select Roles** dialog in XenCenter. This requires the Assign/Modify role permission, which is only available to a Pool Administrator.
- Modify the user's containing group membership in Active Directory (so that the user becomes part of a group that is assigned a different role).

Assigning or changing a role to a user or group

You can change or assign roles to users or groups using XenCenter or xe CLI. To do this task in XenCenter, follow this procedure:

1. In the **Resources** pane, select the pool or server that contains the user or group.

2. Click on the **Users** tab.

3. In the **Users and Groups with Access** pane, select the user or group to which you want to assign permissions.

4. Click on **Change Role**, as shown in the following screenshot:

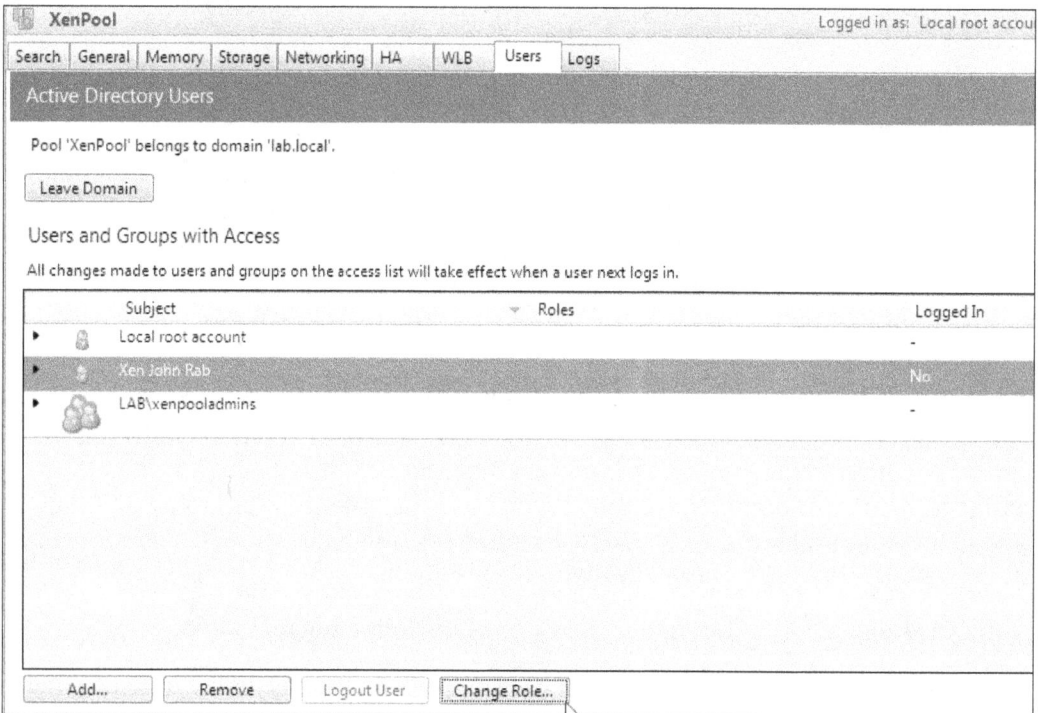

5. In the **Select Roles** dialog, select the role you want to apply and click on **Save**:

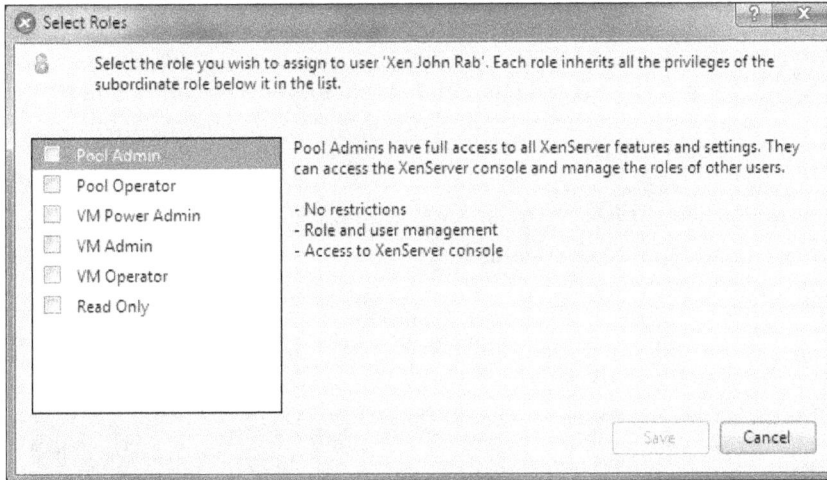

6. If you want to change the role of a user, click on **Change Role** again and select another role.

> You can't remove a role for a user using XenCenter! To do this, you have to use the xe subject-role-remove command in xe CLI. You will learn this very soon.

In the following screenshot, you can see that the **VM Operator** role has been assigned to the **Xen John Rab** user:

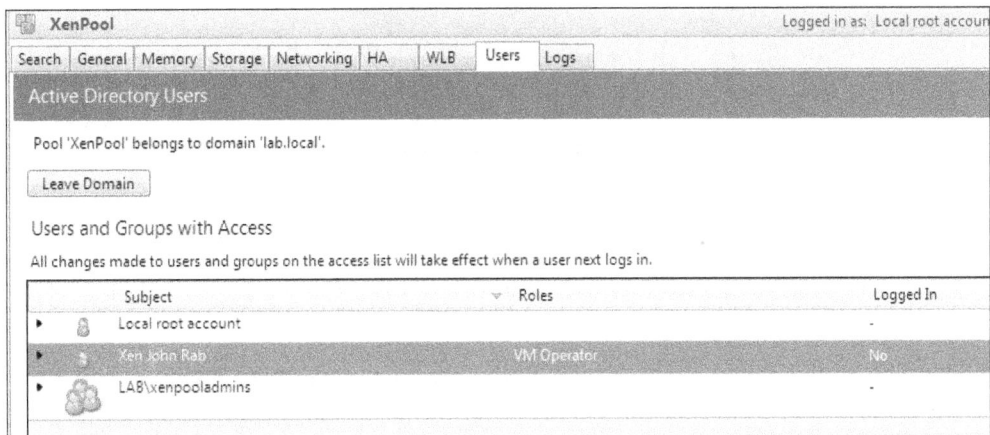

When you are assigning a role, you can select multiple users simultaneously by pressing the *Ctrl* key and selecting the user accounts.

> Like in Active Directory when working with group membership, when you change a role of a user, this user must log out and log back in again for the new role to take effect. You can force this log out by clicking on the **Logout User** button.

After we have discovered how to assign roles using XenCenter, we can move on and see how to use the xe CLI to do this task.

First, we introduce the xe command `role-list`:

```
xe role-list
```

```
uuid ( RO)              : 7955168d-7bec-10ed-105f-c6a7e6e63249
            name ( RO): vm-power-admin
      description ( RO): The VM Power Administrator role has full access to VM and
template management and can choose where to start VMs and use the dynamic memor
y control and VM snapshot features


uuid ( RO)              : aaa00ab5-7340-bfbc-0d1b-7cf342639a6e
            name ( RO): vm-admin
      description ( RO): The VM Administrator role can manage VMs and templates


uuid ( RO)              : fb8d4ff9-310c-a959-0613-54101535d3d5
            name ( RO): vm-operator
      description ( RO): The VM Operator role can use VMs and interact with VM con
soles


uuid ( RO)              : 7233b8e3-eacb-d7da-2c95-f2e581cdbf4e
            name ( RO): read-only
      description ( RO): The Read-Only role can log in with basic read-only access
```

This command displays the list of the roles available in XenServer and for each role it also returns the associated unique identifier (UUID).

So if you prefer to use the xe CLI to manage roles for a subject, execute the following command:

```
xe subject-role-add uuid=<subject uuid> role-name=<role_name>
```

For example, to assign the role VM Operator to user Xen John Rab, execute the following command:

```
xe subject-role-add uuid=f1ae1ebf-3f8b-3e6e-a3bd-6cc1a568b7cc
role-name='vm-operator'
```

Remember to identify subject identifiers for the user!

> You can use also `role-uuid=<role-uuid>` instead of the `role-name` property.

To change a user's role it is necessary to remove them from their existing role, and add them to a new role.

To remove a role from a subject, execute the following command:

```
xe subject-role-remove uuid=<subject uuid> role-name=
<role_name_to_remove>
```

For example, to remove the role `VM Operator` for user `Xen John Rab`, execute the following command:

```
xe subject-role-remove uuid=f1ae1ebf-3f8b-3e6e-a3bd-6cc1a568b7cc
role-name='vm-operator'
```

After you have removed the role, you can add the new role to the user.

Summary

In this chapter, we have learned about user authentication concepts, Active Directory integration and how to manage them. Specifically we have covered:

- User management overview
- Authenticating users with Active Directory
- Adding new users in XenServer using XenCenter and xe CLI
- Role Based Access Control overview
- Assigning roles to users and groups

User authentication with Active Directory is very useful when you have a large XenServer deployment and you want to manage the tasks your administrators or users can do on the virtual infrastructure.

Furthermore, you can delegate some tasks to other users such as VM power management.

In the next chapter, we will introduce storage concepts and discuss storage management.

3
Managing Storage Repositories

In the previous chapter, we discussed user authentication in XenServer and how to manage it. In this chapter, we will introduce the storage concepts and discover how to manage a Storage Repository in XenServer. Storage in XenServer is an interesting topic because it is one of the core aspects you have to evaluate when you start a virtualization project and you want virtualized physical machines.

In this chapter, we will cover the following topics:

- Storage overview
- Storage technologies and protocols
- Storage in XenServer
- Creating storage repositories
- Managing storage repositories
- Multipathing overview

Storage overview

XenServer is able to manage different types of storage, locally and remotely connected. Before discovering how storage is configured and managed by XenServer, we will review some storage concepts.

Virtual machines use disk resources allocated to them by the XenServer host, through Control Domain (Dom0). These disk resources are parts of real disk space available as a Storage Repository. Because XenServer is based on Linux, it is a good idea to review how Linux manages disk storage. In Linux, typically the physical disk itself is split into partitions and it is accessed through a device file.

As an example, for the first **Small Computer System Interface (SCSI)** disk on the system, the device filename might be /dev/sda (SCSI disk "a"). Partitions of that disk will have device filenames such as /dev/sda1, and /dev/sda2 — /dev is the directory that contains all the device files.

Typically, when the system boots, a disk is automatically mounted over /, which is the root directory of the filesystem.

Disks can be mounted onto the Linux filesystem using the mount command.

> The basic syntax for the mount command is:
>
> **mount device directory**
>
> where the device parameter is the partition or device you want to mount and the directory parameter is the directory where you want to mount the partition or device.

Usually before you can mount a disk, you must format it if a filesystem is not available on it. When you install XenServer, the default filesystem type used is ext3.

The following figure shows you these concepts graphically. Here you can see that partition sda1 is mounted to directory /mnt/mymount:

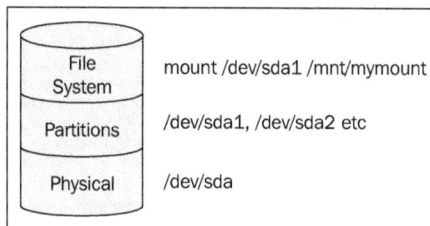

File System	mount /dev/sda1 /mnt/mymount
Partitions	/dev/sda1, /dev/sda2 etc
Physical	/dev/sda

Linux provides a method of allocating space on mass-storage devices that is more flexible than a conventional partitioning schema. This method is known as **Logical Volume Manager (LVM)** and gives you the possibility to combine physical volumes into many logical volumes.

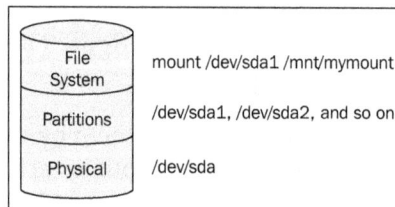

File System	mount /dev/sda1 /mnt/mymount
Partitions	/dev/sda1, /dev/sda2, and so on
Physical	/dev/sda

In the following example you see all of the **Physical Volumes (PV1, PV2, PV3)** as part of a single **Volume Group (VG1)**.

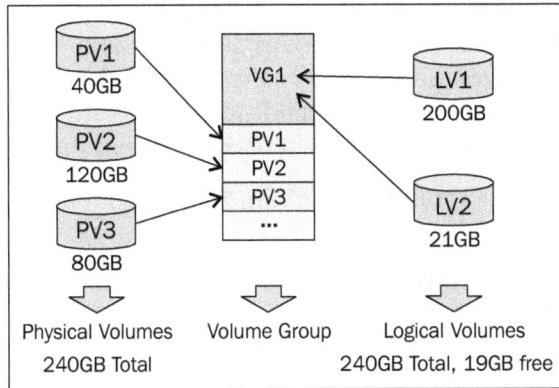

The Logical Volume Manager can support one or more VGs and a VG acts as a pool of storage from which you can create Logical Volumes (LVs). In this example there are two LVs that can now be used as though they were physical volumes.

Because a PV is represented in Linux as a device file (for example, `/dev/sda`), that device file may represent local storage or a **Logical Unit Number (LUN)** on a **Storage Area Network (SAN)**.

As with PVs, LVs do not have to be formatted to be part of a Linux filesystem; they can be used as raw storage, which is how XenServer uses them. When LVM is being used to support SRs, you will find one LV on the XenServer for each **Virtual Disk Image (VDI)**. We will learn more about virtual disk images later in the chapter.

> You can find more details about LVM at the following web address: `http://en.wikipedia.org/wiki/Logical_Volume_Manager_(Linux)`.

Storage technologies and protocols

Within the world of storage, you can find three main architectures:

- Direct Attached Storage (DAS)
- Storage Area Network (SAN)
- Network Attached Storage (NAS)

Direct Attached Storage

A **Direct Attached Storage** (**DAS**) is a storage subsystem that is directly attached to a server or workstation using a cable. Typically, a DAS system is based on an enclosure containing several hard disk drives. In some cases, storage shelves can be connected to multiple servers so the data or the disks can be shared (for example for fault tolerance). DAS systems also offers fault-tolerance features and are able to "hot swap" failed disks and to rebuild disk from parity on other disks.

Common storage protocols for DAS are SATA, SAS, and Fibre Channel.

[Prefer SAS hard drives over SATA hard drives in order to achieve high performance.]

Storage Area Network (SAN)

A **Storage Area Network** (**SAN**) is a dedicated storage network that provides access to consolidated, block-level storage. SANs primarily are used to make storage devices, such as disk arrays, accessible to servers so that the devices appear as locally attached to the operating system.

The cost and complexity of SANs dropped in the early 2000s, allowing wider adoption across both enterprise and small to medium-sized business environments. A SAN alone does not provide the "file" abstraction, only block-level operations.

A SAN typically has its own dedicated network of storage devices that are generally not accessible through the regular network by regular devices. In order to connect a device to the SAN network a specialized extension card called **Host Bus Adapter** (**HBA**) is required if you use Fibre Channel as the storage protocol.

After introducing storage technologies, we now have a look at storage protocols in order to understand the main differences.

Network Attached Storage (NAS)

Network Attached Storage (**NAS**) is a file-level computer data storage connected to a computer network providing data access to heterogeneous clients. NAS not only operates as a file server, but is specialized for this task either by its hardware, software, or configuration of those elements. NAS systems are networked appliances which contain one or more hard drives, often arranged into logical, redundant storage containers or RAID arrays. Network Attached Storage removes the responsibility of file serving from other servers on the network and they typically provide access to files using standard Ethernet and network file sharing protocols such as NFS or SMB/CIFS.

Storage protocols

The first protocol we introduce is the **Network File System** (**NFS**).

Network File System (NFS)

The **Network File System** (**NFS**) protocol is an application-layer (OSI layer 7) network protocol. In general NFS is a low complexity protocol which only allows access to files over an Ethernet network.

NFS was initially developed by Sun in 1983. Latest versions of NFS have been developed by the **Internet Engineering Task Force** (**IETF**).

NFS is most frequently used within Linux or Unix environments, but is also available for other platforms such as Windows (Windows Services for Unix/NFS Client or Server) or Apple Mac OS.

Initially NFS was based on UDP for performance reasons. Starting with version 3 NFS added support for TCP/IP based networks.

Fibre Channel (FC)

Fibre Channel (**FC**), is a transport protocol (similar to TCP used in IP networks) which predominantly transports SCSI commands over Fibre Channel networks. Despite its name, Fibre Channel signaling can run on both twisted pair copper wire and fiber-optic cables.

In order to enable a system to access a Fibre Channel network, it is necessary to implement a Host Bus Adapter (HBA). Fibre Channel HBAs are available for all major open systems, computer architectures, and buses and some are OS dependent. Each HBA has a unique **World Wide Name** (**WWN**), which is similar to an Ethernet MAC address in that it uses an **Organizationally Unique Identifier** (**OUI**) assigned by the IEEE.

There are two types of WWNs on a HBA; a node WWN (WWNN), which can be shared by some or all ports of a device, and a port WWN (WWPN), which is necessarily unique to each port.

Fibre Channel can be used in three different topologies:

- **Point-to-Point (FC-P2P)**: Two devices are connected back to back. This is the simplest topology, with limited connectivity.

- **Arbitrated loop (FC-AL)**: In this design, all devices are in a loop or ring, similar to token ring networking. Adding or removing a device from the loop causes all activity on the loop to be interrupted. The failure of one device causes a break in the ring. Fibre Channel hubs exist to connect multiple devices together and may bypass failed ports. A loop may also be made by cabling each port to the next in a ring.

- **Switched fabric (FC-SW)**: All devices or loops of devices are connected to Fibre Channel switches, similar conceptually to modern Ethernet implementations. The switches manage the state of the fabric, providing optimized interconnections.

Switched fabric is the most flexible topology, enabling all servers and storage devices to communicate with each other. It also provides for failover architecture in the event a server or disk array fails. FC-SW involves one or more intelligent Fibre Channel switches, each providing multiple ports for nodes.

Because switches can be cascaded and interwoven, the resultant connection cloud has been called the *fabric*.

Internet Small Computer System Interface (iSCSI)

The last protocol we analyze is **Internet Small Computer System Interface (iSCSI)** which is a mapping of the regular SCSI protocol over TCP/IP, more commonly over Gigabit Ethernet. Unlike Fibre Channel, which requires special-purpose cabling and switches, iSCSI can be run over long distances using an existing network infrastructure. TCP/IP uses a client/server model, but iSCSI uses the terms *initiator* (for the data consumer) and *target* (for the LUN). An initiator falls into two broad types:

- A software initiator uses code to implement iSCSI. Typically, this happens in a kernel-resident device driver that uses the existing network card (NIC) and network stack to emulate SCSI devices for a computer by speaking the iSCSI protocol. Software initiators are available for most mainstream operating systems, and this type is the most common mode of deploying iSCSI on computers.

- A hardware initiator uses dedicated hardware that mitigates the overhead of iSCSI, TCP processing, and Ethernet interrupts, and therefore may improve the performance of servers that use iSCSI. An iSCSI Host Bus Adapter (HBA) implements a hardware initiator and is typically packaged as a combination of a Gigabit Ethernet NIC, some kind of TCP/IP offload technology (TOE) and a SCSI bus adapter (controller).

To ensure that only valid initiators connect to storage arrays, administrators most commonly run iSCSI only over logically-isolated backchannel networks.

For authentication, iSCSI initiators and targets prove their identity to each other using the Challenge-Handshake Authentication Protocol (CHAP), which includes a mechanism to prevent clear text passwords from appearing on the wire.

> Remember to check if your storage devices and host bus adapters are supported in the XenServer 6 Hardware Compatibility List provided by Citrix. In production environments, always use certified devices.
>
> Visit the website http://hcl.xensource.com for details.
>
> You can find more details about all the storage types we have introduced in this chapter at the following web addresses:
>
> http://en.wikipedia.org/wiki/Direct-attached_storage
>
> http://en.wikipedia.org/wiki/Network-attached_storage
>
> http://en.wikipedia.org/wiki/Storage_area_network

Storage in XenServer

Now that you have an overview of storage technologies and protocols, it is time to introduce the concepts related to storage objects and attributes in XenServer. Storage objects are the following:

- Storage Repository (SR)
- Virtual Disk Images (VDIs)
- Physical Block Devices (PBDs)
- Virtual Block Devices (VBDs)

The following figure shows you how the storage objects are presented and how they are related to each other:

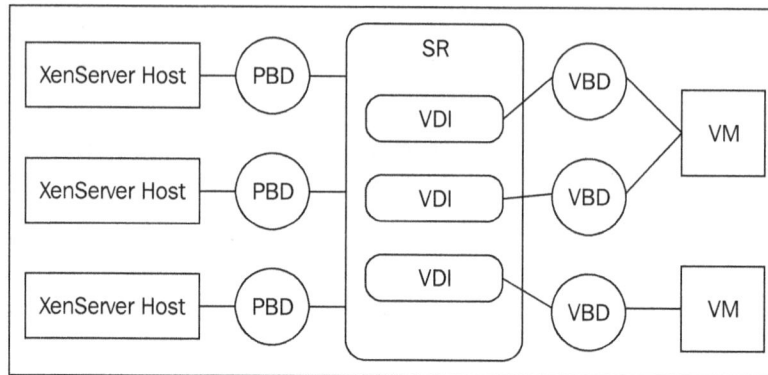

Storage Repository (SR)

The main object in XenServer storage is the **Storage Repository** (**SR**). This term is used to identify a storage target used by XenServer to store Virtual Disk Images (VDIs), which is the object representing the virtual disk used by a virtual machine.

Generally, the target storage for an SR can be:

- Local storage on the XenServer host: An LUN on an iSCSI SAN or an LUN on a Fibre Channel SAN.
- Storage through a NetApp or Dell EqualLogic storage appliance: Network File Systems

You can find one or more of these Storage Repository types in a typical XenServer environment. Also, a Storage Repository can be shared by more than one XenServer host; this is for example when you have an iSCSI SAN and storage is "visible" from all the XenSever hosts belonging to your XenServer pool.

Remember that a shared Storage Repository is a requirement to be able to start a virtual machine on any host of the pool using the XenMotion feature.

Virtual Disk Images (VDIs)

Virtual Disk Images are a storage abstraction that is presented to a virtual machine. VDIs are the fundamental unit of virtualized storage in XenServer. Similar to Storage Repositories, VDIs are persistent, on-disk objects that exist independently of XenServer hosts.

The format of a VDI will be one of the following three types depending on the type of SR it is contained in and the features which are needed:

- **Virtual Hard Disk (VHD)**: VHD is a technology used in Microsoft Virtual PC (originally created by Connectix, then bought by Microsoft). This format is also used by Microsoft's Hyper-V technology and is how XenServer supports VMs created by Hyper-V. Virtual disk images based on this format are essentially flat files. The VHD format supports *sparse allocation* and *fast cloning*. It is also shareable when the containing SR is of type NFS. VHD files may also be chained, allowing two VDIs to share common data. In cases where an NFS-based VM is cloned, the resulting VMs will share the common on-disk data at the time of cloning. Each will proceed to make its own changes in an isolated copy-on-write (CoW) version of the VDI. This feature allows NFS-based VMs to be cloned quickly from templates, facilitating very fast provisioning and deployment of new VMs. The VHD format also supports snapshots.

- **Logical Volume Manager (LVM)**: LVM is used on a raw block device (either local or SAN-based), and a VDI ends up being a Logical Volume (LV) in a Volume Group (VG). This format supports VDI resizing. It is also sharable when the storage originates from a SAN.

- **Supported storage appliances**: For the NetApp appliance, the VDI ends up as a LUN in a NetApp volume. The Dell EqualLogic filer will also store a VDI as a LUN. This format supports sparse allocation, VDI resizing, fast cloning, and is shareable.

Storage attributes

In the *Virtual Disks Images* (*VDIs*) section we spoke about some attributes related to storage. Now it is time to explain them.

The first attribute we introduce is "shared". Yes, I know this is easy to understand!

Shared means that the storage is based on a Storage Area Network (SAN) or NFS, and so can inherently be shared by multiple XenServers in a pool. This is essential for the virtual machine's performance and migration.

The second attribute is "Sparse allocation". The expansion of a Virtual Disk Image file is allocated as the virtual machine writes data to it (the VM is writing to what it thinks is a local drive). The VM VDI files take up only as much space as is required. For example, if a 20 GB VDI is allocated for a new VM and an operating system is installed, the VDI file will only reflect the size of the operating system data that has been written so far (plus some format overhead), not the entire 20 GB. This attribute is also known as "Thin Provisioning".

The "Resizable" attribute is used on a detached VDI to increase the size of that VDI. The VM operating system should have the capability to extend its format into the new space.

"Fast Cloning" is the last attribute we introduce, where a new virtual disk image is created for a virtual machine, but is in essence a pointer to an existing VDI. Any blocks that are read from the new VDI will actually come from the old VDI, but any changes to blocks or newly added blocks are put in the new VDI. This means a VM can be cloned almost instantaneously because the space is allocated on an as-needed basis. For VHD types of VDIs, this can lead to long chains if this process is repeated many times.

Physical Block Devices (PBDs)

Physical Block Devices (**PBDs**) represent the interface between a physical server and an attached Storage Repository. PBDs are connector objects that allow a given SR to be mapped to a XenServer host. PBDs store the device configuration fields that are used to connect to and interact with a given storage target. For example, NFS device configuration includes the IP address of the NFS server and the associated path that the XenServer host mounts. PBD objects manage the run time attachment of a given SR to a given XenServer host.

Virtual Block Devices (VBDs)

Virtual Block Devices (**VBDs**) are connector objects (similar to the Physical Block Devices described earlier) that allows mappings between Virtual Disk Images and virtual machines. In addition to providing a mechanism for attaching (also called *plugging*) a VDI into a VM, VBDs allow for the fine-tuning of parameters regarding QoS (Quality of Service), statistics, and the bootability of a given VDI.

> You can find more details about XenServer storage at the following web address: http://support.citrix.com/article/CTX119088.

Creating Storage Repositories

In the previous paragraphs we have learnt that a XenServer Storage Repository is a storage container on which virtual disks are stored. Both Storage Repositories and virtual disks are persistent, on-disk objects that exist independently of XenServer. Storage Repositories can be shared between servers in a resource pool and can exist on different types of physical storage device, both internal and external, including local disk devices and shared network storage.

A number of different types of storage are available when you create a new Storage Repository using the **New Storage Repository** wizard and, depending on the type of storage selected, a number of advanced storage features can be configured in XenCenter, including:

- **Dynamic multipathing**: You can configure storage multipathing using round robin mode load balancing on Fibre Channel and iSCSI Storage Repositories.

- **Thin provisioning**: You can choose the type of space management used on NetApp, Dell EqualLogic, and StorageLink SRs. By default, allocated space is thickly provisioned and all virtual allocation guarantees are fully enforced on the filer, guaranteeing that virtual disks will never run out of space and consequently experience failed writes to disk. Thin provisioning allows the disks to be better utilized, as physical capacity is allocated only as a VM needs it—when it writes—allowing for over-provisioning of the available storage and maximum utilization of your storage assets.

Now, it is time to discover how to create a Storage Repository in XenServer. This task can be done using XenCenter or xe CLI—xe CLI provides you with more flexibility, so you can start to manage SRs working with the console and when you are familiar with it move on to the command line.

Based on my experience, XenCenter is enough for the common tasks.

Creating a Storage Repository

New Storage Repositories are created using the **New Storage** wizard in XenCenter (available on the toolbar or on the **Storage** menu | **New SR**).

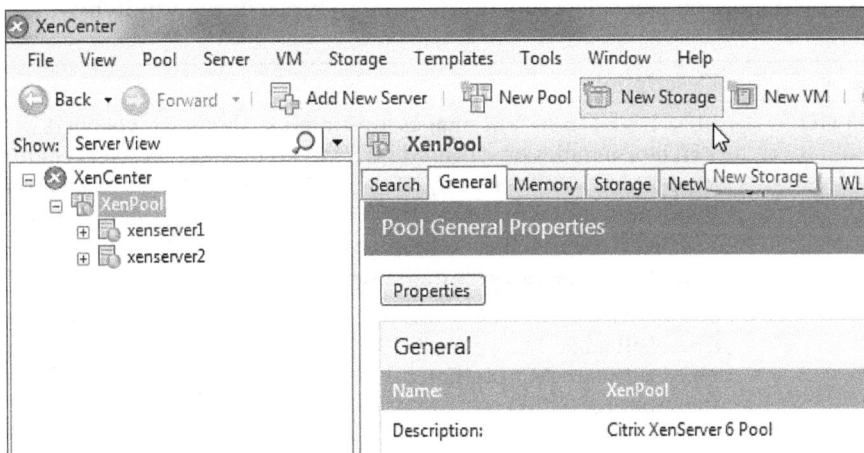

You select the physical storage type on the first page of the **New Storage Repository** wizard and then follow the steps in the wizard as it takes you through the configuration process for that storage type. The set of available settings in the wizard depends on the storage system type you select on the first page.

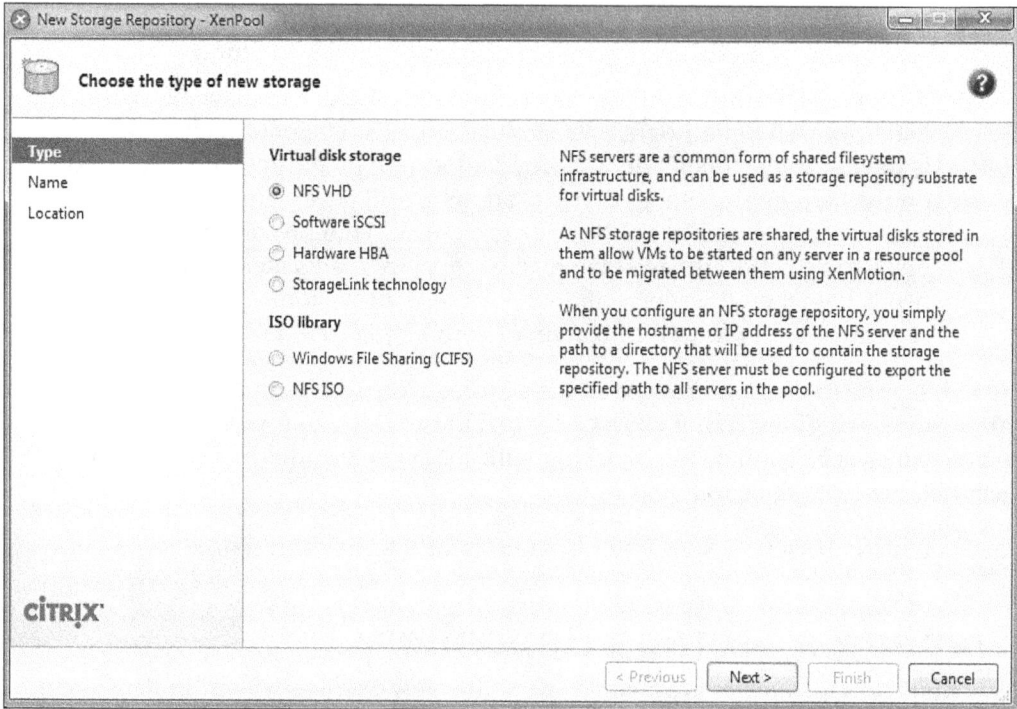

On the **Type** page, you can select one of the storage types in the following table:

Type	Description
NFS VHD	In NFS VHD SRs, VM images are stored as thinly-provisioned VHD format files on a shared NFS target. Existing NFS servers that support NFS V3 over TCP/IP can be used immediately as a Storage Repository for virtual disks. NFS SRs can be shared, allowing any VMs with their virtual disks in an NFS VHD Storage Repository to migrate between servers in the same resource pool.
Software iSCSI	Software iSCSI SRs use a shared Logical Volume Manager (LVM) on a SAN attached LUN over iSCSI. iSCSI is supported using the open-iSCSI software iSCSI initiator or by using a supported iSCSI Host Bus Adapter (HBA).

Type	Description
Hardware HBA	Hardware HBA SRs connect to a Fibre Channel (FC), Fibre Channel over Ethernet (FCoE) or shared Serial Attached SCSI (SAS) LUNs via an HBA. You need to carry out the configuration required to expose the LUN before running the **New Storage Repository** wizard – the wizard will automatically probe for available LUNs and display a list of all the LUNs found.
StorageLink Technology	This option allows you to configure a StorageLink SR that provides native access to automated fabric/initiator and array configuration features in NetApp/IBM N Series or Dell EqualLogic PS Series arrays. The exact features available for a given StorageLink SR depend on the capabilities of the array.
Windows File Sharing (CIFS)	CIFS ISO SRs handle CD images stored as files in ISO format available as a Windows (CIFS) share.
NFS ISO	NFS ISO SRs handle CD images stored as files in ISO format available as an NFS share. This type of SR can be useful for creating shared ISO libraries, for example, VM installation images.

We will introduce StorageLink Technology later in this chapter.

Alternatively, if you prefer using the xe CLI, run the `sr-create` command. This command creates a new SR on the storage substrate (potentially destroying any existing data), and creates the SR API object and a corresponding Physical Block Device record, enabling VMs to use the storage. On successful creation of the SR, the PBD is automatically plugged. If you append the parameter `shared=true` to the command, a PBD record is created and plugged for every XenServer host in the resource pool.

The following is the syntax for the `sr-create` command:

```
sr-create name-label=<name> physical-size=<size> type=<type> content-
type=<content_type> device-config:<config_name>=<value> [host-
uuid=<XenServer host UUID>] [shared=<true | false>]
```

where:

- `name-label` is the name of the SR.
- `physical-size` is the total physical size of the SR expressed in bytes.
- `type` is the type of the SR used to specify the SR backend driver to use (for example NFS).

- `content-type` is the the type of the SR's content. It is used to distinguish ISO libraries from other SRs. For Storage Repositories that store a library of ISOs, the content-type must be set to `iso`. In other cases, Citrix recommends that this be set either to `empty` or to the string `user`.

- `Device-config` is the parameter that points to the device offering the storage services.

- `Host-uuid` is the parameter related to the XenServer host where you want to create the SR. You use this parameter when you set the parameter `Shared` to `False`.

- `Shared` is the value that is set if the SR is capable of being shared between multiple XenServer hosts.

Going on through the chapter, you will find out how to execute the `sr-create` command for creating some types of storage repository; so don't worry if you don't understand the syntax right now.

Creating a new NFS VHD Storage Repository

The NFS VHD type stores disks as VHD files on a remote NFS filesystem.

NFS is an ubiquitous form of storage infrastructure that is available in many environments. XenServer allows existing NFS servers that support NFS V3 over TCP/IP to be used immediately as a Storage Repository for virtual disks (VDIs). VDIs are stored in the Microsoft VHD format only. Moreover, as NFS SRs can be shared, VDIs stored in a shared SR allow VMs to be started on any XenServer hosts in a resource pool and be migrated between them using XenMotion with no noticeable downtime.

> The NFS server must be configured to export the specified path to all XenServer hosts in the pool, or the creation of the SR and the plugging of the PBD record will fail.

As mentioned at the beginning of this chapter, VDIs stored on NFS are sparse. The image file is allocated as the VM writes data into the disk. This has the considerable benefit that VM image files take up only as much space on the NFS storage as is required. If a 100 GB VDI is allocated for a new VM and an OS is installed, the VDI file will only reflect the size of the OS data that has been written to the disk rather than the entire 100 GB.

> Since virtual disks on NFS Storage Repositories are created as sparse, you must ensure that there is enough disk space on the SR for all required virtual disks.

To configure an NFS VHD Storage Repository, follow the given procedure:

1. Open the **New Storage Repository** wizard and click on 🗑 New Storage on the toolbar.

2. Alternatively:
   - On the **Storage** tab for the selected pool or server, click on **New SR**
   - On the **Storage** menu, click on **New SR**
   - In the **Resources** pane, select a server or pool then right-click and click on **New SR** on the shortcut menu

3. Select **NFS VHD** as the physical storage type, then click on **Next**.

4. On the **Name** page, enter the name of the new SR. By default, a description of the SR will be generated automatically by the wizard, including a summary of the configuration options you select as you progress through the wizard. Click on **Next** to continue.

> **Best practice**: Enter your own description, clearing the
> **Auto-generate description** checkbox and typing in the
> **Description** box.

5. On the **Location** page, specify the NFS storage target details:

Parameter	Description
Share Name	The IP address or DNS name of the server and the path. For example, server:/ShareName where server is the DNS name or IP address of the server computer, and ShareName is a folder or filename path. In this example, we will use `192.168.0.11:/mnt/SharedDisk1`
Advanced Options	You can enter any additional configuration options here.

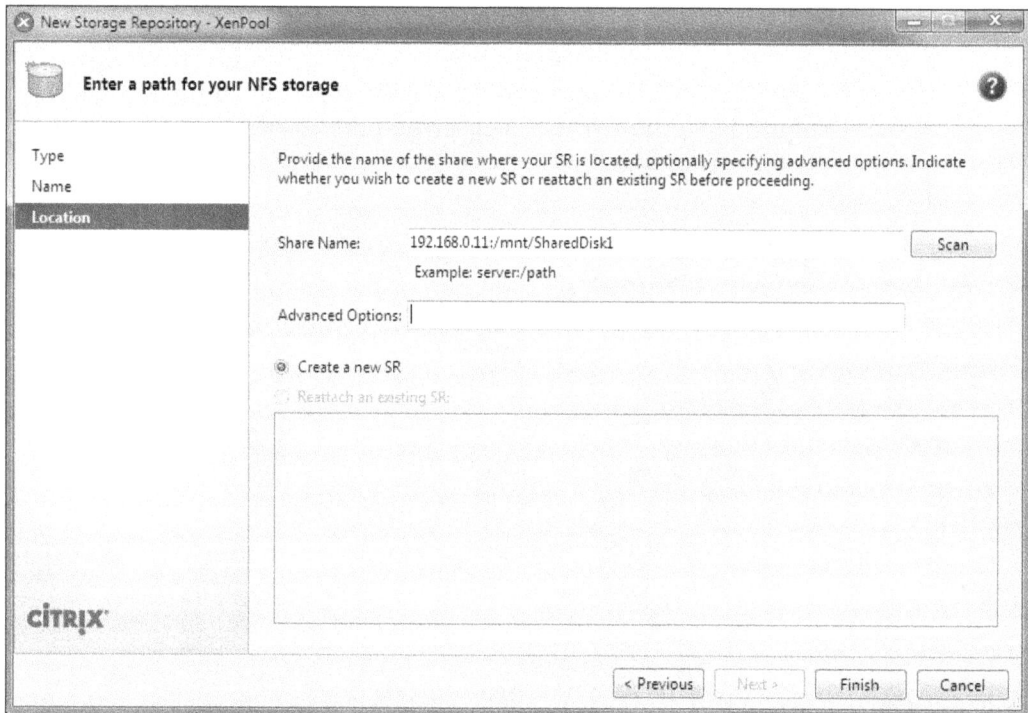

6. Click on **Scan** to have the wizard scan for existing NFS SRs in the location you specified.

7. Click on **Finish** — XenCenter will complete the new SR configuration and present you with the Storage Repository on the console.

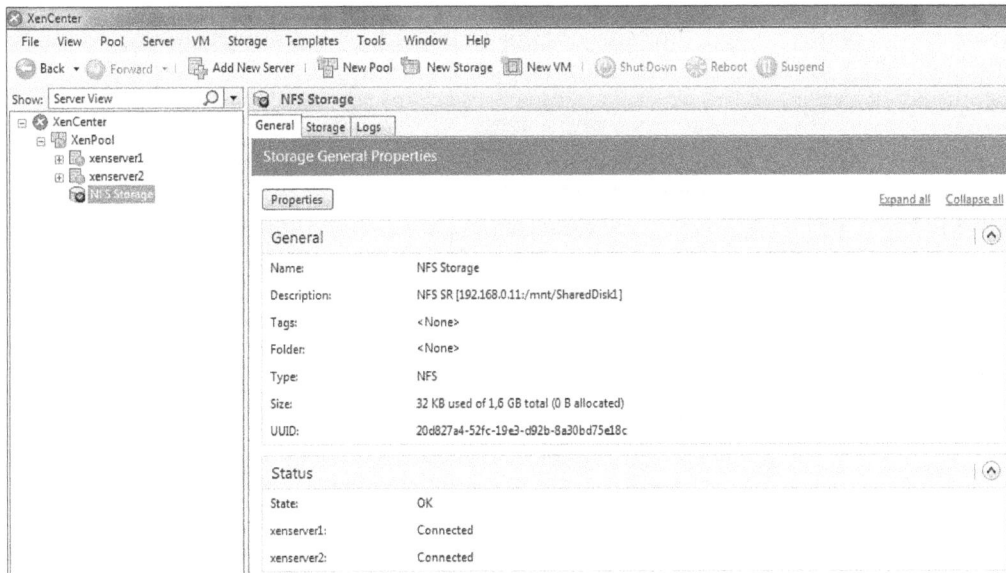

Now, we will take a look at the procedure to create an NFS VHD Storage Repository using xe CLI and the `sr-create` command.

In our example, we will run the following command to create a shared NFS SR on `192.168.0.11:/mnt/SharedDisk1`:

```
xe sr-create name-label="NFS Storage" type=nfs content-type=user device-
config:server=192.168.0.11 device-config:serverpath=/mnt/SharedDisk1
shared=true
```

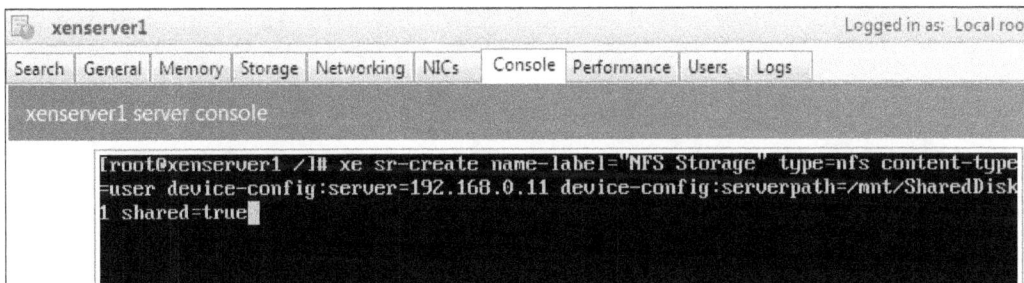

Remember that `server` and `serverpath` are required values for the `device-config` parameter.

Creating a new software iSCSI Storage Repository

XenServer provides support for shared SRs on iSCSI LUNs. iSCSI is supported using the open-iSCSI software iSCSI initiator or by using a supported iSCSI Host Bus Adapter (HBA).

Shared iSCSI support using the software iSCSI initiator is implemented based on the Logical Volume Manager (LVM) and provides the same performance benefits provided by LVM VDIs in the local disk case. Like NFS, shared iSCSI SRs using the software-based host initiator are capable of supporting VM migrations using XenMotion—VMs can be started on any XenServer host in a resource pool and migrated between them without downtime.

iSCSI SRs use the entire LUN specified at creation time and may not span more than one LUN. CHAP support is provided for client authentication, during both the data path initialization and the LUN discovery phases.

Remember that all iSCSI initiators and targets must have a unique name to ensure they can be uniquely identified on the network.

An initiator has an iSCSI initiator address, and a target has an iSCSI target address. Collectively these are called **iSCSI Qualified Names (IQNs)**.

iSCSI targets commonly provide access control using iSCSI initiator IQN lists, so all iSCSI targets/LUNs to be accessed by a XenServer host must be configured to allow access by the host's initiator IQN. Similarly, targets/LUNs to be used as shared iSCSI SRs must be configured to allow access by all host IQNs in the resource pool.

XenServer hosts support a single iSCSI initiator which is automatically created and configured with a random IQN during host installation. The single initiator can be used to connect to multiple iSCSI targets concurrently.

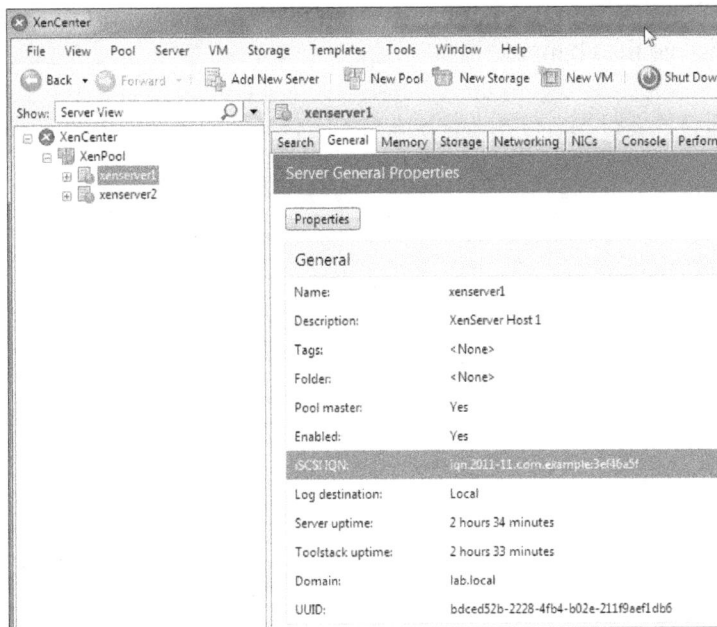

The XenServer host IQN value can be adjusted using XenCenter. To do this task, follow the given procedure:

1. Select the desired host and open the host's properties.

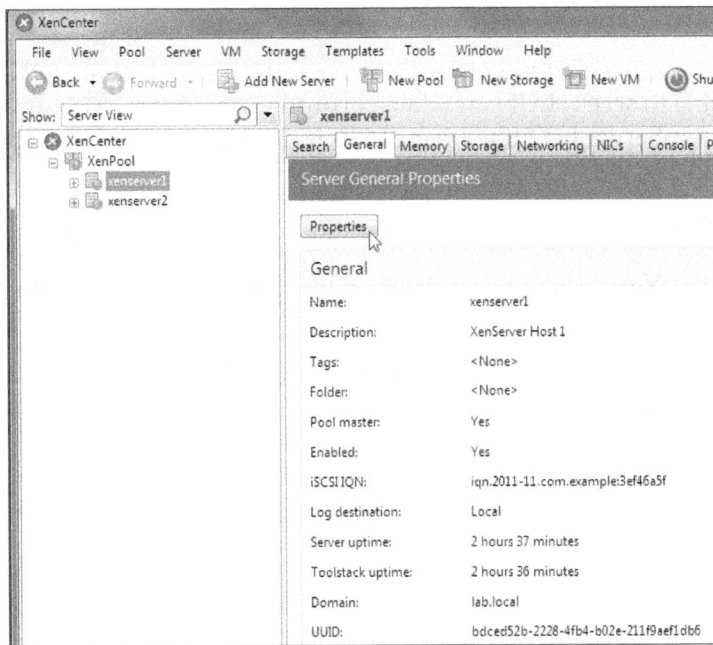

2. Modify the **iSCSI IQN** field with the IQN name you want to set and click on **OK** to save the change.

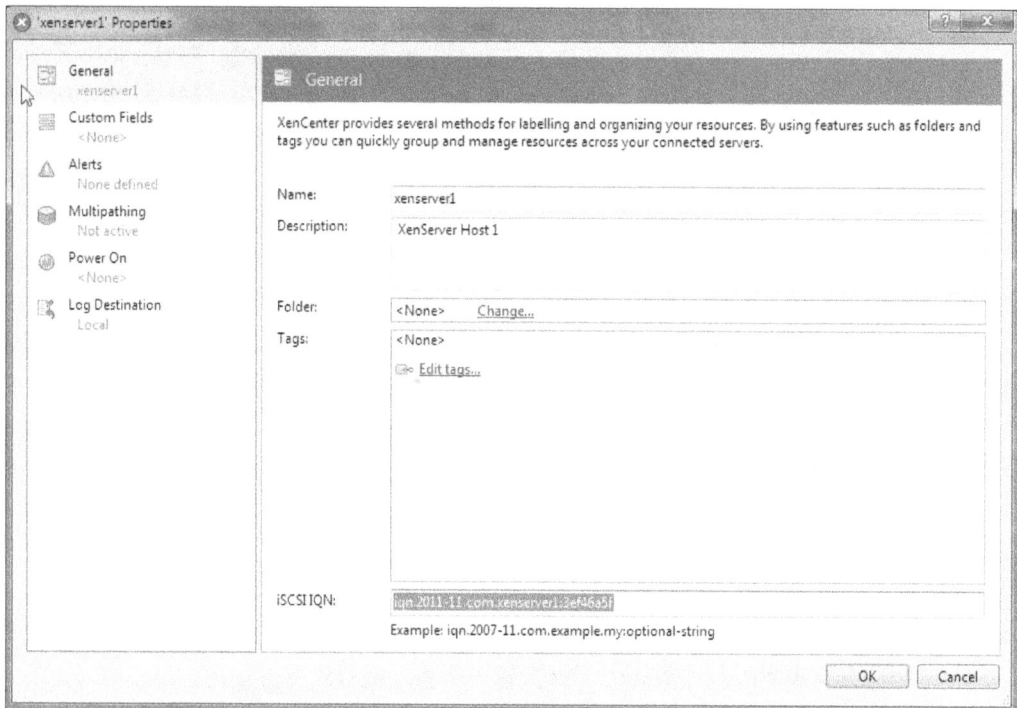

Remember that every iSCSI target and initiator must have a unique IQN, otherwise you will not able to access LUN and data corruption can occur. Also, if you need to change the XenServer host IQN, remember to detach the iSCSI Storage Repositories first.

To configure a new software iSCSI Storage Repository, follow the given procedure:

1. Open the **New Storage Repository** wizard and click on the **New Storage** button on the toolbar.

2. Select **Software iSCSI** as the physical storage type, then click on **Next**.

3. On the **Name** page, enter the name of the new SR and click on **Next** to continue.

4. On the **Location** page, specify the iSCSI target details:

Parameter	Description
Target Host	The IP address or DNS name of the iSCSI target.
Use CHAP	If the iSCSI target is configured to used CHAP authentication, select the **Use CHAP** checkbox and fill in the following details: • **CHAP User**: The CHAP authentication username credential that should be applied when connecting to the target • **CHAP Password**: The CHAP authentication password credential that should be applied when connecting to the target

5. Click on **Discover IQNs** to discover the iSCSI target IQN and choose the IQN for your storage appliance.

6. Click on **Discover LUNs** to specify the LUN on which the Storage Repository will be created.

7. Click on **Finish** to complete the new SR configuration and close the wizard. XenServer will scan the storage for LUN acquisition and will start.

We will now take a look at the procedure to create iSCSI Storage Repository using xe CLI and the `sr-create` command.

In our example, we will run the following command to create a shared iSCSI SR on target `192.168.0.11`:

```
xe sr-create name-label="iSCSI Storage" type=lvmoiscsi content-
type=user device-config:target=192.168.0.11 device-config:port=3260
device-config:targetIQN=iqn.2011-11.com.xenserver1:3ef46a5f device-
config:SCSIid=3300000002db1eaba shared=true
```

XenServer will add the storage at the end of the process. If you pay attention to the command you will notice the `SCSIid` parameter. How to find it? Right Question!

In order to find `SCSIid`, run the same command without the `device-config:SCSIid` parameter. XenServer will display some information about the `iscsi-target`:

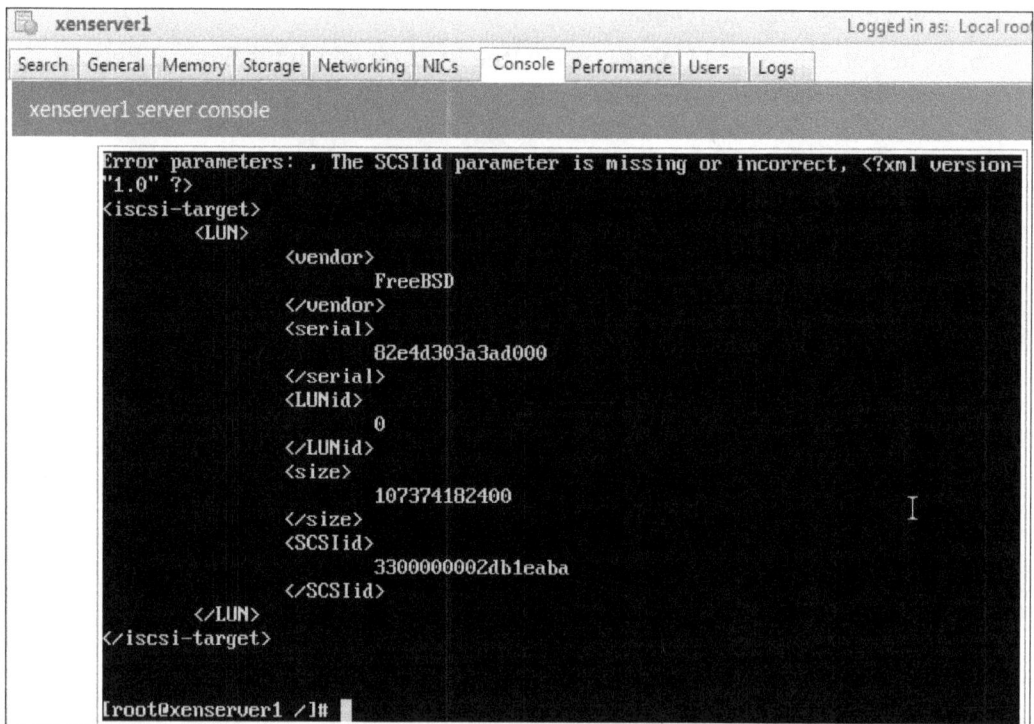

```
                                                    xenserver1                                    Logged in as: Local root

 Search  General  Memory  Storage  Networking  NICs   Console  Performance  Users  Logs

 xenserver1 server console

Error parameters: , The SCSIid parameter is missing or incorrect, <?xml version=
"1.0" ?>
<iscsi-target>
        <LUN>
                    <vendor>
                            FreeBSD
                    </vendor>
                    <serial>
                            82e4d303a3ad000
                    </serial>
                    <LUNid>
                            0
                    </LUNid>
                    <size>
                            107374182400
                    </size>
                    <SCSIid>
                            3300000002db1eaba
                    </SCSIid>
        </LUN>
</iscsi-target>

[root@xenserver1 /]#
```

Here you can find section `<SCSIid>` — this is the ID you have to provide to XenServer with the `device-config=SCSIid` parameter.

> If you want to play with iSCSI storage in a lab environment, you can use FreeNAS, a free solution to build a lab environment for XenServer. Download it from `http://www.freenas.org`.

Creating a new hardware HBA Storage Repository

Hardware HBA Storage Repositories connect to *Fibre Channel* (FC), *Fibre Channel over Ethernet* (FCoE), or shared *Serial Attached SCSI* (SAS) LUNs via a Host Bus Adapter. Before creating an HBA SR, you need to carry out the configuration required to expose the LUN to the XenServer pool.

Refer to your HBA manufacturer for details on configuring the host adapter.

When you start the **New Storage Repository Wizard**, the wizard will automatically probe for available LUNs and display a list of all the LUNs found.

1. Open the **New Storage Repository** wizard and click on the **New Storage** button on the toolbar.
2. Alternatively:
   - On the **Storage** tab for the selected pool or server, click on **NewSR**
   - On the **Storage** menu, click on **NewSR**
   - In the **Resources** pane, select a server or pool then right-click and click on **NewSR** on the shortcut menu
3. Select **Hardware HBA** as the physical storage type and then click on **Next**.
4. On the **Name** page, enter the name of the new SR. Click on **Next** to continue.
5. The wizard scans for available LUNs and then displays a page listing all the LUNs found. Select a LUN from the list.
6. Click on **Finish** to complete the new SR configuration and close the wizard.

Creating a new StorageLink Repository

A StorageLink Storage Repository can provide direct access to high-performance storage, allowing the VMs in your XenServer environment to benefit from array-side enterprise storage services such as replication, de duplication, thin provisioning, snapshots and cloning, data protection, and performance optimization.

StorageLink SRs use storage adapters to access different storage arrays on all common storage technologies including both NAS and SAN over either Fibre Channel or iSCSI. The features available on a given StorageLink SR depend on the capabilities of the underlying array. StorageLink SRs can co-exist with other SR types on the same storage array hardware, and multiple StorageLink SRs can be defined within the same resource pool.

Because the StorageLink SR can be used to access different storage arrays, the exact features available for a given StorageLink SR depend on the capabilities of the array. Each SR uses a LUN-per-VDI model where a new LUN is provisioned for each virtual disk (VDI). StorageLink supports the following array types:

- NetApp/ IBM N Series
- Dell EqualLogic PS Series

> The Dell EqualLogic API uses SNMP for communication. It requires SNMP v3 and therefore requires firmware v5.0.0 or greater. If your EqualLogic array uses earlier firmware, you will need to upgrade it to v5.0.0. The firmware can be downloaded from the Dell EqualLogic Firmware download site at `https://www.equallogic.com/support/download.aspx?id=1502`.

To create a **StorageLink** repository, follow the given procedure:

1. Open the **New Storage Repository** wizard and click on the **New Storage** button on the toolbar.

2. Alternatively:
   - On the **Storage** tab for the selected pool or server, click **NewSR**
   - On the **Storage** menu, click on **NewSR**
   - In the **Resources** pane, select a server or pool then right-click and click on **NewSR** on the shortcut menu

3. Select **StorageLink Technology** as the physical storage type and then click on **Next**.

4. On the **Name** page, enter the name of the new SR. Click on **Next** to continue.

5. On the **Storage Adapter** page, select one of the available storage system adapters and then click on **Next** to continue.

6. On the **Storage System** page, select the storage system that will host the storage for this SR:

   ° In the **Array** target box, enter the hostname or IP address of the array management console.

   ° Under **Credentials**, enter the username and password to use for connection to the array management console.

   ° Click on **Discover** to scan the target array for storage systems. After discovery has completed, select a storage system from the Storage System list, then click on **Next** to continue.

   On the **Settings** page, define the SR settings. The set of available settings for each new SR depends on the storage system vendor/model and the configuration of the storage pool you've selected.

Parameter	Description
Storage pool	Identify the storage pool within the specified storage system to use for allocating storage. On some types of storage system you can use the **Show all** checkbox to list all storage pools here.
RAID types	Select the level of RAID to use for the SR, as supported by the storage array
Provisioning type	Set the provisioning type (Default, Thick, or Thin)
Provisioning options	Set the provisioning options (for example, deduplication)
Protocol	Set the storage protocol used to connect the managed server to the storage (iSCSI, Fibre Channel, or Auto to have the system choose)
Use CHAP authentication	If the server is configured to used CHAP authentication, select this checkbox and fill in the username and password to be used

7. Click on **Finish** to complete the new StorageLink SR configuration and close the wizard.

Creating a new ISO Storage Repository

ISO Storage Repository is useful when you need to share ISO images such as operating systems or software ISO that you use to create virtual machines. Two ISO SR types are provided for handling CD images stored as files in ISO format:

- The NFS ISO SR type handles CD images stored as files in ISO format available as an NFS share

- The CIFS ISO SR type handles CD images stored as files in ISO format available as a Windows share

In the following example, we will create an ISO repository using the `ISO` shared folder located on the Windows server named `dc.lab.local`.

1. Open the **New Storage Repository** wizard. Click on 🗄 New Storage on the toolbar.

2. Alternatively:

   ° On the **Storage** tab for the selected pool or server, click on **NewSR**

   ° On the **Storage** menu, click on **NewSR**

   ° In the **Resources** pane, select a server or pool then right-click and click on **NewSR** on the shortcut menu

3. Under **ISO Library**, select **Windows File Sharing (CIFS)** as the physical storage type and then click on **Next**.

4. On the **Name** page, enter the name of the new SR and type a description.

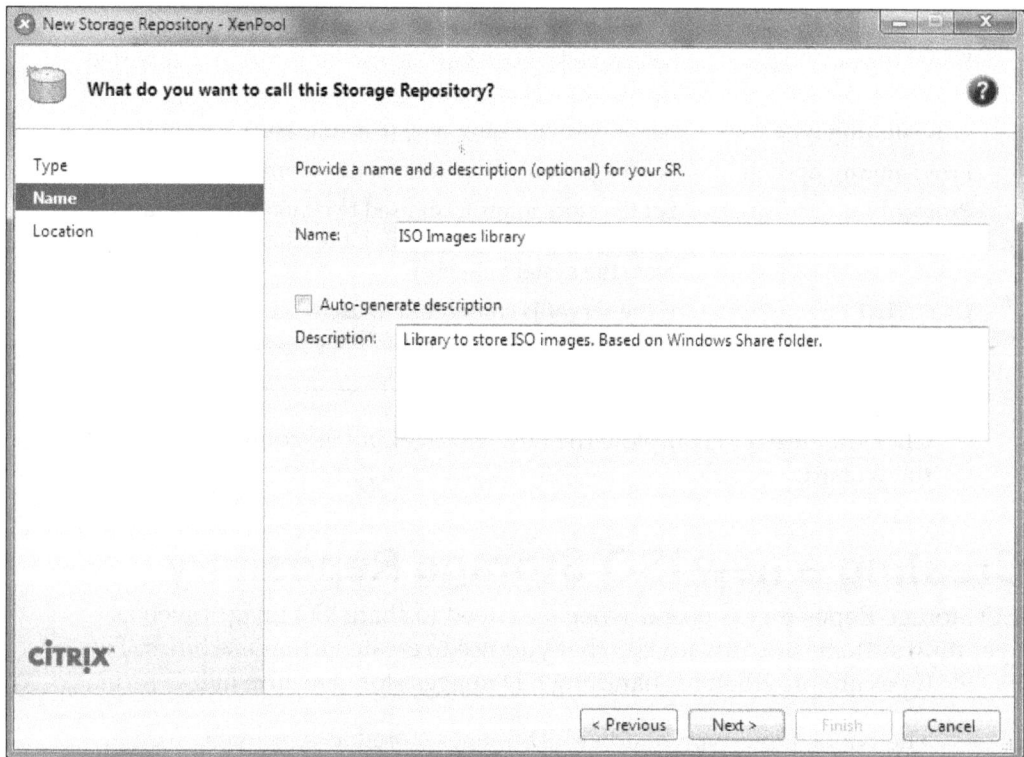

5. Click on **Next** to continue.

6. On the **Location** page, specify the ISO storage target details:

Parameter	Description
Share Name	Type `\\server\ShareName` where `server` is the DNS name or IP address of the server computer, and `ShareName` is the folder that will store ISOs files.
	In this example, we will use `\\dcr.lab.local\ISO`.
Use different user name	If you want to connect to a CIFS server using a different username, select this checkbox and then enter your login username and password.
	In this example, we will use user `LAB\Administrator`.

7. Click on **Finish** to complete the configuration. XenServer will create the ISO library and you will be ready to share ISO images for virtual machine installations!

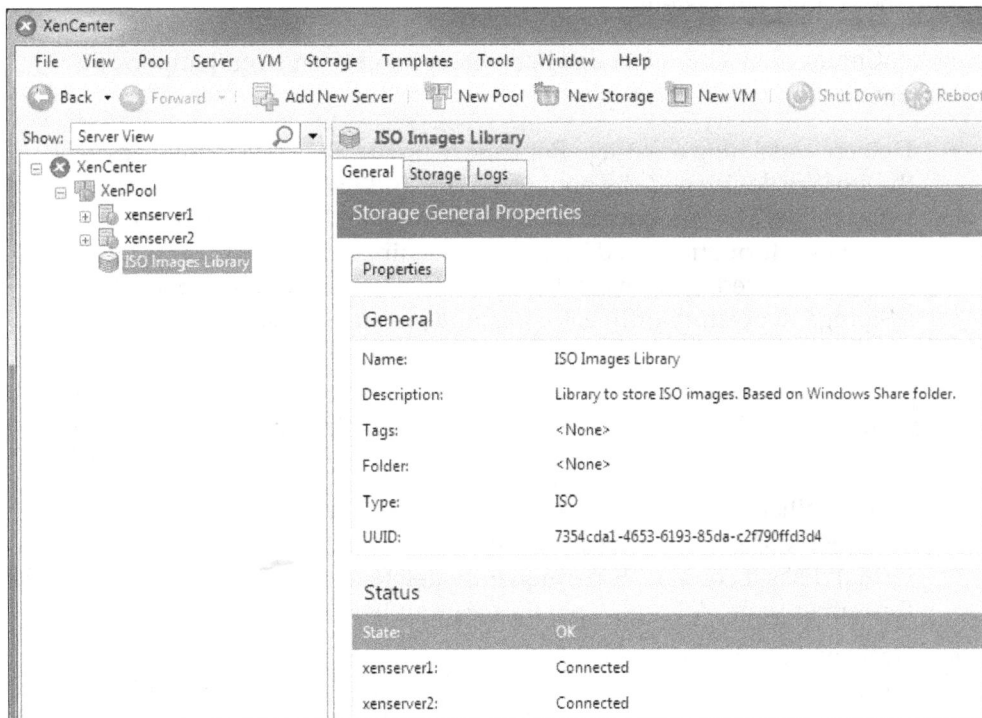

If you prefer, use NFS for the ISO Library. After starting **New Storage Repository** wizard, follow the given procedure:

1. Select **NFS ISO** as physical Storage Repository and click on **Next**.
2. On the **Name** page, enter the name of the new SR and type a description.
3. Click on **Next** to continue.
4. On the **Location** page, specify the ISO storage target details:
5. On the **Location** page, specify the `share name` related to the ISO storage target, type `server:/Path` where `server` is the DNS name or IP address of the server computer and `Path` is the NFS folder that will store the ISO files. In this example, we will use `\\192.168.0.11:\mnt\ISO`.

Managing Storage Repositories

At this point, we know how to create Storage Repositories in XenServer. Now it is time to know how to manage them, for example when you have to do maintenance tasks on the storage subsystem.

Using XenCenter or xe CLI, a Storage Repository can be removed temporarily or permanently:

- **Detach**: Detaching a Storage Repository breaks the association between the storage device and the pool or server, and its virtual disks become inaccessible. The contents of the virtual disks are preserved, however, and the meta-information used by virtual machines to access the virtual disks is also preserved. Detach can be used when you need to temporarily take a Storage Repository offline, for example, for maintenance.

> You can reattach a previously detached Storage Repository.

- **Forget**: When you Forget an SR, the contents of the virtual disks on the SR are preserved but the information used to connect virtual machines to the virtual disks it contains is permanently deleted. The SR is removed from the **Resources** pane. A Forget operation cannot be undone.

- **Destroy**: When you Destroy an SR, both the information used to connect virtual machines to the virtual disks on the SR and the underlying virtual disks themselves are permanently destroyed. The SR is removed from the **Resources** pane. A Destroy operation cannot be undone.

You cannot remove a Storage Repository if it holds virtual disks of a currently running virtual machine.

Always backup your virtual disks when you plan to forget or destroy a Storage Repository.

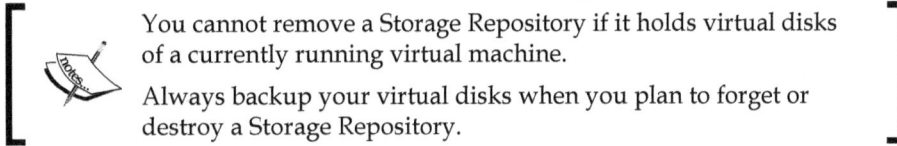

If you want to Detach, Forget, or Destroy a Storage Repository, follow the given procedure:

1. Shut down any VMs using the Storage Repository.
2. Select the SR in the **Resources** pane and then do one of the following:
   - Right-click and click on **Detach Storage Repository** on the **Resources** pane shortcut menu if you want to detach it
   - Right-click and click on **Forget Storage Repository** on the **Resources** pane shortcut menu if you want to forget it
   - Right-click and click on **Destroy Storage Repository** on the **Resources** pane shortcut menu if you want to destroy it

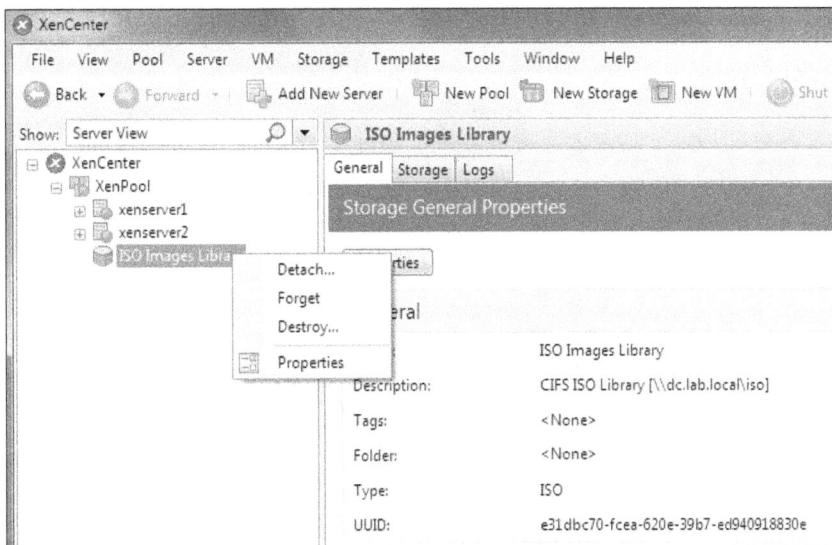

3. In this example, we select **Detach**. A warning will be displayed informing us that virtual disks will not be accessible.

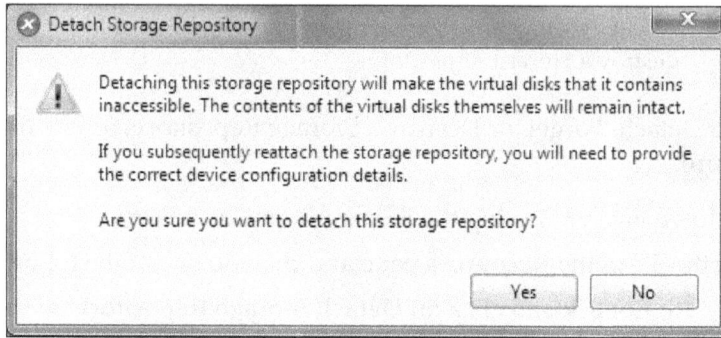

4. Click on **Yes** to confirm. XenServer will detach the Storage Repository.

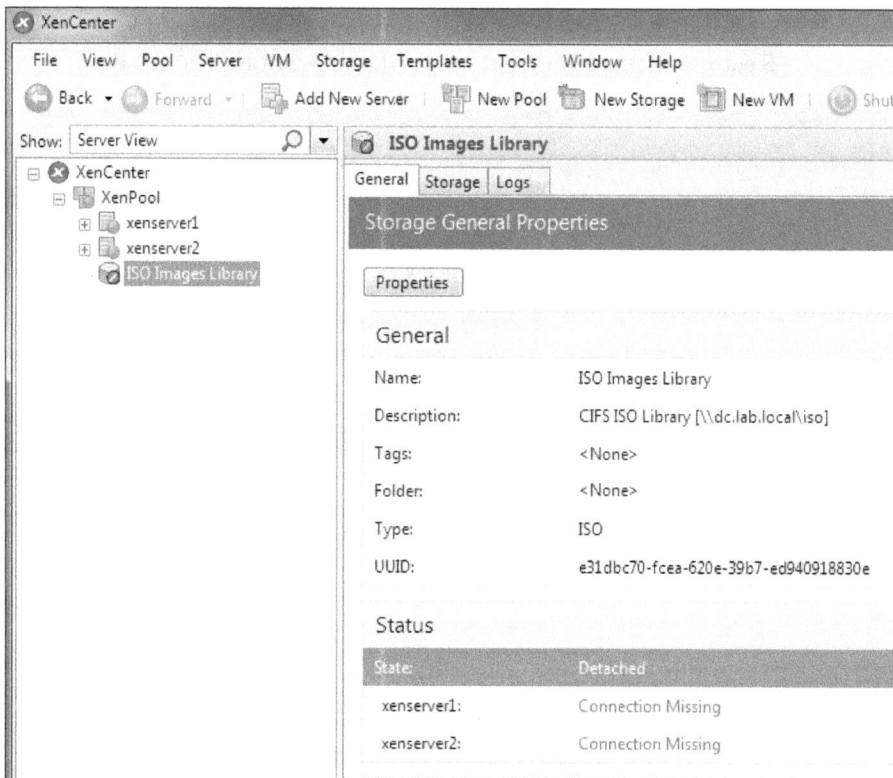

The same operations, as you can imagine at this point, can be performed using xe CLI. In order to forget a Storage Repository, we execute the following command:

```
xe sr-forget uuid=<sr_uuid>
```

> Executing the sr-forget command is the equivalent of the SR Detach in XenServer.

In order to destroy a Storage Repository, we execute the following command:

```
xe sr-destroy uuid=<sr_uuid>
```

where uuid is the unique identifier of the Storage Repository. Using the xe CLI, we have another command that gives us the chance to *unplug* the Storage Repository:

```
xe pbd-unplug uuid=<pbd_uuid>
```

where uuid is the Physical Block Device UUID related to the Storage Repository. In our example, we will execute the following command to unplug the ISO Images Library repository:

```
xe pbd-unplug uuid=6ba7ec84-59ee-6645-c0a8-4c54cb546141
```

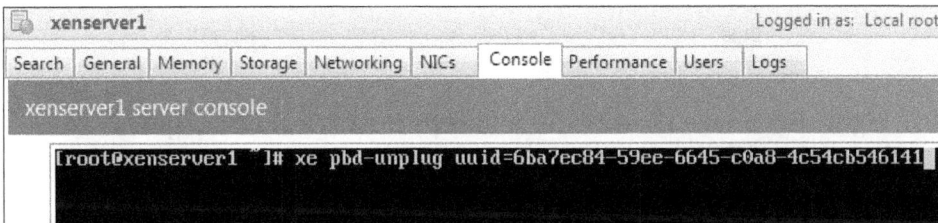

In the previous command we have used the UUID value `"6ba7ec84-59ee-6645-c0a8-4c54cb546141"`. In order to find the UUID value for the PBD we have to follow the given procedure:

1. Click on the **Storage Repository** you want to unplug, in our example, **ISO Images Library**.

2. Right-click on the **UUID** value and copy it. This is the Storage Repository UUID.

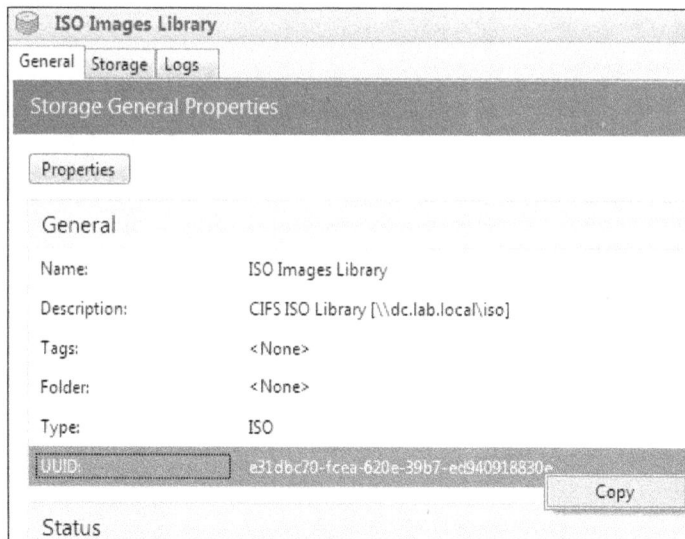

3. Open the XenServer console related to the host where you want to detach the Storage Repository; we do this on the `XenServer1` host. Execute the following command to identify the PBD UUID:

```
xe pbd-list sr-uuid=<sr-uuid> host-uuid=<host-uuid>
```

where the `sr-uuid` parameter is the UUID value you have found before and `host-uuid` parameter is the UUID of the XenServer host where we want to unplug the repository. In our example, we run the command:

```
xe pbd-list sr-uuid=e31dbc70-fcea-620e-39b7-ed940918830e host-
uuid=8791cc9e-e1e0-43f0-9104-d608bb033b9b
```

> We have learned how to find `host-uuid` in *Chapter 1, Introducing XenServer Resource Pools*.

In the following screenshot you can see the syntax of the `xe` command `pbd-list` executed on the `xenserver1` host of the pool:

```
xenserver1                                          Logged in as:  Local root accd

Search | General | Memory | Storage | Networking | NICs | Console | Performance | Users | Logs

xenserver1 server console

[root@xenserver1 ~]# xe pbd-list sr-uuid=e31dbc70-fcea-620e-39b7-ed940918830e ho
st-uuid=8791cc9e-e1e0-43f0-9104-d608bb033b9b
uuid ( RO)                    : f08cbd98-18a4-b54b-fe4a-85db8a11b94e
          host-uuid ( RO): 8791cc9e-e1e0-43f0-9104-d608bb033b9b
            sr-uuid ( RO): e31dbc70-fcea-620e-39b7-ed940918830e
       device-config (MRO): username: LAB\Administrator; location: //dc.lab.lo
cal/iso; type: cifs; cifspassword: password
       currently-attached ( RO): true
```

XenServer displays some information about the ISO Images Repository. Note the `uuid (RO)` value—this is the PBD value we are looking for! In our case, it is:

```
f08cbd98-18a4-b54b-fe4a-85db8a11b94e
```

At this point, we have the value to run the `xe pbd-unplug` command we have used before.

Reattaching an SR

We detached our ISO library earlier. It is now time to reattach it after we have finished performing our maintenance tasks.

A detached storage device has no association with any pool or server, but the data stored on it is preserved. When you reattach a Storage Repository to a managed server, you need to provide the storage configuration information in the same way as when you add a new Storage Repository. To reattach the Storage Repository, follow the given procedure:

1. Select the SR in the **Resources** pane, right-click and click on **Reattach**.

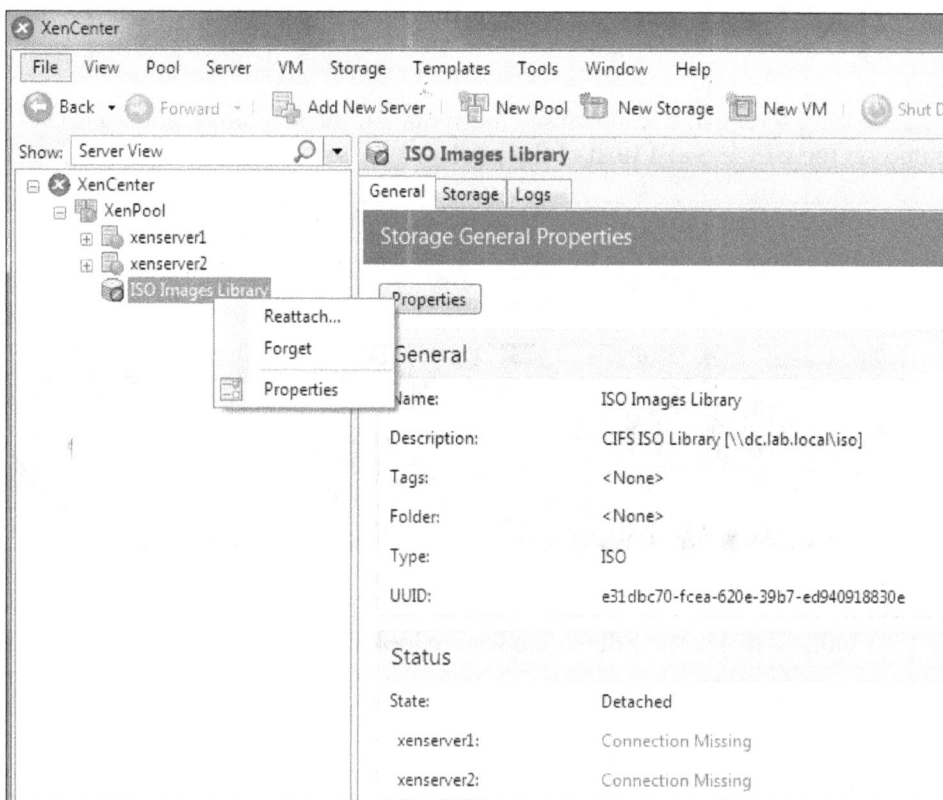

2. XenServer remembers the name and the description you have set before. Click on **Next** to proceed or make changes if you want.

3. On the **Location** page, specify the ISO storage details related to the share name and username for the connection.

4. Click on **Finish** to complete. XenServer will reattach your Storage Repository!

Adding a Storage Repository

In XenServer you can add or *introduce* a Storage Repository that previously has been forgotten. In order to introduce a Storage Repository, we have to create the Physical Block Device (PBD) and manually plug the PBD to the appropriate XenServer hosts to activate the Storage Repository.

In our example, we have decided to forget the iSCSI Storage because we have bought a new iSCSI storage appliance, which is faster and bigger. So in XenCenter, we select the repository, right-click and choose **Forget**.

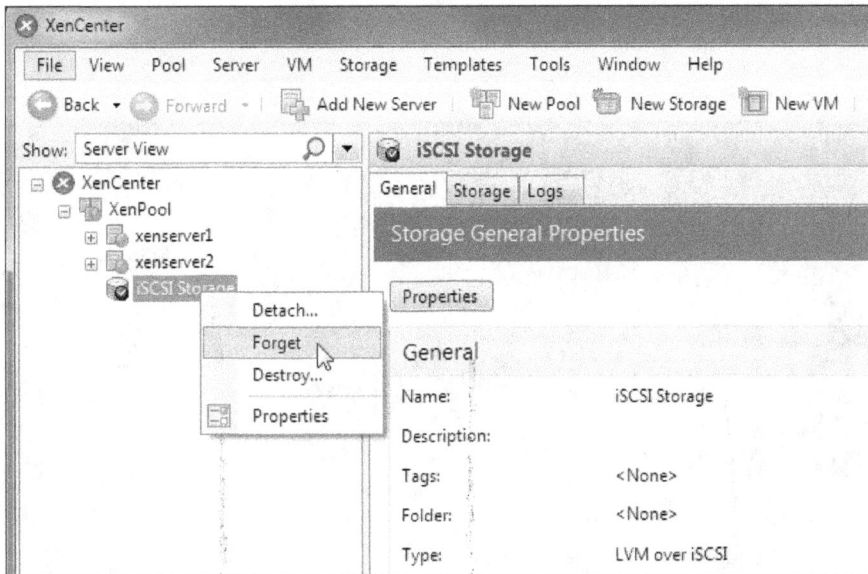

Later, your colleague Jane informs you that she needs to have access to the repository again—a virtual file server machine was configured in that storage. No problem! You can plug the iSCSI storage again.

To do this task, we have to use xe CLI and execute some commands such as `sr-probe`, `pbd-create`, and `pbd-plug`.

1. We start executing `sr-probe`:

   ```
   xe sr-probe type=<type> device-config:<config_name>=<value>
   ```

   This command performs a backend-specific scan, using the provided `device-config` parameter. If device-config is complete for the SR backend, then this will return a list of the SRs present on the device, if any. If the device-config parameters are only partial, then a backend-specific scan will be performed, returning results that will guide you in improving the remaining `device-config` parameters.

We remember only the device type, `lvmoisci`, and the IP address of the storage device, `192.168.0.11`, about the forgotten iSCSI storage . The `sr-probe` command will help us to find the remaining parameters, TargetIQN and SCSIid.

So we run the command:

```
xe sr-probe type=lvmoiscsi device-config:target=192.168.0.11
```

Notice that the command returns you `TargetIQN`. Well done! We have discovered the first, missing parameter.

2. Execute the `sr-probe` command again adding the `device-config:TargetIQN` parameter:

```
xe sr-probe type=lvmoiscsi device-config:target=192.168.0.11
device-config:targetIQN=iqn.2011-11.com.xenserver1:3ef46a5f
```

Again, `sr-probe` helps us and returns the SCSIid!

Now, we have all the parameters and we can run the final
`sr-probe` command:

```
xe sr-probe type=lvmoiscsi device-config:target=192.168.0.11
device-config:targetIQN=iqn.2011-11.com.xenserver1:3ef46a5f
device-config:SCSIid=3300000002db1eaba
```

sr-probe will return the Storage Repository UUID we need to re-introduce the storage

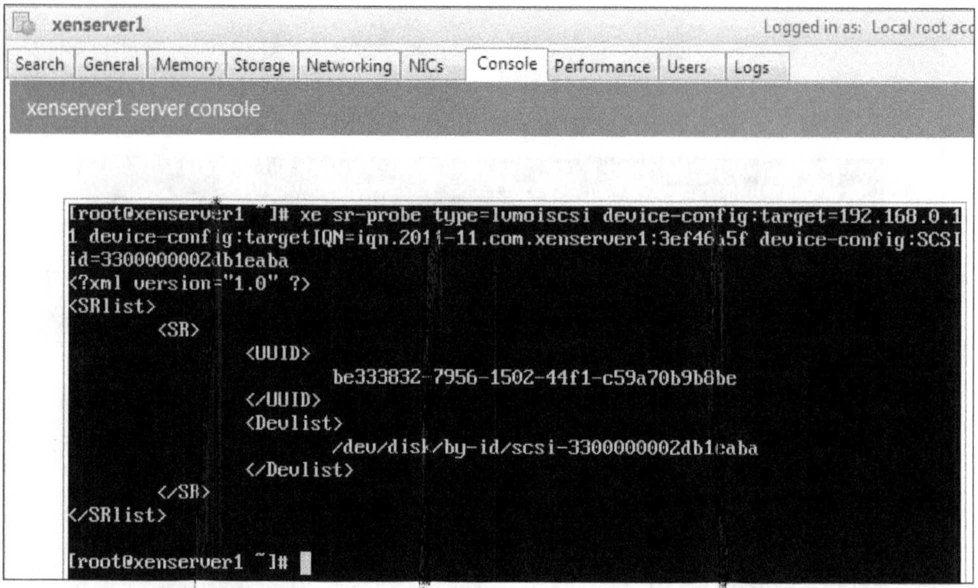

3. The Storage Repository we are looking for is be333832-7956-1502-44f1-c59a70b9b8be. We need this value to execute the next command, that is the sr-introduce command:

    ```
    xe sr-introduce name-label=<name> type=<type> content-type=<type>
    uuid=<sr_uuid>
    ```

    where:

    °   The name-label parameter is the name we assign to the SR
    °   The type parameter is the type of the SR, used to specify the backend driver XenServer has to use
    °   The content-type parameter is the type of the SR's content, used to distinguish ISO libraries from other SRs
    °   The uuid parameter is the unique identifier/object reference for the SR

The command places an SR record into the XenServer database.

In our example, we execute:

```
xe sr-introduce content-type=user name-label="Restored iSCSI
Storage" shared=true uuid=be333832-7956-1502-44f1-c59a70b9b8be
type=lvmoiscsi
```

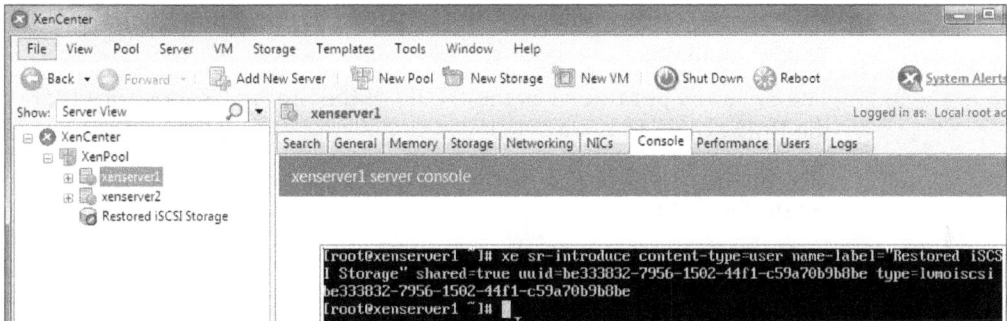

XenServer will add the Storage Repository in XenCenter as **Detached**.

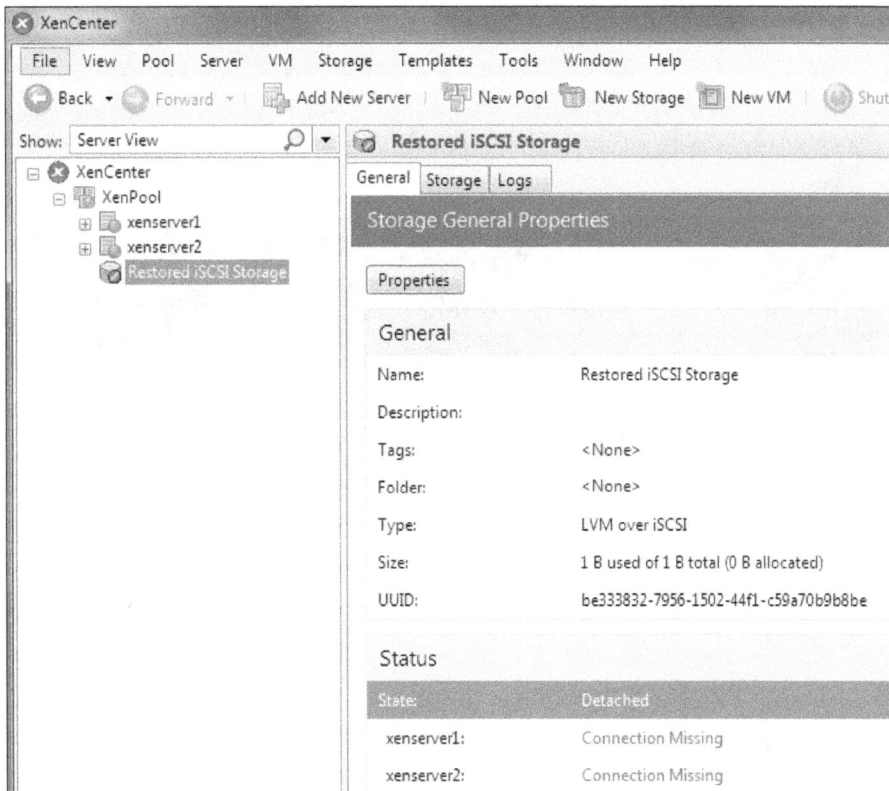

4. Now we have to create the PBD related to the Storage Repository. We will use the `pbd-create` command:

    ```
    xe pbd-create host-uuid=<uuid_of_host> sr-uuid=<uuid_of_sr>
    device-config:<parameter>
    ```

    where:

    ◦ The `host-uuid` parameter is the UUID of the host on which the PBD will be available

    ◦ The `sr-uuid` parameter is the UUID of the Storage Repository that the PBD points to

    ◦ The `device-config:<parameter>` is the parameter required to create the PBD

    So in our example, we execute the command:

    ```
    xe pbd-create host-uuid=bdced52b-2228-4fb4-b02e-211f9aef1db6 sr-
    uuid=be333832-7956-1502-44f1-c59a70b9b8be type=lvmoiscsi device-
    config:target=192.168.0.11 device-config:targetIQN=iqn.2011-11.
    com.xenserver1:3ef46a5f device-config:SCSIid=3300000002db1eaba
    ```

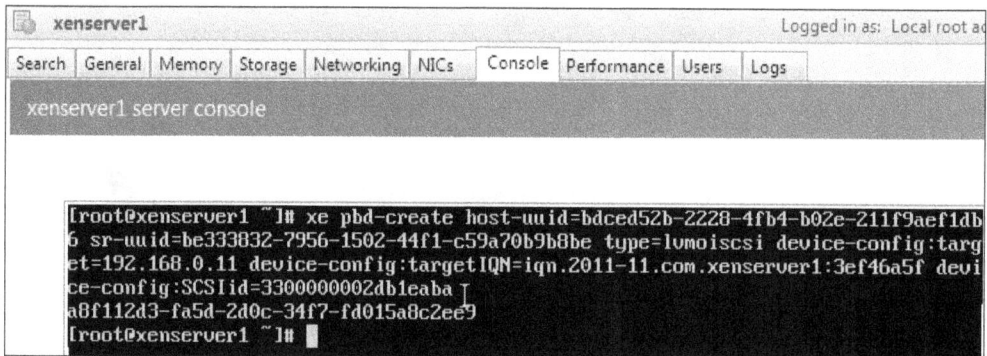

5. The command returns you the UUID, `a8f112d3-fa5d-2d0c-34f7-fd015a8c2ee9`, of the newly created PBD. We will use this UUID to plug the PBD in order to attach the Storage Repository.

6. To do this, we use the command `pbd-plug` which we have introduced earlier. So in this example, we execute:

```
xe pbd-plug uuid=a8f112d3-fa5d-2d0c-34f7-fd015a8c2ee9
```

Using this command, we have reattached the iSCSI Storage on the host XenServer1.

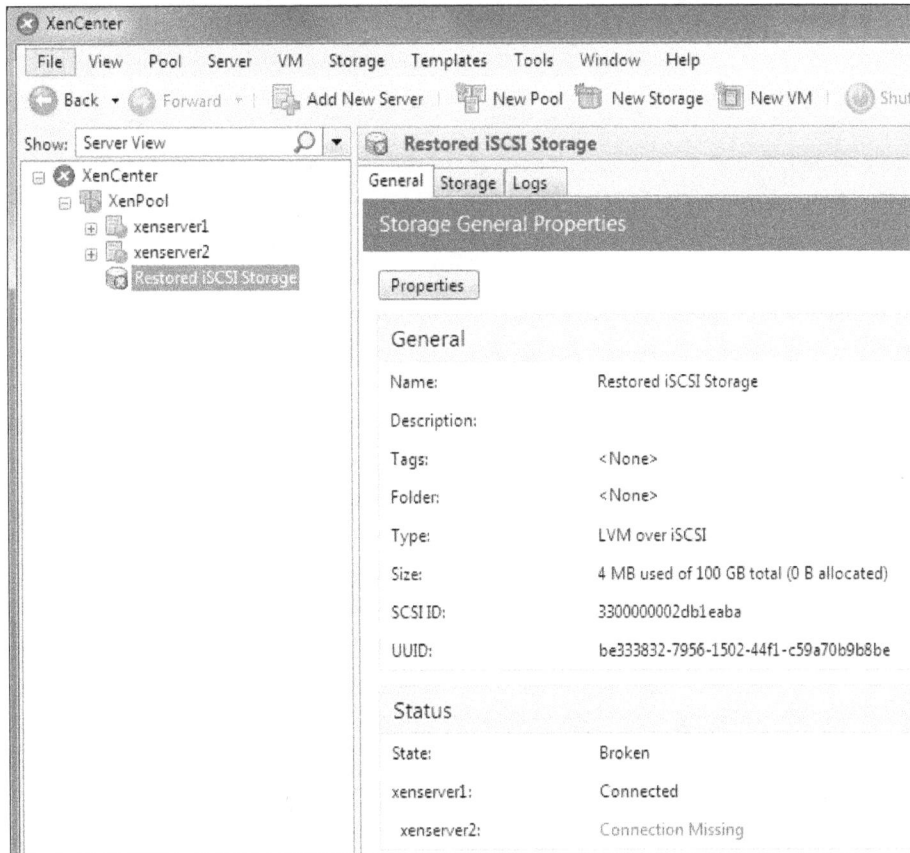

Our job is not finished yet. We have to repeat steps 6 through 7 for each host in the resource pool. Boring? Don't worry, this operation can now also be performed using the Repair Storage Repository function in XenCenter. In order to repair a Storage Repository, follow the given procedure:

1. Select the Storage Repository, right-click and choose **Repair**.

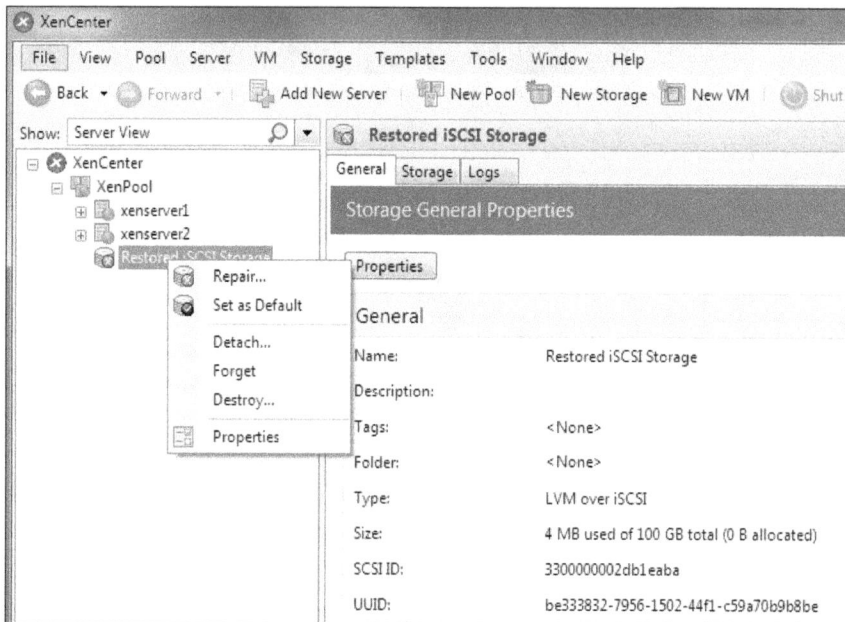

2. Click on **Repair**:

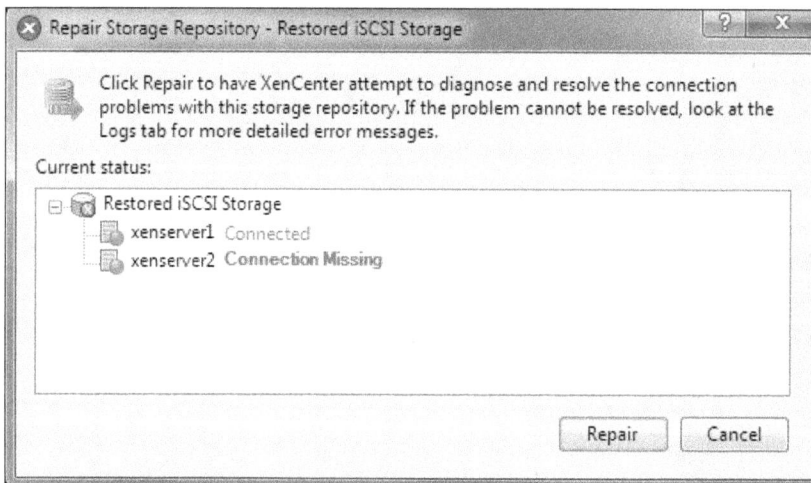

3. XenServer will create and establish the connection also to the other hosts of the pool.

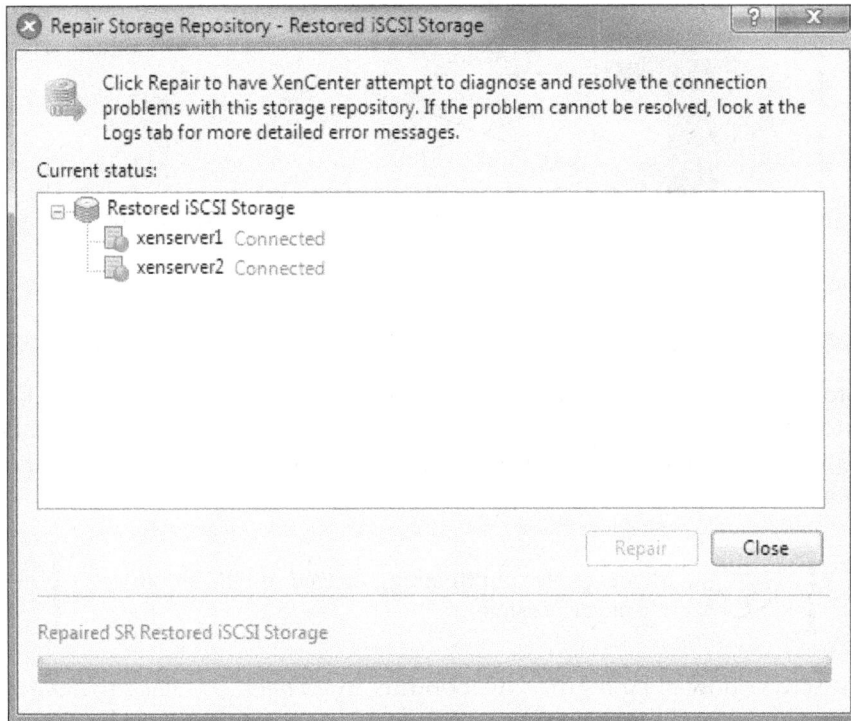

Storage multipathing

XenServer supports dynamic **multipathing** for Fibre Channel and iSCSI Storage Repositories.

Multipath I/O is a fault-tolerance and performance enhancement technique. Multipathing solutions use redundant physical path components (such as adapters, cables, and switches) to create logical paths between the server and the storage device. In the event that one or more of these components fail, causing the path to fail, multipathing logic uses an alternate path for I/O so that virtual machines can still run.

By default, multipathing uses round robin mode load balancing, so both paths will have active traffic on them during normal operation.

In the following figure, you can see a XenServer host with multipathing enabled —
each Host Bus Adapter is connected to a switch using a different path.

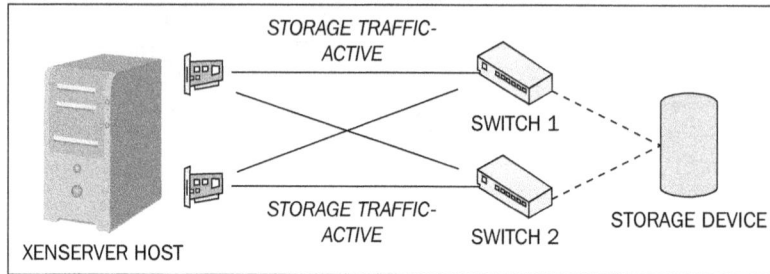

Remember that your FC and iSCSI storage devices must support multipathing too.

If your storage devices do not support multipath, you can also use NIC bonding
in order to provide redundancy for network storage traffic. However, remember
that NIC bonding cannot be configured when your storage devices are based on
Fibre Channel.

> Always prefer multipathing instead of NIC bonding
> whenever possible.

We will discover how to configure NIC bonding in *Chapter 7, Managing XenServer
Networking*, when we discuss XenServer networking so you need not be worried if
you don't understand this concept well at this moment.

You enable and disable storage multipathing in XenCenter via the **Multipathing**
tab on the server's **Properties** dialog.

> Before you enable multipathing:
>
> - Verify that multiple targets are available on your
>   storage server
> - The server must be placed in Maintenance Mode — this
>   ensures that any running virtual machines with virtual
>   disks in the affected Storage Repository are migrated
>   before the changes are made

Enabling multipathing

To enable multipathing in XenServer, follow the given procedure:

1. In the **Resources** pane, select the server and then put it into Maintenance Mode.

2. On the **General** tab, click on **Properties** and then click on the **Multipathing** tab.

3. To enable multipathing, select the **Enable multipathing on this server** checkbox. To disable multipathing, clear the checkbox.

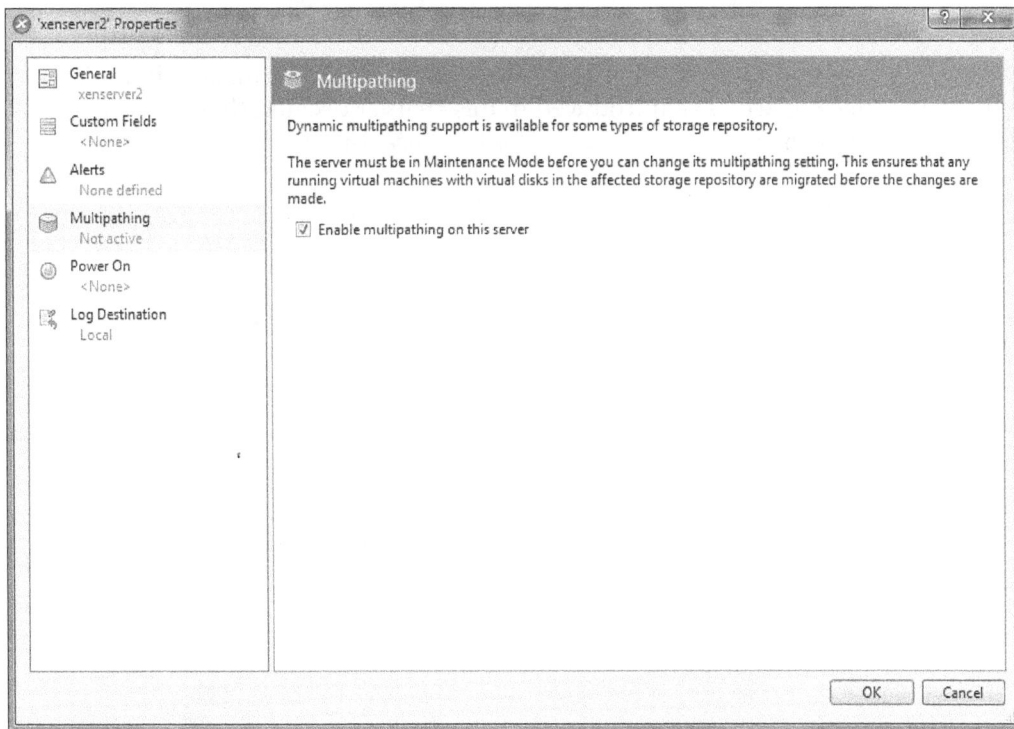

4. Click on **OK** to apply the new setting and close the dialog box. There is a short delay while XenCenter saves the new storage configuration.

5. Take the server back out of Maintenance Mode. Select it in the **Resources** pane, right-click, and click on **Exit Maintenance Mode**.

Summary

In this chapter, we have learned concepts about storage technologies and protocols. Also, we have discovered how to create and manage some types of Storage Repositories in XenServer. Specifically:

- Storage overview
- Storage technologies and protocols
- Storage concepts in XenServer
- Creating Storage Repositories and managing Storage Repositories
- Multipath overview

Storage is one of the core areas that you have to manage in a virtual environment. Review the concepts we have introduced in this chapter because they can help you to decide which storage technologies you can use for your environment.

In the next chapter, we will introduce virtual machine management.

4
Creating Virtual Machines

In the previous chapter, we discussed storage in XenServer. Now we can move on and introduce virtual machines creation in XenServer. At the end, you will have the ability to create your personal virtual machines with virtualization. You never have to wait for server order approval, manufacture, and delivery to your enterprise. Your new servers are ready in a few minutes. In this chapter, we will cover the following topics:

- Virtual machines overview
- Virtual machines creation overview
- Creating virtual machines

Overview of virtual machines

A virtual machine (VM) is a computer that, like a physical computer, runs an operating system and installed applications — the only difference is that hardware devices are virtual not physical. Also, the operating system that is running on a virtual machine is unaware that it is executing in a virtual environment.

Usually, you also refer to VMs with the term *Guest*, like a guest of a hotel or your home, virtual machines are created and hosted on your virtualization infrastructure, and can use all the virtual devices such as networks and storage that the hypervisor provides them.

In XenServer, you can run different client or server operating systems, Linux and Windows.

In the *Appendix A, Supported Guest Operating Systems and Virtual Machine Templates*, you can find the supported guests operating systems that you can install in a virtual machine — note the maximum amount of memory and disk space you can allocate to the guest machine.

Virtual machines have some limits on the virtual devices you can configure. The following table details the limits for virtual CPU, disks, and network interfaces based on different installed OS:

Virtual Device	Windows VMs	Linux VMs
Virtual CPU	16	32
Virtual Disk drives	7	7
Virtual CD-Rom drives	1	1
Virtual NIC	7	7

From the table, you can see that seven virtual disks can be configured for a single virtual machine — this number includes the CD-Rom drive too. So, if you plan to install a virtual CD-ROM, remember that a maximum of six hard drives can be configured on the guest machine.

> XenCenter supports a maximum of 16 vCPU. If you want to add more than 16 vCpu for a Linux guest use the xe CLI `vm-vcpu-hotplug` command.
>
> SUSE Linux Enterprise Server 10 SP1 and Red Hat Enterprise Linux 4.x support a maximum of three virtual network interfaces.
>
> Red Hat Enterprise Linux 5.0/5.1/5.2 supports a maximum of three, but can support seven when you install the XenServer Tools. The same applies for Oracle and CentOS 5.0/5.1/5.2.

XenServer Tools

When you create a virtual machine and install an operating system on it, XenServer uses standard device emulation to present a storage IDE controller and a network card to the VM. This is done in order to allow the guest operating system to complete its installation using built-in drivers, but provide you with a virtual machine with reduced performance due to the overhead inherent in emulation of the controller drivers.

XenServer solves this "problem" with XenServer Tools — a set of optimized paravirtualized network and storage drivers. These drivers, when installed on the guest operating system, replace the emulated devices and provide the best performance for your virtual machines.

A virtual machine where you have installed an updated version of XenServer Tools (according to your XenServer version) is *optimized*. You can see this on the **General** tab in the **Properties** pane of the machine.

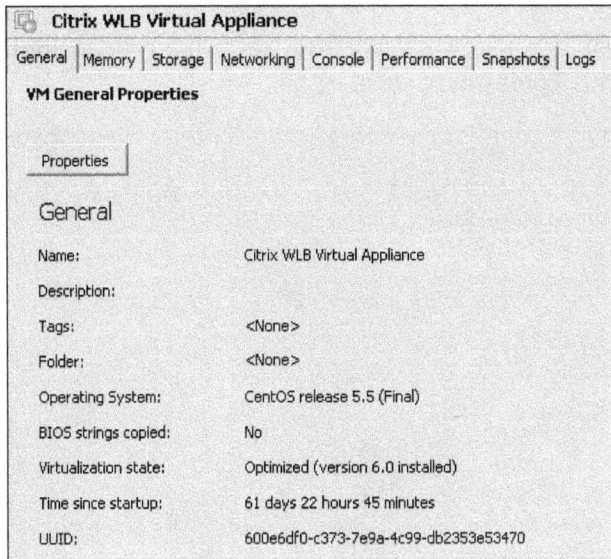

If you are working with a VM that does not have XenServer Tools installed, a **XenServer tools not installed** message in blue underlined text will be visible on the **General** tab in the **Properties** pane.

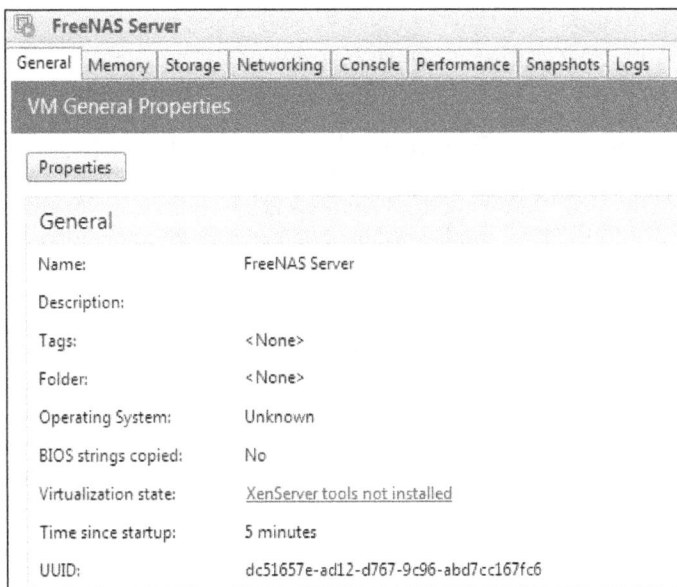

A message will also be displayed here if XenServer has been updated and the VM has an older version of XenServer Tools from an earlier release. In this case, the message displayed is **Tools out of date**.

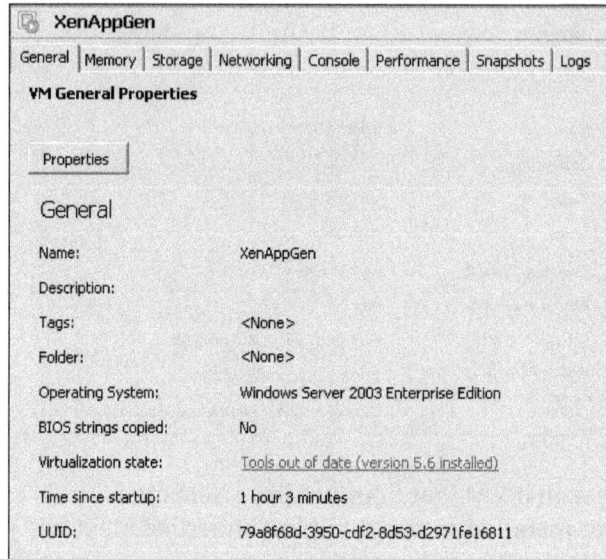

```
XenAppGen

General | Memory | Storage | Networking | Console | Performance | Snapshots | Logs

VM General Properties

    Properties

    General

    Name:                    XenAppGen
    Description:
    Tags:                    <None>
    Folder:                  <None>
    Operating System:        Windows Server 2003 Enterprise Edition
    BIOS strings copied:     No
    Virtualization state:    Tools out of date (version 5.6 installed)
    Time since startup:      1 hour 3 minutes
    UUID:                    79a8f68d-3950-cdf2-8d53-d2971fe16811
```

XenServer Tools must be installed for each virtual machine (Windows and Linux) in order for the VM to have a fully supported configuration.

> In order to install XenServer Tools on a Windows VM, the VM must be running the Microsoft .NET Framework Version 4.0 or later. If a VM is running Windows 2003, you need to install the Windows Imaging Component before installing XenServer Tools.

A Windows VM will function without them but performance will be significantly reduced unless the tools are installed. Without the tools being installed, you cannot:

- Shut down or reboot a VM correctly
- Suspend a VM
- Migrate a running VM (XenMotion)

- Work with snapshots
- Dynamically adjust the number of vCPUs assigned to a running Linux VM—Windows VMs require a reboot for this to take effect

> Running a VM without installing the XenServer Tools is not a supported configuration.

Overview of virtual machines creation

Once you have deployed your XenServer infrastructure, you can start creating virtual machines (VMs).

Virtual machines can be created in different ways:

- Using VM templates
- Converting a physical machine to virtual
- Importing an exported VM
- Cloning an existing VM

We will introduce them here and discuss them in depth later in the chapter.

Using VM templates

Virtual machines are prepared from templates. A *template* is a virtual machine encapsulated into a file, making it possible to rapidly deploy new VMs. Each template contains installation metadata—the setup information needed to create a new VM with a specific guest operating system, and with the optimum storage, CPU, memory, and virtual network configuration.

XenServer provides you a set of templates out of the box—each of them is developed in order to run a specific operating system because Linux and Windows operating systems require several different settings in order to run optimally. VMs in a XenServer environment may be fully virtualized (**Hardware Virtual Machine— HVM**) or paravirtualized.

In the HVM mode, the VM is fully virtualized and can run at near-native processor speeds on virtualization-enabled hardware, without any modification to the guest operating system.

In the paravirtualized (non-HVM) mode, the guest operating system is tuned and optimized to run in a virtual environment, independent of the underlying processor capabilities. The result is better performance and greater flexibility.

Paravirtualized drivers are available for Windows and Linux VMs to enhance disk and network performance. These drivers are supplied in the XenServer Tools package.

Converting a physical machine to virtual

Physical to Virtual Conversion (P2V) is the process by which an existing Windows operating system on a physical machine — its filesystem, configuration, and so on — is converted to a virtualized instance of the operating system.

After conversion, this is then transferred and started as a VM on the XenServer host.

Citrix has made available a tool for converting existing physical instances of a Windows server called *XenConvert*.

XenConvert runs on the physical Windows machine and converts it live into a VHD-format disk image or an XVA template suitable for importing into a XenServer host. The physical host does not need to be restarted during this process and device drivers are automatically modified to run in a virtual environment.

Importing an exported VM

You can create a VM by importing an existing exported VM. Like cloning, exporting and importing a VM is a fast way to create additional VMs of a certain configuration so that you can increase the speed of your deployment. You might, for example, have a special-purpose server configuration that you use many times. Once you have set up a VM the way you want it, you can export it, and import it later to create another copy of your specially-configured VM. You can also use export and import to move a VM to a XenServer host that is in another resource pool.

Cloning an existing VM

You can create new VMs and templates by copying (cloning) an existing VM or template. XenServer has two mechanisms for copying VMs and templates:

- **Full copy**: Makes a complete copy of the VM's disks.

- **Fast clone** (Copy-on-Write): Writes only modified blocks to disk, using hardware-level cloning features for copying the disks from the existing VM to the new VM. This mode is only supported for file-backed VMs (VHD files). Fast clone is designed to save disk space and allow faster cloning tasks, but can slightly slow down normal disk performance.

> A template can be fast cloned multiple times without slowdown. You can only copy a VM directly within the same resource pool.

Creating virtual machines

When you want to create a new virtual machine, you usually create the VM using a template for the operating system you want to run on the VM. Citrix provides out of the box templates for Windows and Linux operating systems. See *Appendix A, Supported Guest Operating Systems and Virtual Machine Templates*, for a detailed list of available templates.

Obviously you can use a template you have created previously: We will cover template creation later in the chapter, so don't worry about this.

> Since XenServer is the virtualization hypervisor which Citrix suggests you use in order to virtualize Citrix XenApp Servers, Citrix has included by default in XenServer some templates you can use to deploy XenApp virtual machines. These templates are tuned to optimize XenApp performance and are related to XenApp 5 for Windows 2003 and 2008 and XenApp 6.x for Windows 2008 R2.
>
> You can find more information on Citrix XenApp here at http://www.citrix.com/English/ps2/products/product.asp?contentID=186&ntref=prod_top.

It is now time to see how to create our first virtual machine. Let's move on to the next section.

Creating a Windows virtual machine

In this section, we will learn how to create a Windows virtual machine. The process is very simple:

1. Select the template related to the Windows operating system we want to deploy into the guest.

2. Install the operating system and at the end we install the XenServer Tools package.

The Windows operating system can be installed either from an install CD in a physical CD-ROM drive on the XenServer host, or from an ISO image.

> If you want to create an ISO image from your DVD media, you can use ISO Recorder. It is a free utility that you can download from `http://isorecorder.alexfeinman.com/isorecorder.htm`.

In XenCenter, the **New VM** wizard takes you through the process of creating a new virtual machine (VM), step-by-step:

1. To start the New VM wizard, click on **New VM** on the toolbar.

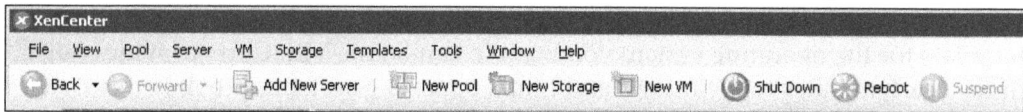

2. Alternatively, you can also start the New VM Wizard by performing one of the following operations:

   ° Press *Ctrl+N*

   ° Click on **New** on the VM menu

   ° Right-click on host in the **Resources** pane and then click on **New VM** on the shortcut menu

Using the wizard, you can configure the new VM exactly as you prefer, adjusting various configuration parameters for CPU, storage, and networking resources. Depending on the VM template you choose on the first page of the wizard, you will see different VM configuration options presented on subsequent pages.

In a XenServer environment where **Role Based Access Control (RBAC)** is implemented, the New VM wizard will perform checks when it starts up to ensure that you have a role with sufficient permissions to allow you to create new VMs. If your RBAC role does not have sufficient permissions you will not be able to continue with the virtual machine creation.

> For Role Based Access Control details, review *Chapter 2, Managing User Authentication.*

In the following example, we will create a Windows 7 virtual machine named `Win7-Master-VM`. We will use it later in the chapter during template creation, import and export, and cloning operations.

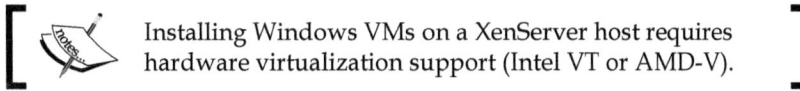

> Installing Windows VMs on a XenServer host requires hardware virtualization support (Intel VT or AMD-V).

To create the `Win7-Master-VM` virtual machine, follow the given procedure:

1. On the XenCenter toolbar, click on the **New VM** button to open the New VM wizard. Select a VM template and click on **Next**.

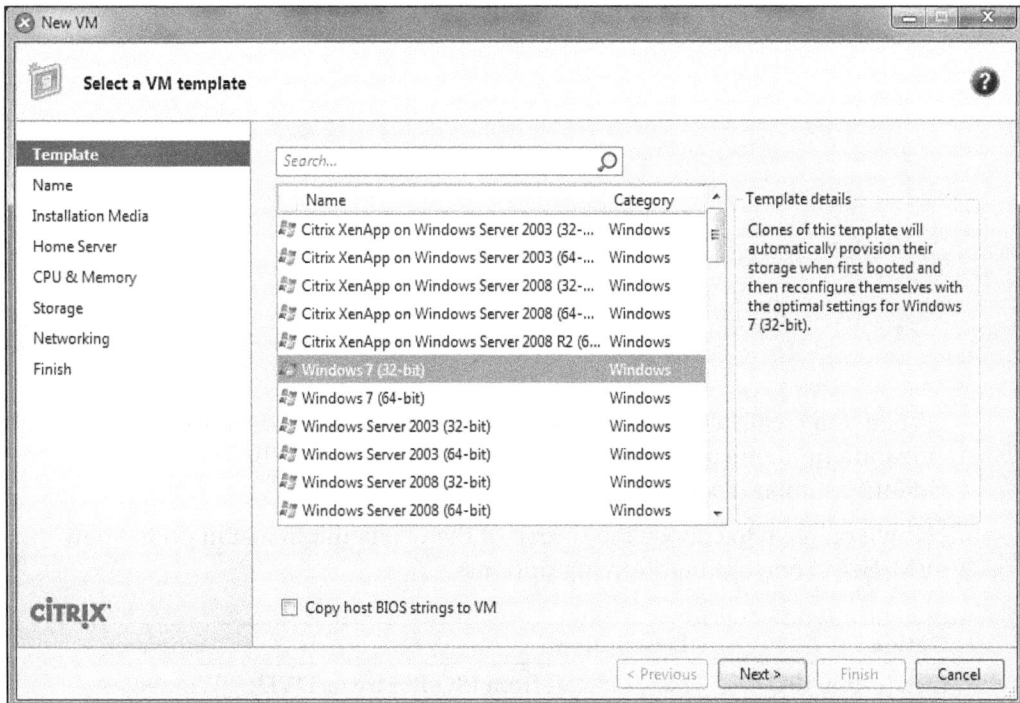

If the OS that you intend to install on your new VM is compatible only with the original hardware (for example, an OS installation CD that was packaged with a specific computer such as Windows OEM), check the **Copy host BIOS strings to VM** checkbox.

2. Enter a name and an optional description for the new VM and click on **Next**.

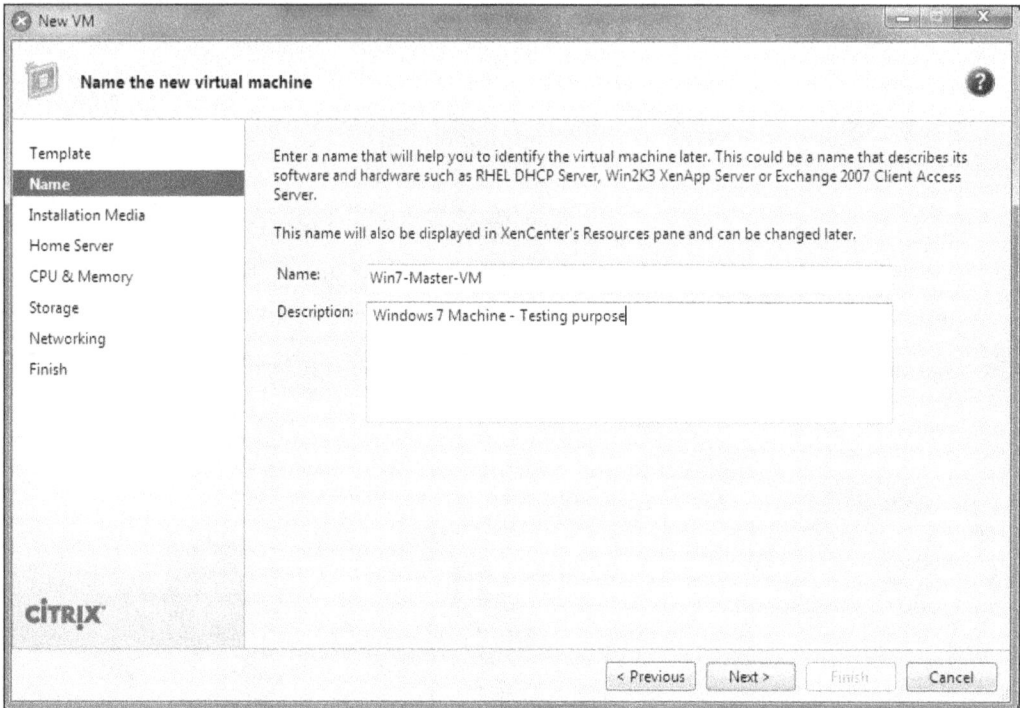

When you create a virtual machine, remember to use a descriptive and meaningful name and insert a description for the VM—this will help you identify similar machines.

Now you have to choose the source of the OS media to install on the new VM. Select one of the following options:

Option	Description	Templates
Install from ISO library or DVD drive	Select **Install from ISO library or DVD drive** and then choose an ISO image or a DVD drive from the drop-down list.	Windows® and Linux
Boot from network	Select this option to use PXE/network booting for Windows and Other install media templates.	Windows

Option	Description	Templates

Install from URL	CentOS, SUSE Linux Enterprise Server, and Red Hat Linux operating systems can be installed from a network install repository. Select Install from URL and enter a URL which must include the server IP address and the repository path in the following form:
	
	`nfs://server/path`
	
	`ftp://server/path`
	
	`http://server/path`
	
	For example, `nfs://10.10.32.10/SLES10`, where `10.10.32.10` is the IP of the nfs server and `/SLES10` is the location of the install repository.
	
	You can also optionally provide additional operating system boot parameters, if required.
		Linux

3. In this example we select to install the Windows 7 operating system using the ISO image and click on **Next** to continue.

4. Choose whether you want to nominate the *home server* that will host the VM. A home server is the server which will provide the resources for a VM in a pool. When you nominate a home server for a VM, XenServer will always attempt to start up the VM on that server if it can; if this is not possible, then an alternate server within the same pool will be selected automatically. By default, XenServer automatically selects the most suitable server, based on the available resources.

5. Select **Place the VM on this server** and select a host from the list. If you prefer, nominate a specific host as home server.

> If you are creating a BIOS-customized VM, the OEM server from which you copy the BIOS strings will automatically be selected as the home server for the new VM.

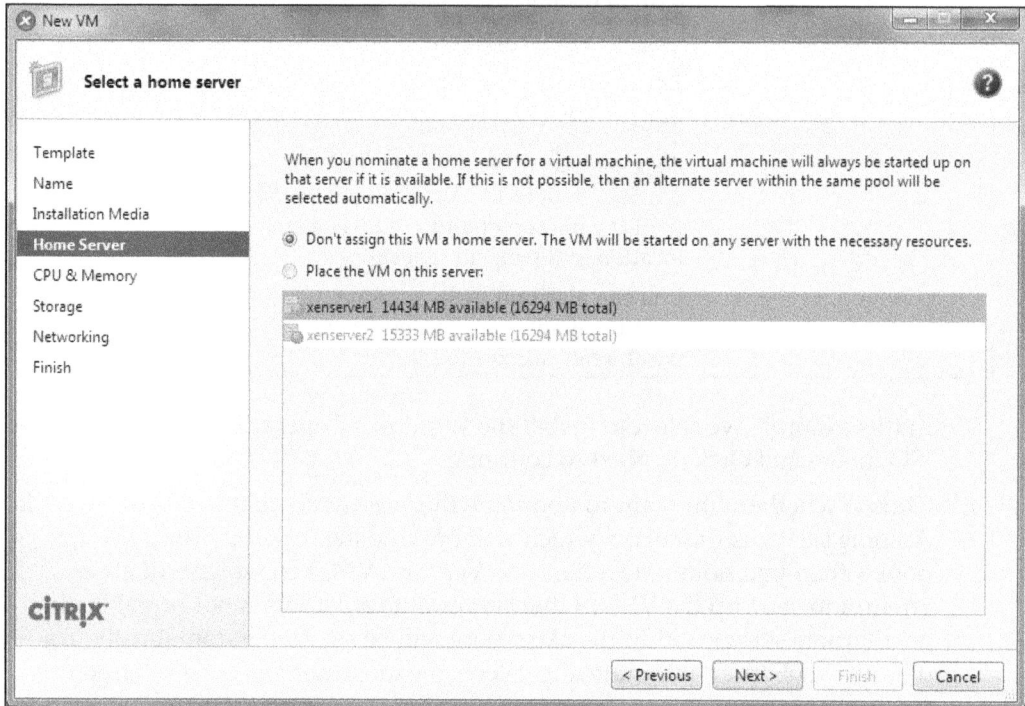

6. Choose **Next** to proceed. Specify the number of vCPUs and the amount of memory you want to assign to the VM. For a Windows 7 VM, the default is **1** virtual CPU and **2048 MB** of RAM.

Best practice: To ensure you get the best performance out of the new VM, the number of vCPUs you assign to it should not exceed the number of physical CPUs on the server.

When deciding how much memory you initially allocate to a new VM, consider the kind of applications that will run on the VM.

Remember that other virtual machines can be using the same resources.

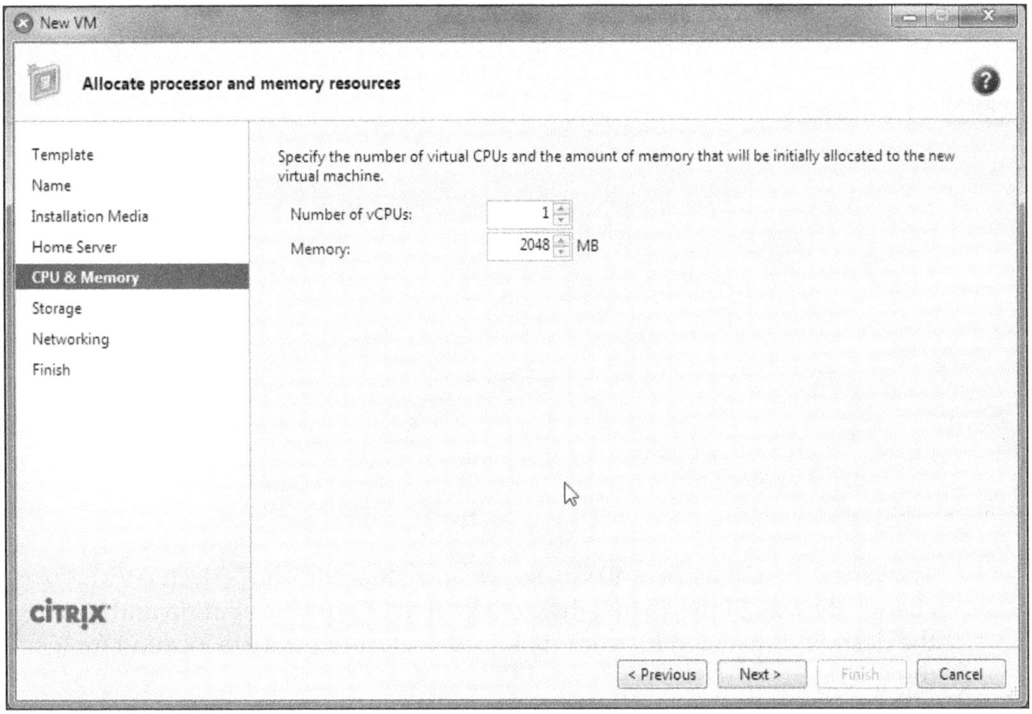

New VM

Allocate processor and memory resources

Template
Name
Installation Media
Home Server
CPU & Memory
Storage
Networking
Finish

Specify the number of virtual CPUs and the amount of memory that will be initially allocated to the new virtual machine.

Number of vCPUs: 1

Memory: 2048 MB

CITRIX

< Previous   Next >   Finish   Cancel

---

7. Select **Next** to continue. Configure the storage for the new VM — by default, the Windows 7 template sets the disk size for a Windows 7 virtual machine to **24 GB**.

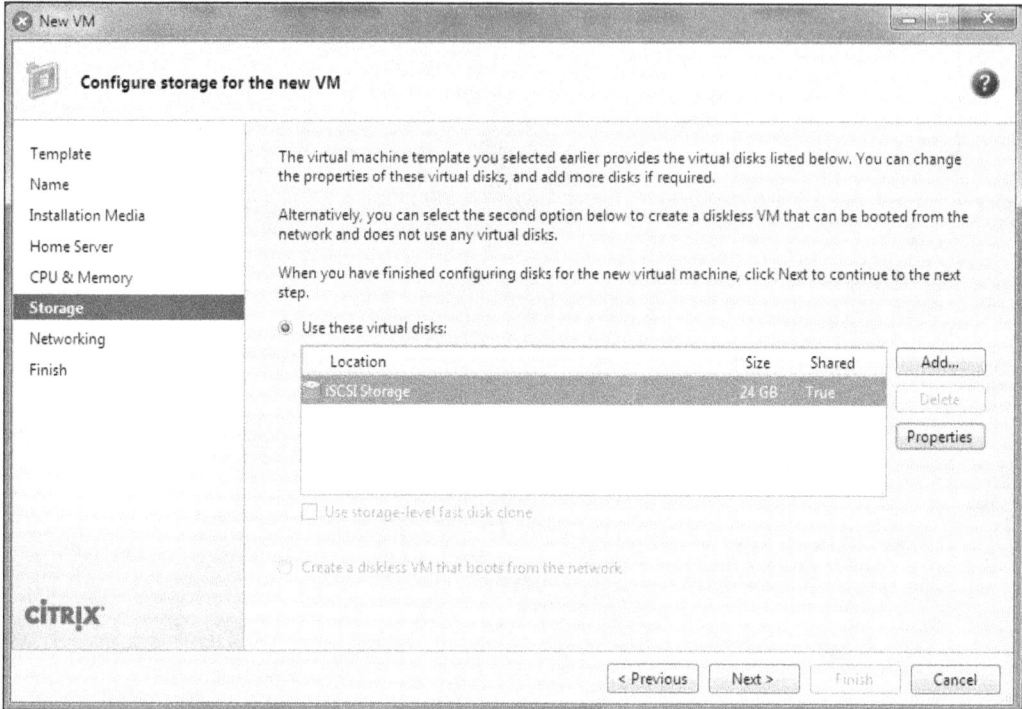

8. The recommended size is 40 GB, so we allocate it for Win7-Master-VM .To change the size of the virtual disk, click on the **Properties** button and set the desired dimension for your disk. Also, select the storage location for the vDisk.

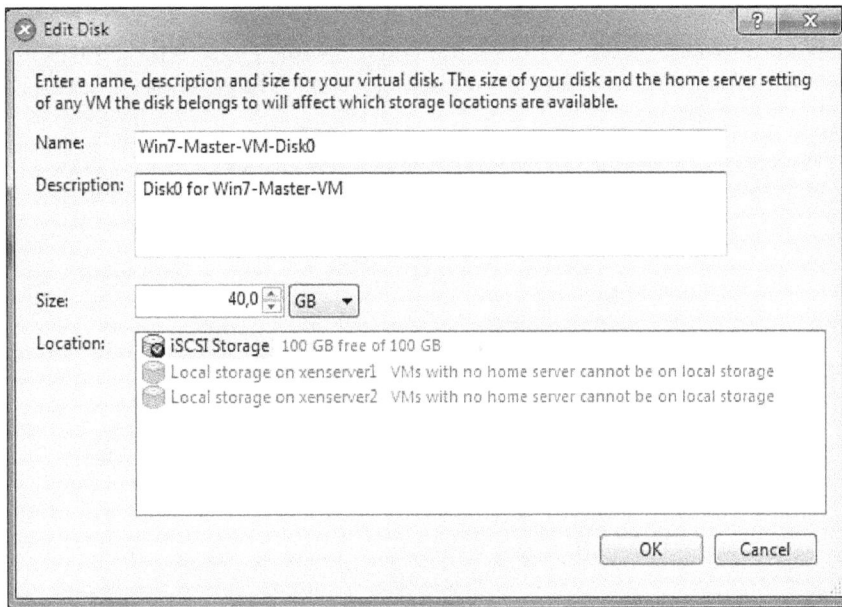

Always remember to rename the virtual disk with a meaningful name that refers to your virtual machine. Also, insert a description for the vDisk — this helps you identify it.

9. If you want, you can also add more disks by clicking on the **Add** button. If any of the virtual disks in the template or snapshot you are using to create the new VM are on the same storage repository, you can select **Use storage-level fast disk clone**. Selecting this option, the new VM will be created very quickly.

10. Also, if you have selected the **Boot from network** option on the OS Installation media page earlier in the wizard, you can create a diskless VM that boots by PXE using **Create a diskless VM that boots from the network**. Click on **Next** to continue.

11. Configure networking on the new VM. You can configure up to four virtual network interfaces from the **Networking** page of the New VM wizard. To configure more than four, use the VM's **Networking** tab after it has been created.

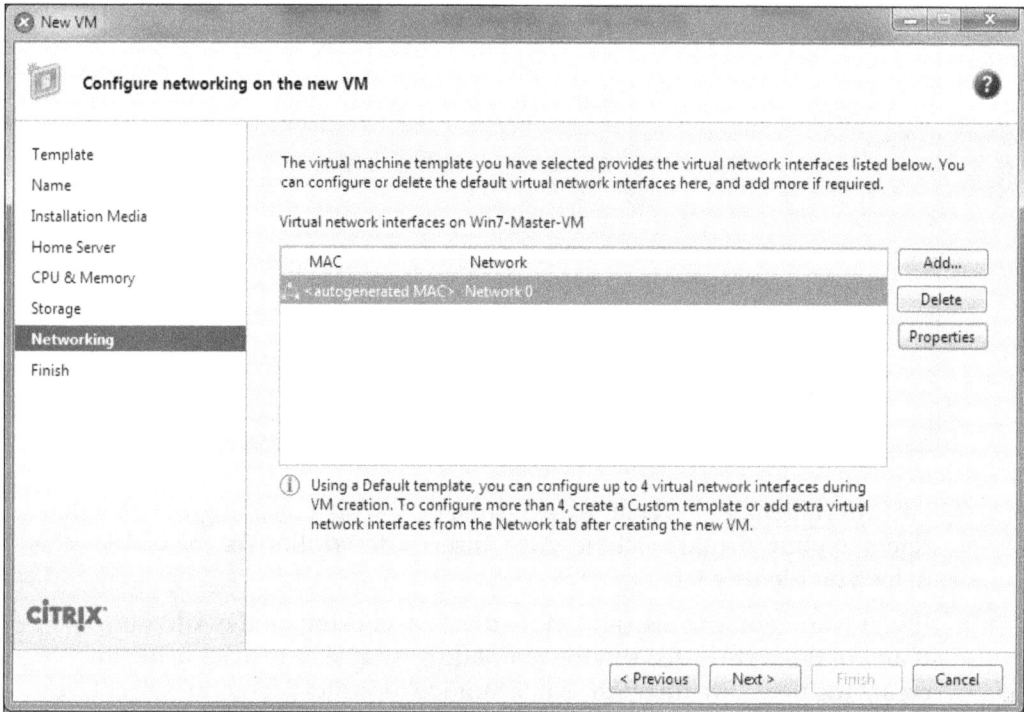

12. By default, an automatically-created random MAC address will be used for all virtual network interfaces. To enter a different MAC address, click on **Properties** and enter a new address in the **Virtual Interface Properties** dialog box, using hexadecimal characters in the format **aa:bb:cc:dd:ee:ff**.

13. In **Properties**, you can also enable a Quality of Service (QoS) priority.

Virtual Interface Properties

Select your network and MAC address for this virtual interface.
You can also optionally define a QoS limit.

Network: Network 0

MAC address:
○ Auto-generate a MAC address
○ Use this MAC address: aa:bb:cc:dd:ee:ff

QoS settings:
☐ Enable a QoS limit of: _____ Kbytes/s

[OK]   [Cancel]

14. Click on **Next** to continue. The wizard shows you a final summary with
    the settings that you have chosen. Review them and then click on **Finish**
    to create the new VM. By default, XenServer will start the machine
    automatically. To prevent the automatic start-up, uncheck the box **Start
    the new VM automatically**.

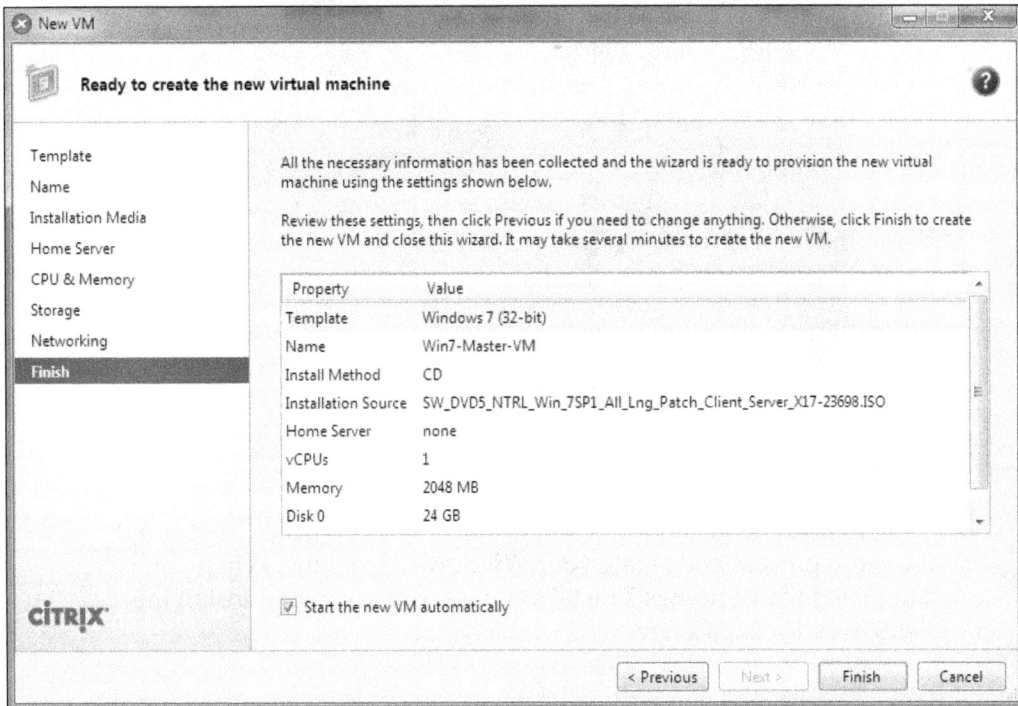

New VM

Ready to create the new virtual machine

Template
Name
Installation Media
Home Server
CPU & Memory
Storage
Networking
Finish

All the necessary information has been collected and the wizard is ready to provision the new virtual
machine using the settings shown below.

Review these settings, then click Previous if you need to change anything. Otherwise, click Finish to create
the new VM and close this wizard. It may take several minutes to create the new VM.

Property	Value
Template	Windows 7 (32-bit)
Name	Win7-Master-VM
Install Method	CD
Installation Source	SW_DVD5_NTRL_Win_7SP1_All_Lng_Patch_Client_Server_X17-23698.ISO
Home Server	none
vCPUs	1
Memory	2048 MB
Disk 0	24 GB

CITRIX

☑ Start the new VM automatically

[< Previous]   [Next >]   [Finish]   [Cancel]

15. The process of creating the new VM may take some time. Progress is displayed in the XenCenter status bar and on the **Logs** tab.

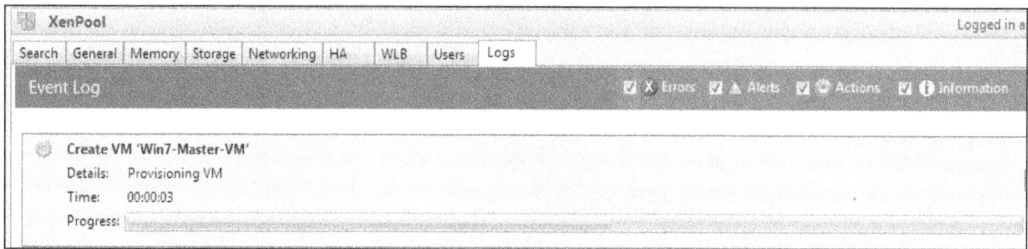

16. On the **Resources** pane, select the VM, and then click on the **Console** tab to see the VM console.

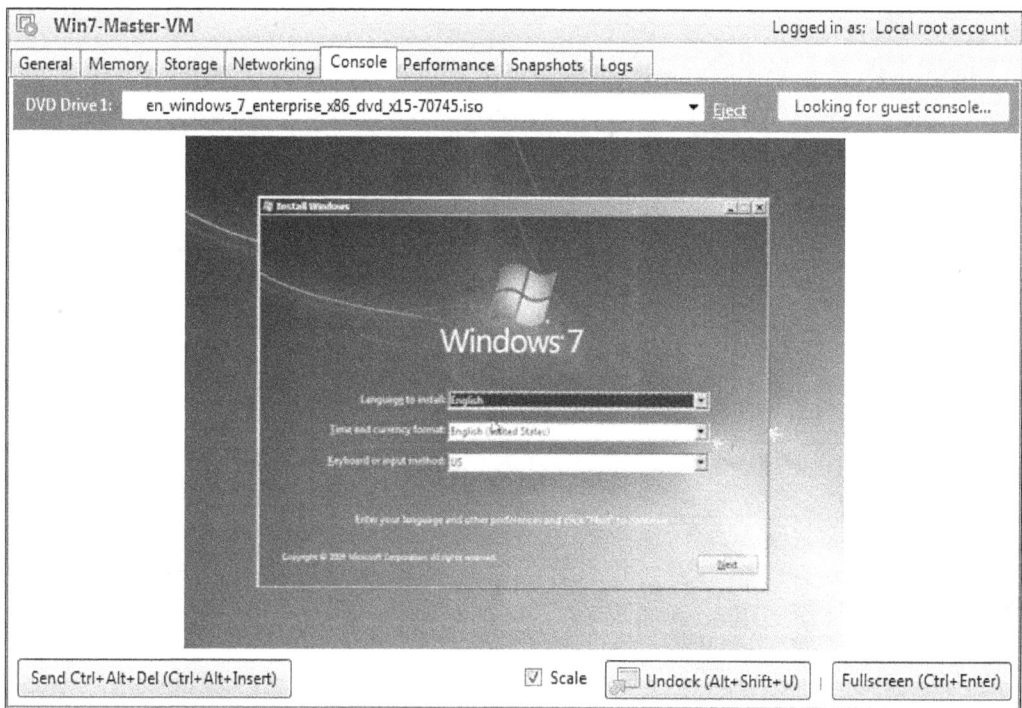

17. You are ready to install Microsoft Windows 7 Enterprise. Go through the setup process and create your Windows 7 machine. When you have completed the Windows 7 installation, we can go on and install the XenServer Tools package.

Installing the XenServer Tools package

Installing the XenServer Tools package is the first task you should accomplish after you deploy a new virtual machine. In this section, we cover the installation of XenServer Tools on the Win7-Master-VM machine we have created in the previous section.

The installation process is easy. Follow the given procedure:

1. Connect the ISO image of the XenServer Tools. To do this, select **Win7-Master-VM machine**, click on the **Storage** tab and select the **xs-tools.iso** file.

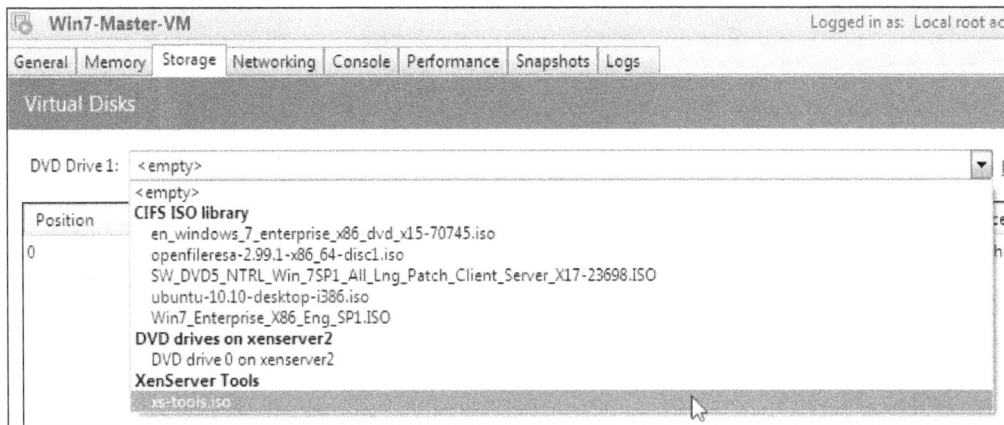

2. Log on on to the virtual machine console and run xensetup.exe to start the XenServer Tools installation process. The setup requires elevation so click **Yes** to the User Account Control request.

3. Accept the License Agreement and click on **Next** and select the destination folder where XenServer Tools will be installed — C:\Program Files\Citrix\ XenTools is the default location.

4. At the end of the setup, restart the virtual machine to complete the installation process. The virtual machine is now **optimized**.

> XenServer Tools requires a full version of Microsoft .NET 4.0 Framework. XenServer Tools installs it during the setup.
>
> **Best practice**: Disconnect the CD-ROM setting it to "empty" after you have used it. Leaving the CD connected degrades performance as the device is scanned when browsing or enumerating drives.

Creating a Windows virtual machine using xe CLI

In the following example, we will create another Windows 7 virtual machine named `Win7-XE-Practice` using xe CLI.

Creating a Windows machine

Connect to a XenServer host member of your pool. To create the Windows machine, execute the `xe` command:

```
xe vm-install template=<template-name> new-name-label=<vm-name> sr-name
```

where:

- The `template` parameter is the name of the template you want to use
- The `new-name-label` parameter is the name of the new VM
- The `sr-name` parameter is the name of the Storage Repository where XenServer will create the virtual disk associated to the VM

> When using the xe command, if you press the *Tab* key on the keyboard, XenServer proposes you a list of available commands and parameters helping you to remember the right syntax.

So, we will run the command:

```
xe vm-install template=Windows\ 7\ \(32-bit\) new-name-label=Win7-XE-
Practice sr-name-label=iSCSI\ Storage
```

Note the syntax for the template name and the Storage Repository name.

XenServer will return the UUID of the new Windows machine and the machine will be created. Note that a standard description will be set and a standard name for the virtual disk will be set. Also, no network interface will be added to the machine. In order to adjust these settings we have to execute some other `xe` commands.

Now, set a description for your virtual machine. To do this, we use `xe vm-param-set`. This command gives you the chance to set many parameters related to your VM.

```
xe vm-param-set uuid=<vm-uuid> name-description=<vm-description>
```

where `name-description` is the description you want to add to the VM.

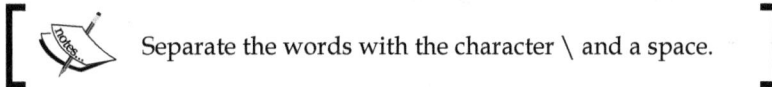

> Separate the words with the character \ and a space.

In our example, run the command:

```
xe vm-param-set name-description=Windows\ 7\ Machine\ -\ Testing\ XE
uuid=77d4875d-ab86-d5f5-79f1-36276d6cb965
```

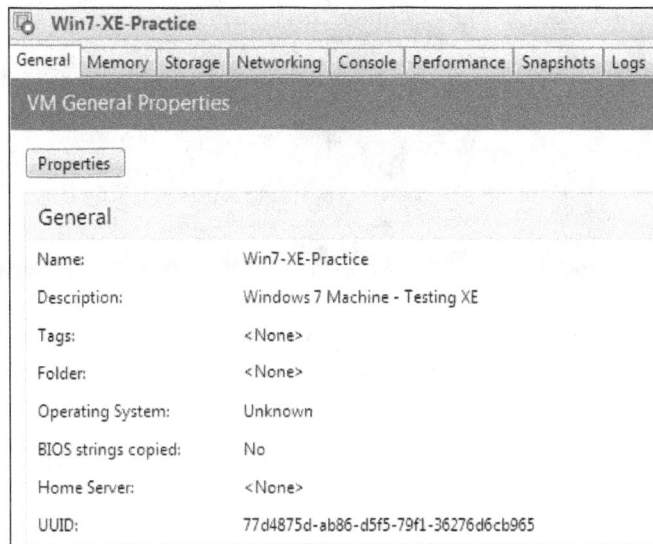

🗔 **Win7-XE-Practice**							
General	Memory	Storage	Networking	Console	Performance	Snapshots	Logs

VM General Properties

Properties

General

Name:	Win7-XE-Practice
Description:	Windows 7 Machine - Testing XE
Tags:	<None>
Folder:	<None>
Operating System:	Unknown
BIOS strings copied:	No
Home Server:	<None>
UUID:	77d4875d-ab86-d5f5-79f1-36276d6cb965

Renaming the virtual disk

Now, we want to rename the virtual disk. We don't like the 0 name that XenServer decides to use. First, we have to discover the UUID related to the virtual disk and later we have to set the desired name. To discover the UUID for the disk, we use the xe command, vm-disk-list. This command lists the virtual disks associated with the machine.

```
xe vm-disk-list uuid=<vm-uuid>
```

In our example, we execute:

```
xe vm-disk-list uuid=77d4875d-ab86-d5f5-79f1-36276d6cb965
```

```
xenserver1                                                      Logged in as: Local ro

Search  General  Memory  Storage  Networking  NICs   Console  Performance  Users  Logs

xenserver1 server console

[root@xenserver1 ~]# xe vm-disk-list uuid=77d4875d-ab86-d5f5-79f1-36276d6cb965
Disk 0 VBD:
uuid ( RO)                  : 4fcf7536-54a8-3abc-fca2-360a7b056efa
    vm-name-label ( RO): Win7-XE-Practice
        userdevice ( RW): 0


Disk 0 VDI:
uuid ( RO)                  : f2fa6eb8-0966-4500-b459-7ef97815aeea
        name-label ( RW): 0
     sr-name-label ( RO): iSCSI Storage
      virtual-size ( RO): 25769803776

[root@xenserver1 ~]#
```

Note the UUID of the Disk 0 VDI. We need this value in order to set the name of the virtual disk. Now, we will use the xe vdi-param-set command. This command is used to modify settings for a VDI object.

```
xe vdi-param-set name-label=<disk-name-label> name-description=<disk-
description> uuid=<vdi-uuid>
```

where:

- The name-label parameter is the name we want to set for the virtual disk
- The name-description parameter is the description we want to set for the virtual disk
- The uuid parameter is the unique identifier reference for the virtual disk

In our example, we run the command:

```
xe vdi-param-set name-label=Win7-XE-Practice\ Disk0 name-
description=Disk\ 0\ for\ Win7-XE-Practice\ VM uuid=f2fa6eb8-0966-4500-
b459-7ef97815aeea
```

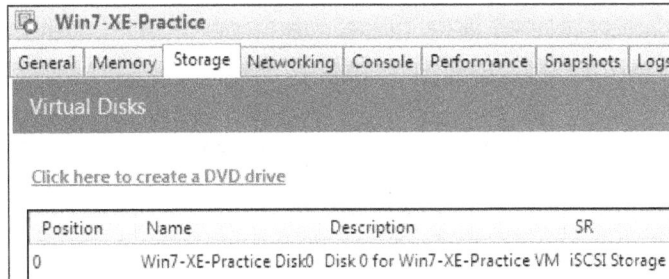

Resizing the disk

The size of the disk is set to 24 GB by default. We want to increase it so we use the `xe vdi-resize` command.

```
xe vdi-resize uuid=<vdi-uuid> disk-size=<new-size-disk>
```

where the `vdi-uuid` parameter is the unique identifier reference for the Virtual Disk Image (VDI) and the `disk-size` parameter is the new value for the size of the virtual disk specified in bytes or using the IEC standard suffixes KiB (210 bytes), MiB (220 bytes), GiB (230 bytes), and TiB (240 bytes).

In our example, we execute the following command:

```
xe vdi-resize uuid=f2fa6eb8-0966-4500-b459-7ef97815aeea disk-size=40GiB
```

Installing a DVD drive on a virtual machine

In the previous screenshot, you can notice that the virtual machine has no DVD drive. We need it to install the operating system. How do we add it? Click on **Click here to create a DVD drive**? Yes, correct answer if you want to use XenCenter but how to do it if you want to use xe CLI?

To connect to the ISO image related to Windows 7, we use the `xe vm-cd-add` command. This command permits you to add a new virtual CD based on an ISO image or physical drive on the host:

```
xe vm-cd-add vm=<vm_name> cd-name=<cd-name> device=<device-pbd-id>
```

where:

- The `vm` parameter is the name of the VM.
- The `cd-name` parameter is the name of the new CD—values can be an ISO image from a storage repository or a physical drive on the XenServer host.
- The `device` parameter is the device number associated with the DVD drive's Physical Block Device. In our example, we will execute the following command:

```
xe vm-cd-add vm=Win7-XE-Practice cd-name=en_windows_7_enterprise_
x86_dvd_x15-70745.iso device=1
```

Note that we use `device=1` because virtual disk `Win7-XE-Practice Disk0` is the device 0.

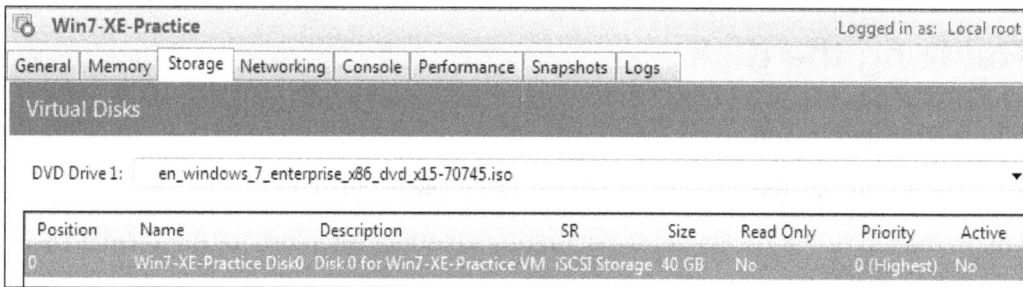

Now we are ready to start this virtual machine. Start the machine with the `xe` command `xe vm-start`:

```
xe vm-start name-label=<wm-name>
```

In our example, we execute the following command:

```
xe vm-start name-label=Win7-XE-Practice
```

Summary

In this chapter, we have learned how to create virtual machines. Also, we have discovered how to convert a physical machine to a virtual machine and perform import and export operations in XenServer.

Spend some time practicing virtual machine creation. When you embrace server and desktop virtualization, you will be required to create new virtual machines often. In the next chapter, we will introduce virtual machine management.

5

Managing Virtual Machines

In the previous chapter, we discussed how to create virtual machines in XenServer.

Now we can introduce virtual machine management in XenServer. At the end, you will have the ability to virtualize your actual server workloads. Server virtualization can help you save businesses money and simplify management overhead by allowing you to reduce the number of physical servers you need to provide IT services. This approach is known as "server consolidation".

In this chapter, we will cover the following topics:

- Managing virtual machines
- Converting a physical machine
- Managing vApps

Managing virtual machines

In the previous chapter, we have learned how to create a virtual machine based on the Microsoft Windows 7 operating system.

Now it is time to discover how to manage the virtual machines you can have in a XenServer environment.

Cloning, converting to template, and converting from physical machine are common tasks which you have to execute in XenServer.

We will use the Windows 7 VM, Win7-Master-VM, which we have created in the previous chapter.

Cloning a virtual machine

Cloning a virtual machine is useful when you need to set up many identical machines in your environment.

The only supported way to clone a Windows VM is by using the Windows utility, "System Preparation Tool", also known as `sysprep`, to prepare the VM.

Computers running Windows operating systems are uniquely identified by a **security ID (SID)**. This security ID must be unique for each Windows machine especially if it is a member of a Windows domain. For this reason, when you clone a Windows VM, it is important to take steps to ensure the uniqueness of the SID. Cloning an installation without taking the recommended system preparation steps can lead to duplicate SIDs and other problems.

> For more information, refer to the Microsoft Knowledge Base article 314828, "The Microsoft policy for disk duplication of Windows installations" available at `http://support.microsoft.com/kb/314828`.

`Sysprep` modifies the local computer SID to make it unique to each computer.

If you need to clone a Windows XP Professional or Windows Server 2003 machine, the `sysprep` binaries are on the Windows product CDs in the `\support\tools\deploy.cab` file.

Otherwise, if you need to clone a Windows 7 or Windows 2008 R2 machine, the `sysprep` tool is included with the operating system and you can find it in the `C:\Windows\System32\Sysprep` folder.

We will now execute `sysprep` on Win7-Master-VM in order to "*generalize*" the virtual machine. This "*generalized*" machine will be the base for our future Windows 7 template.

> For more information on the sysprep tool, visit the Microsoft web page at `http://technet.microsoft.com/en-us/library/cc783215(WS.10).aspx`.

To generalize the virtual machine, follow the given procedure:

1. Log on on to the virtual machine console.

2. Open a command prompt with administrative privileges.

3. Change the current directory to c:\windows\system32\sysprep with the Windows command cd c:\windows\system32\sysprep.

4. Type sysprep.exe and press *Enter* to start the Sysprep tool.

5. On the Sysprep tool, select the **Generalize** checkbox and select **Shutdown** from the **Shutdown Options** drop-down menu.

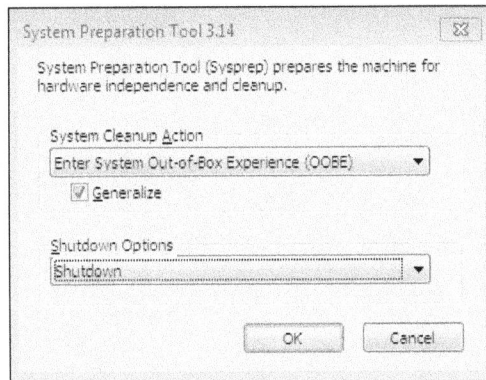

6. Click on **OK** to start the generalize process. At the end, the Windows machine will be powered off.

Now, it is time to see how to clone the virtual machine.

> The clone task requires that the virtual machine is powered-off or suspended.

Follow the given procedure to accomplish this task:

1. Select **Win7-Master-VM** in XenCenter.

2. Right-click and select **Copy VM...**.

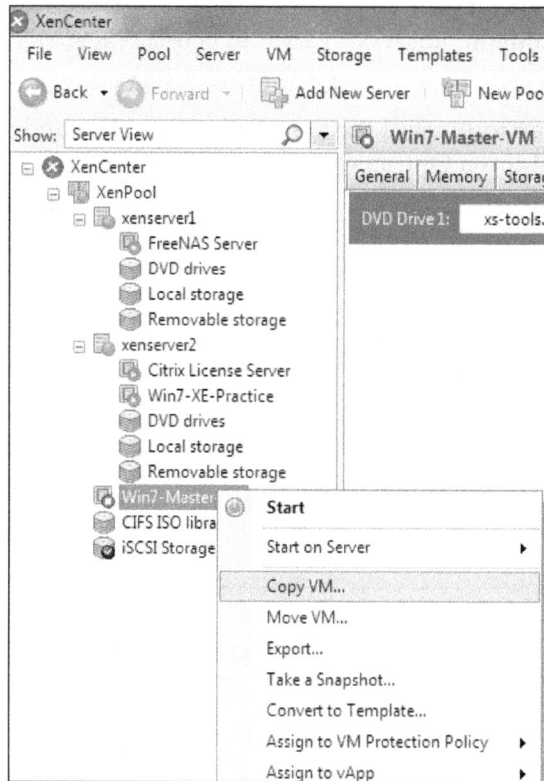

3. Enter the name of the new cloned virtual machine and insert a description.

4. Select the copy mode—**Fast clone** or **Full copy**. If you choose **Full copy**, then also select the Storage Repository (SR) where you want to copy the VM's virtual disks.

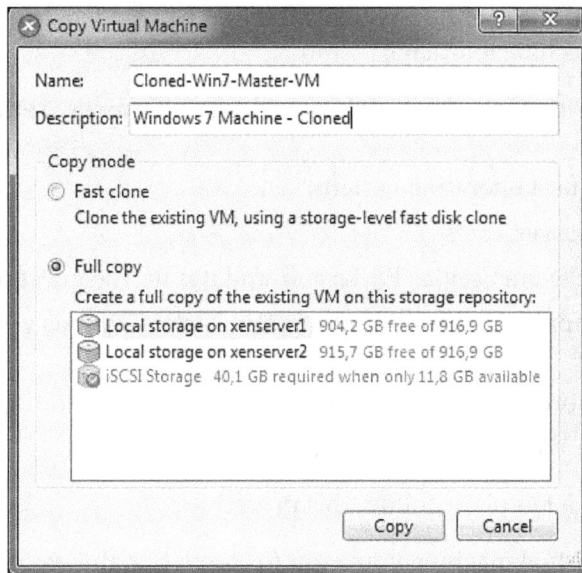

Remember to use **Full Copy** when you plan to create a template from an existing virtual machine and you want to create the copy on a different Storage Repository.

5. Click on **Copy** to start the cloning process. You can monitor the task on the **Logs** tab.

6. When the process is completed, the virtual machine will be displayed in XenCenter.

Creating a template

Early in this chapter, we have introduced the concept of *template*. XenServer permits you to create your fully customized template starting from an existing machine you have prepared before with an appropriate guest operating system, memory, CPU, storage, network, and other settings you want to have on the template.

But before going on, it is useful to review all the steps you usually perform to prepare a virtual machine template:

1. Create the virtual machine with your desired hardware settings in XenCenter.
2. Install the guest operating system.
3. Install XenServer Tools.
4. Apply all relevant Service Packs and updates for the guest operating system.
5. Install any applications and perform any customizations you want to have on the template.
6. Execute Sysprep if the VM is based on a Windows operating system.
7. Convert the VM to a template.

To convert a VM to a template, follow this procedure:

1. Select the virtual machine you want to convert, in this example, we will use **Cloned-Win7-Master-VM**.
2. Right-click and select **Convert to Template...**.

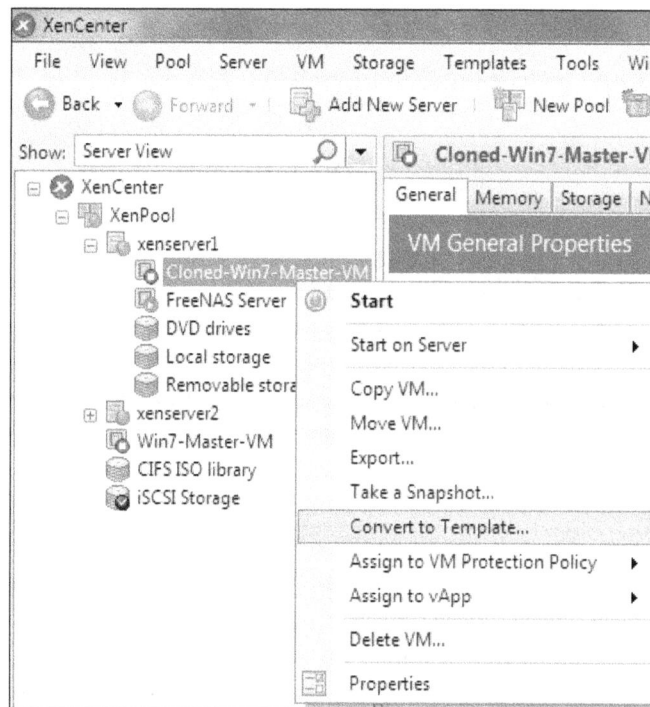

3. XenServer asks you if you are sure you want to convert the VM—this is a one-way operation because you cannot ever revert a template to VM. Click on **Convert** to continue with the process.

4. XenServer converts the VM and shows it to you as a template in XenCenter.

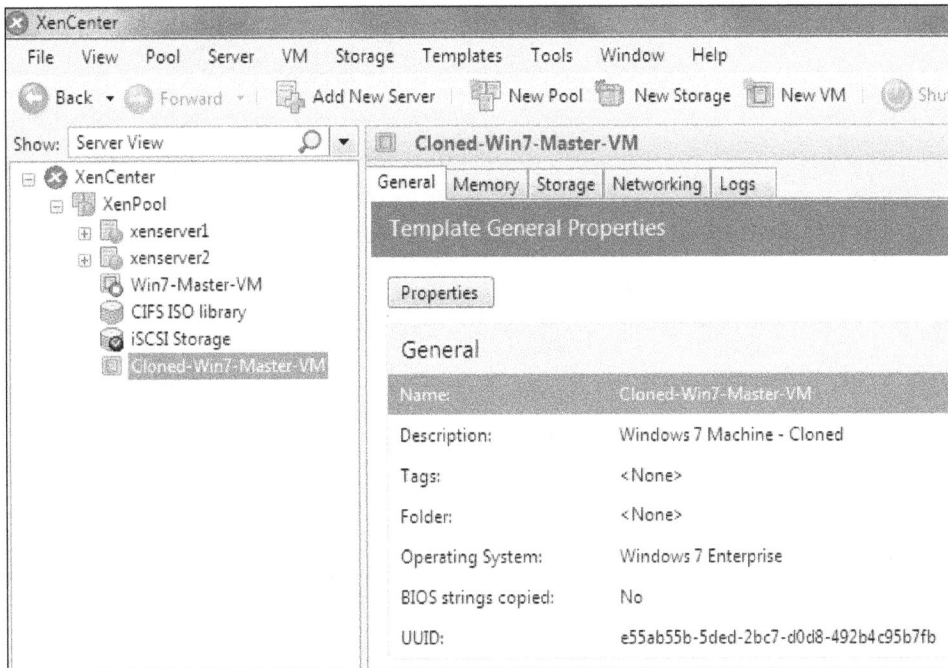

5. As the last step, we want to set a descriptive name for the new template. So we can click on the **Properties** button on the **General** tab of the template or use xe CLI to change the name and the description.

We will use the xe CLI to do this task and execute the command:

```
xe vm-param-set name-label=Custom\ Windows\ 7\
Template name-description=Windows\ 7\ Template\
with\ XenTools uuid=e55ab55b-5ded-2bc7-d0d8-492b4c95b7fb
```

The command renames the VM with the name **Custom Windows 7 Template** and changes the VM description to **Windows 7 Template with XenTools**.

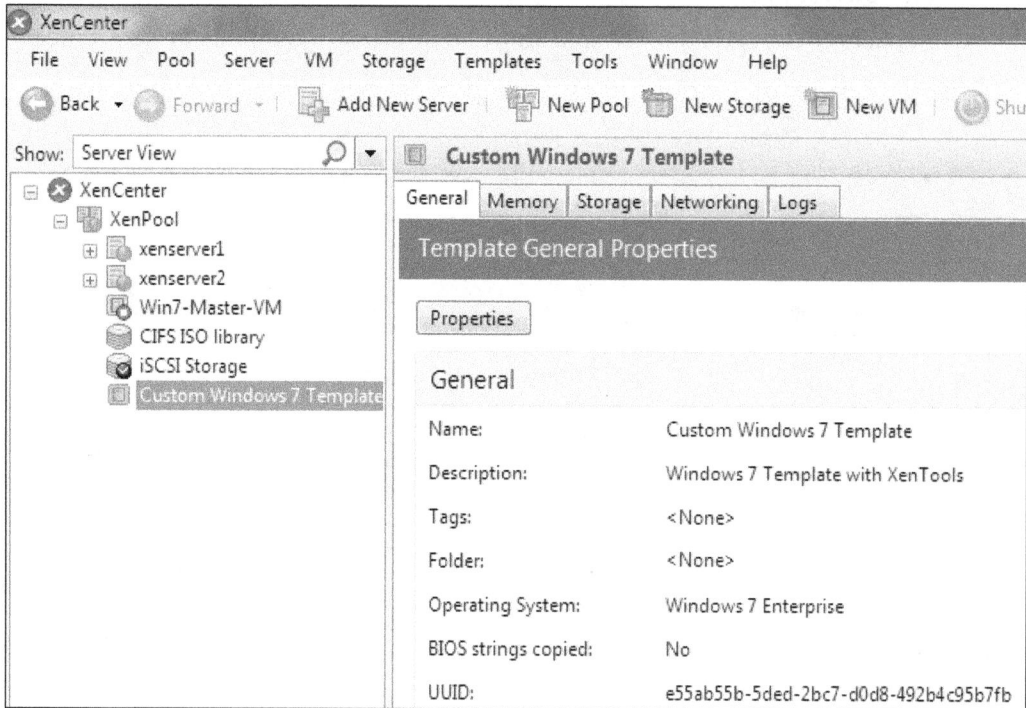

You can create a new virtual machine starting from your custom template following this procedure:

1. Right-click on your custom template.
2. Select **New VM Wizard…**.
3. Complete the wizard using the virtual machine creation procedure we have described earlier.

Importing and exporting virtual machines

XenServer allows you to import VMs from and export them to a number of different formats. Using the XenCenter Import wizard, you can import VMs from *disk images* (VHD and VMDK), Open Virtualization Format (OVF), and XenServer XVA format. You can even import VMs that have been created on other virtualization platforms, such as VMware or Microsoft.

Using the XenCenter Export wizard, you can export VMs to Open Virtualization Format files (OVF and OVA) and XenServer XVA files.

When importing and exporting VMs, a temporary VM named *Transfer VM* is used to perform the import/export of OVF/OVA packages and disk images.

The Transfer VM is a VM provided by XenServer that you use when you want to perform import or export operations of a virtual machine and in order to transfer the virtual machine's contents between the disk image file location and a XenServer Storage Repository (SR). Note that one Transfer VM runs for each import or export of a disk image.

> When importing or exporting VMs with more than one disk image, only one disk image transfers at a time.

Note that only users with the RBAC role of Pool Admin can perform import and export operations if you have enabled Role Based Access Control (RBAC) in your XenServer environment.

Open Virtualization Format (OVF)

Open Virtualization Format (OVF) is an open standard for packaging and distributing virtual appliances consisting of one or more virtual machines (VMs).

An OVF package is always composed of a file with the .ovf extension, known as OVF descriptor, which describes the packaged virtual machine and contains metadata for the package. Also, the OVF package will typically contain one or more disk images. The descriptor file specifies the virtual hardware requirements of the VM and can also include other information such as descriptions of virtual disks, guest operating systems, and a license agreement (EULA).

An **Open Virtual Appliance (OVA)** is an OVF package compressed in a single tar file archived with the .ova extension.

Note that an OVF package created on one hypervisor might not automatically work on a different hypervisor because of different interpretations of the OVF specification. So if you try to export a virtual machine to an OVF package, you don't have the guarantee that the virtual machine included in the package will be cross-hypervisor compatible. In order to ensure a basic level of interoperability for OVF packages, XenServer includes a feature known as Operating System Fixup. You use this feature when you must import a virtual machine from other hypervisors and disk image formats (VHD and VMDK).

Virtual Hard Disk (VHD) is a file format typically used to represent hard disk drives in virtual machines created with Microsoft products such as Virtual PC or Hyper-V. **Virtual Machine Disk (VMDK)** is a file format developed by VMware as a container for virtual disk drives used in virtual machines.

Fine! We have introduced the main concepts for the supported format. In the next sections we will see some examples of the import process.

Importing a virtual machine from an OVF/OVA package

You can import virtual machines (VMs) that have been saved as OVF/OVA files using the Import wizard. The wizard will take you through many of the steps needed to create a new VM in XenCenter as we discovered earlier in this chapter.

If you are bored with all these concepts, don't worry! It is now time to move on to practice. In the next example, we will import a Windows 2003 machine exported as an OVF package from the Oracle VirtualBox software.

You can import an OVF package by following the given procedure:

1. Open the **Import** wizard selecting **Import** from the **File** menu.
2. Locate the package you want to import (with a `.ovf`, `.ova` or `.ova.gz` file extension), then click on **Next** to continue.

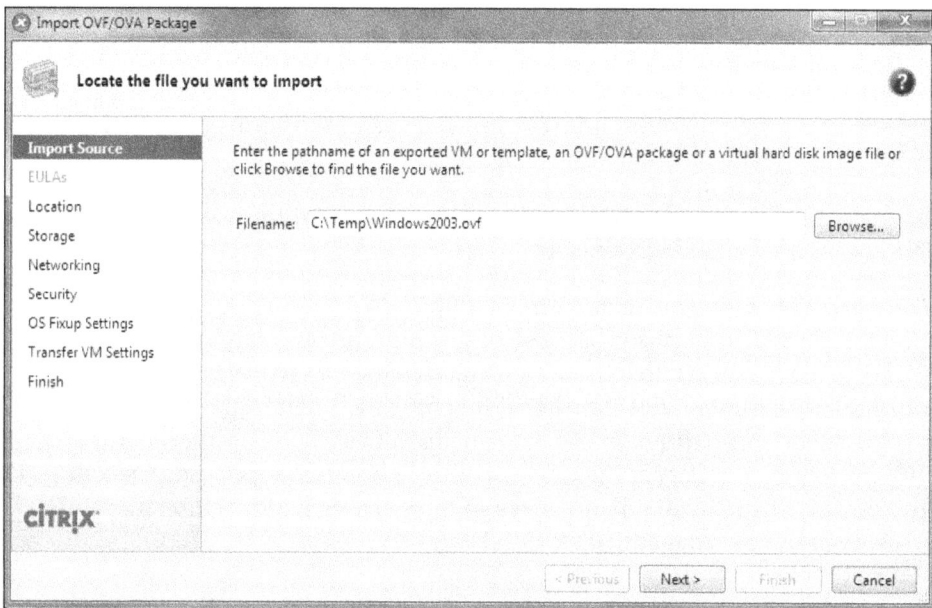

3. If the package you are importing includes any EULAs, accept them and then click on **Next** to continue. If no EULAs are included in the package, the wizard will skip this step and move straight to the next page.

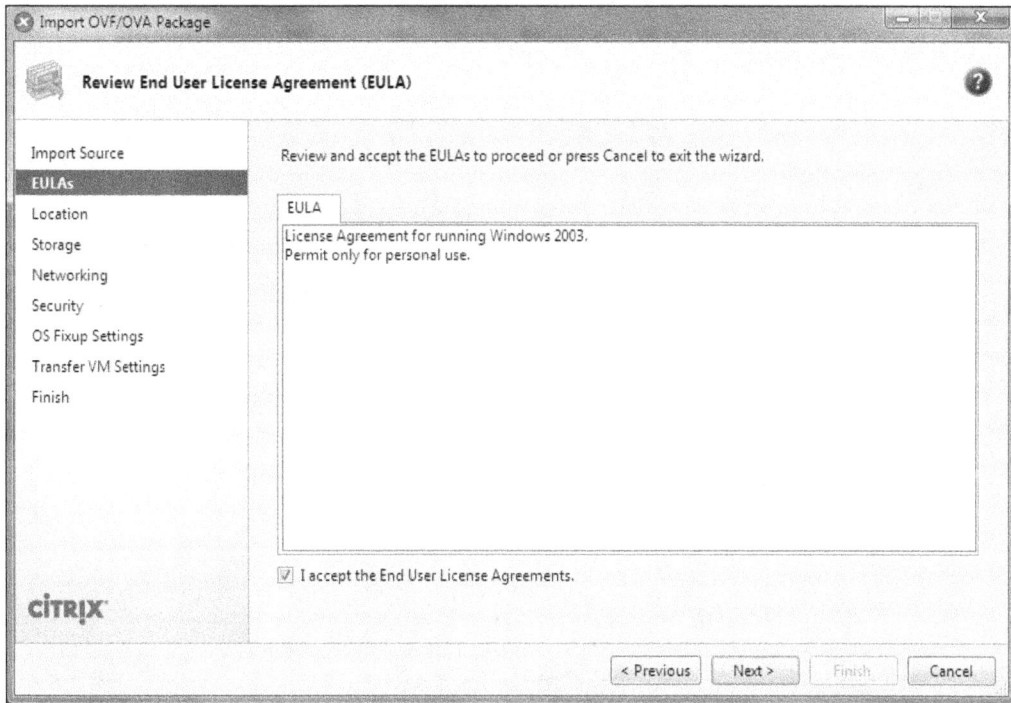

4. On the **Location** page, choose from the **Import VMs** drop-down list the pool or the server where you want to place the virtual machine you are importing.

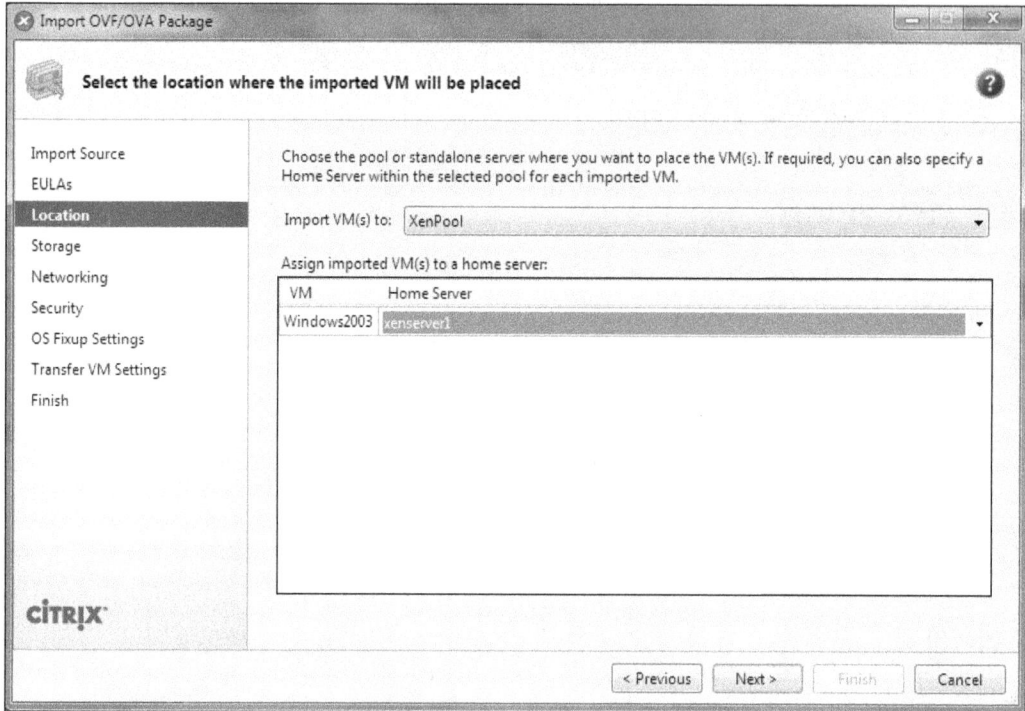

5. If you want to nominate a home server for the VM, select the host from the list in the **Home Server** column. XenServer will always attempt to start up a VM on its home server if it can.

6. In our example, we will import the VM to the **XenPool** and we will nominate host **xenserver1** as the home server for the machine.

7. Click on **Next** to continue.

8. On the **Storage** page, select one or more Storage Repositories (SRs) where the disk images of the imported VMs will be placed, and then click on **Next** to continue.

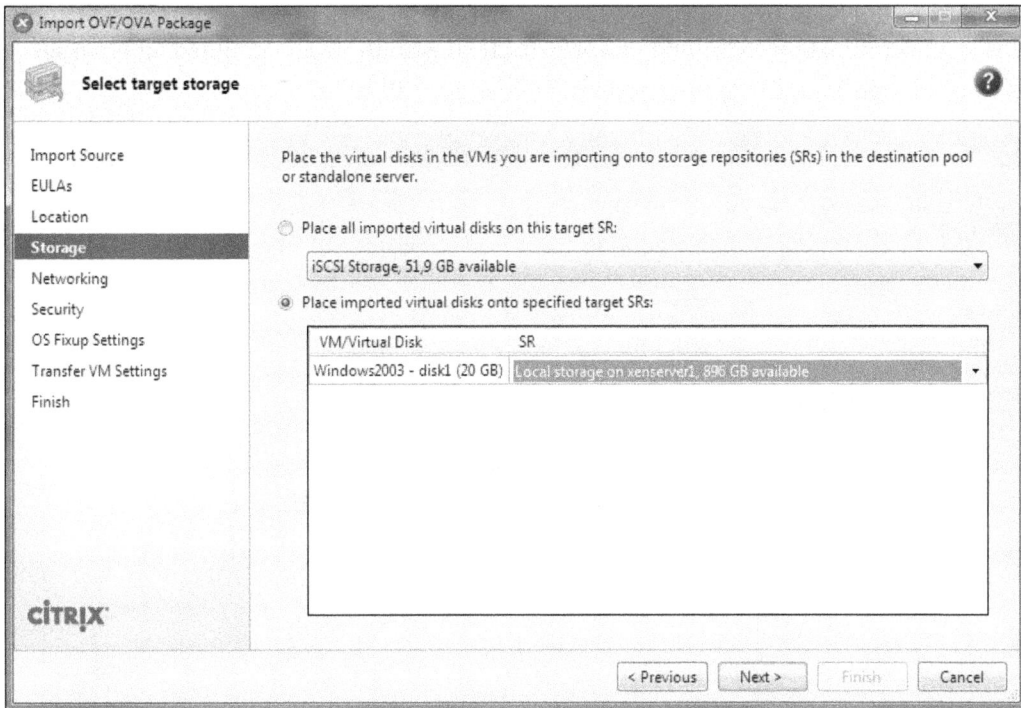

9. To place all the imported disk images on the same SR, click on **Place all imported virtual disks on this target SR** and select an **SR** from the list.

10. You can also place the disk images of the importing VMs onto different SRs. To do so, click on **Place imported VMs on the specified target SRs**. Then, for each virtual disk, select the target SR from the list in the **SR** column. You can select this option, for example, when you have a virtual machine with two disk drives, one for the operating system and one for data, and you have a Storage Repository dedicated only to data disk drives. In this case you will place the data disk on this dedicated storage.

In our example, we will place the virtual disk on the local storage of the `xenserver1` host.

11. On the **Networking** page, map the virtual network interfaces in the VMs you are importing to target networks in the destination pool. After you have set the network information, click on **Next** to continue.

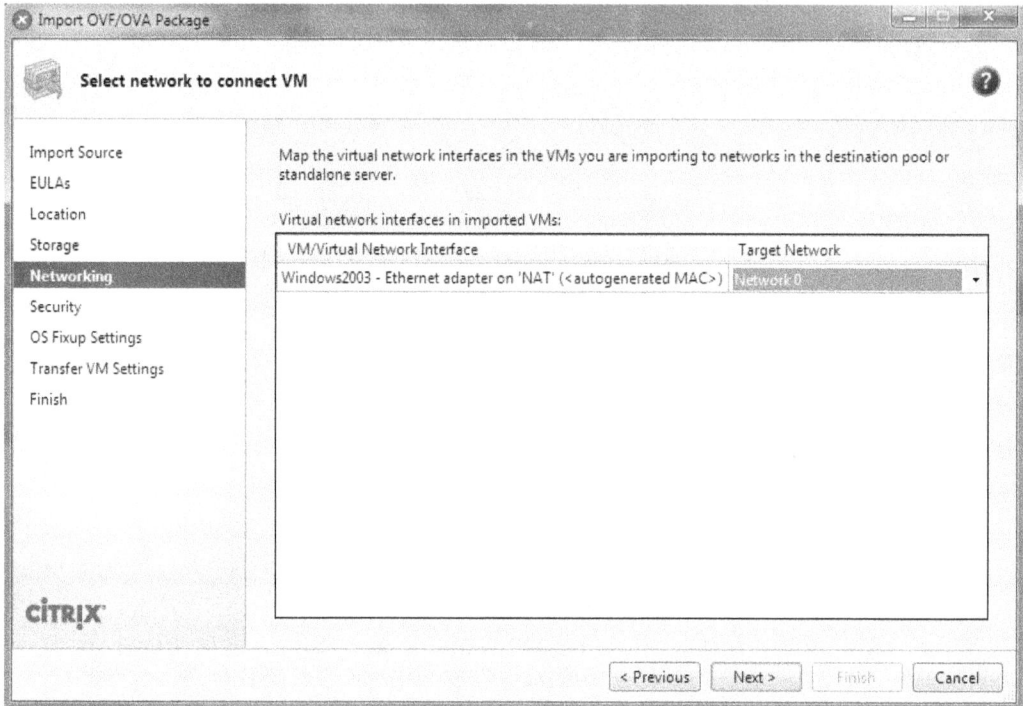

12. If the selected OVF/OVA package is configured with security features such as certificates or a manifest, specify the necessary information on the **Security** page and then click on **Next** to continue.

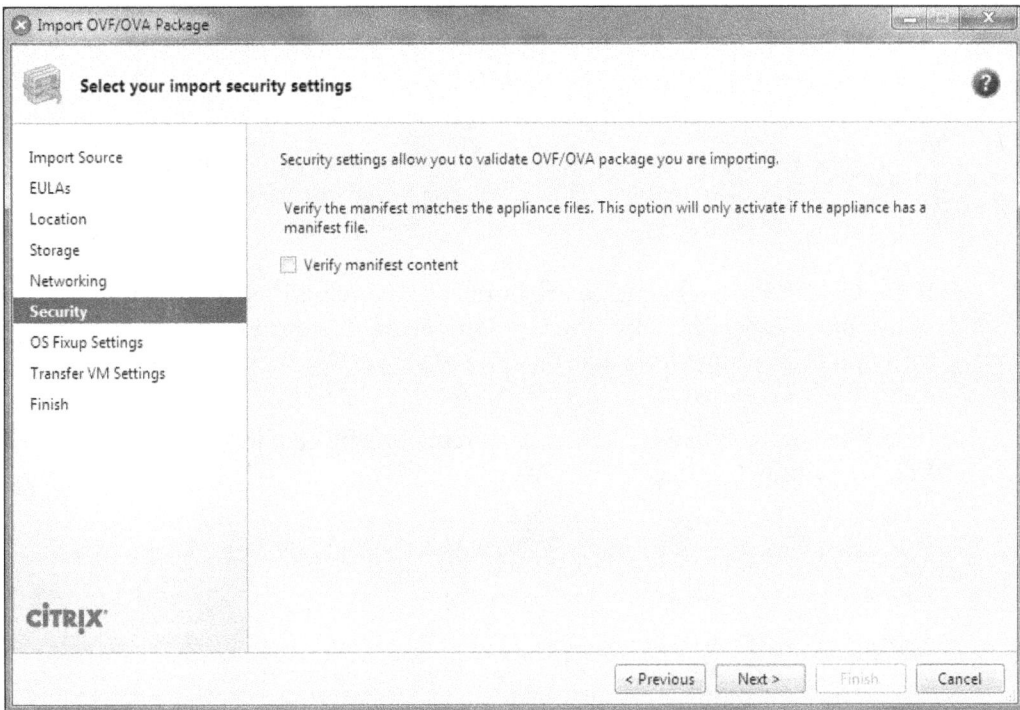

Different options appear on this page depending on which security features have been configured on the OVF package:

- ° If the package is signed, a **Verify digital signature** checkbox appears here. Click this checkbox if you want to verify the signature. Click on **View Certificate** to display the certificate used to sign the package. If the certificate appears as untrusted, it is likely that either the Root Certificate or the Issuing Certificate Authority is not trusted on the local computer.

○ If the package includes a manifest, a **Verify manifest content** checkbox appears here. Select this checkbox to have the wizard verify the list of files in the package.

> When packages are digitally signed, the associated manifest is verified automatically and so the **Verify manifest content** checkbox does not appear on the **Security** page.

13. If the VMs in the package you are importing were built on a hypervisor other than XenServer, select the **Use Operating System Fixup** checkbox and select an ISO Storage Repository where the Fixup ISO can be copied so that XenServer can use it.

    If no ISO library is available, you can create one by clicking on the **New ISO Library** button.

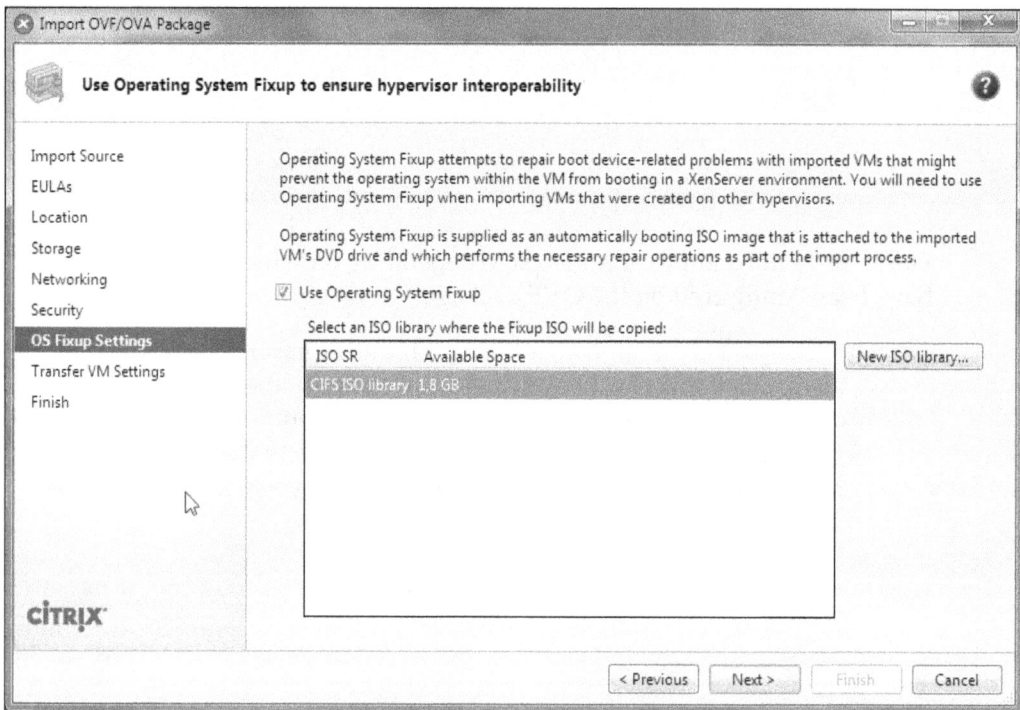

14. Click on **Next** to continue.

15. On the **Transfer VM Settings** page, configure the networking settings for the Transfer VM and then click on **Next** to continue.

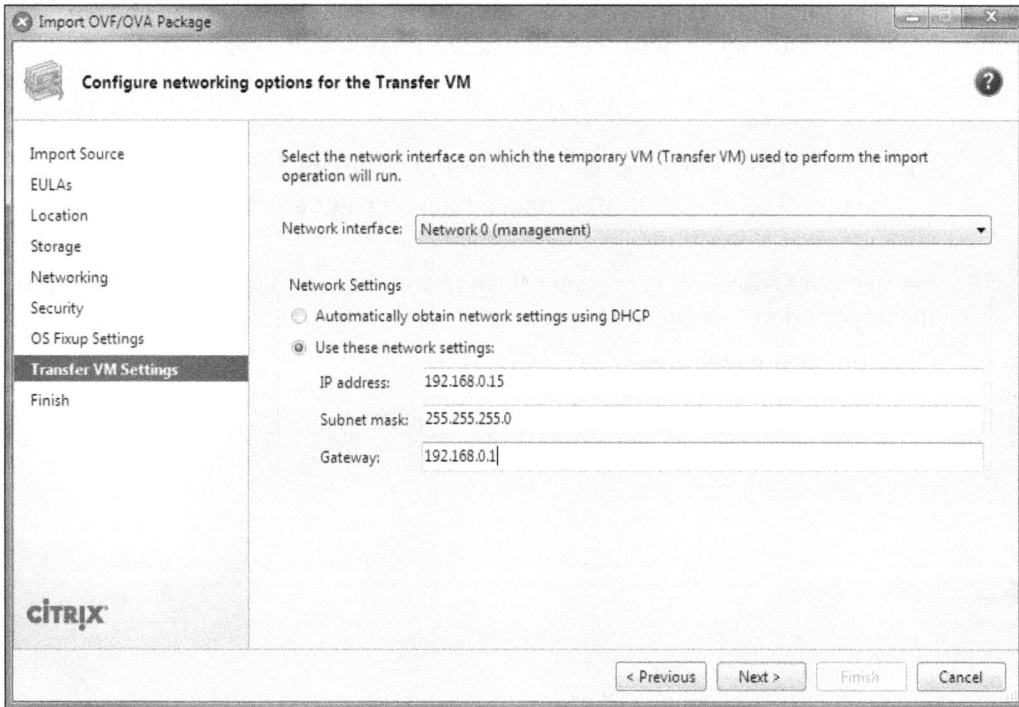

16. Select a network from the list of network interfaces available in your resource pool or XenServer host.

17. By default, XenServer sets the Transfer VM to obtain network information by a Dynamic Host Configuration Protocol (DHCP) server.

18. If you prefer to configure networking settings manually, click on **Use these network settings** and enter the IP address, subnet mask, and gateway.

19. On the **Finish** page, review all the import settings and then click on **Finish** to begin the import process and close the wizard. When the import is finished, the newly-imported VMs will appear in XenServer.

Importing disk images

Like OVF or OVA packages, using XenCenter's Import wizard, you can also import a disk image. The importation procedure is similar to that we have used for importing an OVF\OVA package so we will only look at the main differences.

To import a disk image, following the given steps:

1. Open the Import wizard by selecting **Import** from the **File** menu.
2. Locate the VHD or VMDK disk image file you want to import and then click on **Next** to continue.
3. On the **VM Definition** page, enter the name of the new VM to be created from the imported disk image and specify CPU and initial memory resources.
4. Click on **Next** to continue.

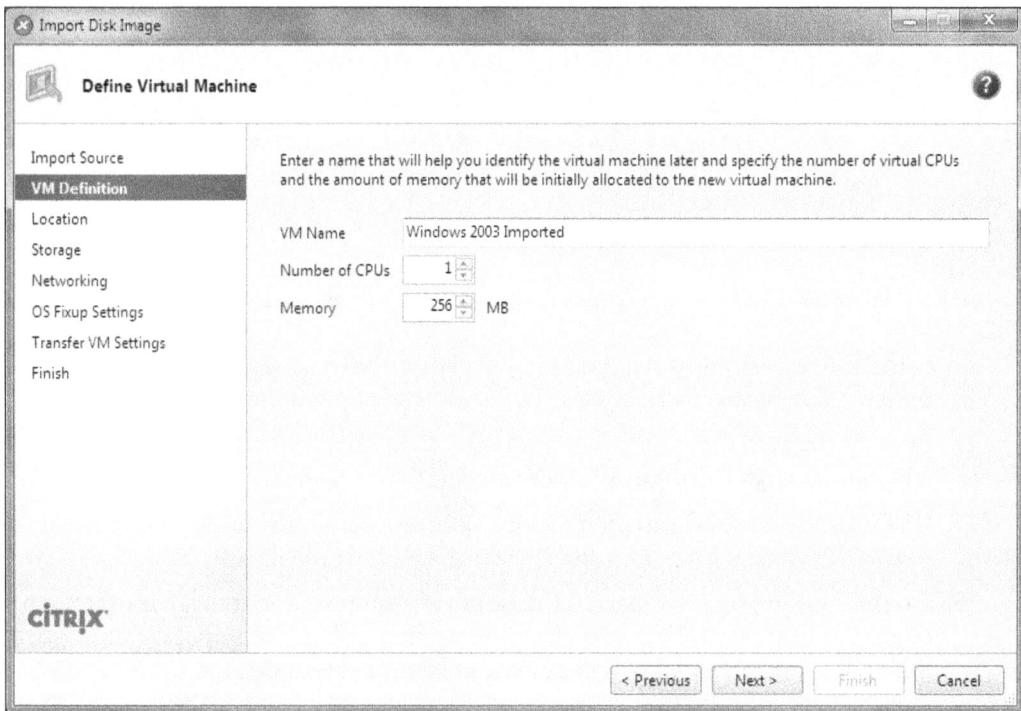

5. On the **Location** page, choose the pool or the XenServer host where you want to place the VM you are importing. Click on **Next** to continue.

6. On the **Storage** page, select one or more Storage Repositories (SRs) where you desire to place the disk images belonging to the VM you are importing and then click on **Next** to continue.

7. On the **Networking** page, select a target network for the new VM's virtual network interface. After you have set the network information, click on **Next** to continue.

8. If the VMs in the package you are importing were built on a hypervisor other than XenServer, select the **Use Operating System Fixup** checkbox and select an ISO storage repository where the Fixup ISO can be copied for XenServer usage. On the **Transfer VM Settings** page, configure the networking settings for the Transfer VM and then click on **Next** to continue.

9. On the **Finish** page, review all the import settings and then click on **Finish** to begin the import process and close the wizard. When the import is finished, the newly-imported VMs will appear in XenServer.

Importing VMs from XVA

You can import VMs, templates, and snapshots that have previously been exported and stored locally in the XVA format (with a .xva file extension) using XenCenter's Import wizard.

You can find examples of virtual machines distributed in XVA format on the Citrix Download website at http://www.citrix.com/English/ss/downloads/index. asp. For example, Citrix Licensing server is also distributed as an XVA package and you can download it from http://www.citrix.com/English/ss/downloads/ details.asp?downloadId=2319562&productId=1679389.

The importation procedure is similar to that we have used for importing an OVF\OVA package.

Also, you can easily import an XVA file by double-clicking on it—the Import wizard will start automatically.

To import the XVA, following the given steps:

1. Open the Import wizard by selecting **Import** from the **File** menu.

2. Locate the XVA file you want to import and click on **Next** to continue.

3. On the **Home Server** page, specify where you want to place the new VM. To place the imported VM in a pool without assigning it a home server, select the pool in the list. If you want to place the imported VM in a pool and assign it to a specific home server, select a server and then click on **Next** to continue.

4. On the **Storage** page, select a Storage Repository (SR) where the imported virtual disks will be placed and then click on **Import** to continue.

5. XenServer prepares the import process and displays the **Networking** page.

6. On the **Networking** page, assign a virtual network available on your resource pool to the virtual network interfaces in the VM you are importing. Click on **Next** to continue.

7. Review the configuration options you have selected. Click on **Finish** to begin the importing process and close the wizard.

If you want to start the machine as soon as the import process has finished and the new VM is created, select the **Start VM after import** checkbox.

Exporting a virtual machine

XenServer lets you export virtual machines, for example, if you want to move them to another pool or just for archiving them.

You can export one or more VMs as an OVF/OVA package or XVA using XenCenter's Export wizard. Note that VMs must be shut down or suspended before they can be exported.

To export a virtual machine, follow the given procedure:

1. Right-click on the virtual machine you want to export or click on menu VM and select **Export...**.

2. On the first page of the wizard, enter a meaningful name for the archive file, specify a location where you want to save the file, and select **OVF/OVA Package** or **XVA** file from the **Format** drop-down menu. Once you do this, click on **Next**.

3. Select the VMs you want to export and then click on **Next**.

4. If you have selected to export the virtual machine as an OVF/OVA package, the **EULAs** page will be displayed. If you want to include some EULA files in your exported package, add them here. Click on **Next** to continue.

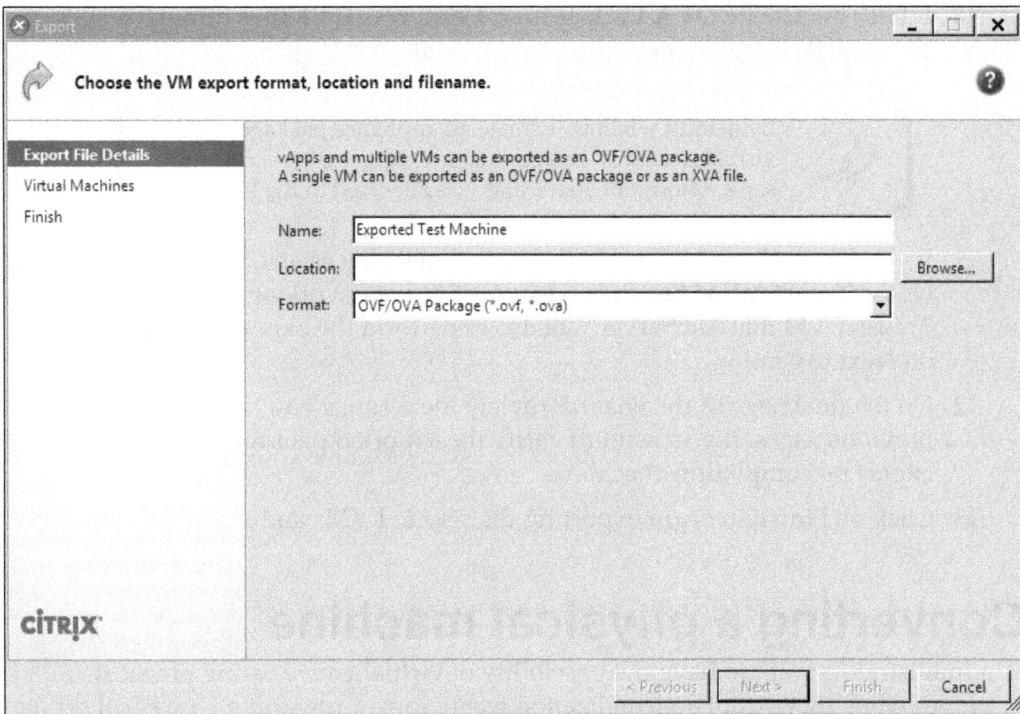

5. If you have selected to export the virtual machine as an OVF/OVA package, the **Advanced Options** page will be displayed. Here you can specify any manifest, signature, and output file options or just click on **Next** to continue.

6. To create a manifest for the package, select the **Create a manifest** checkbox.

    The manifest file is used during the importing process to verify that the files have not changed after the package was initially created.

7. To add a digital signature to the package, select the **Sign the OVF package** checkbox, browse to locate a security certificate, and enter the private key associated with the certificate in the **Private key password** field.

8. To export the selected VMs in OVA format, select the **Create OVA Package** checkbox.

9. To compress the virtual hard disk images included in the package, select the **Compress OVF files** checkbox.

10. If both the **Create OVA Package** and **Compress OVF files** options are checked, the result is a compressed OVA file.

> By default when you create an appliance package, the virtual hard disk images that are exported consume the same amount of space that was allocated to the VM.

11. If you have selected to export the virtual machine as an OVF/OVA package, on the **Transfer VM Settings** page, configure networking options for the Transfer VM that XenServer will use to perform the export process and click on **Next** to continue.

12. On the final page of the wizard, review the settings you have selected on the previous pages. If you want to verify the exported package, select the **Verify export on completion** checkbox.

13. Click on **Finish** to begin exporting the selected VMs and close the wizard.

Converting a physical machine

IT administrators want to have the possibility of virtualizing existing physical machines when they adopt a virtualization technology. Converting a physical server to virtual gives you many benefits, for example, you can reduce power consumption or reduce the number of servers you have to manage and maintain.

In a XenServer environment, you can use Citrix XenConvert to accomplish this task. It is a *physical-to-virtual* (P2V) conversion tool that converts a workload from a server or desktop machine running Windows to a virtual machine in XenServer, virtual appliance, or a virtual disk.

> You can download the latest release of XenConvert for X86 or X64 systems from http://www.citrix.com/English/ss/downloads/details.asp?downloadId=2318170&productId=683148.
>
> Microsoft .Net Framework 4.0 is required to install and use XenConvert.

When you want to operate a conversion, prepare the host machine as follows to achieve best results:

1. Enable Windows Automount on Windows Server operating systems.

2. Disable Windows Autoplay feature.

3. Remove any virtualization software before performing a conversion.

4. Verify if adequate free space exists on the destination, which is approximately 101 percent of used space of all source volumes.

5. Remove any network interface teams because it is not applicable to a virtual machine.

In the following example, we will discover how to convert a physical Windows 7 laptop to a virtual machine. Let's go.

1. Install XenConvert on the machine you want to virtualize and start it.

2. From the drop-down menu, select **This Machine** as source and **XenServer** or **OVF Package** as destination.

   Choose **XenServer** when you want to convert a physical machine that can connect to XenServer or choose **OVF Package** if the physical machine cannot connect to XenServer. This last choice will create a virtual appliance.

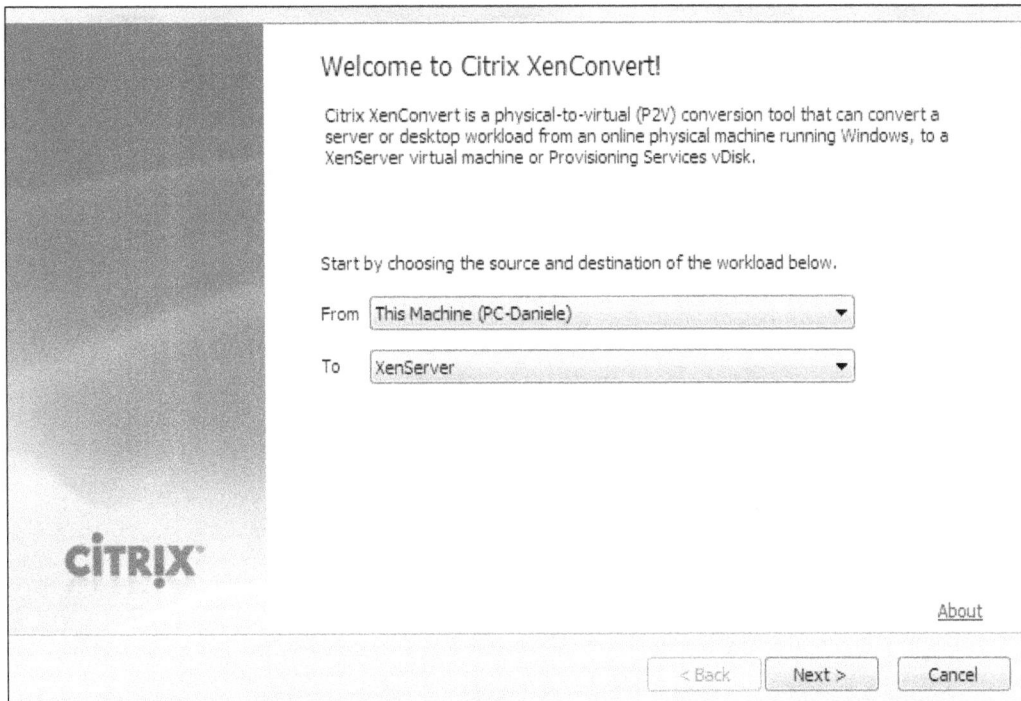

In our example, we choose **XenServer** because we are able to connect to a XenServer pool. Click on **Next** to continue.

3. Converting from a host machine involves copying selected volumes from the physical machine to new virtual disks which XenConvert creates during the conversion process. A *source* volume refers to a volume to copy. A *destination* volume refers to the copy of the source volume on the virtual disk.

4. In the **Source Volume** section, select the volumes you want to include in the conversion. By default XenConvert selects all the discovered volumes in the machine. Choose **None** to remove a volume from the conversion.

5. In the **Destination Volume** section, you can change the unallocated space to reserve space on the virtual disk for creating or extending volumes later.

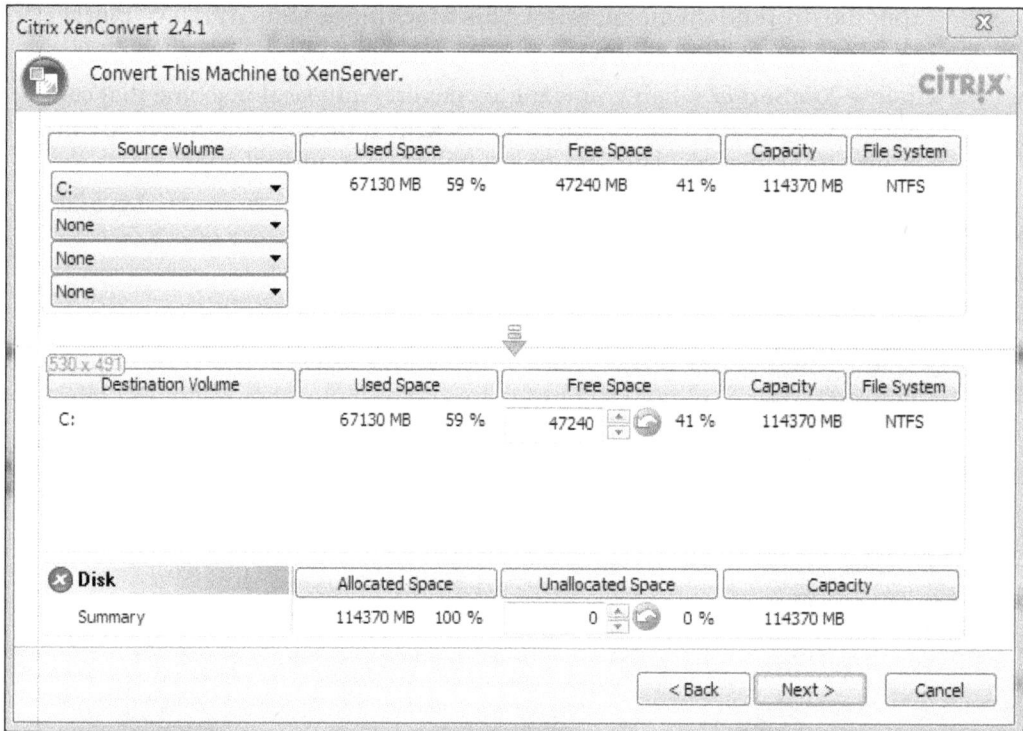

6. Click on **Next** to continue.

7. Specify the required information for connecting to XenServer:

   ◦ **Hostname**: Enter the host name, fully qualified domain name, or IP address of a standalone XenServer or the XenServer Pool Master.

   ◦ **User name**: Enter the name of the account with import privileges. Use root or a user with Pool Admin role.

   ◦ **Password**: Enter the password for the user.

   ◦ **Workspace**: Enter the path of the folder to store the intermediate OVF package that XenConvert will use during the conversion process. In the path you select, XenConvert will store the OVF package.

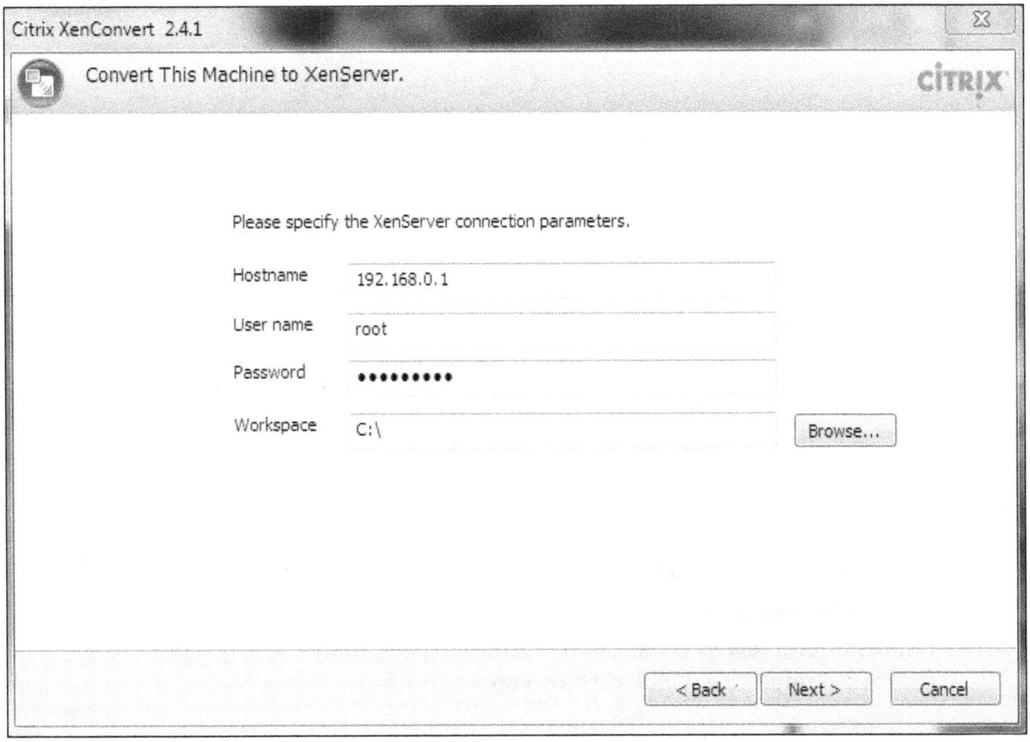

8. Click on **Next** to continue.

9. Type the name of the virtual machine that will be created in XenServer and choose the Storage Repository where you want to place the virtual disks of the converted virtual machine. In this example, we will name the VM `Converted Windows 7 P2V`.

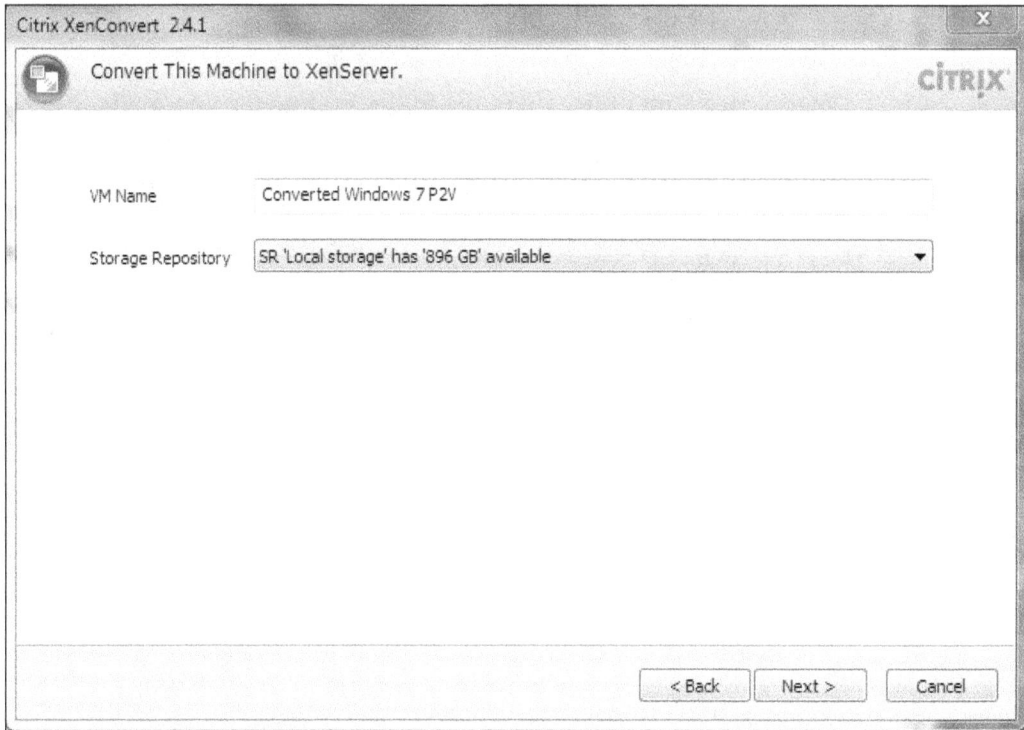

10. Click on **Next** to continue.
11. Review the settings you have entered in the previous steps and check **Log names of converted files** if you want to log the name of each converted file for future reference. Click on **Convert** to continue.

> Logging the names of converted files significantly increases the conversion time.

Citrix XenConvert 2.4.1

Convert This Machine to XenServer.

CITRIX

VM Name	Converted Windows 7 P2V
Source	C:
Destination	SR 'Local storage' on server '192.168.0.1'
Status	Ready to Start
Progress	

☐ Log names of converted files

< Back   Convert   Cancel

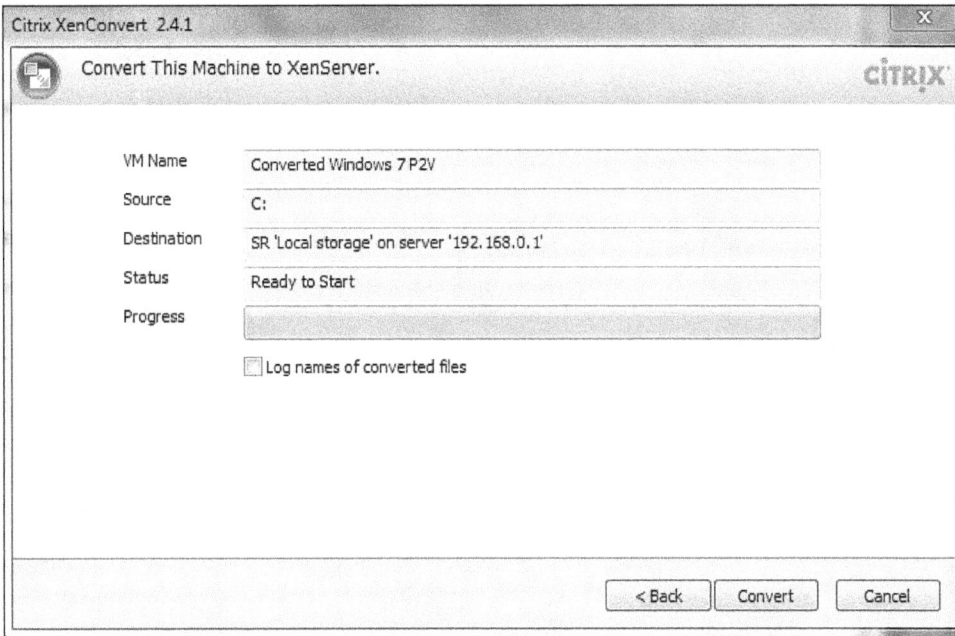

12. XenConvert will start the conversion process. It is complete when the progress bar is full and the **Status** contains a message indicating success or failure. Click on the **Log** button to review the details of the results.

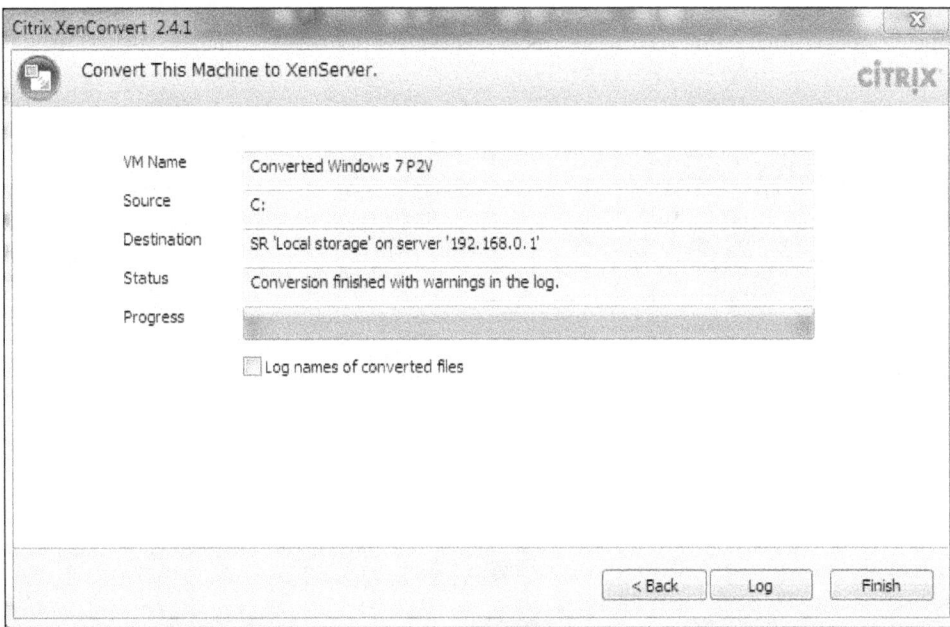

Citrix XenConvert 2.4.1

Convert This Machine to XenServer.

CITRIX

VM Name	Converted Windows 7 P2V
Source	C:
Destination	SR 'Local storage' on server '192.168.0.1'
Status	Conversion finished with warnings in the log.
Progress	

☐ Log names of converted files

< Back   Log   Finish

13. In XenCenter you can find the converted virtual machine! Remember to install XenServer Tools to have a fully optimized and supported machine.

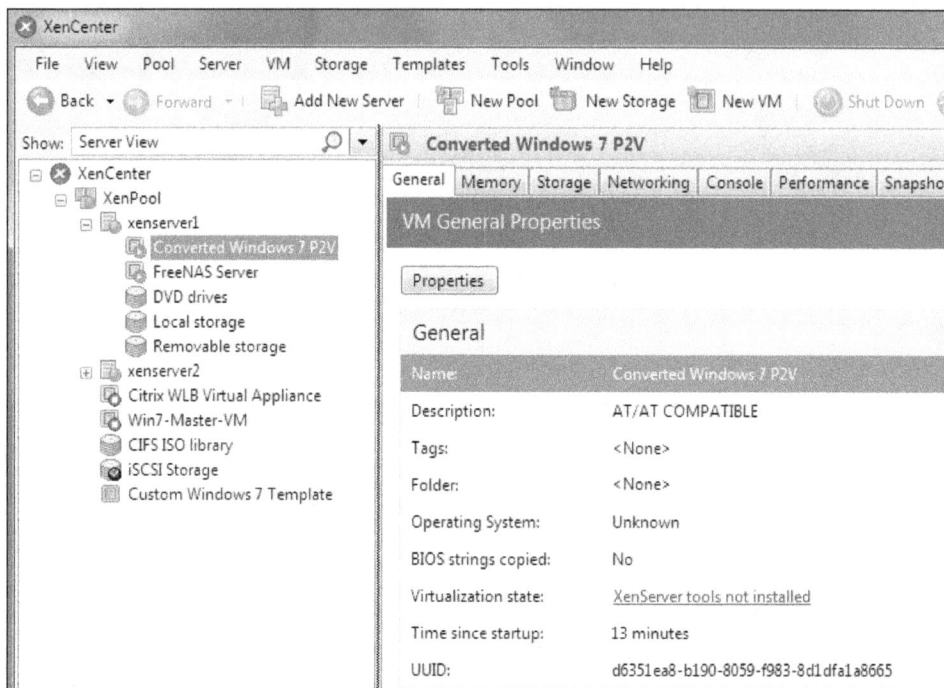

Note that XenConvert does not delete the OVF Package on the physical machine you have just converted. Delete the files manually in order to release allocated space.

Managing vApps

In order to group virtual machines into a logical group, XenServer 6 has introduced a new feature named **vApp**. A vApp is a logical group of one or more VMs which can be started up as a single entity.

When a vApp is started, the VMs contained within the vApp will start in a user predefined order, to allow VMs which depend upon one another to be automatically started. With this feature, you don't have to remember anymore the right order of your virtual machines' startup and accomplish this task manually—XenServer will do the job for you!

You can create, modify, and manage vApps using **Manage vApps** available in the **Pool** menu in XenCenter. When you select a vApp in the list, the VMs it contains are listed in the details pane on the right.

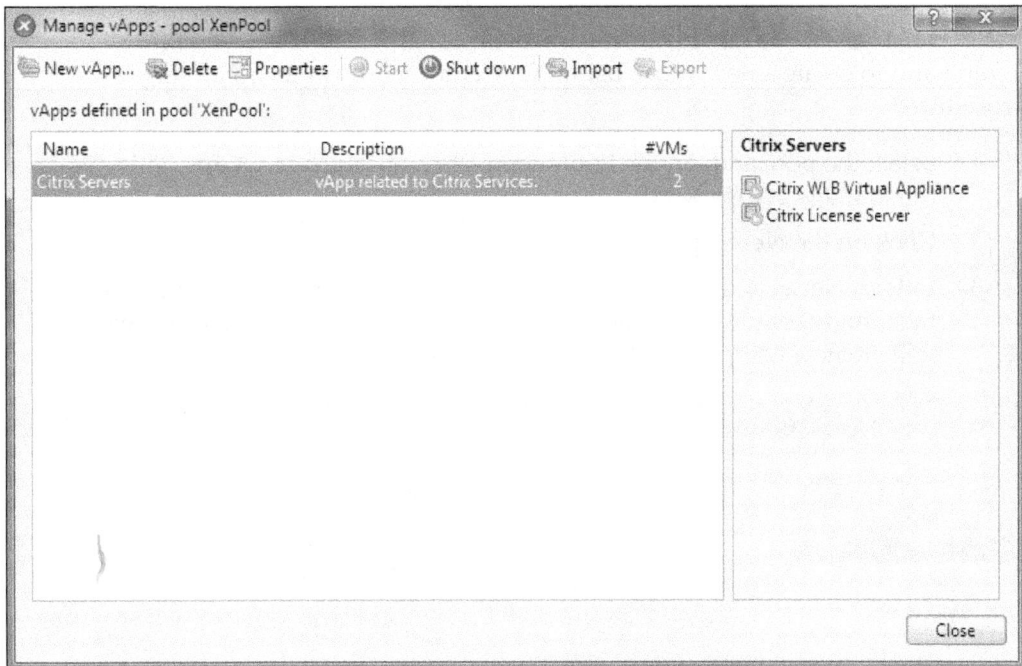

When a virtual machine belongs to a vApp, you can find this information on the VM's **Properties** page in XenCenter:

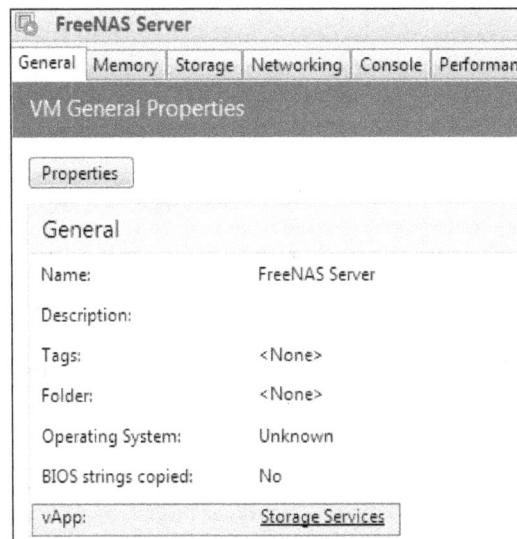

Click on the vApp name to access the vApp Properties page.

Creating a vApp

If you want to create a new vApp using XenCenter, perform the following procedure:

1. Select the pool and, on the Pool menu, click on **Manage vApps**. This displays the Manage vApps window.

2. Click on the **New App...** button.

3. Enter a **Name** and a **Description** for the vApp—use a descriptive and meaningful name. Then click on **Next** to continue. In our example, we will create a vApp related to Citrix services.

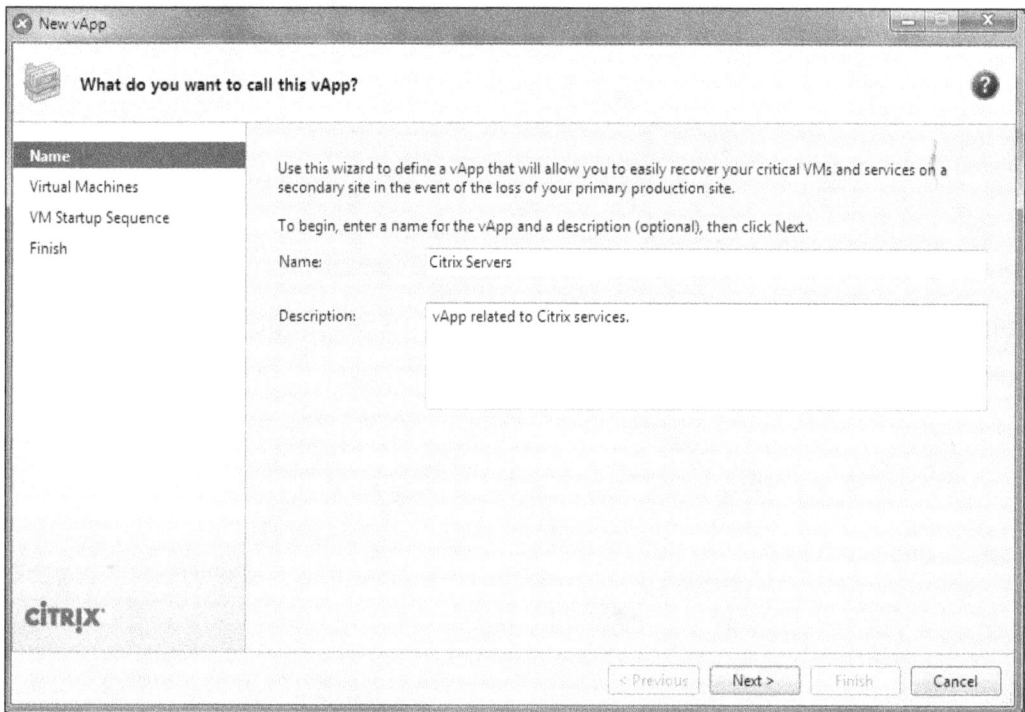

4. Choose which VMs to include in the new vApp and then click on **Next** to continue. You can use the search box to list only VMs with names that include the specified string.

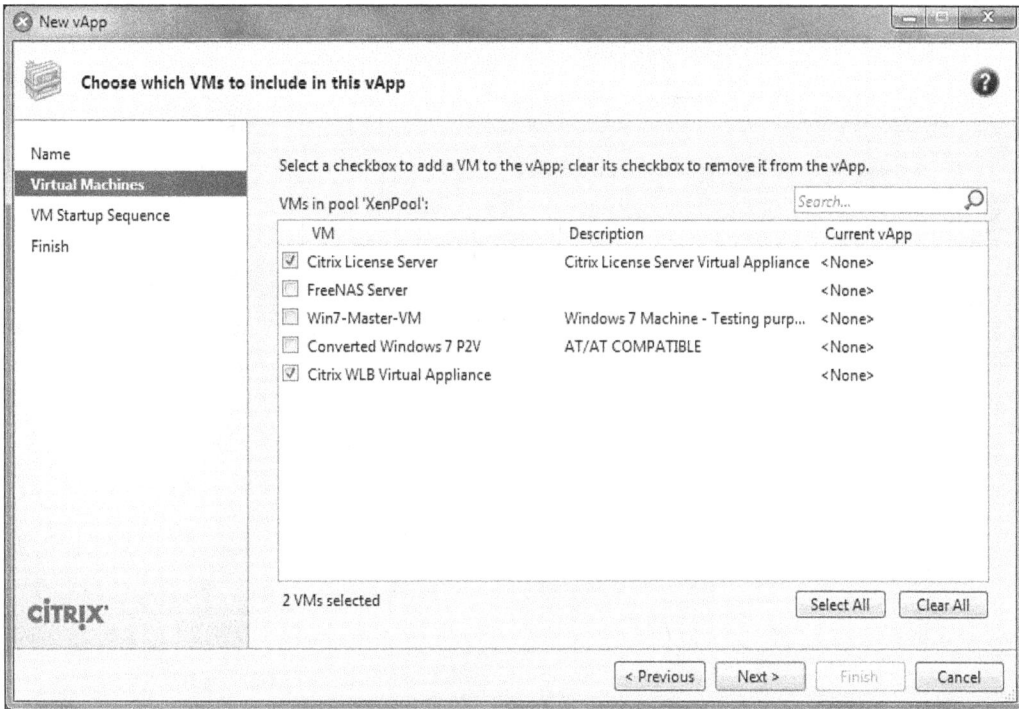

5. Specify the startup sequence for the VMs in the vApp, and then click on **Next**.

   ° **Start Order**: Specifies the order in which individual VMs will be started up within the vApp, allowing certain VMs to be restarted before others. VMs with a start order value of 0 (zero) will be started first, then VMs with a start order value of 1, then VMs with a start order value of 2, and so on.

   ° **Attempt to start next VM after**: This is a delay interval that specifies how long to wait after starting the VM before attempting to start the next VM in the startup sequence.

In our example, we have set a delay of 20 seconds for the start of the VM **Citrix WLB Virtual Appliance**.

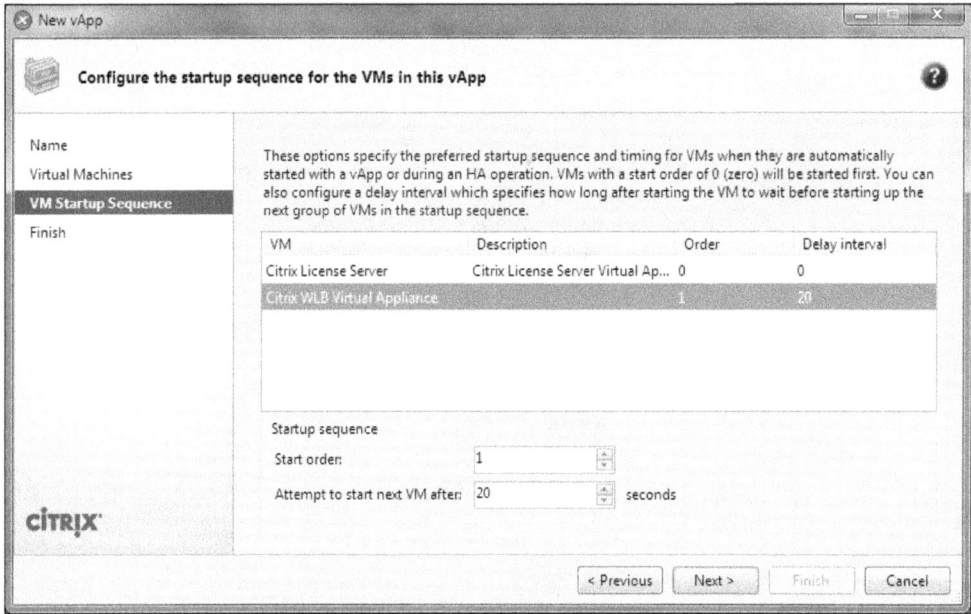

6. On the final page of the wizard, you can review the vApp configuration. Click on **Finish** to create the new vApp and close the wizard.

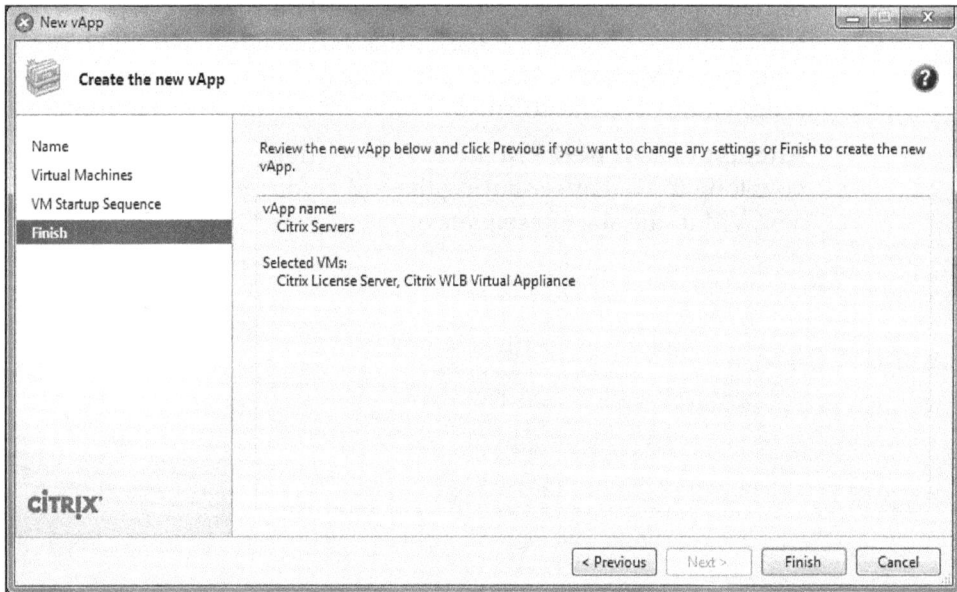

Remember that a vApp cannot include virtual machines belonging to different XenServer resource pools—if you have multiple XenServer resource pools, you have to create different vApps on each pool.

Importing and exporting a vApp

Unlike virtual machines, vApps can only be imported and exported in XenServer using the OVF/OVA.

If you want to import or export a vApp, open the **Manage vApps** dialog box and select the **Import** or **Export** button. Follow the procedure we have described earlier in this chapter to complete the task.

> To export a vApp, virtual machines belonging to it must be powered-off or suspended.

Summary

In this chapter, we have learned how to manage virtual machines. Also, we have discovered how to convert a physical machine and perform import and export operations in XenServer. Specifically, we have covered:

- Managing virtual machines
- Converting a physical machine
- Managing vApps

Spend some time practicing virtual machine management. These tasks are some of the main activities you must be able to do in order to manage your virtualization infrastructure.

In the next chapter, we will introduce virtual machine memory management.

6
Managing XenServer and Virtual Machine Memory

In the previous chapter, we discussed how to manage virtual machines in XenServer.

Now we can introduce memory management in XenServer. At the end of this chapter you will be able to configure memory for your virtual machines in order to provide the best performance for your virtual environment using Dynamic Memory Control.

In this chapter, we will cover the following topics:

- XenServer memory overview
- Virtual machine memory overview
- Managing virtual machine memory

XenServer memory overview

XenServer memory usage is based on how much physical memory exists on the server itself.

In the first chapter of the book, we have discussed the Resource Pools concepts and introduced the "Control Domain" virtual machine, also known as "Dom0".

Dom0 is a small and privileged virtual machine that Xen hypervisor loads when a host running XenServer starts up. The control domain runs the management tool stack and also provides low-level services to other VMs, such as providing physical access to devices.

When calculating the memory that XenServer uses, there are two components to consider. First is the memory that the XenServer virtualization engine known as Xen hypervisor uses. Second is the memory that the control domain uses.

Xen hypervisor uses a fixed amount of memory. This value is set to 128 MB. The Dom0 uses a variable amount of memory based on the total physical memory on the server.

The Dom0 reserves a minimum of 200 MB of memory, but does not use more than 752 MB of memory, so the total range of memory that XenServer might use is 328 MB to 880 MB.

The maximum value of "752 MB" for Dom0 memory is set in a configuration file named `extlinux.conf` located in the `/boot` directory of the XenServer host.

This value is suitable for majority of environments, but when you want to run more than 50 virtual machines on a XenServer host, you can consider increasing this value; you can set the Dom0 memory to a maximum of 2.94 GB.

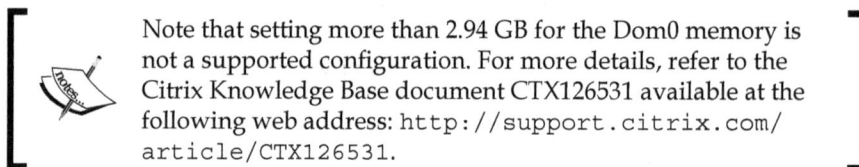

> Note that setting more than 2.94 GB for the Dom0 memory is not a supported configuration. For more details, refer to the Citrix Knowledge Base document CTX126531 available at the following web address: `http://support.citrix.com/article/CTX126531`.

If you want to increase the Dom0 memory value, follow the given procedure:

1. Connect to the console of the XenServer host where you want to apply the memory change.

2. Make a copy of the original configuration file `\boot\extlinux.conf`. This helps you to recover the XenServer from an unbootable state if you experience issues. You can use the Linux command `cp` to do this:

   ```
   cp extlinux.conf extlinux.conf.ori
   ```

3. Open the file `/boot/extlinux.conf` by using an editor such as *VI* or *nano*.

4. On the *label xe* and *label xe-serial* sections, modify the `Dom0_mem` parameter to change the amount of memory assigned to the domain control virtual machine.

   For example, if you want to set 1 GB of memory, change:

   ```
   label xe # XenServer kernel mboot.c32 append /boot/xen.gz dom0_
   mem=752M lowmem_emergency_pool=1M crashkernel=64M@32M console=com1
   vga=mode-0x0311 --- /boot/vmlinuz-2.6-xen root=LABEL=root-
   ecpmuteuroxencons=hvc console=hvc0 console=tty0 quiet vga=785
   splash --- /boot/initrd-2.6-xen.img
   ```

to:

```
label xe # XenServer kernel mboot.c32 append /boot/xen.gz
dom0_mem=1024M lowmem_emergency_pool=1M crashkernel=64M@32M
console=com1 vga=mode-0x0311 --- /boot/vmlinuz-2.6-xen
root=LABEL=root-ecpmuteuroxencons=hvc console=hvc0 console=tty0
quiet vga=785 splash --- /boot/initrd-2.6-xen.img
```

5. Save the changed extlinux.conf file and restart the XenServer host.
   Now we have to check that XenServer was able to allocate 1024 MB for
   Dom0's memory. After rebooting, connect again to the host and open
   the file /proc/xen/balloon. Your file should be as follows:

6. Note the value **Maximum target**. This is the maximum amount of memory we have set in the previous step.

7. We can check the maximum memory target defined for the Dom0 using the xe command vm-param-get:

```
xe vm-param-get uuid=<vm-uuid> param-name=memory-static-max
```

The uuid parameter is the unique identifier (UUID) of the control domain virtual machine.

You can use the command xevm-list to discover the UUID. The command will display the list of all your virtual machines.

You will find one or more virtual machines with the name label **Control Domain on host**. This is the Dom0 virtual machine, so take note of the UUID related to the host of which you want to see the maximum memory static target.

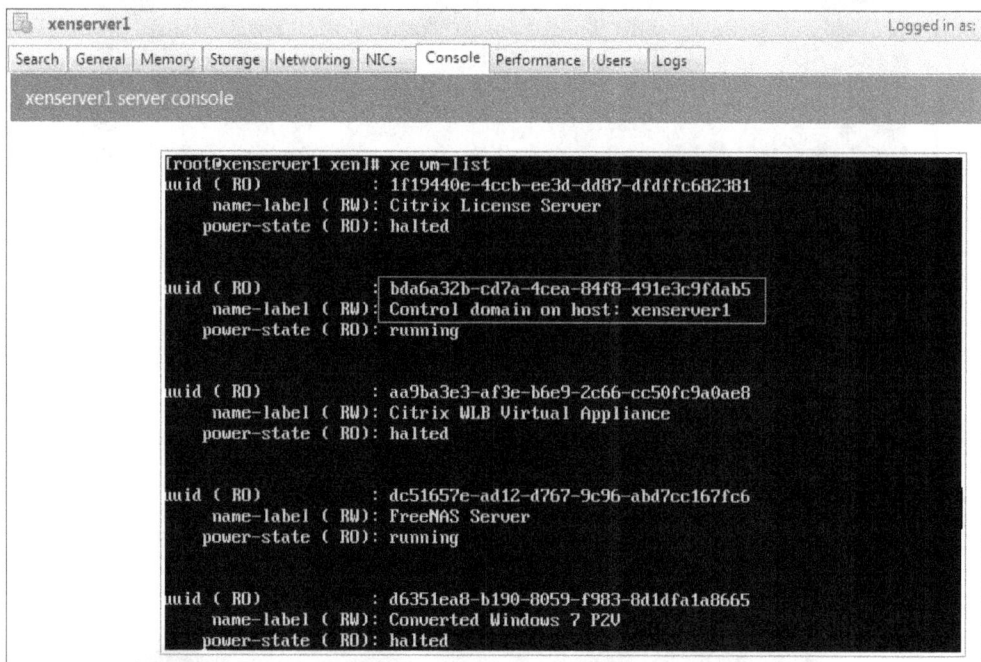

Now that you know the UUID of your control domain virtual machine, you can run the xe command vm-param-get. So in our example, we execute the following command:

```
xe vm-param-get uuid=bda6a32b-cd7a-4cea-84f8-491e3c9fdab5  param-
name=memory-static-max
```

XenServer will display the maximum memory static target associated with the Dom0 virtual machine. This value is expressed in bytes.

Remember to execute the previous procedure for each host in order to change the Dom0 memory value and have the same configuration, if you have more than one host on your XenServer pool.

We have introduced how to change the control domain virtual machine memory in order to be able to run a high number of VMs on the host.

Now, we can introduce how much memory is necessary on our XenServer host to run virtual machines with best performances.

To find out how much memory is needed for your XenServer host, you can use the following formula:

[Memory required for hypervisor/control domain] + [Total memory in all virtual servers] + [Memory needed to support migrated VMs using XenMotion] + [Extra]

The *Memory required for control domain* value is the amount of memory you want to allocate for the control domain virtual machine. By default, this value is 880 MB.

The *Total memory in all virtual servers* value is the total amount of memory you want to allocate for all the virtual machines you have planned to run on a XenServer host.

The *Memory needed to support migrated VMs using XenMotion* value is the amount of memory needed to run optimally migrated virtual machines from other XenServer hosts if you plan to use the XenMotion feature. To better understand this point, imagine you have a XenServer pool with two hosts, each running two virtual machines. If one of the host fails, you should have enough free memory to run all the virtual machines on a unique host. This is a well-known rule named "N+1" where N is the total number of your XenServer hosts.

The *Extra* value is an additional quantity of memory you want to reserve for future growth capacity planning or for expanding the actual amount of memory of your existing virtual machines.

For example, you want to run 20 VMs on your virtual environment based on two XenServer hosts: each host will run 10 VMs. Also each of these VMs will use a maximum of 2 GB RAM and must be available also in case of failure of one host. According to the previous requirements, you need the following minimum amount of memory for the hosts:

880 MB (Memory required for control domain) + 20 GB (Total memory in all servers) + 20GB (Memory needed to support migrated VMs using XenMotion) = 40.88 GB

> Note that in this example, we have not considered the optional *Extra* amount of memory.

In the following section, we will see an overview of virtual machine memory.

Virtual machine memory overview

When you create a new virtual machine, you set a fixed amount of memory using the creation wizard. According to what value you specify, XenServer will allocate this amount of memory to the guest.

Of course, you can change this value from the **CPU and Memory** section of the virtual machine properties.

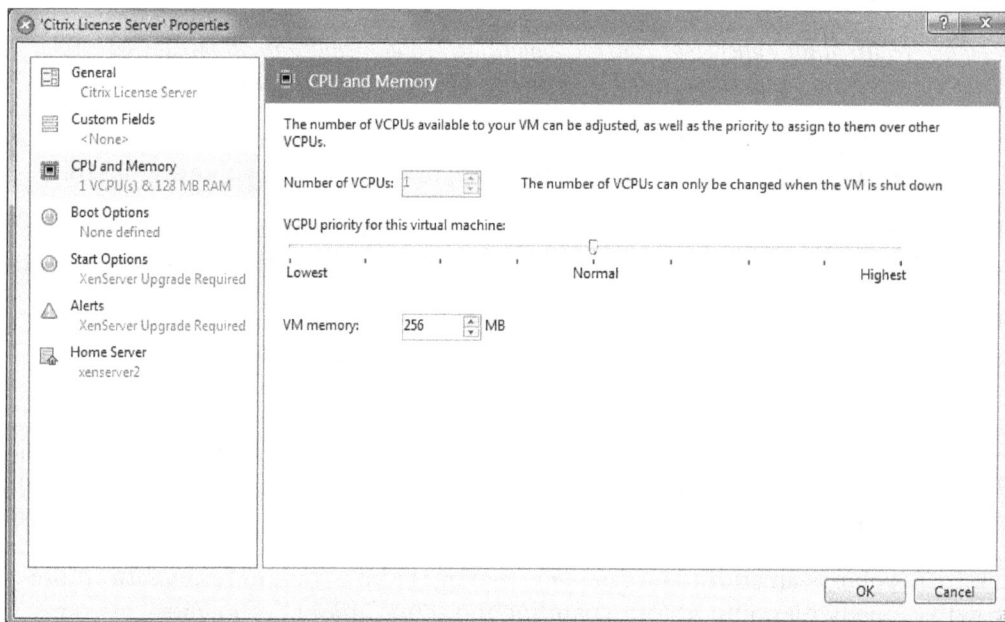

Usually, you don't want to over-allocate memory to a virtual machine if it is not needed because this wastes physical memory. In the same way, you should prevent under-allocating memory because this creates poor performance. By default, when a Windows configuration achieves 75 percent of memory usage, it begins to access the page file and starts swapping.

The goal is to give the VMs the right amount of memory, monitoring the operating system performance and, especially when you have to deploy new applications on an existing or new virtual machine, checking all the applications' requirements in order to verify that a memory bottleneck will not occur on the guest virtual machine.

You can monitor the memory usage of your virtual machine using the **Performance** tab in XenCenter.

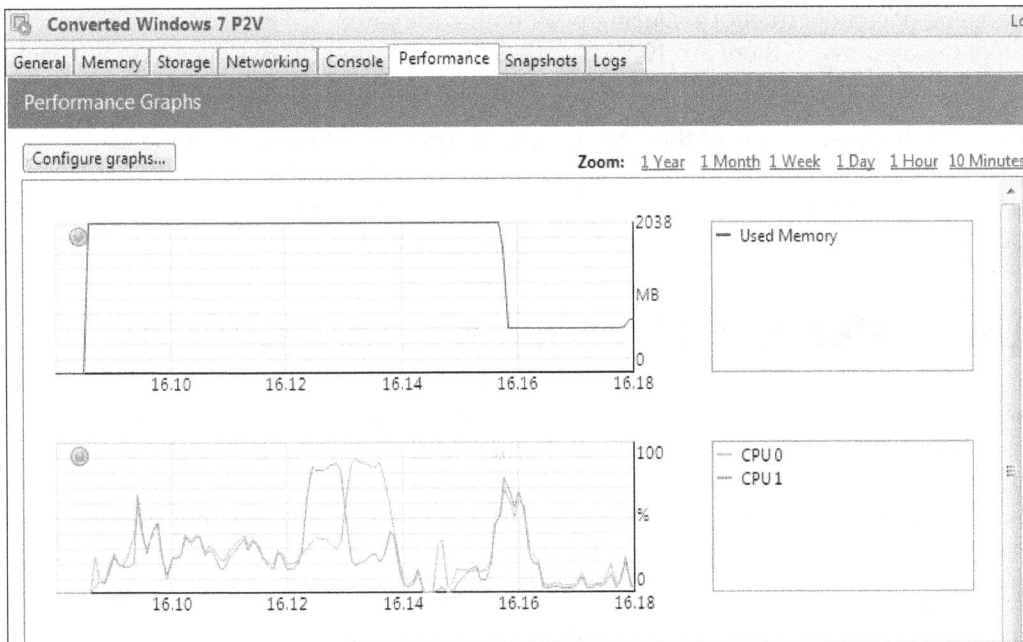

When consolidating older servers into a virtual environment, it is easier to determine the amount of memory required for the VM by looking at the actual memory usage on the physical server to be migrated. After you determine the actual memory usage for a server, increase that number by 25 percent. This gives you a margin of contingency for handling unexpected peaks in the memory usage and enough room to support a future increase in the memory requirements of the virtual machine.

> Note that if the amount of memory needed for the VMs equals or is very close to the physical memory of the XenServer host, then the server can suffer from a lack of memory and enter into a contention state. So, consider increasing your XenServer host memory in order to satisfy the overall memory needs.

Now that we have covered the basic concepts about memory, let me introduce an example which will help us to gain a good understanding of an important feature available in XenServer 6, which we will discuss in the next section.

Assume that you have VMs running with 1 GB of allocated memory and all these VMs are placed on a XenServer host with 10 GB of RAM. During normal operation, the guest operating system and applications inside the virtual machine consume about 30 percent of memory. During peak hours, the same VM can consume almost all of the memory. If there are 10 VMs and each is allocated 1 GB of memory, but each is using 30 percent (about 307 MB), then there is enough physical memory on the host.

But what happens when all the VMs require 100 percent of memory at the same time? You can imagine it—there is no longer enough physical memory. This means that the VMs and the server start swapping memory, and performance degradation occurs rapidly. Also you cannot start any new virtual machines.

Understanding Dynamic Memory Control

In XenServer 6.0 you can adjust the amount of memory allocated to a virtual machine without service interruption. You can set the new value on-the-fly and XenServer reallocates the new amount of memory to the VM. This feature that enables you to dynamically allocate memory is known as **Dynamic Memory Control** (**DMC**) and is very useful because you don't have to shut down the guest to reconfigure the memory settings.

Furthermore, the Dynamic Memory Control feature helps you to start virtual machines in XenServer hosts that have no available memory.

Imagine that virtual machines running on a particular host are consuming all the allocated amount of memory and you need to start a virtual machine *Server1* on the host. If you try to start *Server1* you will receive an error message in XenCenter informing you that there are no available resources to complete the task. In this situation, you must shut down some virtual machines and reconfigure their memory settings to free enough memory to be able to start the *Server1* virtual machine. Usually, in production environments, it is not so easy to complete this task without service interruption.

If you have enabled Dynamic Memory Control, XenServer will automatically reduce the unused memory of running virtual machines in order to free enough memory for completing the "power on" task of the *Server1* virtual machine.

> Note that Dynamic Memory Control is only available for XenServer Advanced or higher editions.
>
> Also, XenServer Tools must be installed on virtual machines in order to use this feature.

Dynamic Memory Control changes the allocated amount of memory to virtual machines using the concept of *dynamic range*. This range is based on minimum and maximum values you have configured in the virtual machine's memory properties. As we have understood from the the previous section, XenServer will add or release proportionally free unused memory inside this range according to the needs of the virtual machines and demand without reboot.

The allocated memory will never fall below the minimum value or exceed the maximum value; virtual machines will use memory within this set range.

Also remember that XenServer always tries to allocate the amount of memory defined in the Dynamic Range for all the running virtual machines according to the host's memory availability. If the host's memory is plentiful, XenServer allocates the value you have set on the Dynamic Maximum Level otherwise if the host's memory is low, the Dynamic Minimum level will be used.

In the following figure, you can see an example where **Virtual Machine 1** and **Virtual Machine 2** are not using all the allocated amount of memory and have 2 GB and 2.5 GB of free memory in the dynamic range respectively. **Virtual Machine 3** is using 4 GB of RAM and is asking for an extra 4 GB. XenServer reclaims this extra amount from **Virtual Machine 1** and **Virtual Machine 2**.

The same behavior can take place if XenServer has to power on a virtual machine.

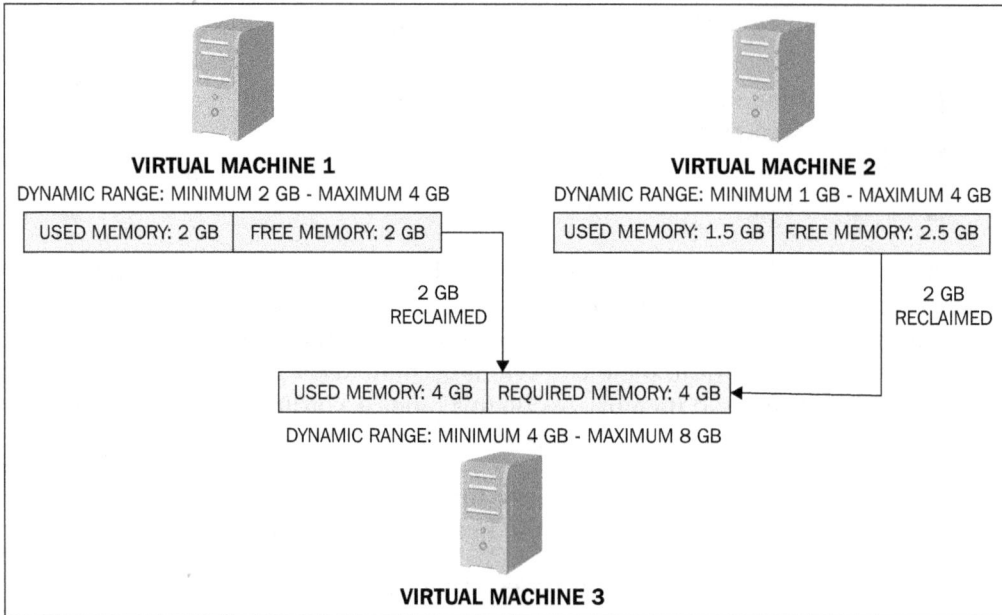

VIRTUAL MACHINE 1
DYNAMIC RANGE: MINIMUM 2 GB - MAXIMUM 4 GB

USED MEMORY: 2 GB | FREE MEMORY: 2 GB

2 GB RECLAIMED

VIRTUAL MACHINE 2
DYNAMIC RANGE: MINIMUM 1 GB - MAXIMUM 4 GB

USED MEMORY: 1.5 GB | FREE MEMORY: 2.5 GB

2 GB RECLAIMED

USED MEMORY: 4 GB | REQUIRED MEMORY: 4 GB
DYNAMIC RANGE: MINIMUM 4 GB - MAXIMUM 8 GB

VIRTUAL MACHINE 3

> Note that if you want XenServer to guarantee the same amount of allocated memory to a virtual machine in every condition, set the dynamic minimum and maximum to the same value.

In addition to the *dynamic range*, it is also important to understand the *static range* concept when we speak about Dynamic Memory Control.

We have discovered that XenServer supports a wide range of operating systems which you can install in the guest virtual machines. However, some of these operating systems do not support changes to memory while running. In this situation, XenServer must inform the virtual machine what is its minimum and maximum static amount of allocated memory. Unlike the dynamic range, the static range cannot be changed dynamically and any modification to these values must be done when the virtual machine is not running.

Also note that Citrix supports only certain guest memory configurations based on the operating system you have installed on the guest. You can find these supported memory limits in the *Appendix A, Supported Guest Operating Systems and Virtual Machine Templates*—avoid changing them for performance reasons.

Managing virtual machine memory

In the previous sections, we covered the basic concepts related to Dynamic Memory Control.

Now, it is time to see how Dynamic Memory Control can be configured using XenCenter or xe CLI.

Using XenCenter, configuring Dynamic Memory Control for a virtual machine is very simple.

To do this, follow the given procedure:

1. Select the virtual machine in XenCenter and click on the **Memory** tab.
2. Click on the **Edit...** tab; the **Memory Settings** dialog will be displayed.

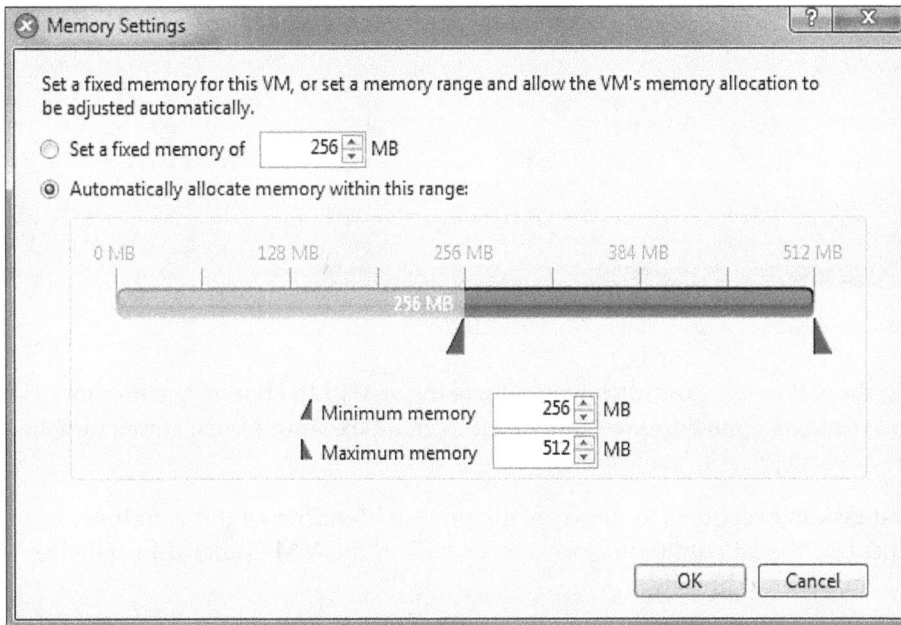

3. Select **Automatically allocate memory within this range** to define a new dynamic range for DMC and input the minimum and maximum memory level you want to set for the virtual machine. If you want to set a fixed amount of memory, select **Set a fixed memory of**.
4. Click on **OK** to complete the configuration.

You can check the amount of memory currently allocated to the XenServer host and to the virtual machines running on it by clicking on the **Memory** tab of the host in XenCenter.

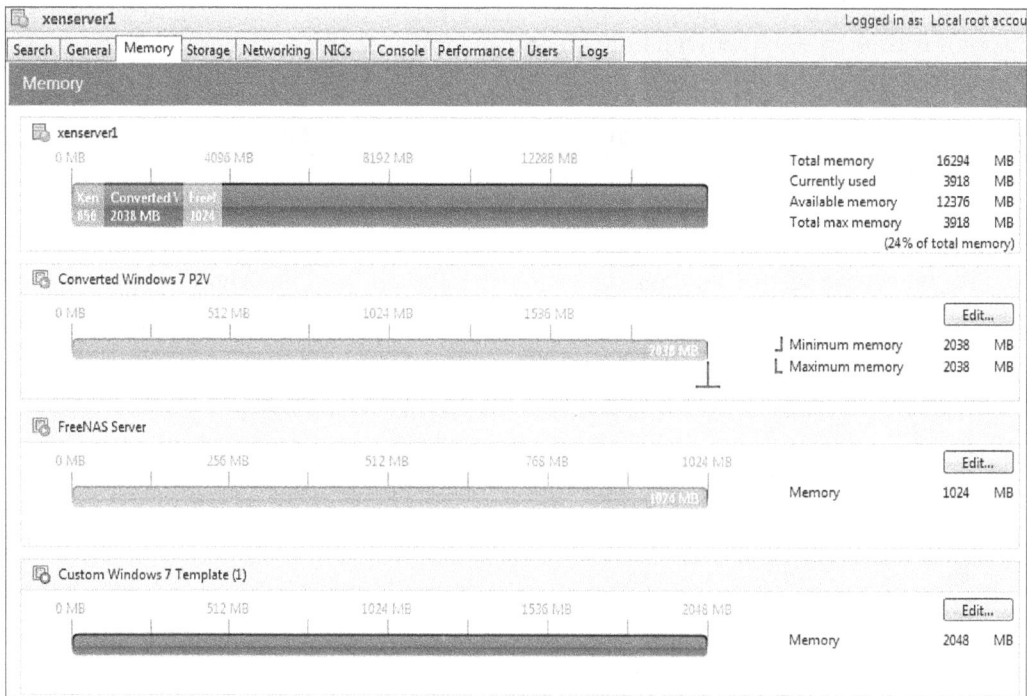

Now in the following examples we will use the xe CLI to change the memory limits for the Windows 7 machine we converted from an existing physical machine in *Chapter 5, Managing Virtual Machines*.

The first task to execute is to discover the unique identifier of the Windows 7 machine. Use the xe command vm-list or look at the **VM General Properties** tab in XenCenter to find it.

In our example, the uuid is d6351ea8-b190-8059-f983-8d1dfa1a8665.

We want to display the actual static and dynamic memory limits for the virtual machine; in case you want to revert the change, it is useful to know them.

We use the xe command xe vm-param-get to do this step.

The following command will display the static memory limits:

```
xe vm-param-get uuid=<vm-uuid> param-name=memory-static-{min,max}
```

This is the same command we have used to view the memory limit for the Dom0 machine at the beginning of the chapter.

In order to get the static memory limits for our Windows 7 guest, execute the following commands:

```
xe vm-param-get uuid=d6351ea8-b190-8059-f983-8d1dfa1a8665 param-name=memory-static-min
```

```
xe vm-param-get uuid=d6351ea8-b190-8059-f983-8d1dfa1a8665 param-name=memory-static-max
```

The result of the execution of these commands is `16777216` bytes (minimum static limit) and `2136997888` bytes (maximum static limit).

The following command will display the dynamic memory limits:

```
xe vm-param-get uuid=<vm-uuid> param-name=memory-dynamic-{min,max}
```

In order to get the dynamic memory limits for our Windows 7 guest, execute the following commands:

```
xe vm-param-get uuid=d6351ea8-b190-8059-f983-8d1dfa1a8665 param-name=memory-dynamic-min
```

```
xe vm-param-get uuid=d6351ea8-b190-8059-f983-8d1dfa1a8665 param-name=memory-dynamic-max
```

The result of the execution of these commands is 2136997888 bytes (minimum dynamic limit) and 2136997888 bytes (maximum dynamic limit). The VM is configured with 2038 MB of virtual memory.

Why are the minimum and maximum limits the same? The Windows 7 machine is configured with a fixed amount of memory and Dynamic Memory Control is not enabled on this VM!

Ok, we have acquired all the information about the starting Windows 7 memory configuration.

Now we can change the static memory limits using the xe command, xevm-memory-static-range-set:

```
xe vm-memory-static-range-set uuid=<vm-uuid> min=<value> max=<value>
```

where the min parameter is the minimum static limit and the max parameter is the maximum static limit.

In our example, we want to set the minimum limit to 512 MB and the maximum to 4096 MB. We do so by executing the following command:

```
xe vm-memory-static-range-set uuid=d6351ea8-b190-8059-f983-8d1dfa1a8665
min=512MiB max=4096MiB
```

Note the suffix *MiB* used by XenServer for megabytes.

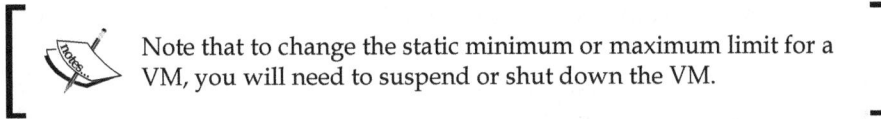

> Note that to change the static minimum or maximum limit for a VM, you will need to suspend or shut down the VM.

After the static limits, we can update the dynamic memory limits using the `xe` command `vm-memory-dynamic-range-set`:

```
xe vm-memory-dynamic-range-set uuid=<vm-uuid> min=<value> max=<value>
```

where `min` parameter is the minimum static limit and the `max` parameter is the maximum static limit.

In our example, we want to set the dynamic minimum limit to 1024 MB and the maximum to 2048 MB. We do so by executing the following command:

```
xe vm-memory-dynamic-range-set uuid=d6351ea8-b190-8059-f983-8d1dfa1a8665
min=1024MiB max=2048MiB
```

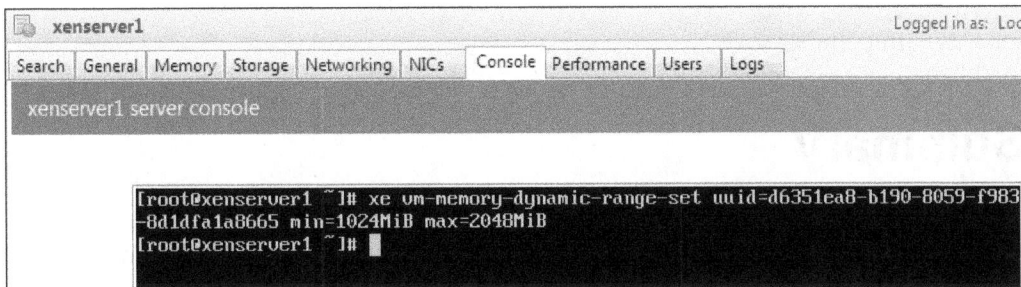

Now the virtual machine is using a dynamic amount of memory. XenServer will allocate the memory in the range between 1024 MB and 2048 MB.

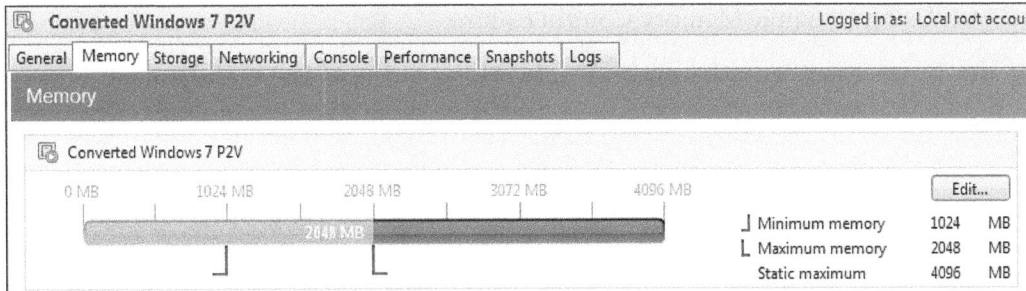

Note the static maximum limit we have set earlier with the `xe` command `vm-memory-static-range-set`. When the static maximum and the dynamic maximum coincide, the static maximum is not displayed on the **Memory** tab.

> When you configure dynamic memory limits, remember not to invalidate the following constraints:
>
> `0 ≤ memory-static-min ≤ memory-dynamic-min ≤ memory-dynamic-max ≤ memory-static-max`
>
> Also, refer to the supported limits for each guest operating system on the table in the *Appendix A, Supported Guest Operating Systems and Virtual Machine Templates*.

If you want to set only one parameter for the memory limit, you can execute the `xe` command `vm-param-set`:

`xe vm-param-set uuid=<vm-uuid> memory-static-{min,max}=<value>`

for a static limit, or:

`xe vm-param-set uuid=<vm-uuid> memory-dynamic-{min,max}=<value>`

for a dynamic limit.

Summary

In this chapter, we learned how XenServer uses memory.

Also we discovered how to manage virtual machine memory using the Dynamic Memory Control feature.

Specifically, we covered:

- Managing Control Domain memory usage
- Using Dynamic Memory Control feature

In the next chapter, we will introduce networking concepts and management.

7
Managing XenServer Networking

In the previous chapter, we discussed how to manage memory in XenServer.

Now we introduce network management in XenServer. At the end of this chapter you will know the XenServer network concepts and you will able to configure the network in order to provide the best connectivity for your virtual machines.

In this chapter, we will cover the following topics:

- XenServer networking
- Managing networking
- Managing network VLANs
- Managing network bonds
- Distributed vSwitch Controller

XenServer networking

XenServer provides virtual networking features that let you build networks for your virtual machines the same way you build networks for physical machines.

So you can connect virtual machines to your production network like physical machines or you can build private networks within a host or pool for testing, development, or security purposes. Also, you can connect virtual machines to your VLAN networks using standard VLAN configurations.

The most important networking components are *physical network interfaces (NIC)*, *virtual interfaces*, and *networks*.

Each physical network interface on your host is represented in XenServer with an object called *PIF*.

Virtual machines connect to networks using virtual NICs, known as *virtual interfaces*. Virtual interfaces let VMs send and receive network traffic. Each virtual NIC configured on a virtual machine is represented in XenServer with an object called *VIF*.

Just like network interfaces in the physical world, each virtual interface must have its own (virtual) MAC address. This address is a unique identifier composed of six groups of two hexadecimal digits, separated by hyphens or colons, and assigned to the network interface by the manufacturer. It is known as a *universally administered address* because the first three octets identify the vendor of the interface.

When you add a new virtual interface for a virtual machine, XenServer automatically generates a new MAC address for the NIC. You can also specify a MAC address manually and in this case, the assigned MAC address is generated as a *locally administered address*.

Each PIF, VIF, and network object in XenServer has a name and a description and is identified by a unique identifier (UUID).

A network is the logical network switching fabric built into XenServer that lets you connect your virtual machines to each other and with other devices in your enterprise. It links the physical NICs to the virtual interfaces and connects the virtual interfaces together.

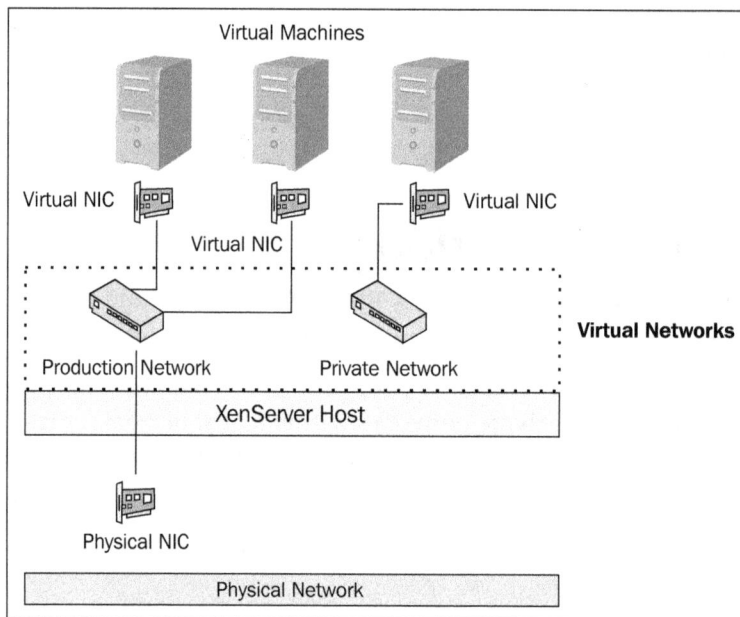

In XenServer you can install and configure up to 16 physical network interfaces per host and you can add up to seven virtual network interfaces per each virtual machine.

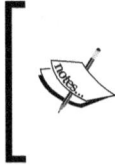

> Remember to check if your physical network interfaces are supported in the XenServer 6 Hardware Compatibility List provided by Citrix. In a production environment, always use certified devices.
>
> Visit the website `http://hcl.xensource.com` for details.

Initial network configuration

In the previous section, we introduced the main concepts related to the network components of your XenServer virtual environment.

Now, we will look at the XenServer as installed default network configuration.

After installation, the XenServer host has all the information it needs to connect to at least one of your external networks.

This is because you have defined networking options such as the *IP Address*, *Netmask*, and *Gateway* for a physical network interface during XenServer setup on the physical host.

This NIC you have configured is known as the *Primary Management Interface*.

The Primary Management Interface is used by XenServer for connecting to your organization's network and to carry management traffic for functions such as communicating with other hosts in a pool, XenCenter, and other components. This is the only NIC that setup configures with an IP address.

During installation, XenServer also creates a separate network for each NIC it detects on the host and uses the additional NICs on the host for managing the virtual machines' traffic only. This means that if the host has, for example, three NICs, XenServer creates three networks, such as Network 0, Network 1, and Network 2.

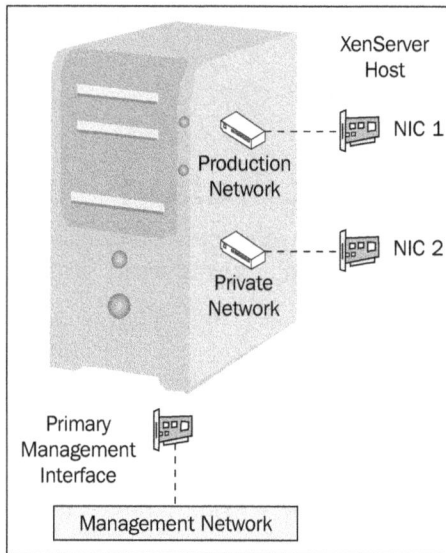

> Remember to plug the physical Ethernet cables into all the NICs and the appropriate switches before installing XenServer.

Networking and XenServer Pools

Networking is a pool-level feature in XenServer.

Because of this peculiarity, after you have created a new pool or joined a host to an existing pool, XenServer automatically replicates the network settings on the pool master to the joining hosts.

Furthermore, when you change networking on the pool master, XenServer synchronizes all hosts in a pool to use the same network settings.

As a result, for XenServer to operate correctly, you must ensure that network settings match across all hosts in the pool; this is because XenServer features such as XenMotion, high availability, and workload balancing enable your virtual machines to be placed to different hosts at any time and automatically without your intervention. Therefore, the VMs must be able to access all of their target networks regardless of which host XenServer they are hosted on.

For this reason, it is critical to have and maintain an identical physical cabling, NIC, and switch configuration for each host across the pool.

Network types

During the initial setup, XenServer detects the physical network interfaces installed on your system; for each of the detected NICs, XenServer creates a network. When you join a host to a resource pool, XenServer configures the networks in order to have a consistent configuration across the pool—physical network interfaces with the same device name are linked to the same network.

In XenServer, using the **Networking** tab in XenCenter or using the xe CLI, you can configure four different types of network:

- **Single-server private network**: This type is not attached to a physical network interface and can be used to provide connectivity between the virtual machines that run on a specific host—network traffic remains isolated on that host and cannot reach other hosts. Just to clarify, think of a bubble (your host) where nothing can go out (your network traffic) but can only move inside it. Usually, you also refer to this type of network as *Internal*.

- **Cross-server private network**: This type is similar to the single-server private network type but differs from it because in this case network traffic can also reach virtual machines running on different hosts in the resource pool and not only on a single, given host.

- **External network**: This type is attached to a physical network interface and enables a virtual machine to connect to resources available through the physical network interface card installed on the host.

- **Bonded network**: In this type, a network is attached to a "bond", created by combining two network interface cards in order to have a single, high-performing, and redundant channel between your virtual machines and the network. This concept is the same as "Teaming".

We will see later in this chapter how to create a new network.

Now, before moving on, we will take a more detailed look at the Cross-server private network.

The cross-server private network is a new feature in XenServer 6.0; in fact, previous versions of XenServer allowed you to create only single-server private networks that allowed VMs running on the same host to communicate with each other. Cross-server and single-server private networks are completely isolated — virtual machines that are not connected to the private network cannot sniff or inject traffic into the network even when they are located on the same physical host.

Also, this type of network provides similar functionality to VLANs but unlike them, cross-server private networks provide isolation without requiring the typical configuration that a network administrator does on a physical network switch to implement VLANs.

Remember that the following conditions must be met when you want to create a cross-server private network:

- All of the hosts in the pool must be using XenServer 6.0 or greater
- All of the hosts in the pool must be using the vSwitch for the networking stack
- The vSwitch Controller must be running and you must have added the pool to it
- The cross-server private network must be created on a NIC configured as a management interface

> Note that creating cross-server private networks requires Citrix XenServer Advanced editions or higher.

Managing networking

We have introduced some of the main concepts related to networking in XenServer. It is now time to put them into practice using our laboratory environment. Later, we will cover VLANs, bonds, and vSwitch Controller.

Changing networking configuration

Using XenCenter, you can click on the **Networking** tab for a server or for the pool to see all the networks and management interfaces currently configured on the server or pool, with information about each one such as link status or MAC address.

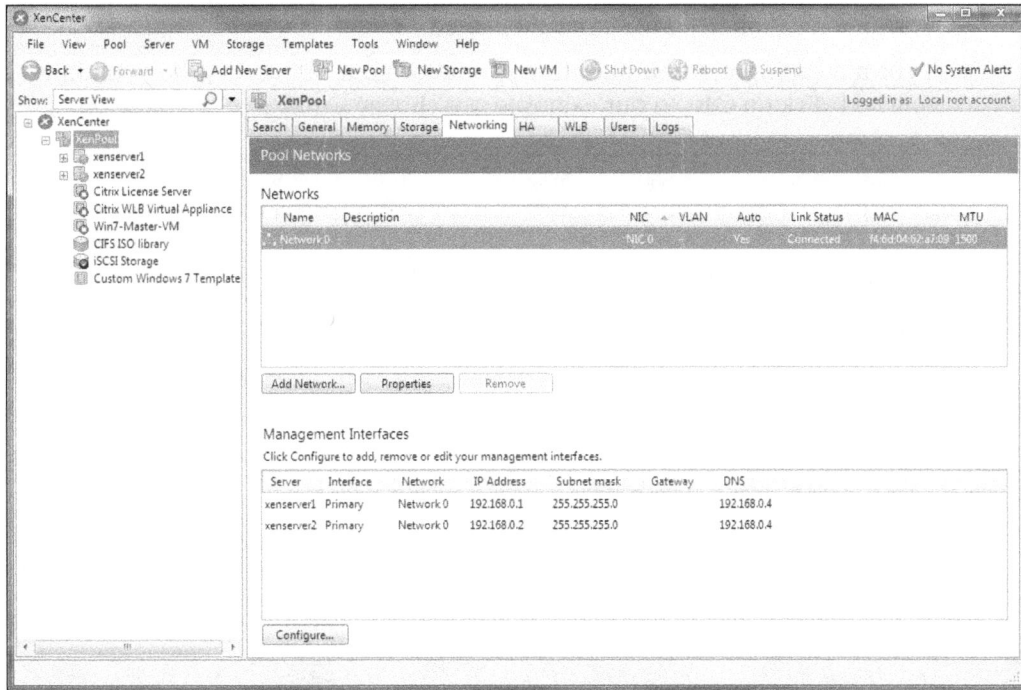

From this tab, you can modify your XenServer networking configuration adding, removing, or modifying virtual networks and management interfaces.

Adding and modifying virtual networks

At the beginning of the chapter, we discovered that XenServer creates a virtual network for each physical network interface found on the system and assigns them a default name. The name associated with the created networks is `Network 0` and so on.

Usually, a good administrator renames them with a descriptive and meaningful name—this is a simple task that you can complete using XenCenter.

So if you want to rename a virtual network, follow the given procedure:

1. Select your XenServer pool and click on the **Networking** tab.

2. Here, you can find all the networks currently configured.

3. Select the virtual network you want to rename and click on **Properties**.

4. The general **Properties** screen is displayed.

5. Type a meaningful name and description for your network. When you have finished click on **OK**. In our example, we choose XenServer-Management.

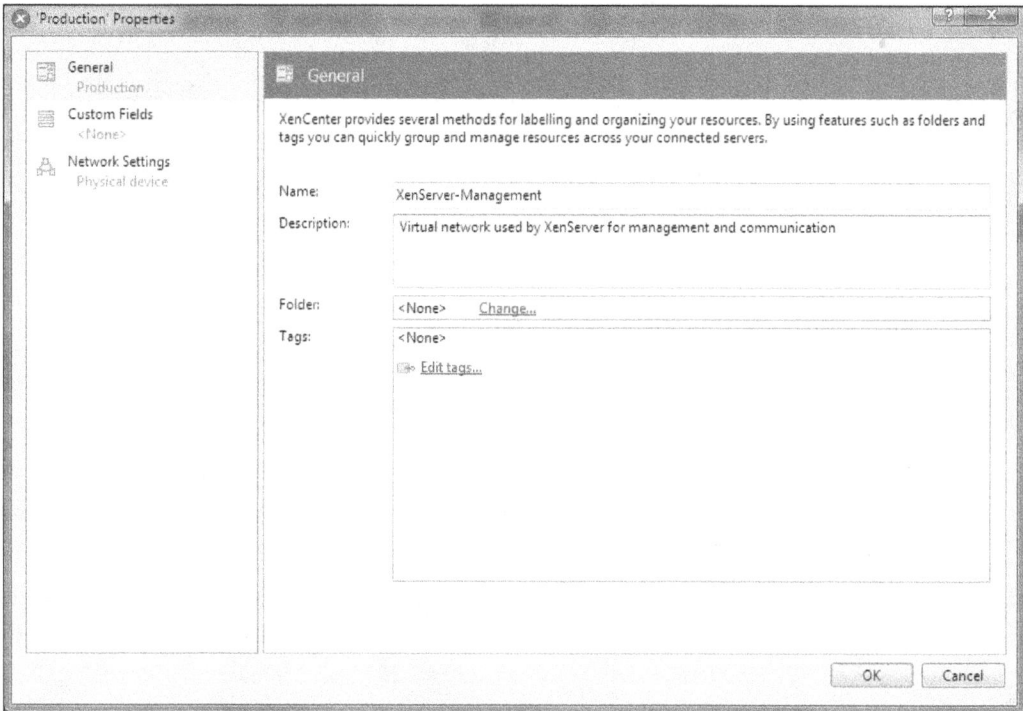

We have renamed Network 0 to XenServer-Management. Why did we decide upon this name?

Easy! It is best practice to separate each type of traffic — VM, storage, and management traffic — into its own network for either security or performance reasons!

To ensure that virtual machines in your environment will not use this network, you must prevent XenServer from adding it to newly deployed virtual machines.

To set this behavior, follow the given procedure:

1. Select the network you have decided to reserve for XenServer communication.
2. Click on the **Properties** button on the **Networking** tab of the pool.
3. In **Properties**, click on the **Network Settings** section.
4. Uncheck the box **Automatically add this network to new virtual machines**.

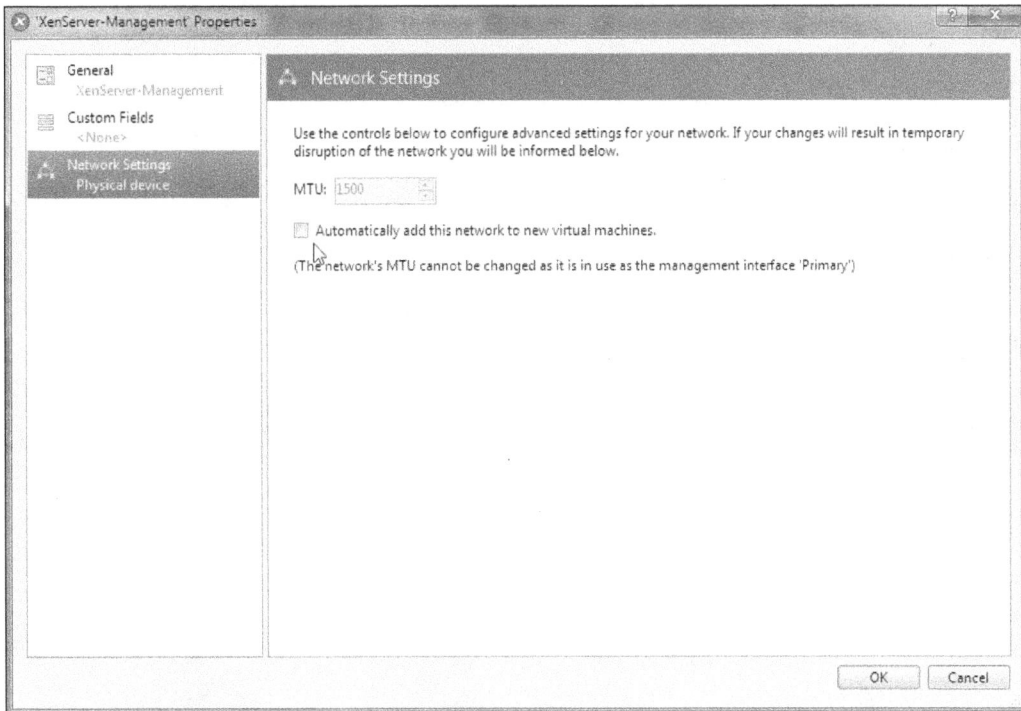

5. Click on OK.

Well, we have segregated the management traffic but how do we manage the network traffic for virtual machines? We have to add a new virtual network!

To add a new network, follow the given procedure:

1. On the **Networking** tab of the pool, click on the **Add Network...** button.

2. Now you have to choose the type of network. We have detailed each one previously in this chapter. Select the **External Network** type. In this type, the network traffic can reach machines outside the XenServer infrastructure.

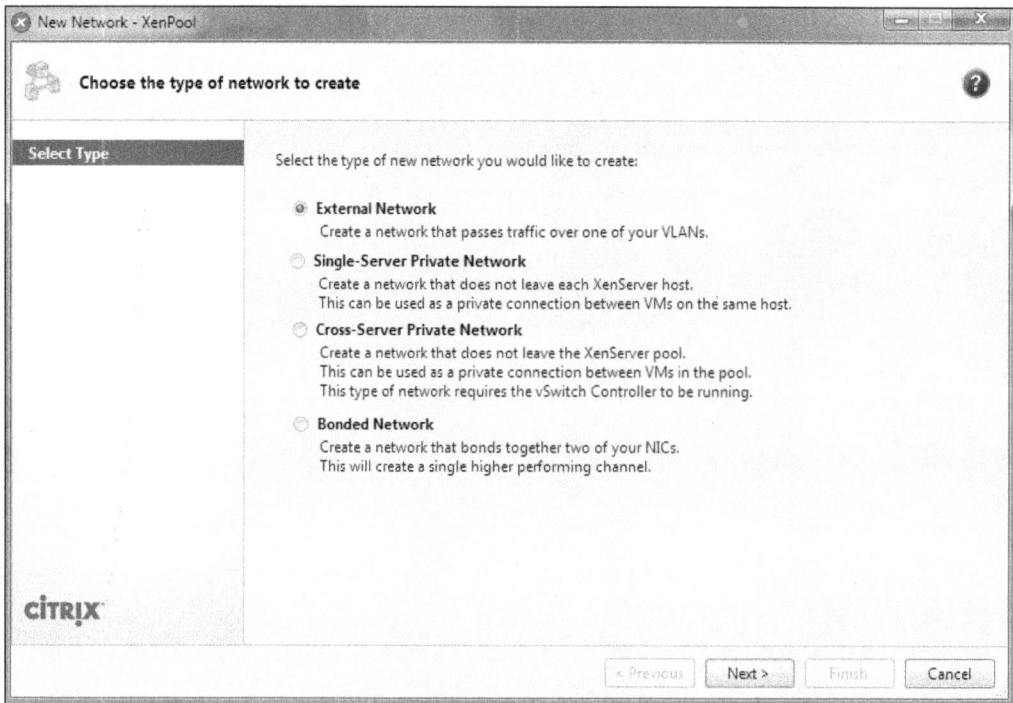

3. Type a meaningful name and description for your virtual machine network. In our example, we choose VMs-Production.

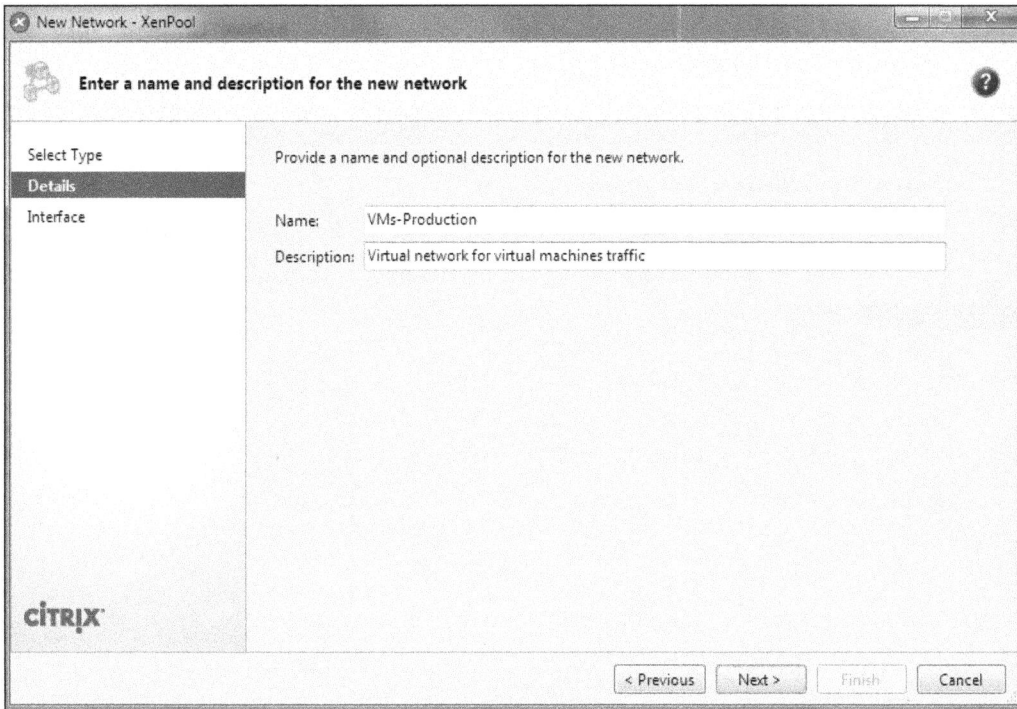

4. Select the physical network interface to which you want to bind this virtual network and select **Automatically add this network to new virtual machines**. Here, you can also set the Maximum Transmission Unit (MTU) value and the **VLAN** tag. The **MTU** value can be set between **1500** to **9216** to allow the use of jumbo frames.

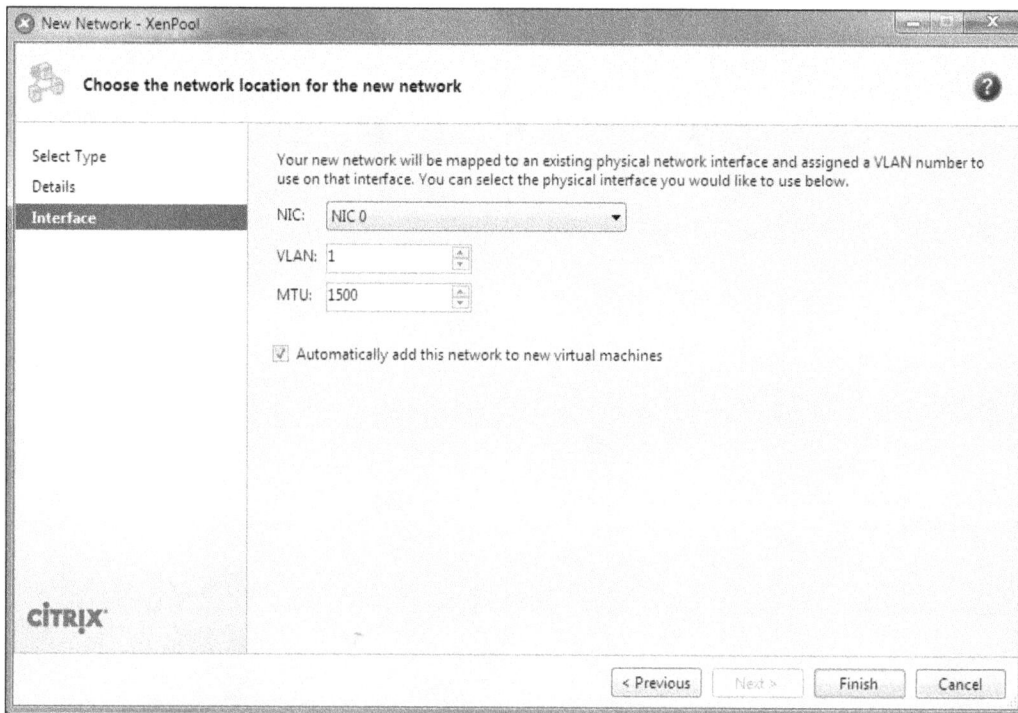

5. Click on **Finish** to complete the network creation.

We have created the network for our virtual machines.

Now we will discover how to create a new private virtual network using xe CLI—this is the time to learn the use of the command xe network-create.

Why do we want to create a private virtual network? In your virtual environment, you could decide to create some virtual machines to set up a laboratory and you may prefer to isolate the network traffic generated by these machines from the production traffic. You achieve this outcome by creating a private network.

To create the private network, we use the following command:

```
xe network-create name-label=<network-name> name-description=<network-description>
```

where the `name-label` parameter is the name we want to set for the virtual network and the `name-description` parameter is the description we want to set for the network.

So, in our example, we will execute the following command on the pool master:

```
xe network-create name-label=Private-Traffic name-description=Virtual Network for private traffic
```

On the **Networking** tab, you can notice the new network without association with a physical network interface.

If you want to remove a virtual network, you can click on the **Remove** button available on the **Networking** tab.

> Note that the xe network-create command always creates an internal network.

Configuring management interfaces

As we have learned earlier in the chapter, XenServer hosts in resource pools have a single management IP address used for management and communication to and from other hosts in the pool.

On the **Management Interfaces** section of the **Networking** tab in XenCenter, the interface used for management and communication is identified as **Primary**.

As we have discovered previously in the chapter, dedicating one or more NICs as a separate storage network for NFS and iSCSI storage devices is the best practice.

Note that in order to segregate storage traffic correctly, dedicating a different NIC in XenServer is not the only task to do, you must also route the traffic on a different network using VLAN or a specific network switch. We will introduce VLAN concepts later in this chapter.

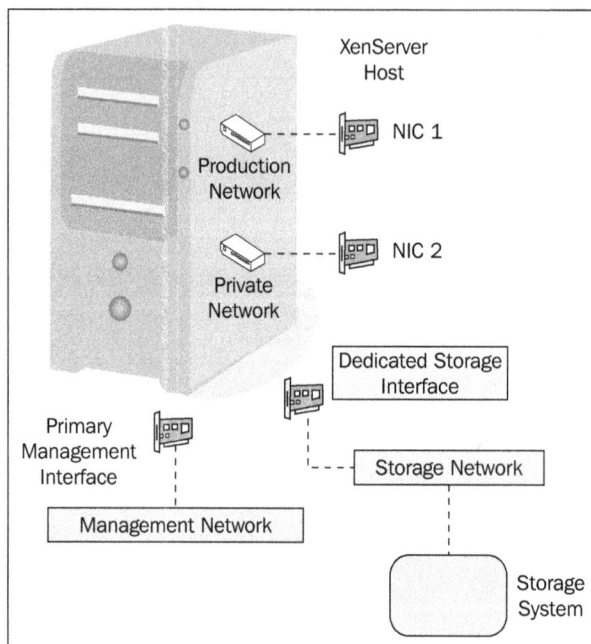

You can configure additional management interfaces in XenCenter. To do so, follow the given procedure:

1. In the XenCenter resource pane, select the host that is the pool master and click on the **Networking** tab.

2. Click on the **Configure** button in the **Management Interfaces** section.

3. The **Management Interfaces** pane is displayed. Click on the **New Interface** button to dedicate a NIC for the storage.

4. Type a meaningful name for the new management interface and create a bond to the network associated with the physical network interface you have designated to route the storage traffic.

5. Set a static IP address configuration by selecting **Use these network settings** on the **Network Settings** section.

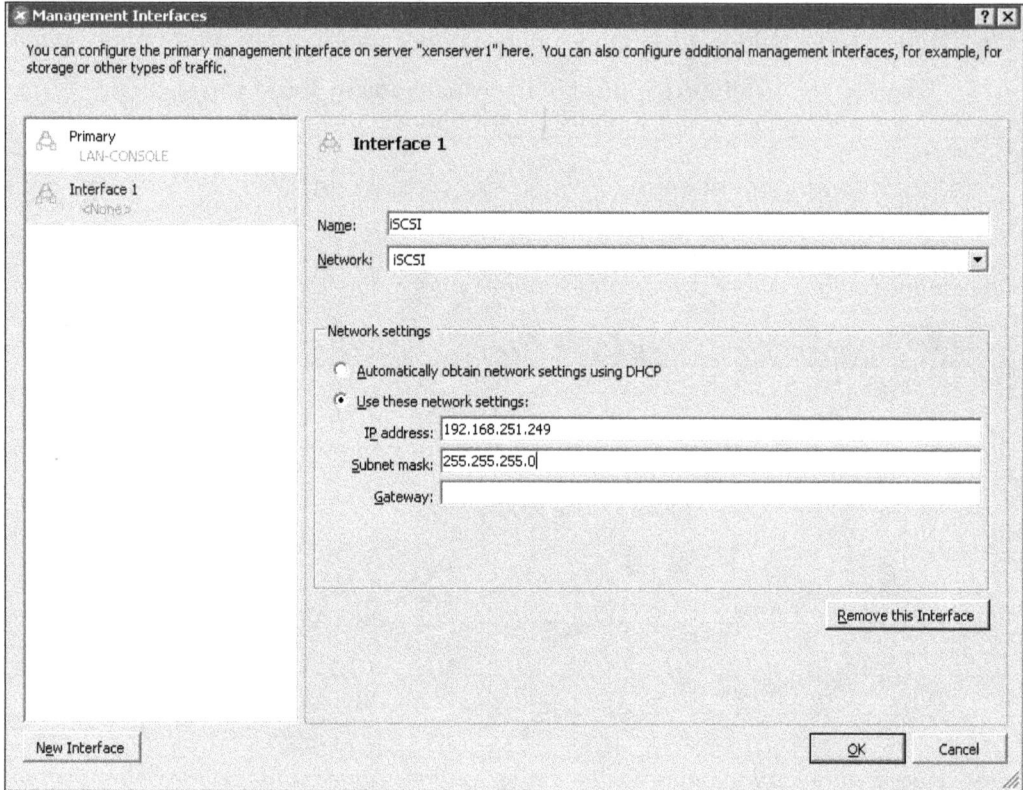

6. Click on **OK** to complete the creation process. XenServer will configure the new management interface on the pool.

You can also configure the management interface by using the xe CLI.

To do so, we start using the command `xe pif-list` to identify the `uuid` of the physical interface we will use for the storage network.

```
xe pif-list host-name-label=xenserver1
```

```
  DEMO-XENSRV01                                          Logged in as:  Local root

Search │ General │ Memory │ Storage │ Networking │ NICs │ Console │ Performance │ Users │ Logs │

  DEMO-XENSRV01 server console


      [root@demo-xensrv01 boot]# xe pif-list host-name-label=xenserver1
      uuid ( RO)                    : 1aea63a2-596b-6112-392f-692fe92c9ebd
                  device ( RO): eth0
       currently-attached ( RO): true
                    VLAN ( RO): -1
            network-uuid ( RO): b41b5a05-bc44-85a9-b3de-678e28ecb089


      uuid ( RO)                    : 90fc2fba-e385-66bd-34cd-f2b87a91663c
                  device ( RO): eth1
       currently-attached ( RO): true
                    VLAN ( RO): -1
            network-uuid ( RO): 775ca7a3-bc78-e04b-7a55-87ae2501712b


      uuid ( RO)                    : e501a0b6-a080-3f0f-e3cb-4c26f30f2568
                  device ( RO): eth2
       currently-attached ( RO): true
                    VLAN ( RO): -1
            network-uuid ( RO): 7d6111a7-4818-6bc7-0b4a-f470d05b38d1


      [root@demo-xensrv01 boot]# █
```

We will create the network storage on the device `eth1` so the associated `uuid` is `90fc2fba-e385-66bd-34cd-f2b87a91663c`.

Now, we will assign a static IP address to the physical interface we will use for the storage network using the command `xe pif-reconfigure-ip`:

```
xe pif-reconfigure-ip uuid=<pif-uuid> mode=<dhcp> | mode=<static>
gateway=<network-gateway-address> IP=<pif-static-ip>
netmask=<pif-netmask> DNS=<dns-address>
```

where the `pif-uuid` parameter is the unique identifier object of the network interface, the `mode` parameter is the IP assignment configuration you want to use, dynamic or static, and `gateway`, `IP`, `netmask`, and `DNS` are the parameters related to the static network configuration you want to set.

In our example, we will use the following command:

```
xe pif-reconfigure-ip uuid=90fc2fba-e385-66bd-34cd-f2b87a91663c
mode=static IP=192.168.251.249 netmask=255.255.255.0
```

After we have set the IP configuration, we set the `disallow-unplug` parameters for the physical interface. This is required when you want to dedicate a management interface to storage. To set this, we use the command:

```
xe pif-param-set disallow-unplug=true uuid=<pif-uuid>
```

So in our example, we execute the command:

```
xe pif-param-set disallow-unplug=true uuid=90fc2fba-e385-66bd-34cd-
f2b87a91663c
```

After this, we run the last command in order to create the management interface for the storage:

```
xe pif-param-set other-config:management_purpose="Storage" uuid=<pif-
uuid>
```

So in our example, we execute the command:

```
xe pif-param-set other-config:management_purpose="Storage" uuid=90fc2fba-
e385-66bd-34cd-f2b87a91663c
```

As we saw using XenCenter, XenServer will create the new management interface where we route the storage traffic.

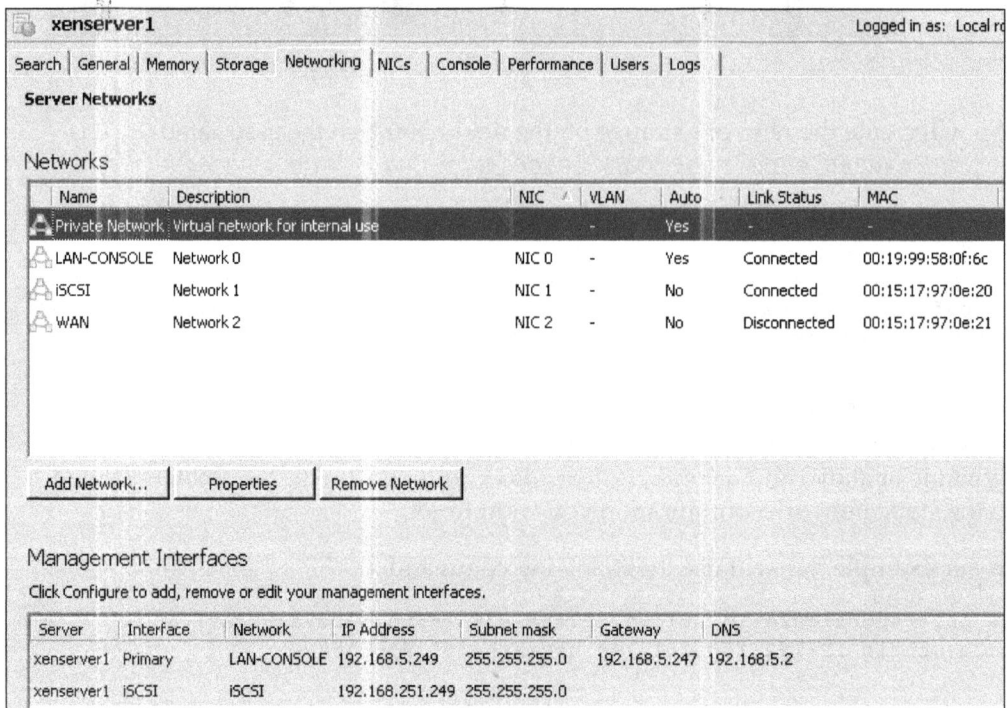

xenserver1   Logged in as: Local ro

Search | General | Memory | Storage | Networking | NICs | Console | Performance | Users | Logs |

Server Networks

Networks

Name	Description	NIC	VLAN	Auto	Link Status	MAC
Private Network	Virtual network for internal use	-		Yes	-	-
LAN-CONSOLE	Network 0	NIC 0	-	Yes	Connected	00:19:99:58:0f:6c
iSCSI	Network 1	NIC 1	-	No	Connected	00:15:17:97:0e:20
WAN	Network 2	NIC 2	-	No	Disconnected	00:15:17:97:0e:21

[Add Network...]   [Properties]   [Remove Network]

Management Interfaces

Click Configure to add, remove or edit your management interfaces.

Server	Interface	Network	IP Address	Subnet mask	Gateway	DNS
xenserver1	Primary	LAN-CONSOLE	192.168.5.249	255.255.255.0	192.168.5.247	192.168.5.2
xenserver1	iSCSI	iSCSI	192.168.251.249	255.255.255.0		

Managing VLANs

Today, **Virtual Local Area Networks (VLANs)** are very common in many companies. By configuring them, network administrators usually separate physical networks into different logical networks for security reasons.

XenServer supports VLANs offering you the possibility to separate the network traffic related to the virtual machines from the traffic dedicated to management interfaces, storage, and XenServer communications. The protocol most commonly used today in configuring VLANs is IEEE 802.1Q. Each network frame contains a *tag* identifier used to distinguish the traffic belonging to a specific VLAN. Commonly, we refer to traffic belonging to a VLAN with the term *tagged* as opposed to the term *untagged,* which is used for referring to network traffic not belonging to a VLAN.

VLAN configuration is usually made on the network switches. The network administrator can configure a switch's port as an *access port* or as a *trunk port.*

In the *access mode,* the switch ports are configured with a specific VLAN tag by the administrator to manage network traffic related to the VLAN. Devices belonging to this VLAN are connected to these ports.

In the *trunk mode,* each switch port is configured to manage the network traffic related to all the VLANs defined by the administrator in the network. In order to distinguish the traffic flow, the *tag* is inserted into the network frame. You must use this mode when you want to carry in and out the VLAN traffic from different switches.

> You can learn more on VLAN history and implementation at the following web address:
> http://en.wikipedia.org/wiki/Virtual_LAN

In XenServer, you can connect a Primary management interface only to a switch port configured in "access mode". Other management interfaces, for example dedicated to storage traffic, can be connected to either "access mode" or "trunk mode" ports indifferently.

Switch ports configured in "trunk mode" are typically used for connecting guest virtual networks. In this case, XenServer will tag and untag the network traffic with the VLAN identifier.

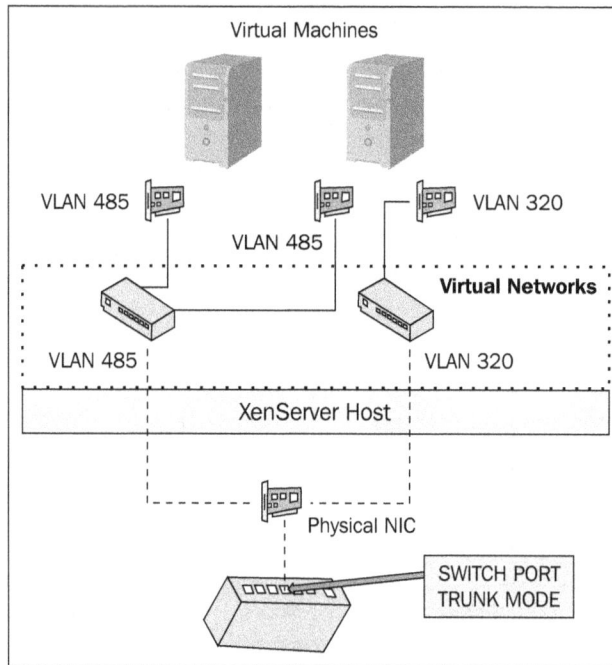

Connecting a virtual machine to a VLAN

You can use XenCenter or the xe CLI if you want to connect a virtual machine to a VLAN.

Before configuring the VLAN network in XenServer, you must connect the network interface on each host to the switch port configured with trunk mode for that specific VLAN.

After you have completed the cabling configuration, create the network in XenServer following the given procedure:

1. In XenCenter, select the pool master in the **Resource** pane and click on the **Network** tab.

2. Click on the **Add Network** button. The **New Network** wizard will be displayed and select **External Network**.

3. Click on **Next**.

4. Type a meaningful name and description for the network. As is best practice, append the VLAN ID to the name. In our example, we choose `Storage-Network VLAN 485`. Click on **Next**.

5. On the **Location** page, specify the **NIC** you physically connected to the switch and enter the VLAN tag for the VLAN in the **VLAN** box.

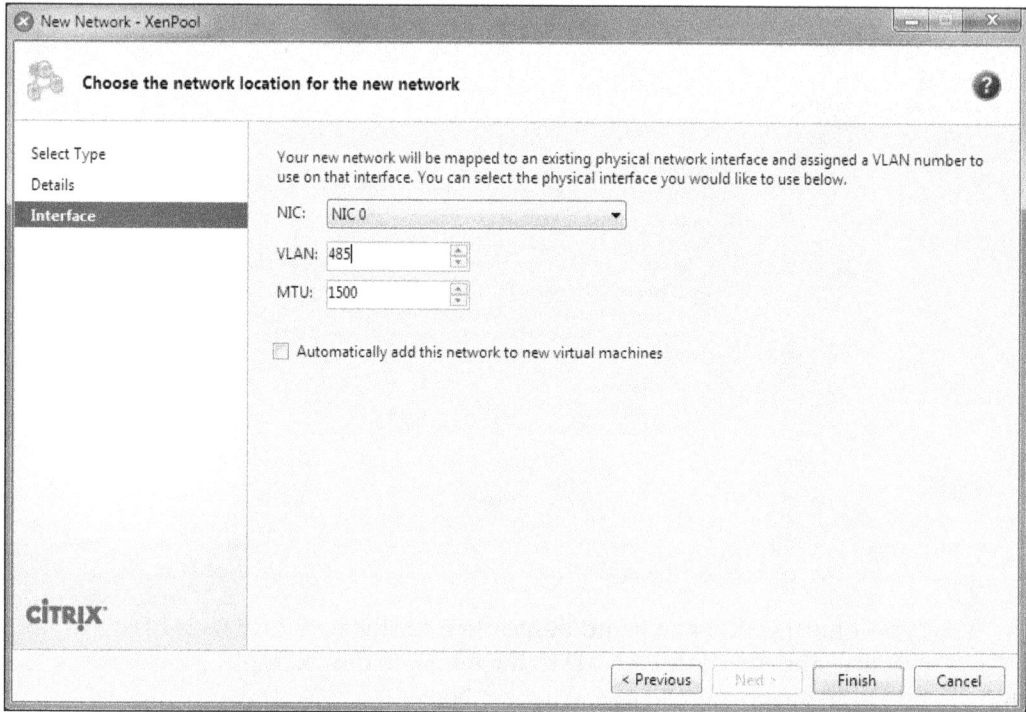

6. Click on **Finish** to complete the network creation. You will find the new network configured in XenCenter.

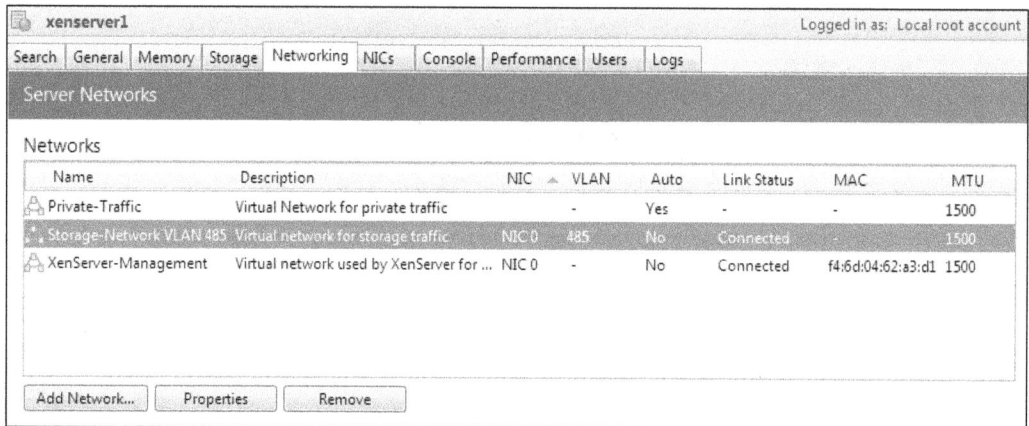

> The numbers of VLAN tags must be between 0 to 4094.

Now, you can connect the appropriate virtual machines to the VLAN configuring a virtual interface that points to the VLAN network. In XenCenter, this is done by selecting the VM in the **Resource** pane, clicking on the **Networking** tab, clicking on **Add Interface**, and then specifying the VLAN network we have created.

Using the xe CLI, we will use two `xe` commands. The first is `network-create` which we have already learned and the other is the `pool-vlan-create` command.

To do this, follow the given procedure:

1. Connect to the pool master of your pool.

2. Execute the following command to create the new network where we will configure the VLAN:

   ```
   xe network-create name-label=Storage-Traffic name-description="Virtual network for storage traffic"
   ```

   Note that XenServer returns you the UUID of the newly created network which in our example is `9c198343-293a-04db-a0df-3c0e9a5cf8f1`. We will use this with the command for creating the VLAN.

   Remember that for the moment the network is not connected to a PIF and therefore is internal.

```
xenserver1                                              Logged in as: Local root accou

Search | General | Memory | Storage | Networking | NICs | Console | Performance | Users | Logs

xenserver1 server console

[root@xenserver1 /]# xe network-create name-label=Storage-Traffic name-descripti
on="Virtual network for storage traffic"
9c198343-293a-04db-a0df-3c0e9a5cf8f1
[root@xenserver1 /]#
```

3. In order to proceed with the configuration, we have to find the physical PIF corresponding to the physical NIC supporting the desired VLAN tag. We use the command:

   ```
   xe pif-list host-name-label=<host-name>
   ```

where the `host-name` parameter is the name of the pool master.

In our example, we execute:

```
xe pif-list host-name-label=xenserver1
```

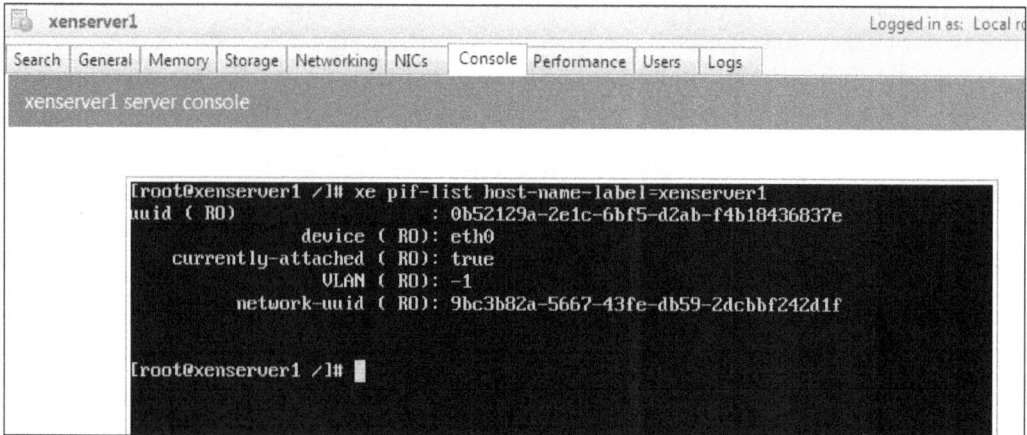

4. Note that XenServer returns you the UUID of the physical PIF, which in our example is `0b52129a-2e1c-6bf5-d2ab-f4b18436837e`.

5. The `xe pif-list` command returns more than one UUID if there are more than one physical network interfaces present on your host — in this case you have to use the UUID related to the physical network interface where you want to create the VLAN network.

You can see an example of this situation in the following screenshot:

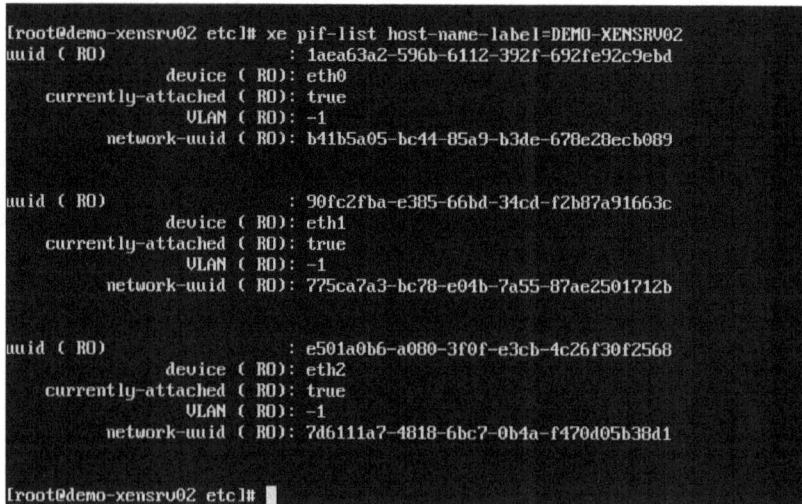

6. Now, we have all the information to create the VLAN network and we can introduce the `xe` command `pool-vlan-create`:

```
xe pool-vlan-create network-uuid=<network-uuid> pif-uuid=<pif-uuid> vlan=<vlan-tag>
```

where:

- The `network-uuid` parameter is the unique identifier of the network we have created in the second step
- The `pif-uuid` parameter is the unique identifier of the physical interface we have identified in the last step
- The `vlan` parameter is the VLAN tag we want to associate to the network.

In our example, we will execute the following command:

```
xe pool-vlan-create network-uuid=9c198343-293a-04db-a0df-3c0e9a5cf8f1 pif-uuid=0b52129a-2e1c-6bf5-d2ab-f4b18436837e vlan=485
```

Note that XenServer returns some new network object identifiers, one for each host configured on the pool. In our example, we have two hosts, so two UUIDs.

Managing bonds

You wish to ensure that any critical server has high availability access to the network.

This is a highly desirable requirement in a virtual environment. XenServer lets you achieve high network availability and create redundancy through **NIC bonding**, also known as NIC teaming.

Using NIC bonding, an administrator configures two physical network interfaces together so they logically function as one network card. If one NIC in the bond fails, the host's network traffic is automatically redirected through the second NIC.

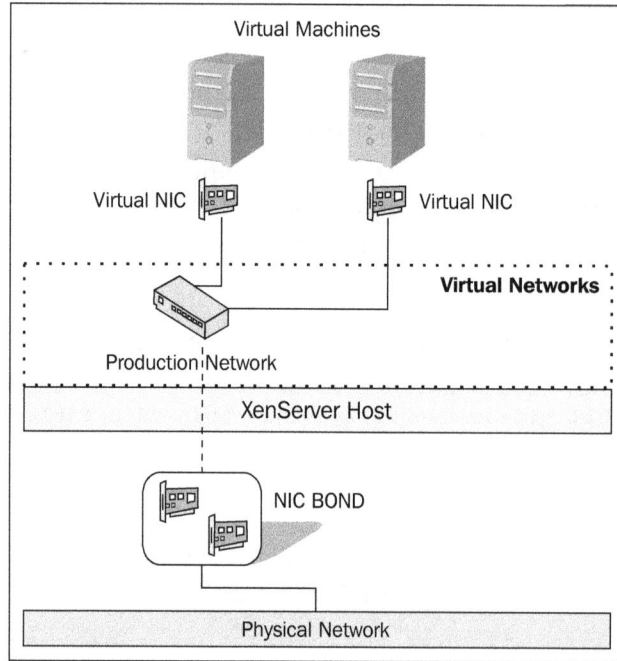

XenServer supports up to eight bonded networks—you can bond network interfaces related to management and virtual machine traffic.

Bonding behavior differs depending on whether it is being configured for management interfaces (primary or dedicated to storage) or for virtual machine interfaces. When you create a bond for management interfaces, the second NIC provides only failover for the management traffic, when you create a bond dedicated to a virtual machine's traffic, bonding provides not only failover but also load balancing.

Switch failures, network outages, and performance issues on one subnet are common, so it is best practice to consider making bonded interfaces more reliable by connecting the network cables to separate switches—if you connect one of the links to a second, redundant switch and a NIC or switch fails, traffic is directed to the other link.

Whether you use bonds for virtual machine traffic or for management interfaces, using separate switches prevents a single point of failure for your pool and your virtual infrastructure.

When you create a NIC bond, you can choose between two types: **Active/Active** mode, with VM traffic balanced between the bonded NICs, or **Active/Passive** mode, where only one NIC actively carries traffic.

Active/Active bonding

Active/Active, which is the default bonding mode, is an Active/Active configuration for traffic originated by and directed to virtual machines—both NICs are used in order to balance the virtual machine's traffic. When a bond is configured for the management traffic, only one NIC is used to route the traffic; the other NIC remains unused and provides failover support.

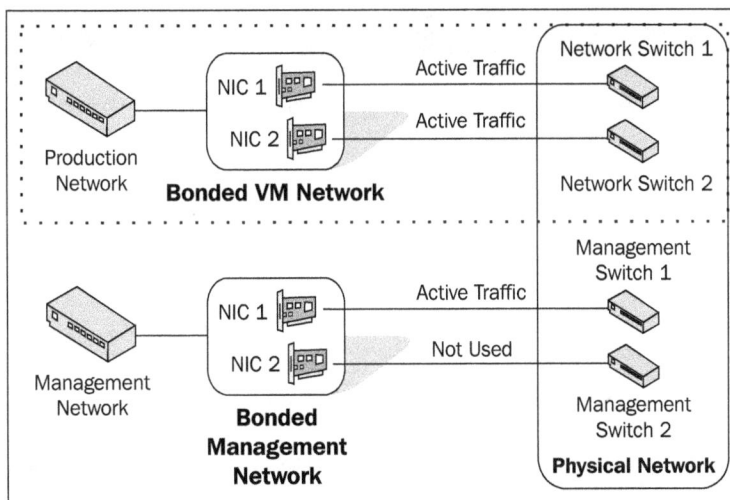

Active/Passive bonding

When you configure a bond to operate in *Active/Passive* configuration, XenServer routes traffic across one NIC in the bond—this is the only active NIC. The second network interface is in a passive state and will be used only if the active network interface fails.

Creating an NIC Bond

We have covered the concept of a NIC bond. Now, it is time to discover how to create it.

In the following example, we will create an Active/Active bond using XenCenter.

To create a new bond in XenCenter, follow the given procedure:

1. In XenCenter, select the pool master in the **Resource** pane and click on the **NIC** tab.

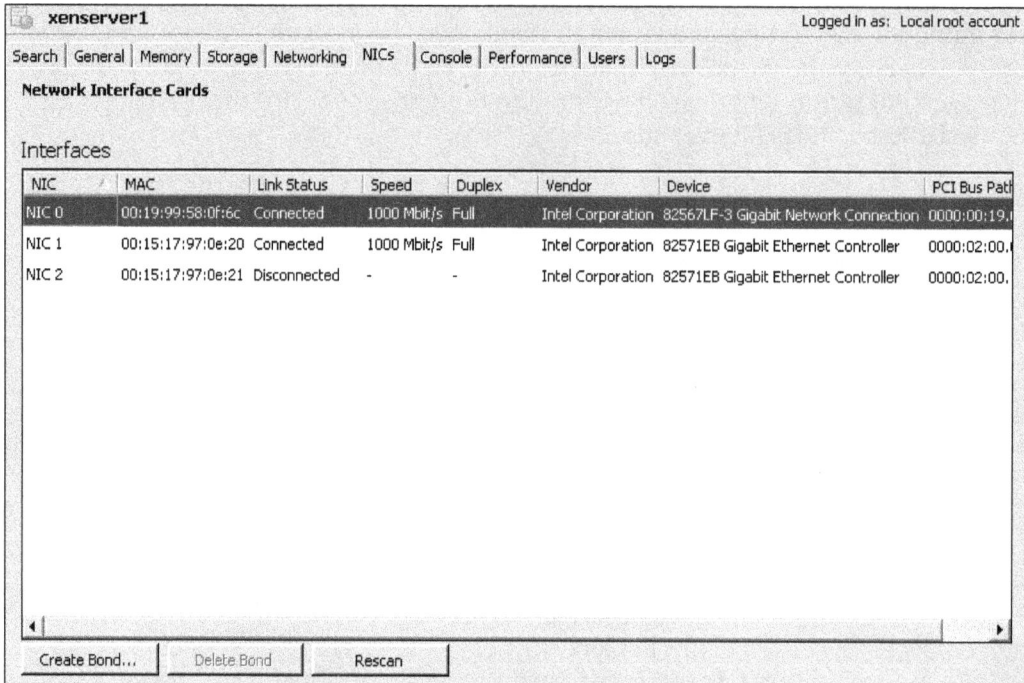

NIC	MAC	Link Status	Speed	Duplex	Vendor	Device	PCI Bus Path
NIC 0	00:19:99:58:0f:6c	Connected	1000 Mbit/s	Full	Intel Corporation	82567LF-3 Gigabit Network Connection	0000:00:19.
NIC 1	00:15:17:97:0e:20	Connected	1000 Mbit/s	Full	Intel Corporation	82571EB Gigabit Ethernet Controller	0000:02:00.
NIC 2	00:15:17:97:0e:21	Disconnected	-	-	Intel Corporation	82571EB Gigabit Ethernet Controller	0000:02:00.

xenserver1 — Logged in as: Local root account

Search | General | Memory | Storage | Networking | NICs | Console | Performance | Users | Logs

Network Interface Cards

Interfaces

Create Bond... | Delete Bond | Rescan

2. Click on the **Create Bond...** button to create a new bond.

3. In the **Create Bond** window, select the two network interfaces that will be joined together. Under **Bond mode**, you can select **Active-active** (default) or **Active-passive**.

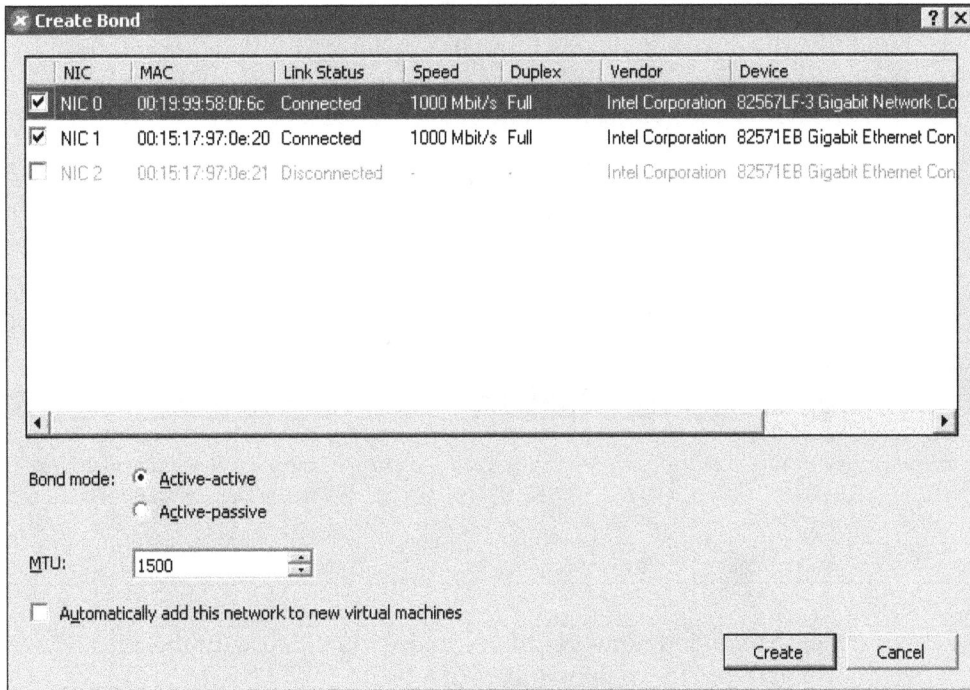

If you want to add this new bonded network to new virtual machines, select **Automatically add this network to new virtual machines**.

4. Click on **Create** to complete the creation process. Note that when you want to create a bond on one network interface used for the primary management interface, XenServer will inform you that the connections to the pool will be temporarily disturbed.

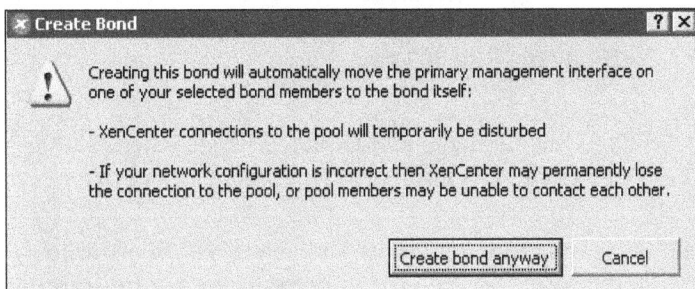

5. Click on the **Create bond anyway** button. XenServer will team up the two interfaces and create the new bond.

6. On the **Networking** or **NIC** tab in XenCenter, you can see the newly created bond identified with the name **Bond 0+1**, where 0 and 1 represent the network interfaces NIC 0 and NIC 1 respectively. If you create a bond with the NIC 0 and NIC 2, the bond name will be *Bond 0+2*.

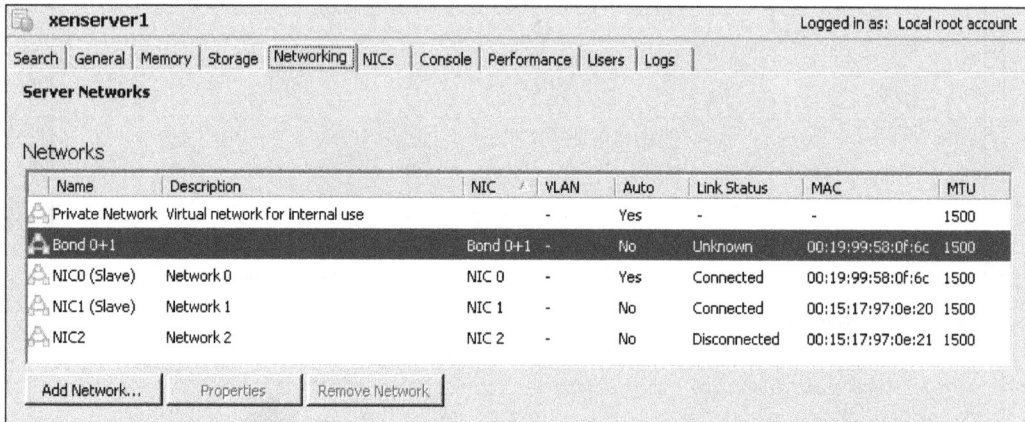

7. Note that the bonded network interfaces are identified with the term **(Slave)** to inform you that they are members of a bond.

8. If you want to remove the bond, you can click on the **Delete Bond...** button available on the **NIC** tab in XenCenter.

Distributed vSwitch Controller overview

In addition to the standard Linux bridge, XenServer 6.0 supports **Open vSwitch** — it is a production quality, multilayer virtual switch licensed under the open source Apache 2.0 license. It is designed to enable massive network automation through programmatic extension, and supports standard management interfaces and protocols such as NetFlow or IEEE 802.1ag.

> You can find more information on Open vSwitch at the following web address: http://openvswitch.org/.

The Open vSwitch is enabled by default in XenServer 6.0. In order to provide a centralized administration of the virtualized networking configuration based on the "vSwitch" and other features, such as Quality of Service (QoS) policies or cross-server private networks, Citrix has developed a virtual appliance known as *Distributed vSwitch Controller* that you can install and configure in your XenServer environment.

Deploying the Distributed vSwitch Controller

The Distributed vSwitch (DVS) Controller is provided by Citrix as an .xva package.

To install the DVS Controller, import the supplied virtual appliance VM image into a XenServer resource pool. We have learned how to import a virtual appliance into a XenServer pool in *Chapter 5, Managing Virtual Machines*.

The standard DVS controller configuration supports deployments of up to 16 XenServers and 256 virtual interfaces connected to it. The maximum supported limit is 64 XenServers and 1024 virtual interfaces.

After you have imported and started the DVS Controller, you can begin the configuration process:

1. First, assign a static IP address to the Distributed vSwitch Controller. By default, the controller first attempts to acquire an IP address from a DHCP server and later asks you to set an IP address manually if the DHCP server is not available.

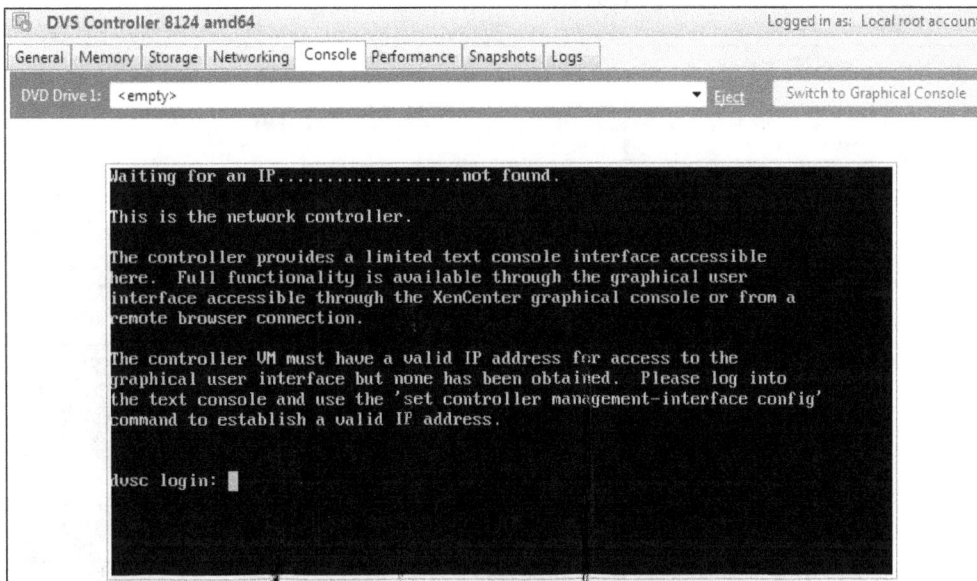

2. After that the DVS controller has been configured with an IP address, you can access a graphical user interface locally or remotely.

> Always prefer a static IP address to dynamic configuration.

3. After you have completed the network configuration, log in with the default username `admin` and password `admin`.

4. Set a static IP address for the controller with the following command:

   ```
   set controller management-interface config static <IP-address>
   <netmask> <gateway-IP>
   ```

   where:

   - The `<IP-address>` parameter is the IP address you want to set, for example, *192.168.0.50*

   - The `<netmask>` parameter is the subnet mask associated with the IP address you have chosen to use, for example, *255.255.255.0*

   - The `<gateway>` parameter is the IP address of the gateway configured on your network, for example *192.168.0.4*

   In our environment, we execute the following command:

   ```
   set controller management-interface config static 192.168.0.50
   255.255.255.0 192.168.0.4
   ```

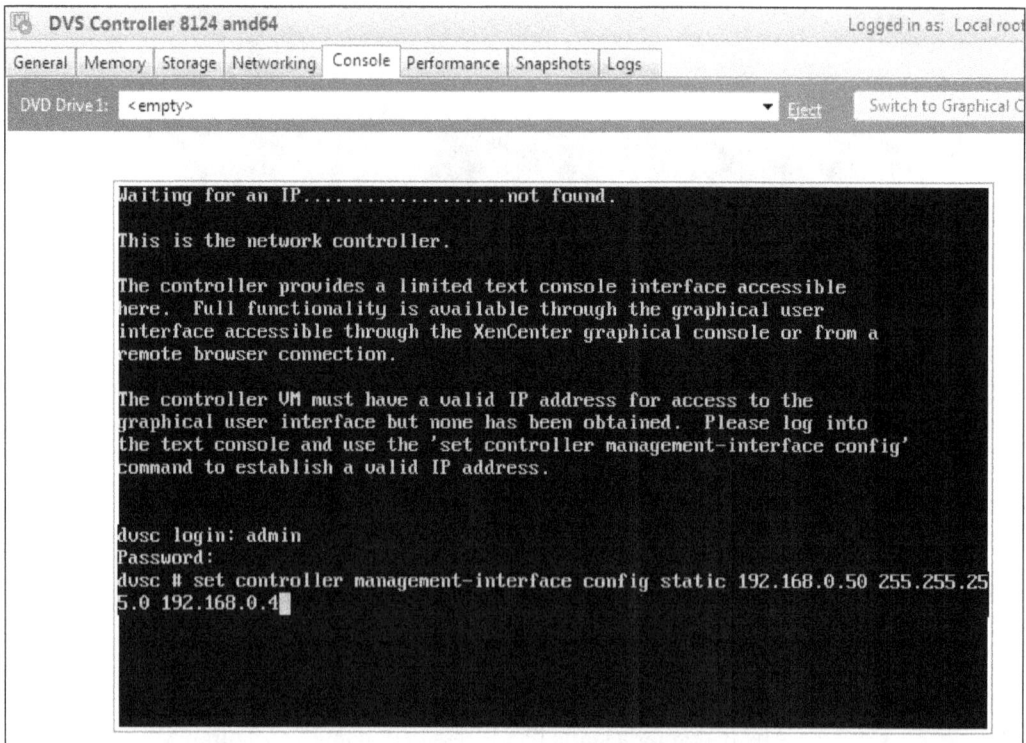

Now, we are ready to proceed with the initial configuration of the DVS Controller.

1. Open a browser and enter the URL `https://server/`, where `server` is the IP address of the interface of the DVS controller.

2. Log in with the default username `admin`.

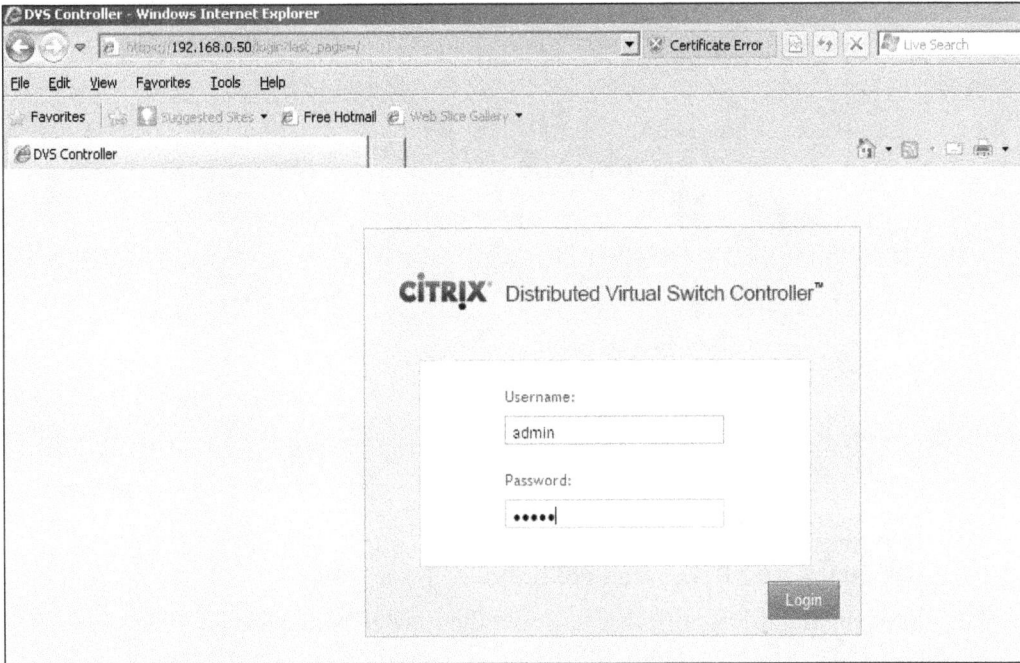

3. In the screenshot, you can notice that an SSL certificate error is displayed on the browser. By default, the vSwitch Controller web server uses a self-signed certificate, which will cause many browsers to show a security error when connecting to the GUI.

4. At the first logon, you will be prompted to change the password. Type a complex password for security reasons.

5. After the password change, you will be redirect by default to the **Visibility & Control** page of the graphical user interface. Here, we can add the resource pools, which the DVS Controller will manage.

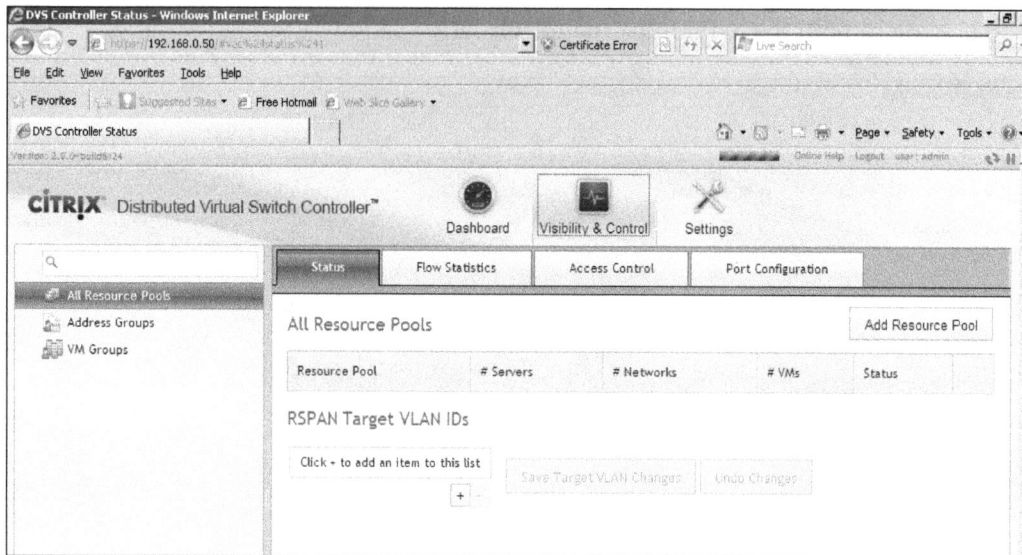

6. Now, we can connect the DVS Controller to our XenServer Pool. To do so, click on the **Add Resource Pool** button.

7. Enter the IP address or DNS name of the master XenServer in the **Pool Master Server (DNS/IP)** field and username and password for administrative access to the server—the user must have full management capabilities in the resource pool. The **Steal** checkbox is used when you want to override any existing vSwitch Controller configuration that was previously set for this resource pool.

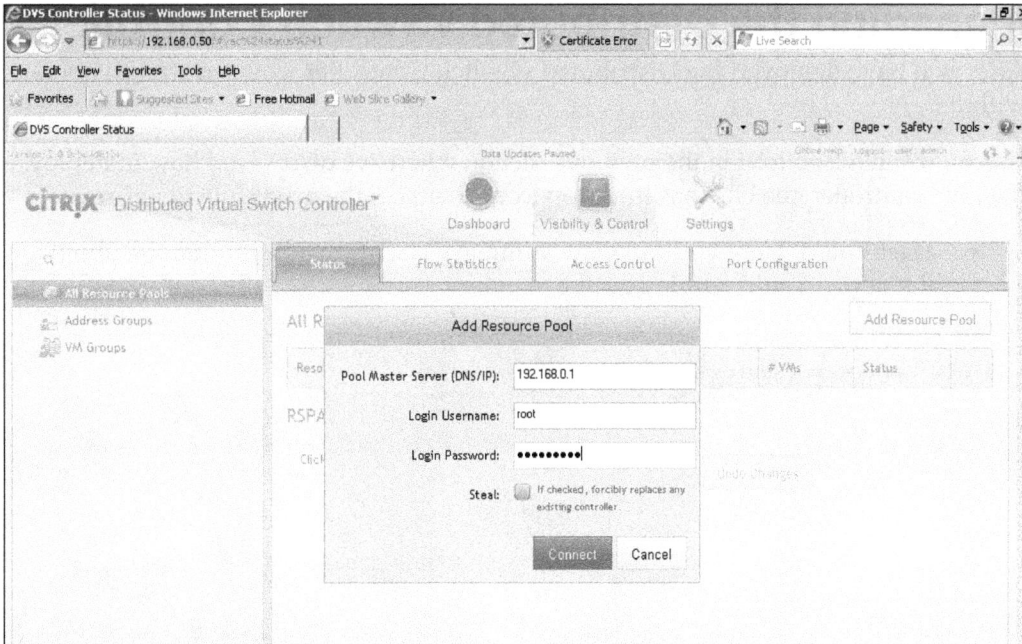

8. Click on **Connect**. The DVS Controller will try to establish a connection with your pool and after that will add the new resource pool to the resource tree, along with all of the associated resources.

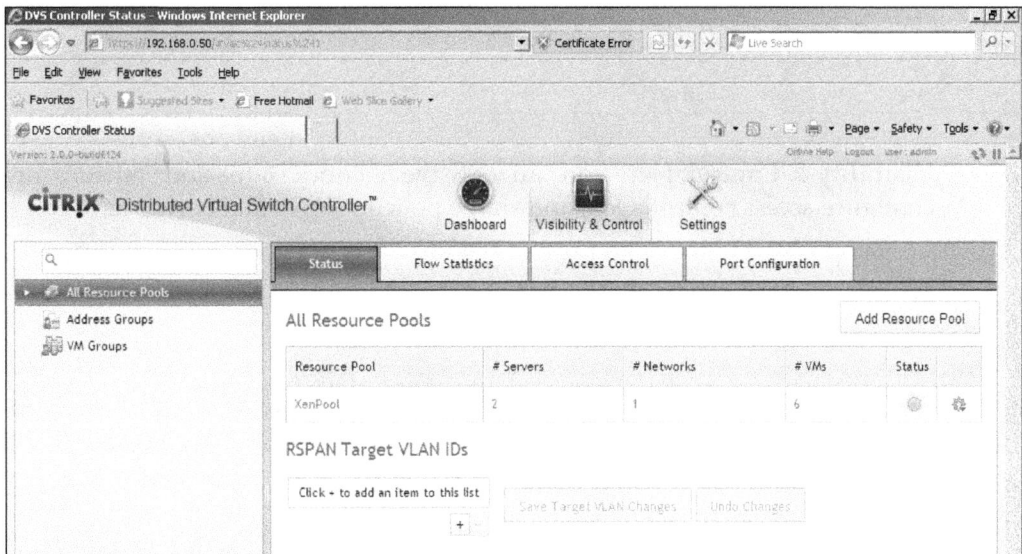

Managing the Distributed vSwitch Controller

After you have deployed the Distributed vSwitch Controller, you can start to operate with it.

As you will have noticed in the previous section where we discovered how to deploy the DVS controller, the GUI has three top icons to access the major functional areas:

- **Dashboard**: Here you can view summary statistics and information about the network and administrative events

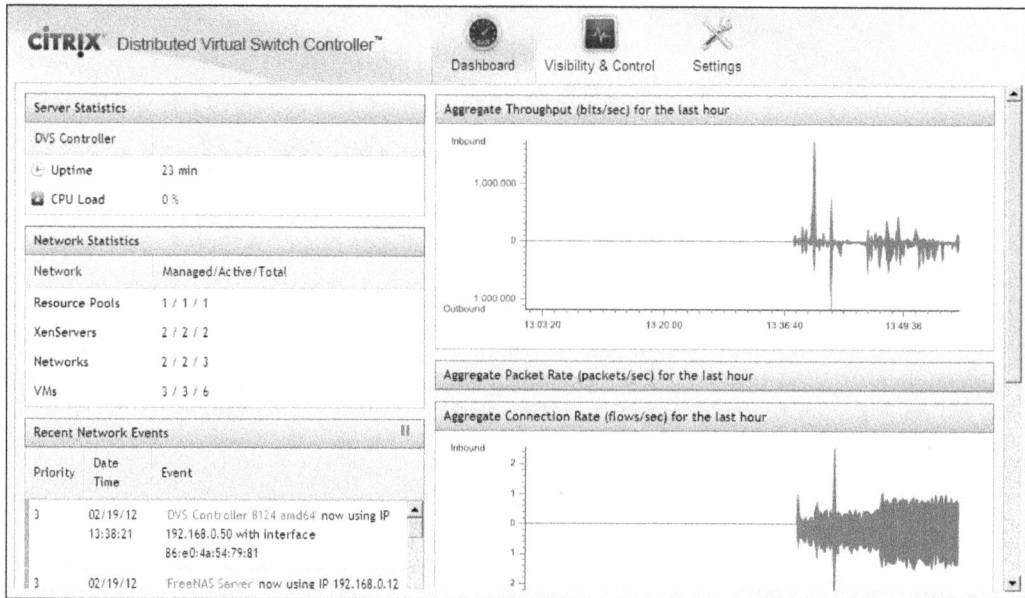

- **Visibility & Control**: Here you can view the network status and statistics, or configure access control, QoS, and traffic policies for virtual networks

- **Settings**: Here you can perform vSwitch Controller maintenance and administrative functions

Furthermore, when you select **Visibility & Control**, a side panel is displayed on the left showing you a resource tree that you can use to browse network elements within the virtual network environment. Similar to the resource tree in XenCenter, elements are organized hierarchically and provide an easy way to browse elements within the system.

At the highest level, the resource tree displays the following items:

- **All Resource Pools**: A list of all the available resource pools. This is the top-level resource for exploring all XenServers, Networks, VMs, and VIFs that are part of each resource pool.

- **Address Groups**: Named sets of IP addresses and subnet ranges to be used to limit the application of a rule in the **Access Control** section or to limit the scope of a query in the **Flow Statistics** section.

- **VM Groups**: Named sets of VMs to be used to simplify viewing the status and flow statistics of a particular collection of VMs.

When you expand a resource pool in the resource tree, the following items are displayed:

- **Pool-wide Networks**: This list includes all networks in the resource pool and is similar to the list in the **Networking** tab of XenCenter. You can expand the list to show the individual networks, expand a network to show the VMs on that network, and expand a VM to show its VIFs on that network.

- **XenServers**: This list is similar to the server hierarchy in XenCenter. You can expand the list to show all the servers in the pool and expand a single server entry to show the networks, VMs, and VIFs associated with that server. The Server Networks listing is similar to what you see if you click on a server in XenCenter and choose the **Networking** tab.

- **All VMs**: This list shows all VMs in the resource pool, whether or not they are configured for a single server. You can expand the list to show the individual VMs, and expand a VM to show its VIFs.

Remember that you can access context menus by right-clicking on most of the items. This provides you a simple way of adding, modifying, and deleting objects in the resource tree.

Viewing the status of a Distributed vSwitch Controller

We have learned that from the **Visibility & Control** section, we can monitor the network behavior.

The **Status** tab provides detailed information in table form about the node that is selected in the resource tree. The type of information that is presented varies according to the selected node.

At the global level, the **Status** page presents a table listing all resources pools with information related to number of servers, networks, and virtual machines.

If you click on the name of the resource pool, you can display status information about the selected XenServer pool.

Also, you can configure "**Fail-Safe" mode** — this is how a vSwitch in the resource pool manages Access Control List (ACL) rules when it is unable to connect with its configured vSwitch Controller.

If the DVS Controller is unavailable, for example due to network issues or Controller restart, all traffic is allowed and previously defined ACLs are no longer applied until the vSwitch is able to reconnect with the vSwitch Controller. This mode is knows as *fail-open* and is enabled by default.

Otherwise, if you configure the DVS Controller in *fail-safe* mode, existing ACLs continue to apply and network traffic that does not match existing ACLs is dropped.

The **Status** tab for **Pool-wide Networks** lists summary information about each network in the resource pool.

The status icon is green if the network is active and properly managed by the vSwitch Controller, red if it has no connected interfaces, and orange if there is an error condition.

Address and virtual machine groups

In the DVS Controller, you have the ability to set up address groups and virtual machine groups. The former gives you the ability to specify the IP addresses to use as the source or destination for ACLs or for reporting.

The latter is a set of VMs that you identify as a group for viewing the status and statistics.

If you want to create an address group, follow the given procedure:

1. Under **Visibility & Control**, select **Address Groups** in the resource tree to open the **Status** page for all address groups.

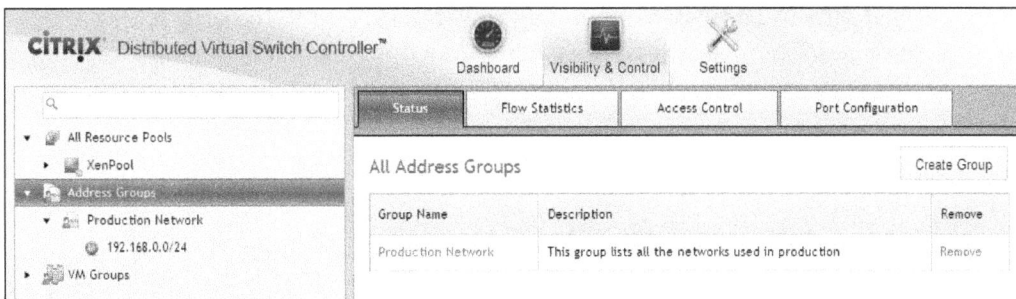

2. Click on **Create Group** and enter a name to identify the group and an optional description—as usual, use a meaningful name. In this example, we will create a group named `Private Networks` for all the internal networks we use in our environment.

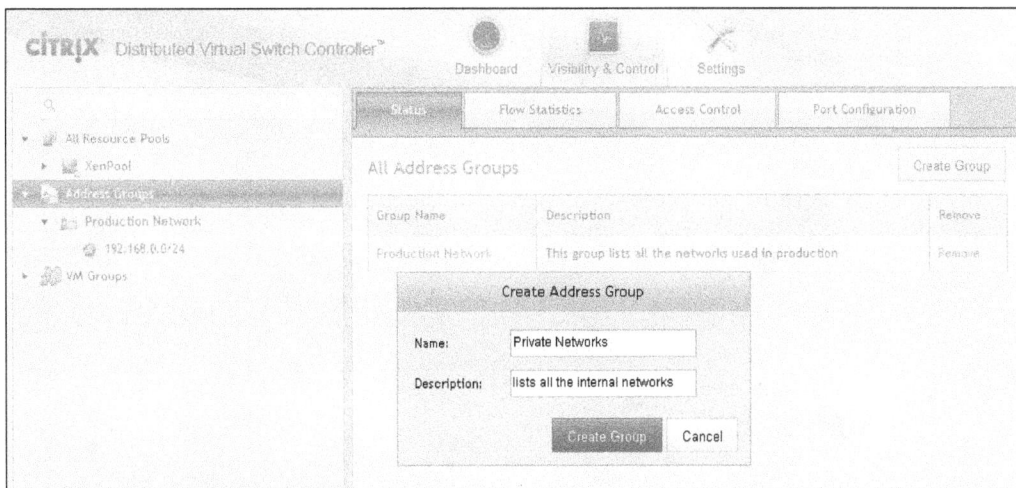

3. Click on **Create Group**.

4. Now we have to add the virtual networks that will belong to this group. The Controller gives you the chance to do this after you have created the new group. Now click on **Add Members**.

5. Specify the IP addresses or subnets you want to add to the group. Use a comma as a separator to specify more than one IP address or subnet. In this example, we will insert networks `10.0.0.0/24`.

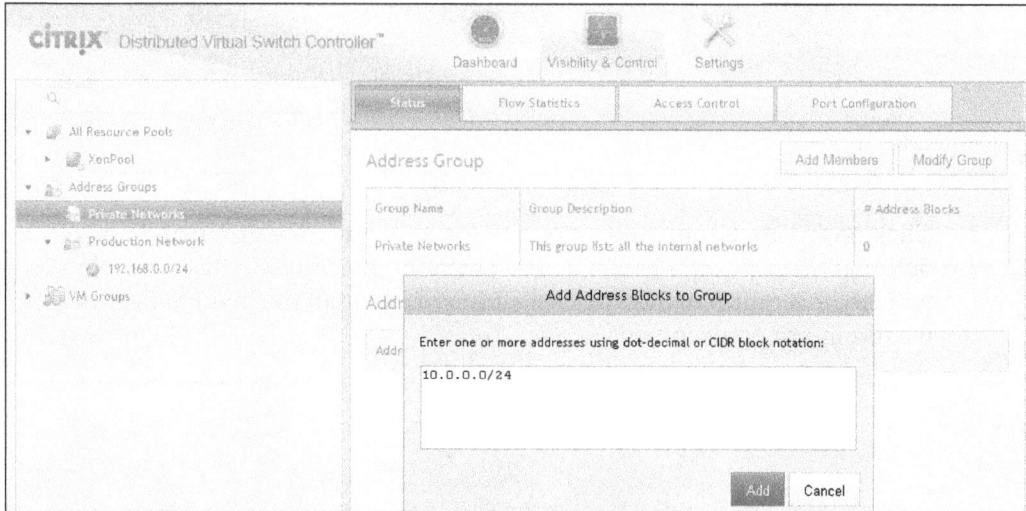

6. Click on **Add** to complete the creation of the group.

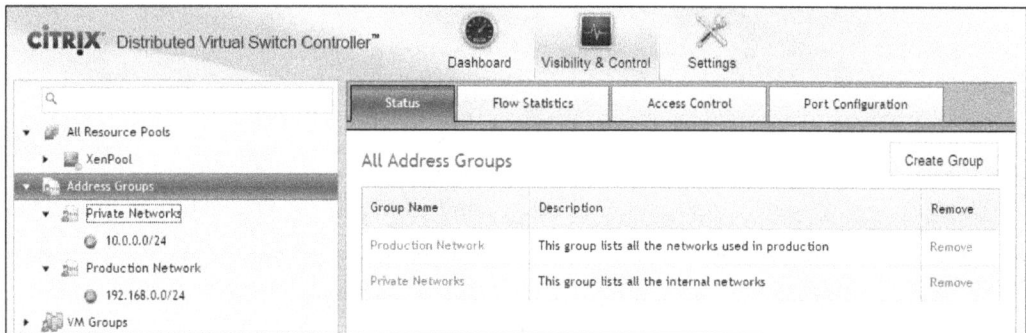

You can use the same procedure to create a Virtual Machine group.

Managing Access Control List rules

You can create and configure Access Control and Quality of Service (QoS) policies from the **Access Control** and **Port Configuration** tabs within **Visibility & Control**.

All policies are applied and enforced at the virtual interface level but remember that you can set policies to all the levels, from a resource pool to a single virtual interface attached to a virtual machine.

If you want to define a new ACL policy, use the following procedure:

1. On the resource tree, select the node where you want to apply the policy. In our example, we will create a rule for the **Storage-Network VLAN 485** network.

2. Click on the gear icon in the header bar for the level where you want to place the new policy. New policies can be added in the following ways:

   ° To add a new mandatory policy, click on the gear icon in the header bar for the level, and choose **Add New Mandatory ACL**

   ° To add a new default policy, click on the gear icon in the header bar for the level, and choose **Add New Default ACL**

   ° To add a new policy above an existing policy entry, click on the gear icon for the entry, and choose **Add New ACL Above**

   ° To add a new policy below an existing rule entry, click on the gear icon for the entry, and choose **Add New ACL Below**

   In the example, we will create a *mandatory* policy.

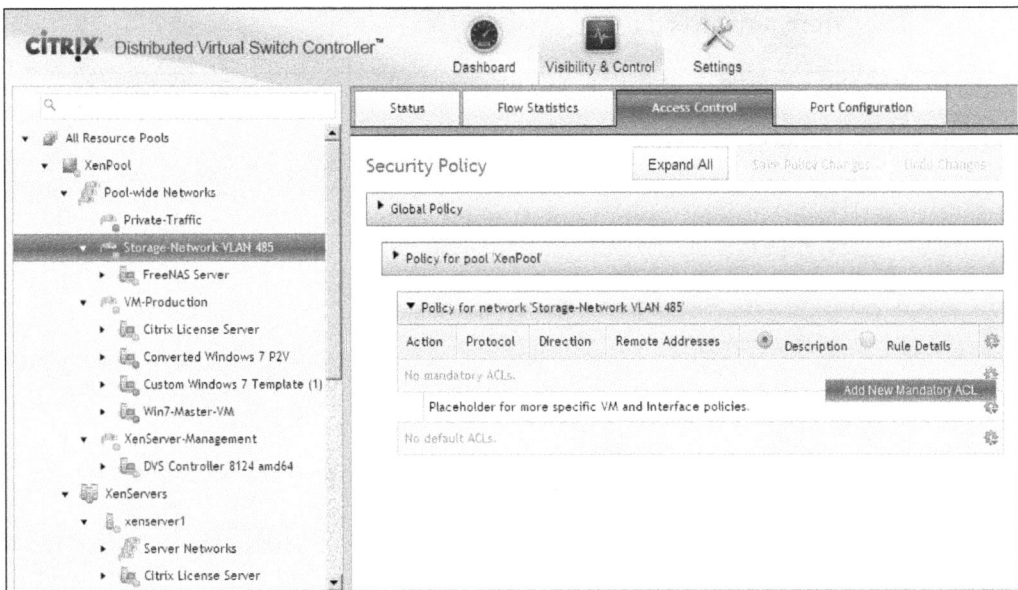

3. The new policy is added to the page with the setting **Allow**, permitted to and from any protocol and direction. To change a particular field within a policy, click on the link representing that field.

4. You can set a change as described in the following table:

Item	Description
Protocol	Choose **Match Any Protocol** to apply the policy to all protocols.
	Choose **Use an Existing Protocol** to specify a protocol. Select the protocol from the drop-down list, and click on **Use Protocol**.
	Choose **Use a New Protocol** to specify custom protocol characteristics.
Direction	Choose whether the policy will apply from or to the specified remote addresses or both
Remote Addresses	Click on the **Any** link to open a pop-up window that lists the available address groups to specify a specific remote address.
Description	To add a text description of the policy
Rule Details	Click on the **Rule Details** button to display a brief summary of the policy.

° In our example, we create a policy that allows only *TCP* protocol from any direction.

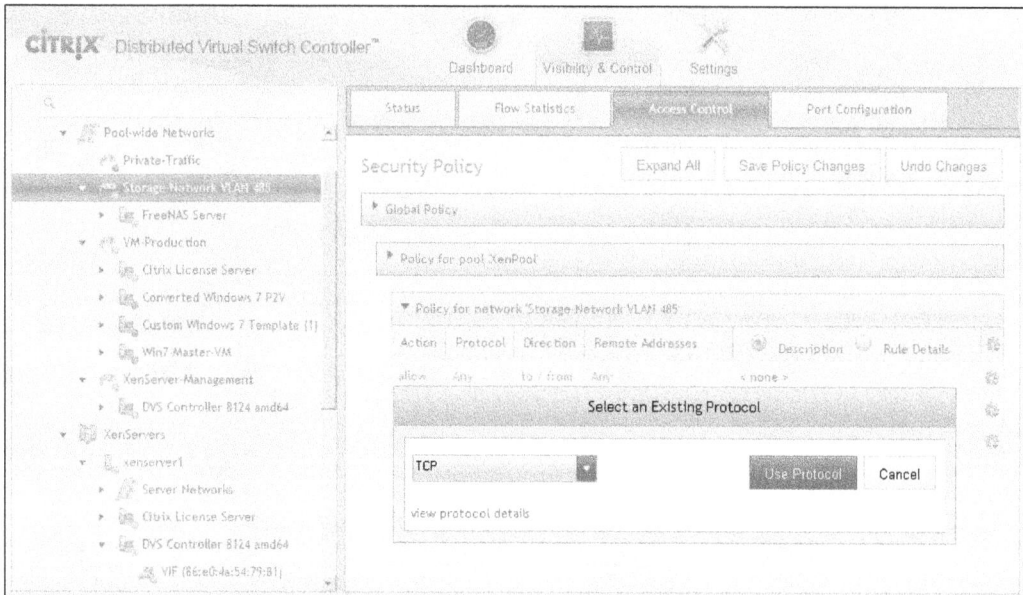

○ Note that by clicking on **view protocol details** you can also set specific parameters for the protocol you have selected.

5. When you have chosen the network protocol you want to use in the policy, click on **Use Protocol** to confirm your choice

6. Enter a meaningful description for the new policy by clicking on the description field.

7. When you have finished configuring the new policy, click on **Save Policy Changes** available at the top of the **Security Policy** area. When you do so, the changes take effect immediately within the virtual network environment.

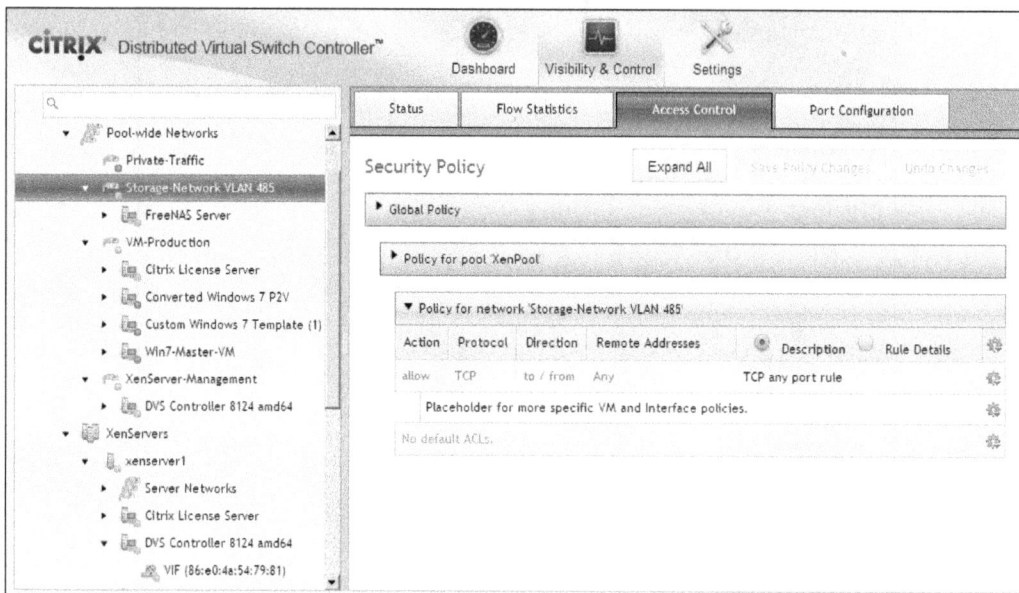

8. You can change the order of policies in a level by clicking on the gear icon for the policy and choosing **Move Up** or **Move Down** or remove a policy by choosing **Delete**.

> Note that you cannot move a rule between levels.

Setting Port Configuration Policies

In your virtual environment you can have some virtual machines that consume a lot of network bandwidth to the detriment of other virtual machines, for example, a database server that provides real time statistics about sales of your company. In this situation, you might want to limit the amount of data this virtual machine can send. In order to achieve this goal, you must configure each virtual interface to have a QoS limit.

You can do this by creating a port configuration policy in the **Port Configuration** tab.

With DVS Controller, you can configure the following policy types:

- Quality of Service (QoS) policies
- Traffic Mirroring: Remote Switched Port Analyzer (RSPAN) policies support mirroring traffic sent or received on a virtual network interface to a VLAN
- Disable MAC address spoof check: MAC address spoof check policies are on by default

To set a QoS policy for a virtual machine, follow the given procedure:

1. Click on **Port Configuration** on the GUI and select the virtual machine where you want to set the policy. In our example, we will set a QoS policy on the **Citrix License Server** machine.

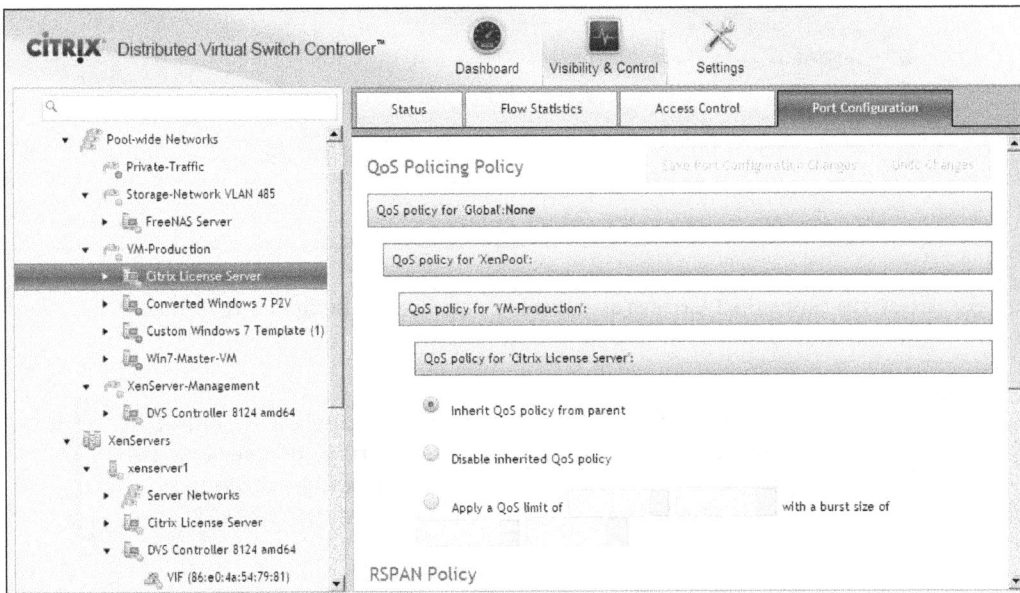

2. By default, the virtual machine inherits a QoS policy from the parent. Select **Apply a QoS limit of** and type the limit you want to apply to the machine. In our example, we have set a limit of **10 Mbit/sec** with the default burst size of **100 Kbits**.

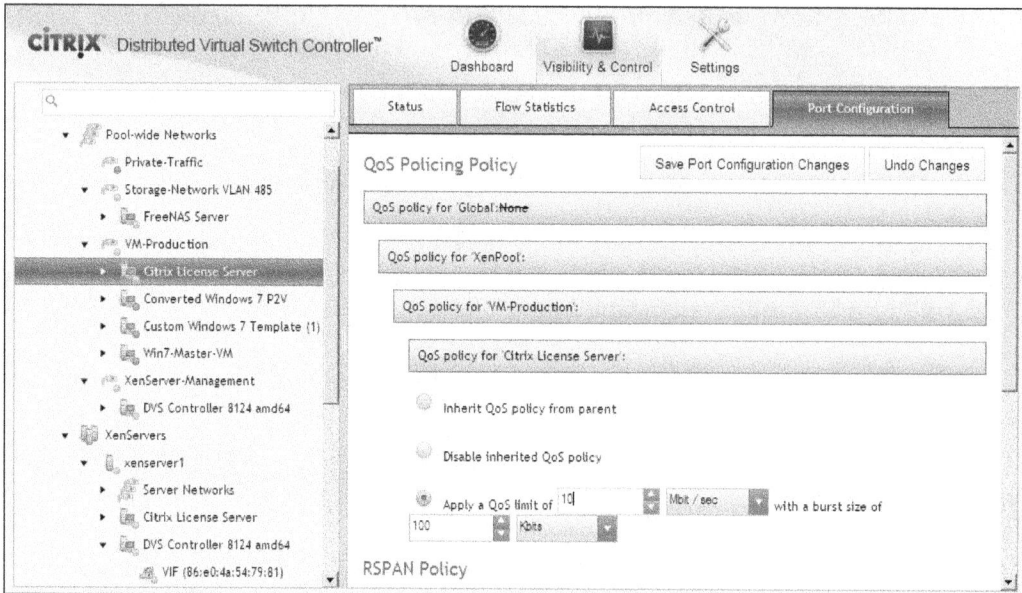

3. Click on **Save Port Configuration** for changes to be applied to the new policy.

> You can find more details on the Distributed vSwitch Controller management and configuration on the Citrix XenServer vSwitch Controller User Guide available at the following web address: http://support.citrix.com/article/CTX130423.

Summary

In this chapter, we have learned how to manage XenServer networking.

We have also discovered how to manage the Distributed Virtual Switch Controller to monitor and manage network traffic.

Specifically, we have seen:

- Managing Virtual Networks and Management Interfaces
- Creating VLANs to segregate traffic
- Creating Network Bonds to provide resiliency
- Deploying the Distributed vSwitch Controller
- Managing Access Control List rules using the Distributed vSwitch Controller

In this chapter the concepts relating to networking in XenServer have been presented to you. Networking is very important in XenServer, so take some time to familiarize yourself with it and also with the Distributed vSwitch Controller. This is a feature that gives you the chance to control very deeply the network traffic in your environment.

In the next chapter, we will introduce high availability and backup concepts for a XenServer environment.

8
Managing High Availability and Snapshots

In the previous chapter, we discussed XenServer networking.

Now we will discover how to make virtual machines highly available and how to manage snapshots in XenServer.

In this chapter, we will cover the following topics:

- High Availability overview
- Configuring High Availability
- Working with snapshots

Overview of High Availability

After you have created virtual machines in your XenServer environment, you should guarantee that services offered by these virtual machines are always available and also limit downtime. For example, a company selling products on the Internet can lose a lot of money if virtual web servers hosting the e-commerce website go down!

The **High Availability (HA)** feature in XenServer is designed to ensure your virtual machines are always available and have an optimal level of service within a resource pool.

When you enable HA in the pool, XenServer continually monitors the health of the hosts. If a host fails, virtual machines running on the failed host are automatically moved to another healthy host. Furthermore, if the failed host is the pool master, the High Availability feature is nominated automatically nominates another host as the new pool master so you can continue to manage the resource pool.

Virtual machines running on a host with HA enabled are known as *protected*.

But how does XenServer detect that a host has failed and is unreachable? It does so using two mechanisms called **storage heartbeat** and **network heartbeat**.

Storage heartbeat is based on a small virtual disk that is created by the HA feature on a shared storage repository. To successfully enable HA on your pool, this shared storage repository must be based on iSCSI, Fibre Channel, or NFS.

Each host in the pool writes to this small virtual disk to indicate to each other that it is alive. Also, each host uses the management interface as a "network heartbeat" to monitor the status of other hosts in the pool. If you are familiar with "clustering" concepts, this behavior is well known to you.

> You can find more details about the High Availability mechanism on the Citrix Knowledge Base document CTX 119717 available at `http://support.citrix.com/article/CTX119717`.

Another concept we have to understand when talking about HA in XenServer is the "host failures to tolerate". This value is defined in the HA configuration and is used by XenServer to determine the number of hosts that can fail at any given time without service interruption. According to this value, XenServer also calculates a failover plan so that virtual machines are always restartable in a host in the pool.

For example, if you have a resource pool based on 10 hosts and you set the "host failures to tolerate" value to 2, XenServer will calculate a failover plan that allows for starting virtual machines on other hosts if two hosts fail.

What happens if a host loses connectivity to the pool? In situations where a failure of a host is not real, XenServer uses the "fencing" process. It is the process of isolating a host in order to protect shared resources and avoid virtual machines starting on two hosts at the same time. When fencing, XenServer immediately restarts itself causing all VMs running on it to be stopped. The other hosts will detect that the VMs are no longer running and restart them.

> You can find more details about fencing at `http://en.wikipedia.org/wiki/Fencing_(computing)`.

Previously we have discovered a requirement we have to satisfy for enabling High Availability: a shared storage as iSCSI, NFS, or Fibre Channel LUN to be used for the heartbeat mechanism.

This shared storage must have a size of 356 MB or greater because XenServer creates two volumes on it: one small volume, 4 MB, for heartbeating and one, 256 MB, for storing pool master metadata to be used in the case of master failover.

Furthermore, you need to satisfy the following requirements:

- The hosts have to belong to a XenServer pool
- XenServer Advanced edition or higher on all hosts
- Static IP addresses for all hosts

These are requirements for the XenServer hosts. Are there any for virtual machines? Sure!

For a VM to be protected by the HA feature, it must be agile. This means that:

- It must have its virtual disks on shared storage (any type of shared storage may be used; the iSCSI, NFS, or FibreChannel LUN is only required for the storage heartbeat and can be used for virtual disk storage if you prefer, but this is not necessary)
- It must not have a connection to a local DVD drive configured
- It should have its virtual network interfaces on pool-wide networks

Also, remember that in a XenServer environment where Role Based Access Control (RBAC) is implemented only users belonging to *Pool Administrator* or *Pool Operator* can configure the High Availability feature.

Setting restart priorities

When you configure HA, you can also assign *restart priorities* to virtual machines. The restart priority is a flag instructing XenServer to protect a virtual machine by HA. If a restart priority is specified, any protected VM that is halted will be started automatically. If a server fails then the running VMs will be started on another server.

In the following table, you can find an explanation related to each available priority level:

HA Restart Priority	Restart Explanation
0	Attempt to start VMs with this priority first.
1	Attempt to start VMs with this priority, only after having attempted to restart all VMs with priority 0.
2	Attempt to start VMs with this priority, only after having attempted to restart all VMs with priority 1.
3	Attempt to start VMs with this priority, only after having attempted to restart all VMs with priority 2.
best-effort	Attempt to start VMs with this priority, only after having attempted to restart all VMs with priority 3.

Also, you can set the parameter **HA Always Run** for a virtual machine. When you set it to **True** that virtual machine is included in the restart plan.

The restart priorities determine the order in which XenServer attempts to start VMs when a failure occurs. The VMs that have restart priorities 0, 1, 2, or 3 are guaranteed to be restarted in case of server failures. VMs with a best-effort priority setting are not part of the failover plan and are not guaranteed to be kept running.

Configuring High Availability

After we have introduced the High Availability's concepts, we can learn how to enable HA.

This feature can be enabled on a pool using either XenCenter or the xe CLI.

Remember that when HA is enabled, some operations that would compromise the plan for restarting VMs may be disabled, such as removing a server from a pool. To perform these operations, HA can be temporarily disabled, or alternately, VMs protected by HA made unprotected. We will cover how to this later in the chapter.

If you want to enable HA using XenCenter, follow this procedure:

1. Connect to your XenServer pool and click on your pool name.
2. Click on **Pool | High Availability...** to start the **High Availability** wizard.

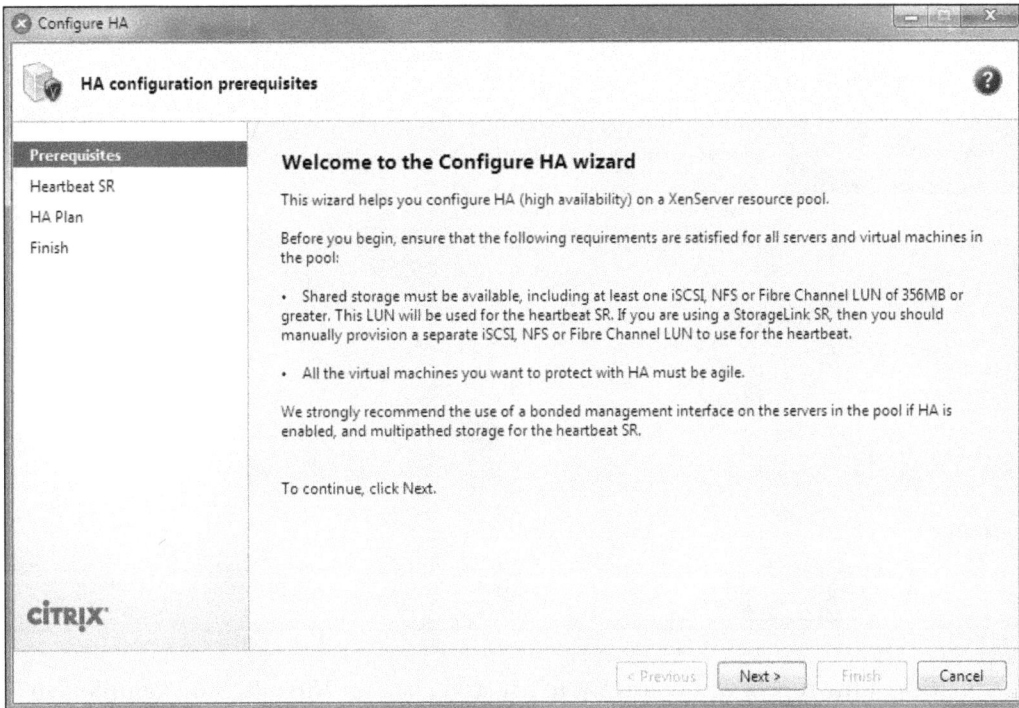

3. The wizard guides you through the process. Click on **Next** to continue.

4. XenServer will scan the storage repository in order to configure the heartbeat SR and prompts you to select the storage repository to use. Also, configured storage repositories that are not suitable for the heartbeat repository will be identified as *not supporting this operation*.

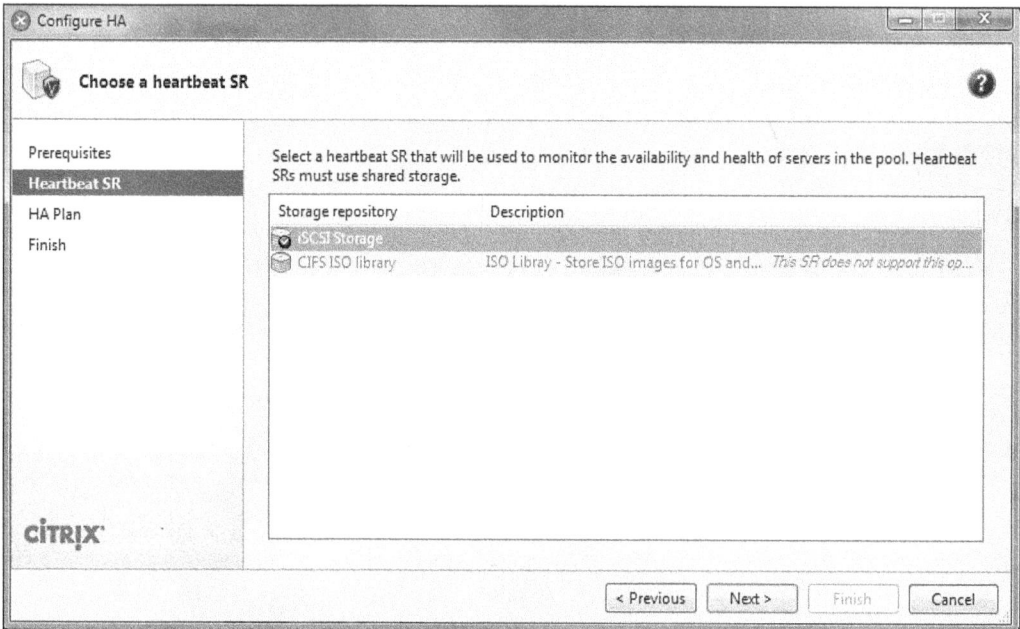

5. Select the repository you want to use and click on **Next**. In our example, we will use an iSCSI storage repository.

6. Now, you can set the required virtual machines startup settings on the HA Plan page. Select one or more virtual machines and set:

Option	Description
HA Restart Priority	Choose a restart priority for each VM: • Choose **Restart** to ensure the selected VM(s) are restarted if sufficient resources are available within the pool • Choose **Restart if Possible** if it is not essential to restart the VM automatically • Choose **Do Not Restart** if you never want the VM to be restarted automatically

Option	Description
Start Order	Specifies the order in which individual VMs will be started up during the HA recovery operation, allowing certain VMs to be restarted before others.
Attempt to start next VM after	This is a delay interval that specifies how long to wait after starting the VM before attempting to start the next virtual machine.

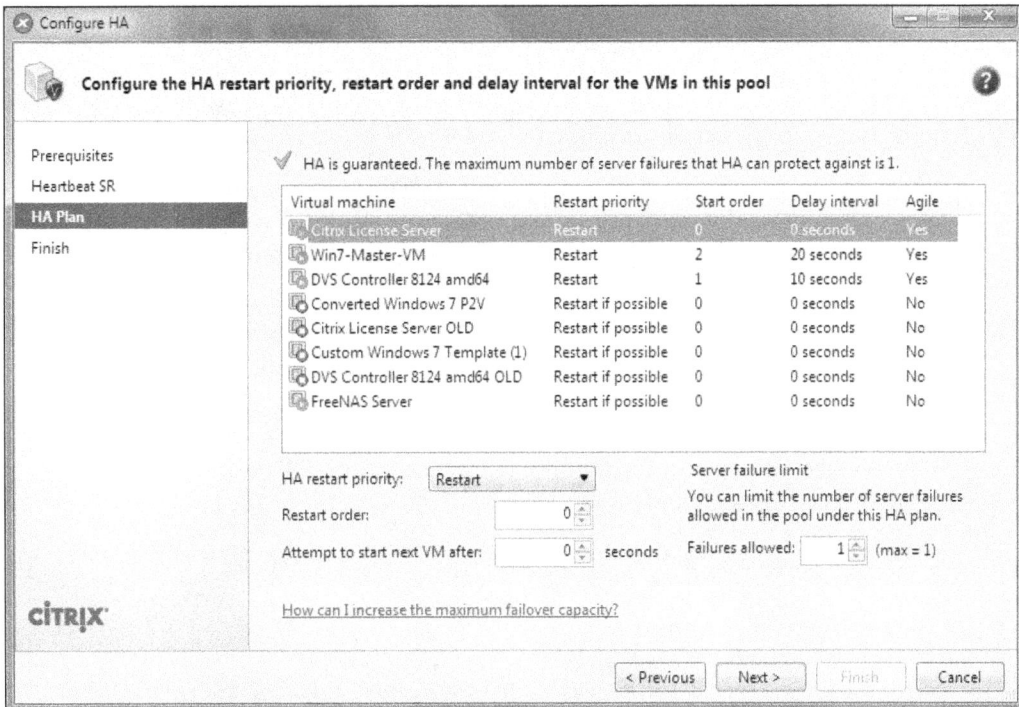

Note that XenServer will try to restart all the agile VMs with a priority of 0 and a delay interval of 0 seconds by default.

In our example, we have set a priority of 1 for the virtual machine DVS Controller 8124 amd64 and a priority of 2 for the virtual machine Win7-Master-VM. Also, we have set a delay interval for these machines of 10 and 20 seconds respectively.

7. On the **Configure HA** page, under **Server failure limit**, you can set the number of server failures to allow within the HA plan. This value should be less than or equal to the maximum failure capacity for the pool, shown in the following screenshot as max:

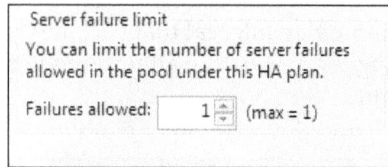

```
Server failure limit

You can limit the number of server failures
allowed in the pool under this HA plan.

Failures allowed:    1 ⬍  (max = 1)
```

In our example, we have set the max equal to 1 because if the pool is based on two XenServer hosts then only one XenServer host has available resources in case of failure of the other host.

If max is zero, the pool will not have available resources and consequently you will not be able to continue with the configuration without either adjusting the HA restart priorities or making more resources available within the pool.

Also, if you try to set a value higher than max, you receive a warning informing you that High Availability cannot be guaranteed.

8. After you have set your desired HA configuration, click on **Next**.

9 The wizard shows you the configuration summary. Click on **Finish** to finalize the process.

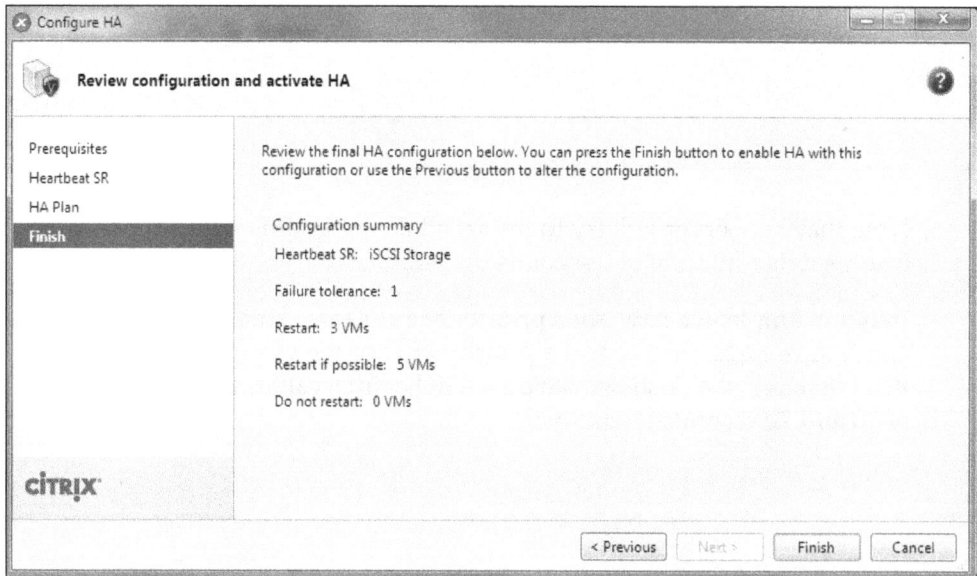

```
Configure HA                                                          _ □ X

  Review configuration and activate HA                                    ?

  Prerequisites         Review the final HA configuration below. You can press the Finish button to enable HA with this
  Heartbeat SR          configuration or use the Previous button to alter the configuration.
  HA Plan
  Finish                  Configuration summary

                          Heartbeat SR:  iSCSI Storage

                          Failure tolerance:  1

                          Restart:  3 VMs

                          Restart if possible:  5 VMs

                          Do not restart:  0 VMs

  CITRIX

                                      < Previous    Next >    Finish    Cancel
```

10. XenServer will enable the HA feature on your pool. On the **HA** tab of XenCenter you can review the actual applied settings and the heartbeating status for network and storage. Also, from here you can modify the HA configuration using **Configure HA...** or disable it using **Disable HA...**, as shown in the following screenshot:

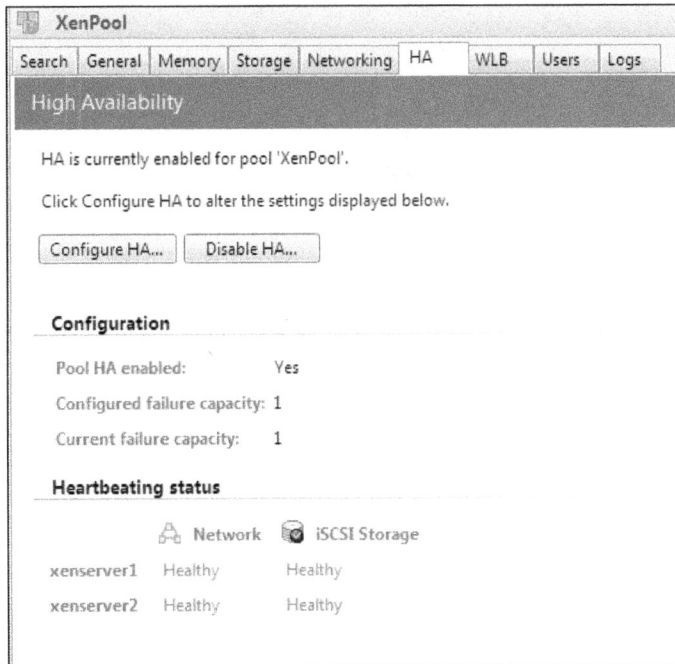

Remember that you can modify the settings for a particular virtual machine from the **Start Options** available on the VM's **Properties** page:

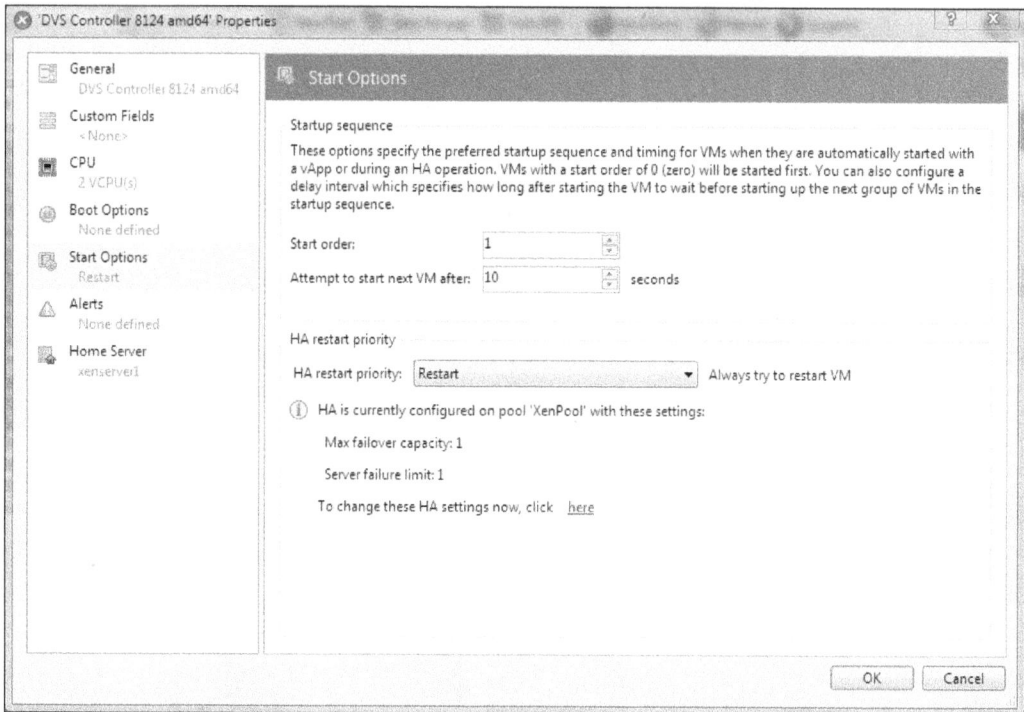

We have discovered how to enable the HA feature using XenCenter. Now, it is time to learn how to do this using the xe CLI.

To enable HA using the xe command line, follow the given procedure:

1. From XenCenter, select the pool master and click on the **Console** tab.

2. First, for each VM you wish to protect, we have to set a restart priority. We can do this with the command xe vm-param-set:

   ```
   xe vm-param-set uuid=<vm-uuid> ha-restart-priority=restart
   order=<priority-number> ha-always-run=true
   ```

   where:

   ◦ The uuid parameter is the unique identifier for the virtual machine we want to protect.

   ◦ The ha-restart-priorty=restart order parameter is the priority we want to set for the virtual machine. This value can be 0 , 1 , 2, or 3.

    °   The `ha-always-run` parameter instructs XenServer to always restart (`true`) or not (`false`) the virtual machine on another host in case of the failure of the host it is resident on.

In this example, we will configure XenServer to always restart the virtual machine `Citrix License Server` with a priority of 1.

3.   First, we have to identify the UUID associated with the virtual machine Citrx License Server. We will use `xe` command `vm-list` to find it. Execute the command `xe vm-list` to retrieve it or select the VM on XenCenter and click on the **General** tab. The UUID value will be displayed.

    So, in order to identify the UUID of `Citrix License Server`, we will execute the following command:

```
xe vm-list name-label=Citrix\ License\ Server
```

    XenServer will return the value `4fbde613-baf9-c103-e159-33109f704a2c`.

4.   Now, we configure the priority for this VM with the command:

```
xe vm-param-set uuid=4fbde613-baf9-c103-e159-33109f704a2c ha-
restart-priority=restart order=1 ha-always-run=true
```

5.   After this, we have to enable High Availability on the pool. To do this, we will execute the following command:

```
xe pool-ha-enable heartbeat-sr-uuids=<sr-uuid>
```

    where the `heartbeat-sr-uuids` parameter is the unique identifier of the central storage heartbeat repository you want to use.

6.   But how will we find the storage repository unique identifier? We use the command `xe sr-list`! Otherwise, select the SR on XenCenter, click on the **General** tab and take note of the UUID value.

```
xe sr-list name-label=<sr-name-label>
```

    where the `name-label` parameter is the name of the storage repository you want to use for the hearbeat.

In our example, we will use the `iSCSI Storage` and execute the following command:

```
xe sr-list name-label=iSCSI\ Storage
```

Note the UUID value. We have the SR unique identifier!

7. To enable the HA in our pool, we execute the following command:

```
xe pool-ha-enable heartbeat-sr-uuids=be333832-7956-1502-44f1-
c59a70b9b8be
```

> XenServer will take a few minutes to activate HA.

8. We have enabled the HA feature. Now, we have to set the maximum number of tolerated failures. This value is the maximum number of hosts that can fail in the pool before there are no available resources to run all the protected VMs in the pool. In order to do this, first we have to discover what is this value.

9. To accomplish this task, we execute the following command:

```
xe pool-ha-compute-max-host-failures-to-tolerate
```

In our example, the number of tolerated failures equals to 1.

10. Now we can specify the number of failed hosts to tolerate which should be less than or equal to the computed value. We will use the following command:

```
xe pool-param-set ha-host-failures-to-tolerate=<host-number>
uuid=<pool-uuid>
```

where:

- ° The `ha-host-failures-to-tolerate` parameter is the number of host failures to tolerate before sending a system alert

- ° The `uuid` parameter is the pool unique identifier of your XenServer pool

11. In order to find the pool UUID, execute the following command:

```
xe pool-list
```

In our example, the UUID of the pool *XenPool* is `8eaa281f-c7ae-20d3-f37d-00e8596e4bc4`.

12. Now, we have all the information needed to set the number of failed hosts to tolerate and we can execute the following command:

```
xe pool-param-set ha-host-failures-to-tolerate=1 uuid=8eaa281f-
c7ae-20d3-f37d-00e8596e4bc4
```

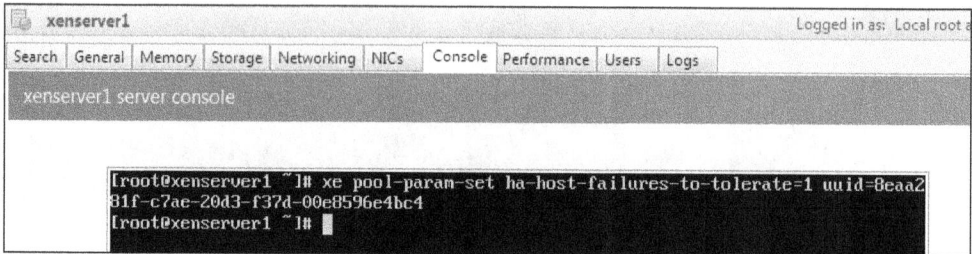

Managing host and virtual machines with High Availability

When you have enabled High Availability in your XenServer pool, you have to take special care when shutting down or rebooting a virtual machine or host.

This is in order to prevent the HA mechanism from assuming that a host has failed.

Shutting down or rebooting a host with HA enabled

To shut down or reboot a host cleanly in an HA-enabled environment, you must first disable the host, then evacuate the host, and finally perform the shutdown or reboot task.

The term *evacuate* refers to the migration of all the running virtual machines to another host using the XenMotion feature.

Using XenCenter, XenServer performs the required steps automatically but also displays a warning about the potential impossibility needed High Availability for the pool, as shown in the following screenshot:

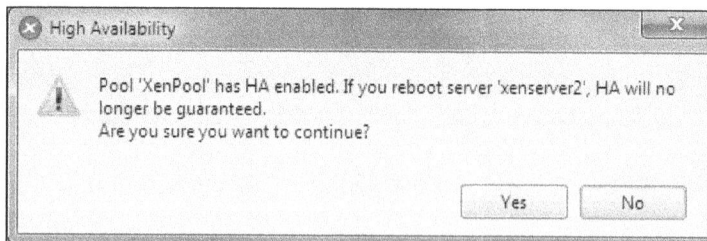

If you are using the xe CLI to shut down or reboot a host, you have to follow this procedure:

1. From XenCenter, select the pool master and click on the **Console** tab.

2. First, disable the specified XenServer host you must shut down or reboot in order to prevent any new VMs from starting on it using the command:

```
xe host-disable host=<host_name>
```

In our example, in order to disable the host xenserver2, we will execute the command:

```
xe host-disable host=xenserver2
```

This command will put your host in maintenance mode. Remember that you cannot put a host in maintenance mode when this operation invalidates VM failover planning and XenServer is unable to guarantee protected VMs restarting after a host failure.

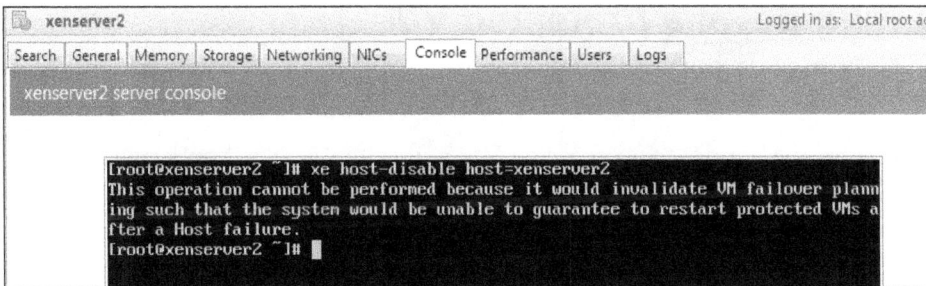

If you are in this condition, decrease the server failure limit in the HA configuration.

> If for some reason a host cannot access the HA state file, it is possible that a host may become unreachable. To recover your XenServer installation it may be necessary to disable HA using the host-emergency-ha-disable command:
>
> ```
> xe host-emergency-ha-disable --force
> ```

3. After you have disabled your host, you have to migrate all running VMs to other suitable hosts on the pool using the command:

```
xe host-evacuate uuid=<host-uuid>
```

where the uuid parameter is the unique identifier of the host you want to shut down or reboot.

In our example, we want to evacuate the host `xenserver2` so we will execute the following command:

```
xe host-evacuate uuid=8791cc9e-e1e0-43f0-9104-d608bb033b9b
```

where `8791cc9e-e1e0-43f0-9104-d608bb033b9b` is the UUID associated with `xenserver2` host.

4. Finally, you can perform power-off or restart your host using the following command:

```
xe host-shutdown host=<host-name> or xe host-reboot host=<host-name>
```

In our example, if we want to reboot the host `xenserver2` we will execute the following command:

```
xe host-reboot host=xenserver2
```

Shutting down a protected VM

When HA is in place you cannot shut down a virtual machine while it is protected. To correctly shut down a protected VM, first you have to disable its HA protection.

When you try to shut down a protected VM using XenCenter, XenServer automatically disables the HA protection but displays a warning dialog box asking you to confirm the shut down operation, as shown in the following screenshot:

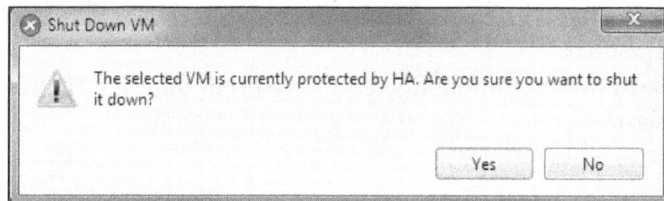

If you shut down a VM from within the guest and the VM is protected, it is automatically restarted; this ensures against a protected VM being left shut down accidentally.

Using the xe CLI, you have to disable the HA feature for the virtual machine by setting the `ha-always-run` parameter to `False` before you can shut down the virtual machine.

In order to do this, use the following command:

```
xe vm-param-set uuid=<vm-uuid> ha-always-run=false
```

where the `uuid` parameter is the unique identifier of the virtual machine you want to shut down.

For example, if we want to power off the `Citrix License Server` virtual machine, we will execute the following command:

```
xe vm-param-set uuid=4fbde613-baf9-c103-e159-33109f704a2c ha-always-run=true
```

Managing snapshots

Snapshots are a useful feature of XenServer, as they provide a "point in time" disk state.

For example, imagine that you want to test an update of an application installed on your virtual machine. Using snapshot, you have the chance to revert to the *pre-update* state if the newly installed update doesn't work as expected.

Also, snapshots provide a fast way for creating templates that can be exported for backup purposes and can be used to quickly create new virtual machines.

When you create a snapshot, the result is a virtual machine very similar to a template. The VM snapshot contains all the VM configuration allowing you to export the snapshot and restore it if you need to.

You will play with snapshots many times! They give you a flexible *modus operandi* impossible to achieve when you have only physical servers.

In XenServer you can take three different types of VM snapshots:

- **Disk-only**: This type stores a VM's configuration information (metadata) and disks (storage) allowing them to be exported and restored for backup purposes. A disk-only snapshot can be created on all virtual machines, Windows and Linux based.

- **Quiesced**: This type takes advantage of the **Windows Volume Shadow Copy Service (VSS)** to generate application consistent point-in-time snapshots.

> XenServer supports quiesced snapshots on Windows Server 2003 and Windows Server 2008 for both 32-bit and 64-bit variants. Windows XP, Windows Vista, and Windows 7 are not supported.
>
> The service Microsoft Software Shadow Copy Provider must be enabled and running before taking a quiesced snapshot.

- **Disk and memory**: In addition to saving the disk state, this type of snapshot also saves the memory state (RAM) of a virtual machine. This can be useful if you are upgrading or patching software or want to test a new application and also want to have the option to revert to the previous state of the VM. Note that you can save the memory status only if the VM is running or suspended. Also, during the snapshotting creation process, the VM is paused for a brief period of time and for this reason cannot be used.

> Disk and memory snapshots are only available in XenServer Enterprise Edition or higher.

Working with snapshots

In the previous section, we have introduced the main concepts related to snapshots.

Now, it is time to discover how to manage them.

You can take a snapshot using XenCenter and the xe CLI.

Creating a snapshot

In the following example, we will see how to record the state of a Windows 7 machine before applying Service Pack 1.

If you prefer to use XenCenter, follow this procedure:

1. From XenCenter, select the virtual machine of which you want to create the snapshot and click on the **Snapshots** tab.

2. On the Virtual Machine **Snapshots** tab, click on the **Take Snapshot** button. If you have previously created snapshots, you will find them here in chronological order.

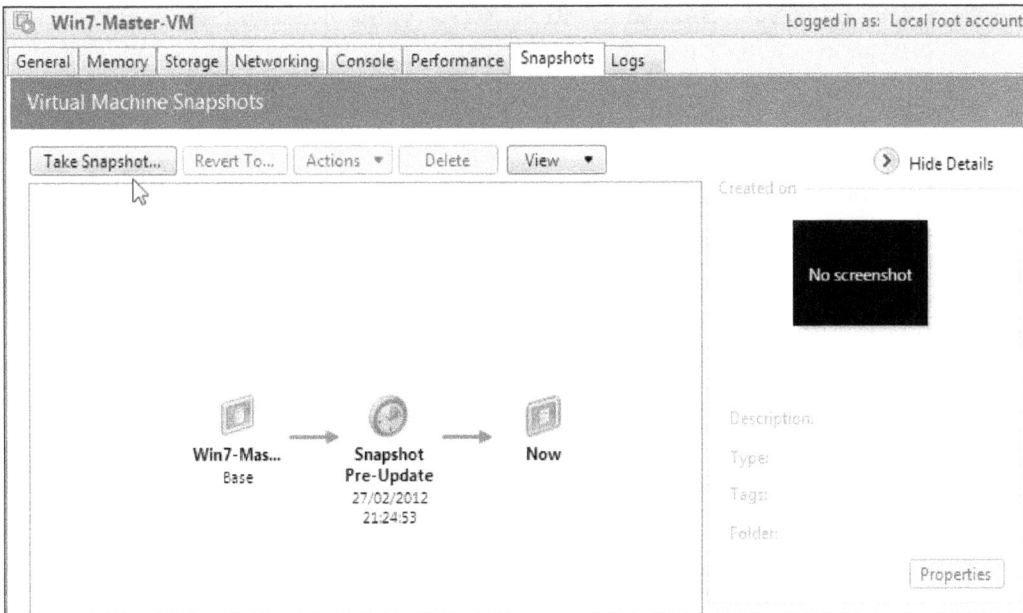

3. In the **Take Snapshot** window, type a meaningful name for the snapshot and also type a description. Also, select the type of the snapshot you want to take. In our example, we select **Snapshot the virtual machine's disks and memory**:

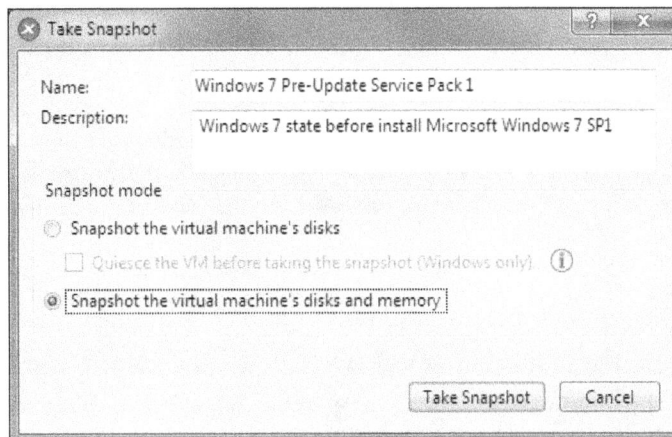

4. Click on the **Take Snapshot** button. XenServer will start the snapshotting process and will display the new snapshot in XenCenter when completed.

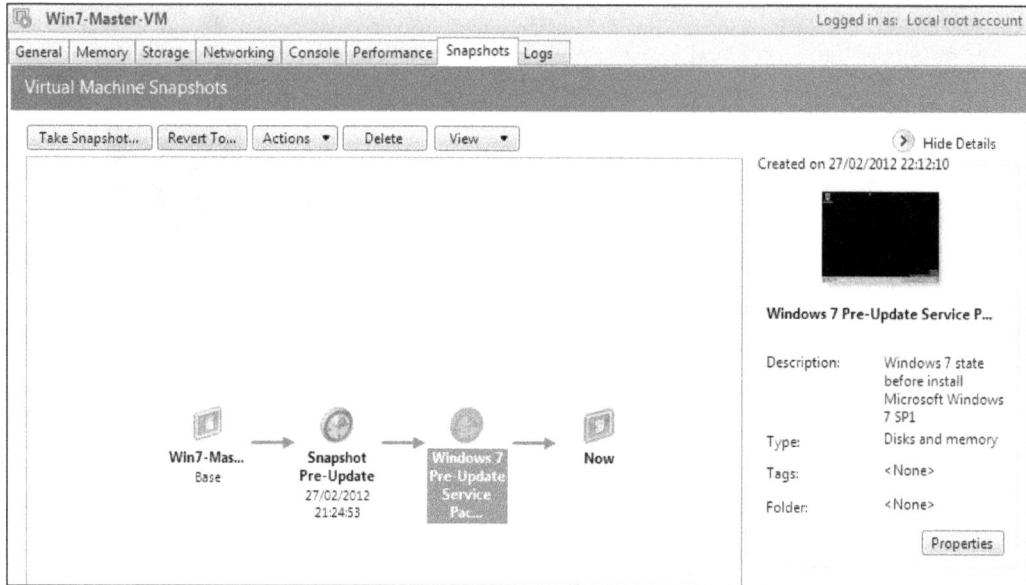

If you click on a snapshot, XenCenter shows you the **Details** pane on the right. Here you can find information associated with the snapshot.

5. Now you can install Microsoft Windows 7 Service Pack 1 and, in case of issues, you can revert to the previous state. We will learn how to revert to a snapshot later in the chapter.

In the previous example, we have discovered how to create a *disk and memory* snapshot. Now, we will learn how to create a *disk-only* snapshot using the xe CLI. In this example, we will operate with the virtual machine `Citrix License Server`.

To do this, follow this procedure:

1. From XenCenter, select the pool master and click on the **Console** tab.

2. To perform the snapshotting task, we will use the following command:

```
xe vm-snapshot vm=<vm-name> new-name-label=<snapshot-name>  new-
name-description=<snapshot-description>
```

where:

  ° The vm parameter is the name of the virtual machine of which you want to take a snapshot

- ° The `new-name-label` parameter is the name you want to assign to the snapshot

- ° The `new-name-description` parameter is the description you want to set for the snapshot

In our example, we execute the command:

```
xe vm-snapshot vm=Citrix\ License\ Server new-name-label=Backup\
Citrix\ License\ Server new-name-description=This\ snapshot\ is\
a\ backup
```

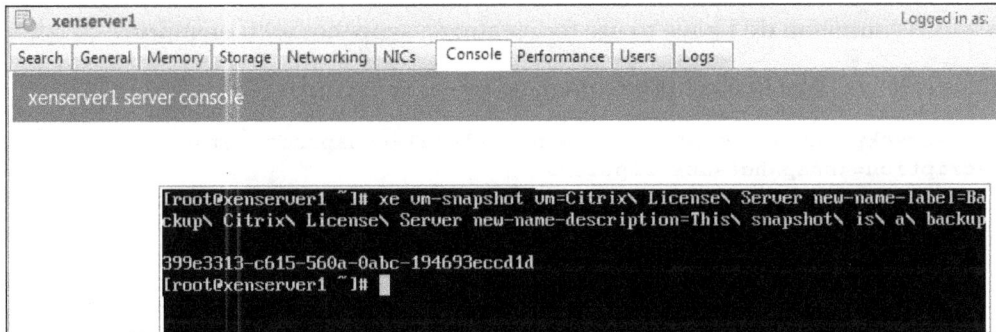

3. After the snapshot creation, XenServer returns the unique identifier of the snapshot. In our case it is `399e3313-c615-560a-0abc-194693eccd1`.

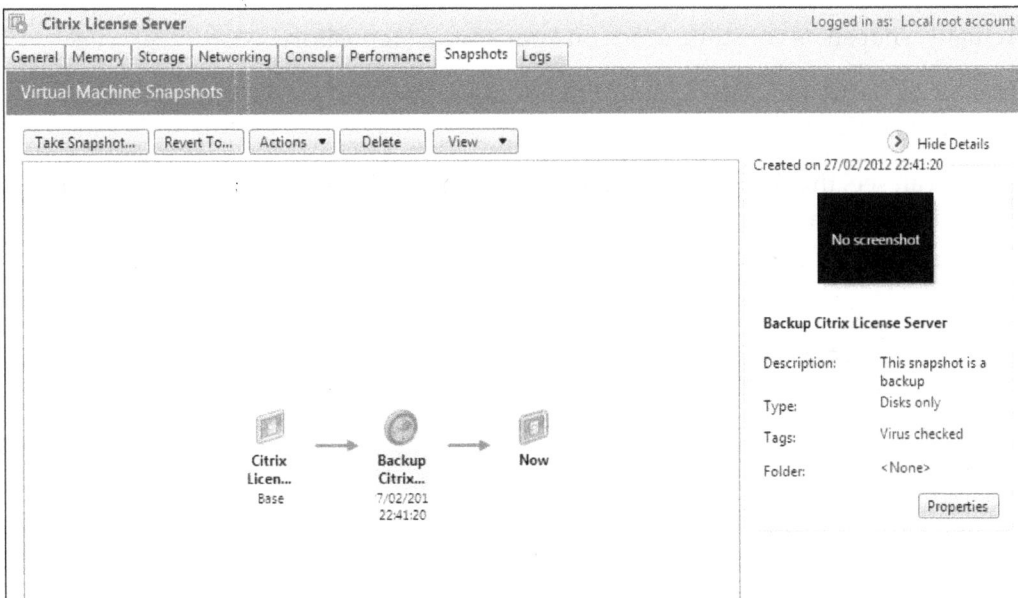

So, we have learned that if we want to create a *disk-only* snapshot we have to use the `xe` command `vm-snapshot`. Do we use the same command to create the other types? No!

If we want to create a *quiesced* snapshot, we have to use the `xe` command `vm-snapshot-with-quiesce`:

```
xe vm-snapshot-with-quiesce vm=<vm-name> new-name-label=<snapshot-name>
new-name-description=<snapshot-description>
```

As you can see, the syntax is very similar to the `xe vm-snapshot` command.

So which command do I have to use for creating a snapshot with memory?

In this case we have to use the xe command `vm-checkpoint`:

```
xe vm-checkpoint vm=<vm-name> new-name-label=<snapshot-name> new-name-description=<snapshot-description>
```

Again, the syntax is very similar to the previous command.

> You can also use the argument `uuid` instead of `vm` in order to select the virtual machine while taking the snapshot.

At this point, we have to focus our attention on an important aspect of taking a snapshot, the storage allocation.

Actually, snapshots consume space on your storage repository.

In order to clarify this, take a look at the storage allocation for the virtual machine `Win7-Snapshot-Test`.

As you can see, this VM has a 40 GB disk located on the local storage repository of the host `xenserver2`:

Also, because the disk is using thin provisioning, only 16 percent of the allocated space is really used:

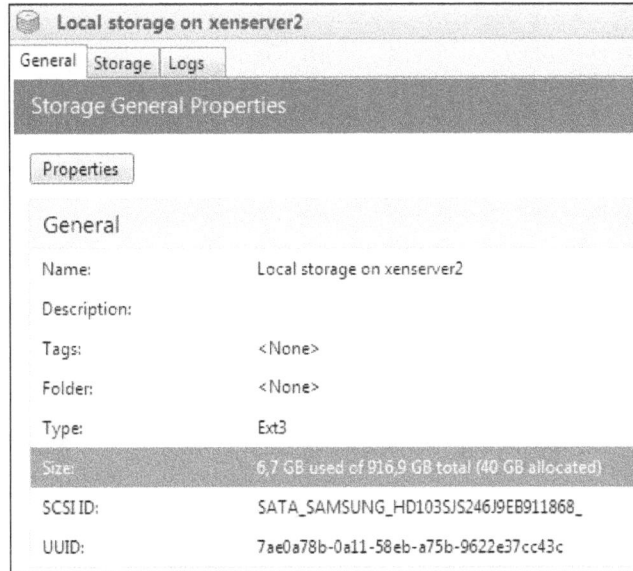

What happens when we take a snapshot? Let's go and discover this!

We take a snapshot of the virtual machine:

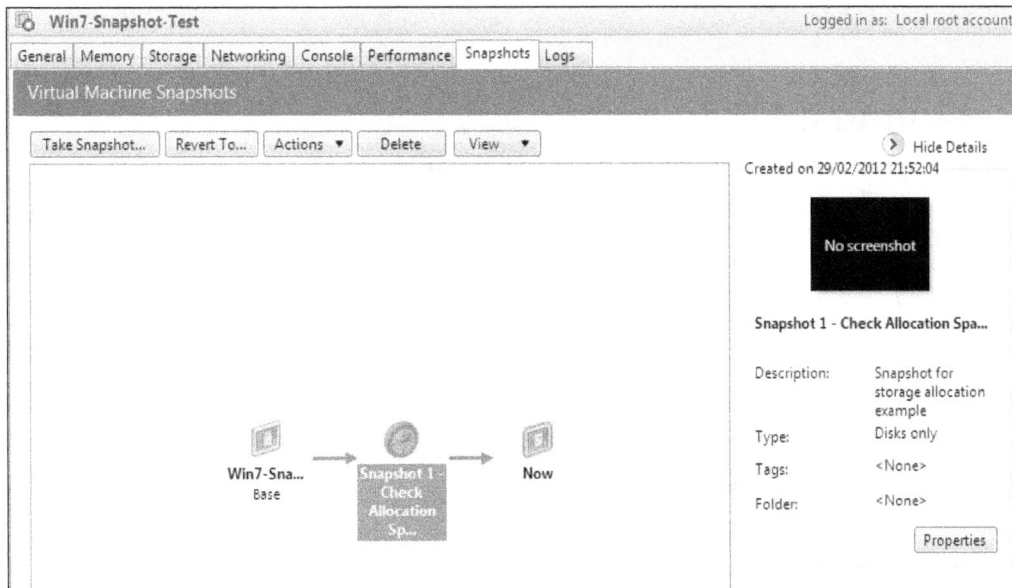

At this point, we check our storage repository: 80 GB is allocated by the virtual machine.

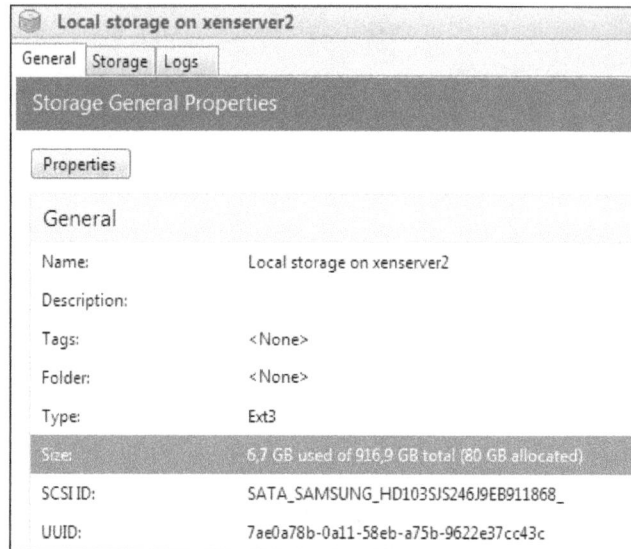

This is because the snapshotting process has created a second additional disk dedicated to the snapshot on the repository. From now on, XenServer will refer to this disk when it has to save all the subsequent writes for the virtual machine.

It is important to keep this in mind when you plan the amount of space for the storage repository.

Restoring a VM to a previous state

When you are working with virtual machines and snapshots, you may have the need to restore a virtual machine to a previous state. For example, you have unsuccessfully installed an application update and you need to restore the normal functionality of the virtual machine.

You can accomplish this task by reverting to a snapshot and this can be done using XenCenter or the xe CLI.

In order to do this in XenCenter, follow this procedure:

1. Select the virtual machine where you have to operate and click on the **Snapshot** tab. In this example, we select the VM **Win7-Master-VM**.

2. Select the snapshot you have previously created and click on the **Revert to...** button. You can also click with the right button of the mouse in order to open the context menu. In our example, we revert to the snapshot named **Windows 7 Pre-Update Service Pack 1**:

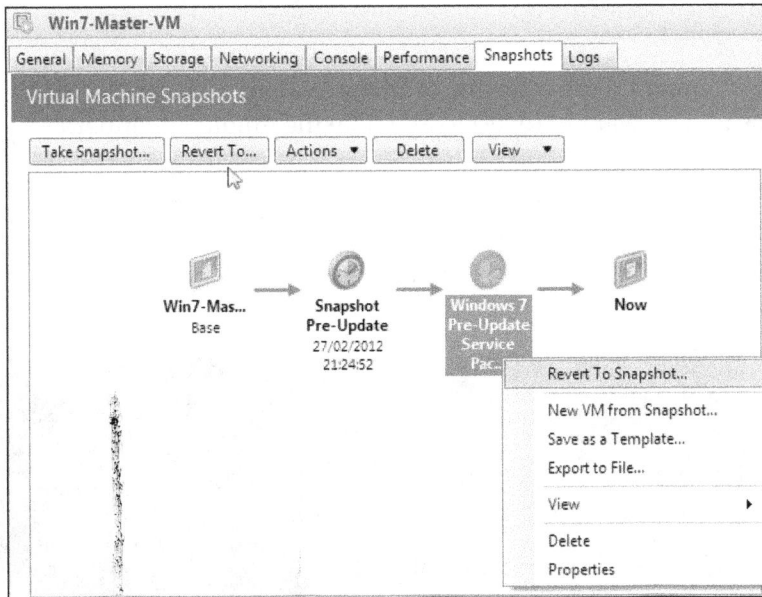

3. XenServer prompts you asking if you are sure you want to revert to the selected snapshot. Also, by default you have the possibility to take a snapshot of the virtual machine's current state before starting with the reverting process. In our example, we don't want to do this so we unselect this option:

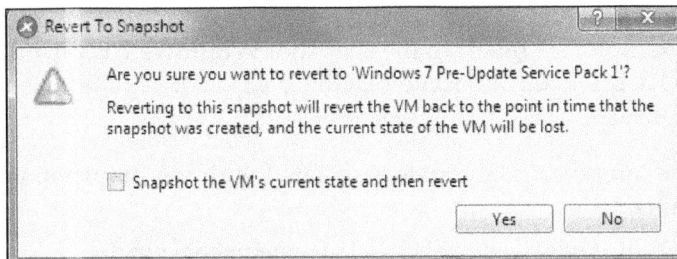

4. Click on **Yes** to start the reverting process. The virtual machine will revert to the point in time that the snapshot was taken. In our example, the Win7-Master-VM machine will return to the state without the Service Pack 1.

If you want to achieve the same result with the xe CLI, follow this procedure:

1. From XenCenter, select the pool master and click on the **Console** tab.

2. First, we have to find the unique identifier of the snapshot that we want to revert to. To do this, we use the following command:

   ```
   xe snapshot-list
   ```

   This command returns the list of all the available snapshots. Identify the snapshot you want to revert to and note the unique identifier:

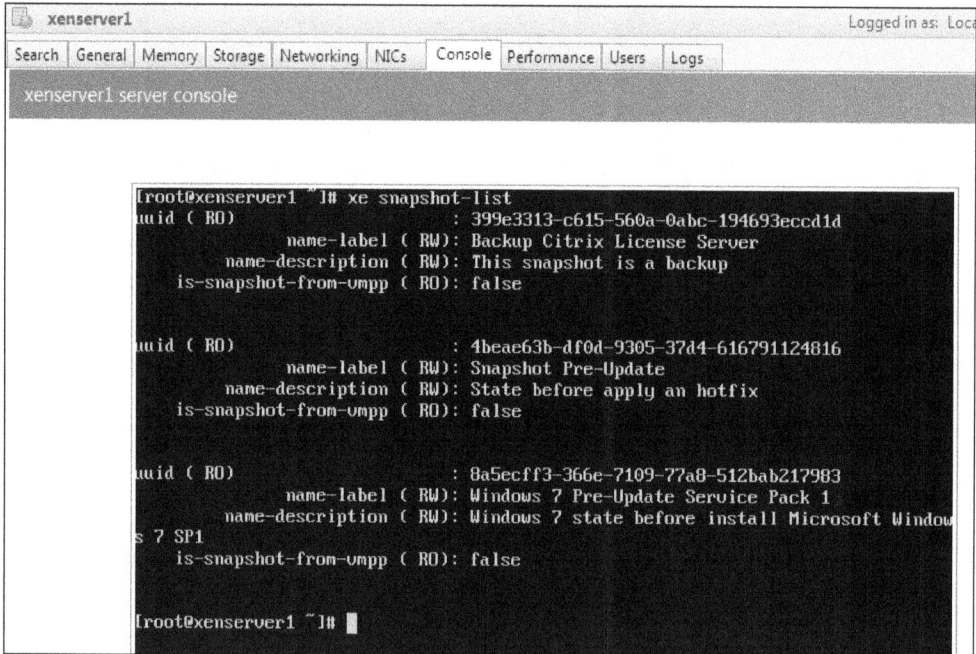

   In our example, we revert to the snapshot **Windows 7 Pre-Update Service Pack 1** so the associated UUID is `8a5ecff3-366e-7109-77a8-512bab217983`.

3. Now, we can revert to the state associated with the snapshot using the command:

   ```
   xe snapshot-revert snapshot-uuid=<snapshot-uuid>
   ```

   where the `snapshot-uuid` parameter is the UUID associated with the snapshot.

So in our example, we execute the following command:

```
xe snapshot-revert snapshot-uuid=8a5ecff3-366e-7109-77a8-
512bab217983
```

XenServer will revert to the selected snapshot and will suspend the virtual machine when the task is completed, so remember to resume it!

Deleting a snapshot

We have discovered how to create and revert snapshots in the previous sections. We have learned that snapshots can be useful when we want to test an update. Now, it is time to see how to delete a snapshot.

You can accomplish this task using XenCenter or the xe CLI.

In order to do this in XenCenter, follow this procedure:

1. Select the virtual machine from which you want to delete a snapshot and click on the **Snapshot** tab. In this example, we select the VM **Win7-Snapshot-Test**.

2. Select the snapshot you have previously created and click on the **Delete** button. You can also click with the right button of the mouse in order to open the context menu. In our example, we delete the snapshot named **Snapshot 1 - Check Allocation Space**.

3. XenServer asks you if you are sure you want to perform this action. Remember that this is a one-way operation. Click on **Yes** to delete the snapshot.

If you want to achieve the same result with the xe CLI, follow this procedure:

1. From XenCenter, select the pool master and click on the **Console** tab.

2. As we have seen for reverting a snapshot, we have to find the unique identifier of the snapshot that we want to delete. To do this, we use the command:

   ```
   xe snapshot-list
   ```

   The command returns the list of all the available snapshots. Identify the snapshot you want to delete and note the unique identifier.

In our example, we want to delete the snapshot **Snapshot 1 - Check Allocation Space** so the associated UUID is `126ccfcb-3e3b-dd38-4c0c-c198d5562854`:

```
 xenserver1                                                          Logged in as: Local r

 Search  General  Memory  Storage  Networking  NICs  Console  Performance  Users  Logs

 xenserver1 server console



      [root@xenserver1 ~]# xe snapshot-list
      uuid ( RO)                    : 126ccfcb-3e3b-dd38-4c0c-c198d5562854
                  name-label ( RW): Snapshot 1 - Check Allocation Space
            name-description ( RW): Snapshot for storage allocation example
          is-snapshot-from-vmpp ( RO): false


      uuid ( RO)                    : 4beae63b-df0d-9305-37d4-616791124816
                  name-label ( RW): Snapshot Pre-Update
            name-description ( RW): State before apply an hotfix
          is-snapshot-from-vmpp ( RO): false


      [root@xenserver1 ~]#
```

3. Now, we can delete the snapshot using the command:

   ```
   xe snapshot-uninstall snapshot-uuid=<snapshot-uuid>
   ```

   where the `snapshot-uuid` parameter is the UUID associated with the snapshot.

   So in our example, we execute the command:

   ```
   xe snapshot-uninstall snapshot-uuid=126ccfcb-3e3b-dd38-4c0c-c198d5562854
   ```

4. This command alerts you that this deletes a VM (remember that a snapshot is similar to a virtual machine) and virtual disk images (VDIs) associated with the snapshot. Type `yes` to confirm or press *Enter* to abort the deletion process.

```
 xenserver1                                                          Logged in as: Local r

 Search  General  Memory  Storage  Networking  NICs  Console  Performance  Users  Logs

 xenserver1 server console



      [root@xenserver1 ~]# xe snapshot-uninstall snapshot-uuid=126ccfcb-3e3b-dd38-4c0c
      -c198d5562854
      The following items are about to be destroyed
      VM : 126ccfcb-3e3b-dd38-4c0c-c198d5562854 (Snapshot 1 - Check Allocation Space)
      VDI: 1e8261bd-c343-4bef-9d72-0ae20898af82 (Win7-Snapshot-Test Disk0)
      Type 'yes' to continue
      yes
      All objects destroyed
      [root@xenserver1 ~]#
```

5. XenServer will delete the snapshot and inform you that all the associated objects have been destroyed.

What happens to the storage allocation?

When snapshots are deleted XenServer automatically reclaims the disk space by freeing unused data. This process is known as **coalescing**.

In some cases, some disk space might remain allocated. To address this, you can use the **Off-line Coalesce** tool. This tool can reclaim all disk space previously allocated to the deleted snapshots.

To execute this tool, follow this procedure:

1. From XenCenter, select the pool master and click on the **Console** tab.
2. Find the UUID of the virtual machine where you need to reclaim disk space and UUID of the host where the virtual machine is located. Use the `xe` commands `host-list` and `vm-list` respectively to retrieve this information.
3. To reclaim the disk space, execute the following command:

   ```
   xe host-call-plugin host-uuid=<host-uuid> plugin=coalesce-leaf
   fn=leaf-coalesce args:vm_uuid=<vm-uuid>
   ```

   where:
   - The `host-uuid` parameter is the unique identifier of the host
   - The `vm-uuid` parameter is the unique identifier of the virtual machine

   In our example, we execute the command for the virtual machine `Win7-Snapshot-Test`:

   ```
   xe host-call-plugin host-uuid=8791cc9e-e1e0-43f0-9104-d608bb033b9b
   plugin=coalesce-leaf fn=leaf-coalesce args:vm_uuid=2016aaf6-0380-
   5329-97b7-b8daf933bbe2
   ```

In this case, the tool informs us that the virtual machine has no unused space to reclaim (`leaf-coalesceable VDIs`).

> Before executing the offline coalesce tool, shutdown or suspend the VM manually.
>
> If the Virtual Disk Images (VDIs) to be coalesced are on shared storage, you must execute the offline coalesce tool on the pool master.
>
> If the VDIs to be coalesced are on local storage, you must execute the offline coalesce tool on the server to which the local storage is attached.

Creating a template from a snapshot

With snapshots, you can also create a virtual machine's template. Furthermore, you can export a complete copy of the virtual machine starting from an existing snapshot and store it as a single .xva package on your local machine or network share.

This approach is useful as a backup solution for your VMs. An exported VM can be used to recover an entire VM in the event of disaster. Also, you use the snapshot template as a simple way of copying a VM or moving a VM to another server in a different XenServer pool.

> When you create a template from a snapshot, remember that the virtual machine's memory state will be removed.

You can create a template from a snapshot using XenCenter following this procedure:

1. Select the virtual machine from which you want to create a template and click on the **Snapshots** tab. In this example, we select the VM **Win7-Snapshot-Test**.

2. Select the snapshot from which you want to create the template or create a new snapshot. In our example, we have created a snapshot named **Snapshot for Template**.

3. Click on the **Actions** button or right-click on the snapshot and select **Save as a Template...**:

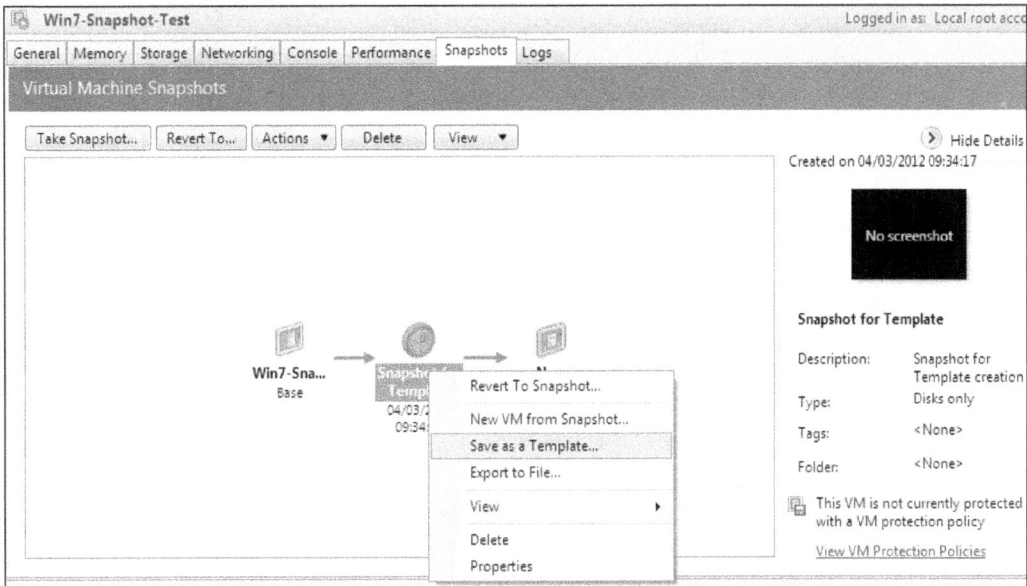

4. Type a meaningful description for the template you want to create and click on the **Create** button:

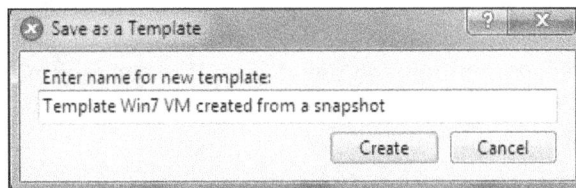

5. XenServer will create the template and display it in XenCenter:

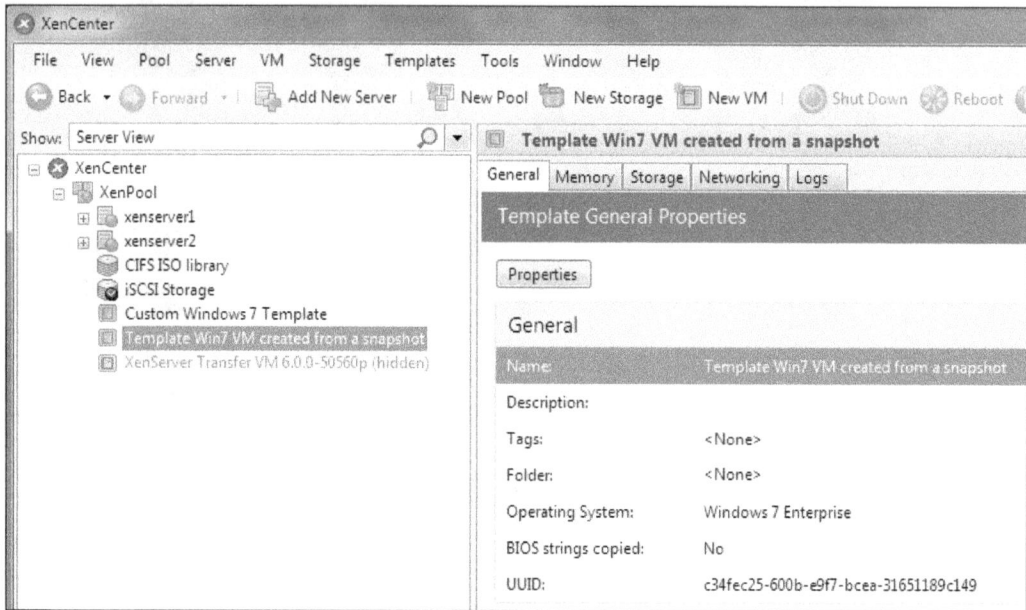

You can also use the xe CLI to create the template.

To do this, follow this procedure:

1. From XenCenter, select the pool master and click on the **Console** tab.

2. As we have seen previously in the chapter, we have to find the unique identifier of the snapshot from which we have to create the template. To do this, we use the command:

   ```
   xe snapshot-list
   ```

   This command returns the list of all the available snapshots. Identify the snapshot and note the unique identifier.

   In our example, the snapshot **Snapshot for Template** has the associated UUID `40635e09-367e-e605-592f-1677255f4b8a`.

3. In order to create the template, we use the xe command `snapshot-copy`:

   ```
   xe snapshot-copy new-name-label=<vm-template-name> uuid=<uuid-snapshot>
   ```

where:

- ◦ The `new-name-label` parameter is the name of the new template
- ◦ The `uuid` parameter is the unique identifier of the snapshot

So in our example, we execute the following command:

```
xe snapshot-copy new-name-label=Template\ From\ Snapshot
uuid=40635e09-367e-e605-592f-1677255f4b8a
```

4. XenServer will create the new template in the XenServer pool and return the UUID associated with the template. You can verify that the template has been created by executing the `xe` command `template-list`:

```
xe template-list name-label=<template-name>
```

where the `name-label` parameter is the name of the template we have created in the previous step.

So in our example, we execute the following command:

```
xe template-list name-label=Template\ from\ Snapshot
```

Creating a virtual machine from a snapshot

We can create a virtual machine starting from an existing snapshot. You can do this using the **Actions** button or by right-clicking on the snapshot and selecting **New VM from Snapshot…**:

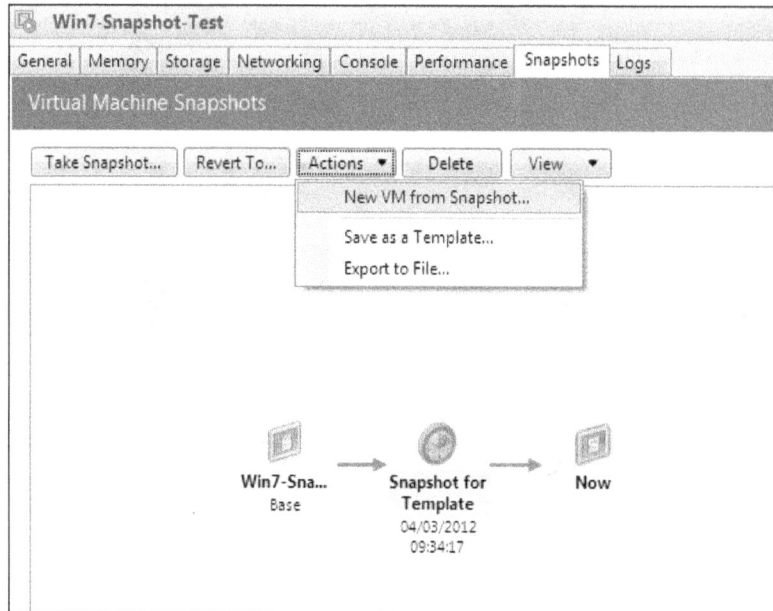

The **New VM** wizard will start and guide you through the creation process using the snapshot you have selected as the template:

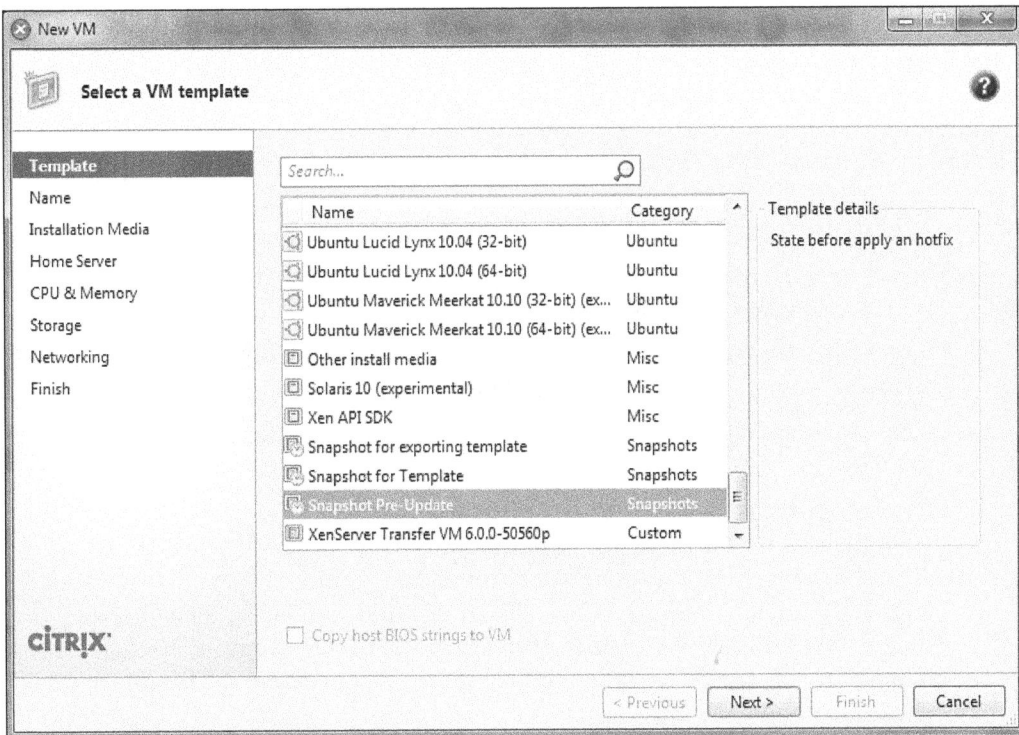

Creating a new VM from a snapshot works in exactly the same way as creating one from a regular VM template, refer to *Chapter 4, Creating Virtual Machines* for further detail.

Using snapshots is a useful manner in which to clone a virtual machine without powering off the virtual machine and an optimum solution in case you want to restore the accidentally deleted original VM you have used to create the snapshot.

Exporting a snapshot

We have learned how to create a template from a snapshot. Now, it is time to discover how to export the snapshot in a .XVA package.

You can do this task using XenCenter or the xe CLI.

Using XenCenter, follow this procedure:

1. Select the virtual machine and click on the **Snapshots** tab. In this example, we select the VM **Win7-Master-VM**.

2. Select the snapshot you want to export. In our example, we have selected the snapshot named **Snapshot Pre-Update**.

3. Click on the **Actions** button or right-click on the snapshot and select **Export to a File...**.

4. In the **Export to file** window, select the folder where you want to save the .XVA file and type a meaningful name for the file. Best practice is to use the virtual machine and the snapshot name as the naming convention in order to quickly identify the .XVA package. By default, XenServer also verifies the exported file on completion of the process. In our example, we use the name Win7-Master-VM-Exported-Snapshot-Pre-Update. Click on **Save** to continue:

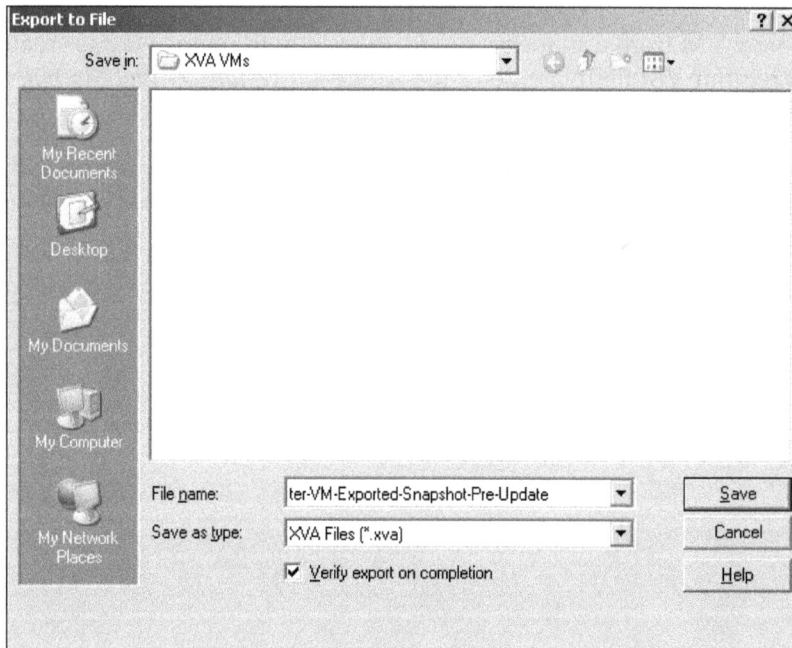

Note that XenServer shows you a warning if there is not enough disk space to complete the export operation. In this situation, select **Choose another destination** or **Cancel** to abort the export process.

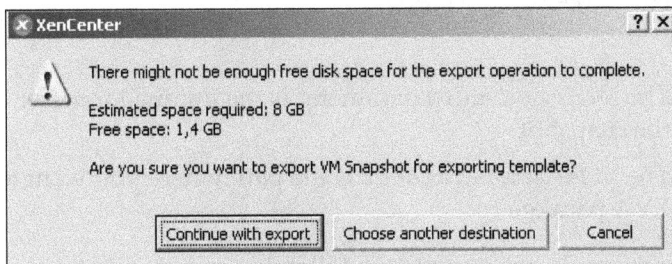

5. XenServer will create the exported XVA package and save it on the path you have specified. In our example, we have selected to save the file in the `F:\XVA VMs` folder.

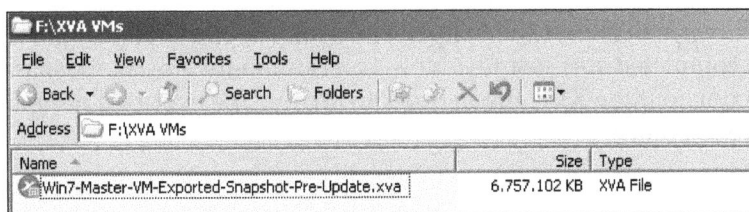

To export a snapshot to a template using the xe CLI, follow this procedure:

1. From XenCenter, select the pool master and click on the **Console** tab.

2. As we have seen previously in the chapter, we have to find the unique identifier of the snapshot from which we have to create the template using the `xe snapshot-list` command.

   In our example, the snapshot **Snapshot Pre-Update** has the associated UUID `4beae63b-df0d-9305-37d4-616791124816`.

3. Use the command `snapshot-export-to-template` to create a new template file:

```
xe snapshot-export-to-template snapshot-uuid=<snapshot-uuid>
filename=<template-filename>
```

where:

   ° The `snapshot-uuid` parameter is the unique identifier of the snapshot

   ° The `filename parameter` is the path where you want to store the XVA pacakge

So in our example, we execute the following command to export the snapshot in the `\home` folder of `xenserver2` host:

```
xe snapshot-export-to-template snapshot-uuid=4beae63b-df0d-9305-
37d4-616791124816 filename=/home/Win7-Master-VM-Exported-Snapshot-
Pre-Update.xva
```

4. XenServer will export the template and inform you that the operation has been completed successfully. Now you can mount a network shared folder and copy to it the XVA file in order to archive the exported template for future reference.

Summary

In this chapter, we have learned how to enable High Availability in a XenServer pool and how to use snapshots in order to record a previous state of a virtual machine.

Specifically we learned:

- Enabling High Availability
- Protecting virtual machines
- Creating and managing snapshots

Familiarize yourself with the concepts introduced in this chapter. They are very important in order to make your virtual machines always available, even in cases of server failure.

In the next chapter, we will introduce workload balancing, backup, and monitoring.

Protecting and Monitoring XenServer

9

In the previous chapter, we discussed XenServer High Availability and Snapshots.

Now we will discover how to protect your XenServer virtual environment and how to monitor XenServer using Workload Balancing.

At the end of this chapter you will be able to back up and monitor your virtual environment.

In this chapter, we will cover the following topics:

- Overview of backup and virtual machine protection
- Overview of Workload Balancing
- Configuring Workload Balancing
- Managing Workload Balancing
- Monitoring performances with Workload Balancing

Overview of backup and virtual machine protection

In the previous chapters, we have learned how to create our XenServer virtual infrastructure, how to deploy virtual machines, and how to manage them.

It is now important to understand how to protect the virtual environment you have configured.

To accomplish this task, you need to back up the XenServer pool database metadata and also each virtual machine.

Backing up your XenServer environment

In order to back up the core information about our virtual environment, we must back up the **pool database metadata**.

In a XenServer resource pool, as seen in *Chapter 1, Introducing XenServer Resource Pools*, the pool master stores a database of metadata containing information about virtual machines and pool resources such as Storage Repositories and networking configurations. In order to back up the pool database metadata, you need to execute the xe command `pool-dump-database` using the xe CLI.

To back up the database, follow the given procedure:

1. From XenCenter, select the pool master and click on the **Console** tab.

2. Execute the following xe command:

   ```
   xe pool-dump-database file-name=<backup-file-name.xbk>
   ```

   where the `file-name` parameter is the path where you want to save the backup and the filename of the backup file.

   In our example, we execute the following command to save the backup file `XenPool-Database-Metadata.xbk` into the path `/mnt/share`. The path `/mnt/share` is related to a Windows shared folder mounted in the XenServer host.

   ```
   xe pool-dump-database file-name=/mnt/share/XenPool-Database-
   Metadata.xbk
   ```

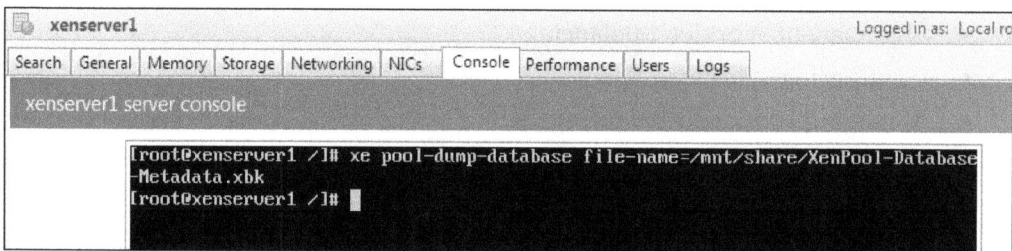

3. XenServer will back up the database metadata into the specified file.

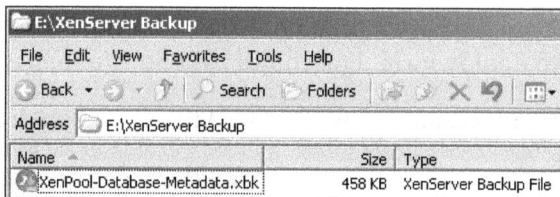

> Use the Linux command `mount -t cifs` to mount a network shared folder where you want to save the backup file.
>
> In our example, we have used:
>
> mount -t cifs //192.168.0.4/`XenServerBackup` /mnt/share -o domain=LAB -o user=Administrator.

In this section we have learned how to back up the pool database. In XenServer you can also back up the control domain files using XenCenter or xe CLI.

But note that this is not enough to restore your XenServer virtual environment completely because resources and virtual machines are not saved.

If you want to back up the XenServer files using XenCenter, follow the given procedure:

1. From XenCenter, select the XenServer host you want to backup.
2. Click on **Server | Back up....**

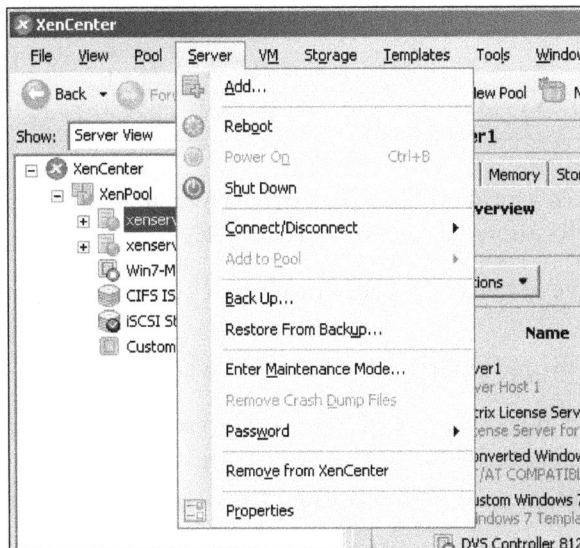

3. Browse to locate the folder where you want to create the backup file and enter a meaningful name for the file. Best practice is to use a name composed of the hostname and the date of the backup. In our example, we use the name **XenServer1-Backup-06032012**.

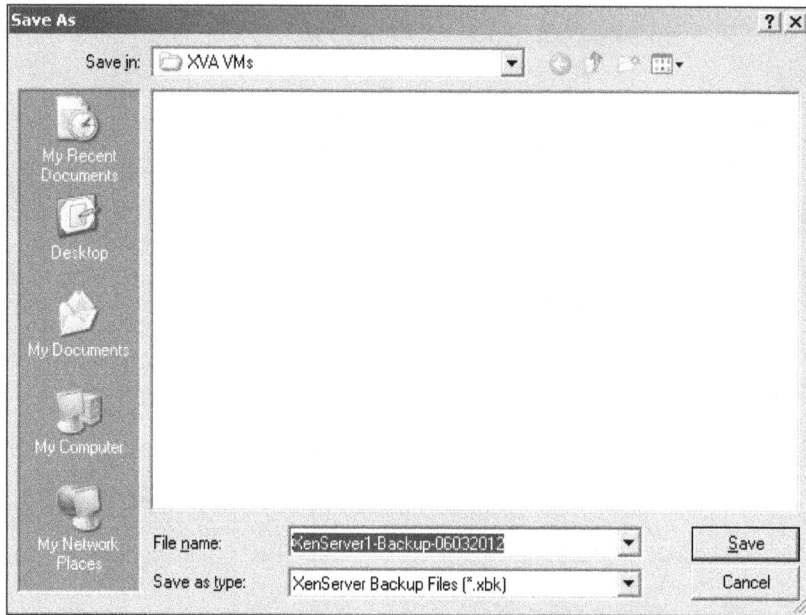

XenCenter uses local and network drives available on your management machine as locations to save the backup file.

4. Click on **Save** to begin the backup. The backup may take some time so be patient.

5. Repeat this procedure for every host you want to backup.

If you prefer to use the xe CLI, you have to use the `xe` command `host-backup` in order to back up your XenServer host:

```
xe host-backup host=<host-name> file-name=<backup-filename>
```

where the `host` parameter is the name of the XenServer host you want to backup and the `file-name` parameter is the path and filename where you want to save the backup.

In our example, to perform the backup of the `xenserver1` host in the path `\home`, we execute the following command:

```
xe host-backup host=xenserver1 file-name=\home\xenserver1-backup-
06032012-xecli.xbk
```

Restoring from failures

If a XenServer host fails, you need to perform recovery actions to restore its state and make it available again. These recovery actions are different based on the role of the failed XenServer host.

If the failed server is a member of the pool and this member could not be repaired, we have to instruct the pool master to forget the member node using the `xe` command `host-forget`:

```
xe host-forget uuid=<host-uuid>
```

where the `uuid` parameter is the unique identifier of the failed host.

For example, execute the following command to forget `xenserver2` host:

```
xe host-forget uuid=9d52c9f0-afad-4ae8-a621-e43296496f06
```

Also, note that XenServer does not update the power state of virtual machines that were running on the failed host: XenServer does this to avoid starting a virtual machine on two hosts at the same time. You can use the `xe` command `vm-reset-powerstate` to set the power state of the VMs to `halted`:

```
xe vm-reset-powerstate vm=<vm-name> --force
```

where the `vm` parameter is the name of the virtual machine for which you want to reset the power state.

For example, to reset the power state of the virtual machine `Win7-Master-VM` execute the following command:

```
xe vm-reset-powerstate vm=Win7-Master-VM -force
```

If the failed host is member of a pool where High Availability is enabled, we have to disable HA using the `xe` command `pool-ha-disable` before using the `xe` command `host-forget`.

Once the member has been forgotten and the VMs' power state has been reset, all the VMs which were running on the failed host can be restarted safely on other XenServer hosts.

> It is very important to ensure that the XenServer host is offline before attempting to start the VMs, otherwise VM data corruption might occur.

Once your virtual machines are running again, you can recover the failed host.

The best way to restore it is to reinstall XenServer software from the installation media and join the host to the XenServer pool again.

If the failed server is the pool master of the pool, another master is elected automatically only if High Availability is enabled, otherwise each member will wait for the master to became available again.

If you are not able to restore the previous pool master, you have to elect another host as pool master.

To do this, follow the given procedure:

1. From XenCenter, select the member server you want to elect as master and click on the **Console** tab.

2. Execute the following command to nominate the `pool master` server:

   ```
   xe pool-emergency-transition-to-master
   ```

3. Once the server has become the master, run the following `xe` command on each member server to point it to the new pool master:

   ```
   xe pool-recover-slaves
   ```

If you repair or replace the server that was the original master, you can simply bring it up, install XenServer, and add it to the pool as a member.

In the catastrophic event that your entire resource pool fails, your only solution is recreating your XenServer pool and later restore the pool database metadata from a previous backup.

To recreate the pool, follow the given procedure:

1. Install new hosts using XenServer installation media but do not join them in a pool.

2. On the host you want to designate as pool master, restore the pool database metadata from the backup using the following `xe` command:

   ```
   xe pool-restore-database file-name=<file-name>
   ```

   where the `file-name` parameter is the path and the filename of your previous backup.

In our example, we use the following command to restore the pool database using the backup file we have created at the beginning of the chapter:

```
xe pool-restore-database file-name=/mnt/share/XenPool-Database-
Metadata.xbk
```

3. Connect to the master host using XenCenter and ensure that all your shared storage and VMs are available again.

4. Join the remaining newly installed member hosts to the new pool and then start up your VMs on the appropriate hosts.

> If your virtual machines were located on local storage, you need to import them from a virtual machine backup.

Protection and recovery of virtual machines

After we have learned how to backup XenServer pool database metadata, we have to discover how to backup virtual machines.

To do this, we can use the **Virtual Machine Protection and Recovery** feature. It provides a simple backup and restore utility for our VMs.

> This feature is available in Citrix XenServer Advanced Edition or higher.

This feature consists of regular scheduled snapshots that are taken automatically according to pool-wide virtual machine protection policies and can be used to restore VMs in case of disaster. These snapshots can be archived to a remote network shared folder or to an NFS share.

Note also that the best approach is to install backup agents on virtual machines just as if they are standard physical servers in order to perform backups of data stored on a virtual machine.

Creating a VM protection policy

You can create a protection policy related to VM protection and recovery using the *New VM Protection Policy* wizard and then you can associate this policy to a virtual machine.

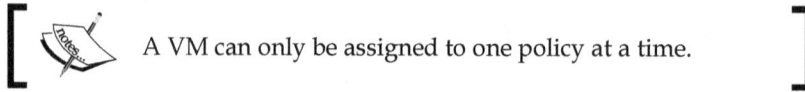

> A VM can only be assigned to one policy at a time.

In order to create a VM protection policy, follow the given procedure:

1. From XenCenter, select the XenServer pool where you want to create the VM protection policy.

2. Click on **Pool | VM Protection Policies...**.

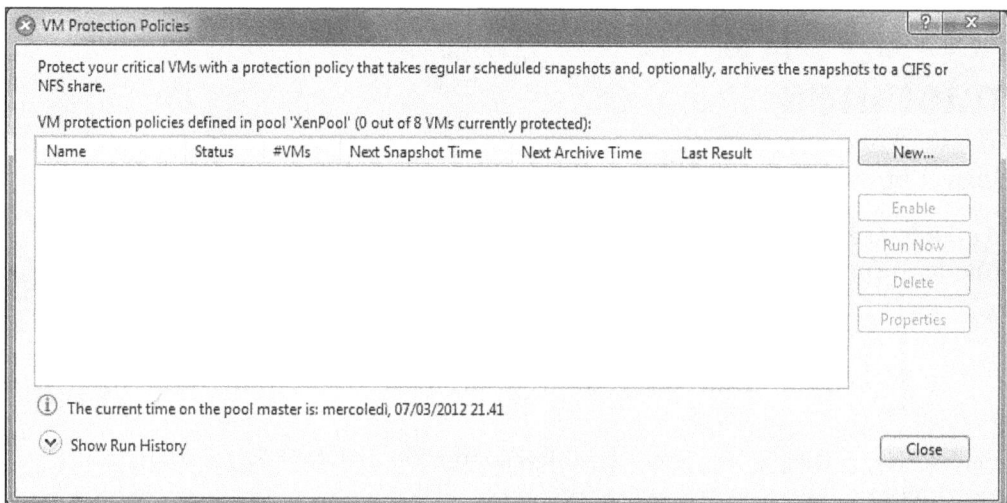

3. Click on **New** to start the VM Protection Policy creation wizard.

4. Enter a name and a description for the new policy and click on **Next**. As best practice, use a meaningful name and insert a description that can help you identify the scope of the policy you are creating. In our example, we create a policy to backup critical virtual machines every day.

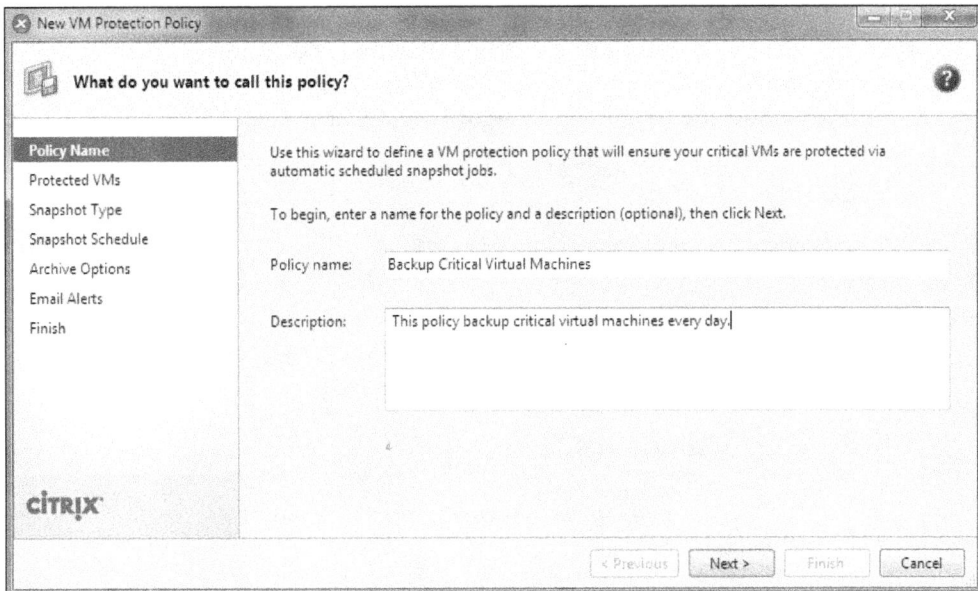

5. Select all the virtual machines you want to protect with this new policy and click on **Next**. In our example, we want to backup the **Citrix License Server** virtual machine daily.

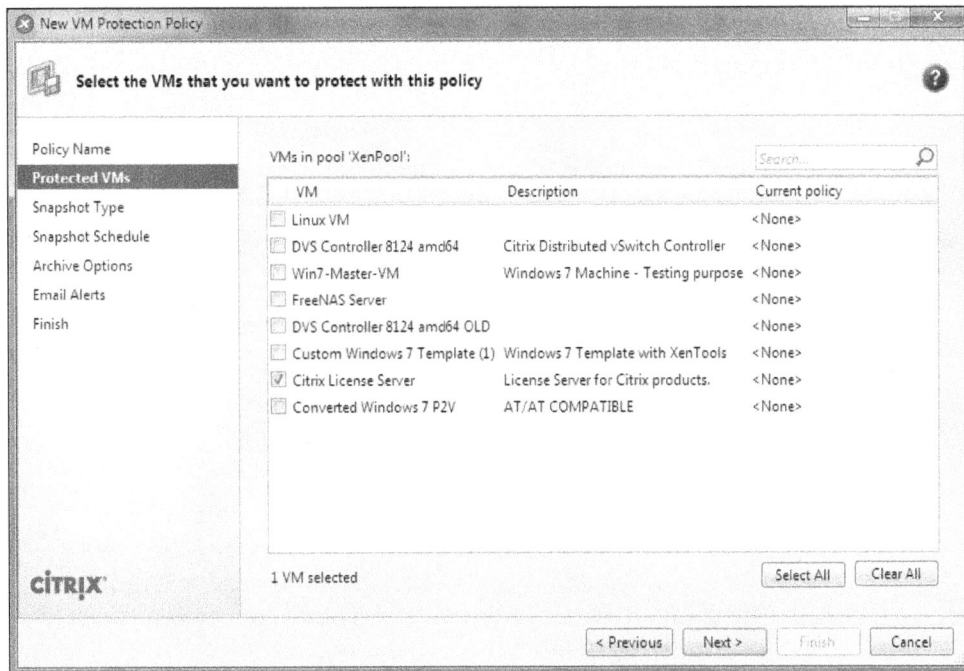

6. Select the snapshot type **Disk only snapshot** or **Disk and memory snapshot** that you want to use in this policy and click on **Next** (refer to *Chapter 8, Managing High Availability and Snapshots,* for details about each type). In our example, we decide to use the **Disk only** snapshot type.

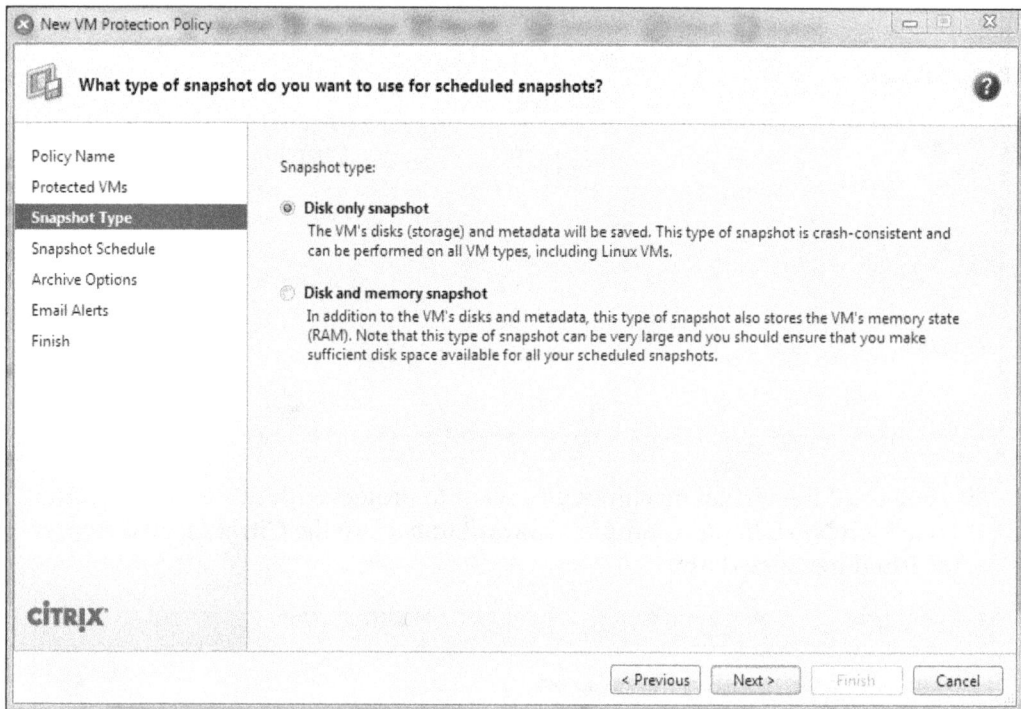

7. Define the snapshot schedule to use in this policy. You can set a hourly, daily, or weekly timeframe:

   ° Using **Hourly snapshots**, a snapshot of the specified VM or VMs will be taken each hour at the specified time.

   ° Using **Daily snapshots**, a snapshot of the specified VM or VMs will be taken each day at the specified time.

   ° Using **Weekly snapshots**, a snapshot of the specified VM or VMs will be taken at the specified time on the specified days of the week. You can select one or more days.

   ° Also specify the snapshot retention policy under **Number of snapshots to keep**—this value specifies how many scheduled snapshots you want to retain. When the number of scheduled snapshots taken exceeds this value, the oldest one will be deleted automatically. By default, this value is set to **7**.

In our example, we have set a daily schedule that occurs at 1 A.M. and we have left the maximum numbers of scheduled snapshots unchanged.

8. When you have configured the schedule and retention policy, click on **Next**.

9. Define an archive schedule for your policy in order to have your scheduled snapshots automatically archived to a remote CIFS or NFS share. You can define a daily or weekly archive schedule that is independent of the snapshot schedule or simply have every scheduled snapshot archived as soon as it is taken using the **Archive after every scheduled snapshot** option.

10. Also, set the archive folder path where XenServer will store the snapshots and the needed credentials to access the specified path. When you have completed the configuration click on **Next**.

In our example, we decide to archive the snapshots as soon as they are taken in the archive path \\192.168.0.4\XenServerBackup. This folder is located on a Windows 2003 machine.

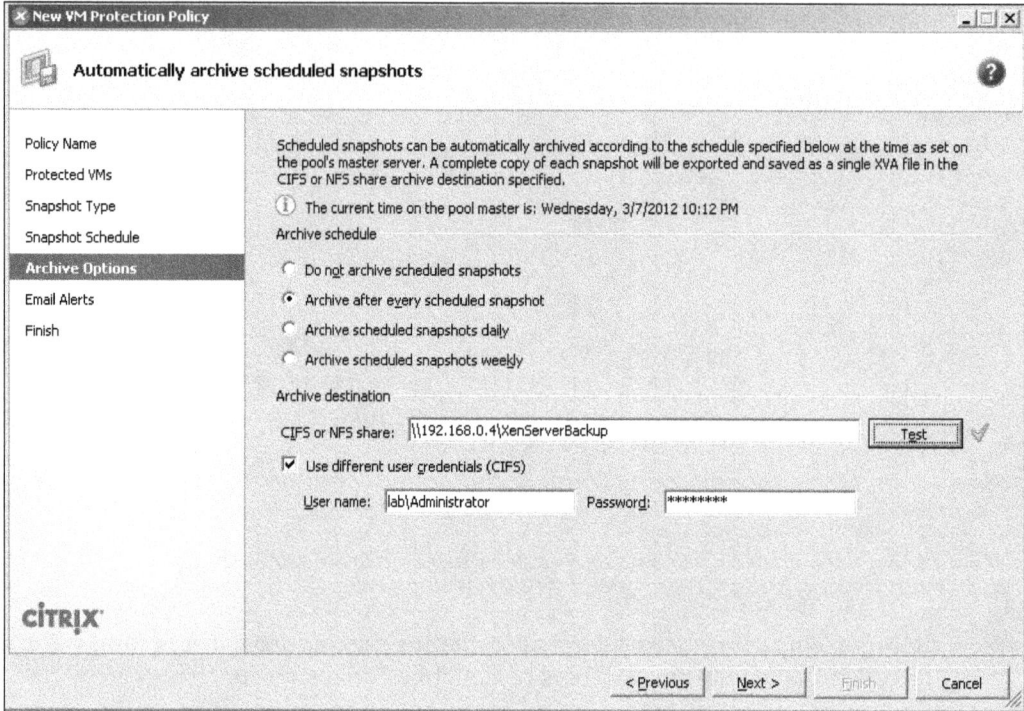

11. XenServer can send you an e-mail when system alerts are generated for any scheduled snapshot or archive operations. If you want to receive the notification, enable it and specify the e-mail address where you want to receive the notification and the mail server you want to use as **SMPT server**. After this, click on **Next** to continue.

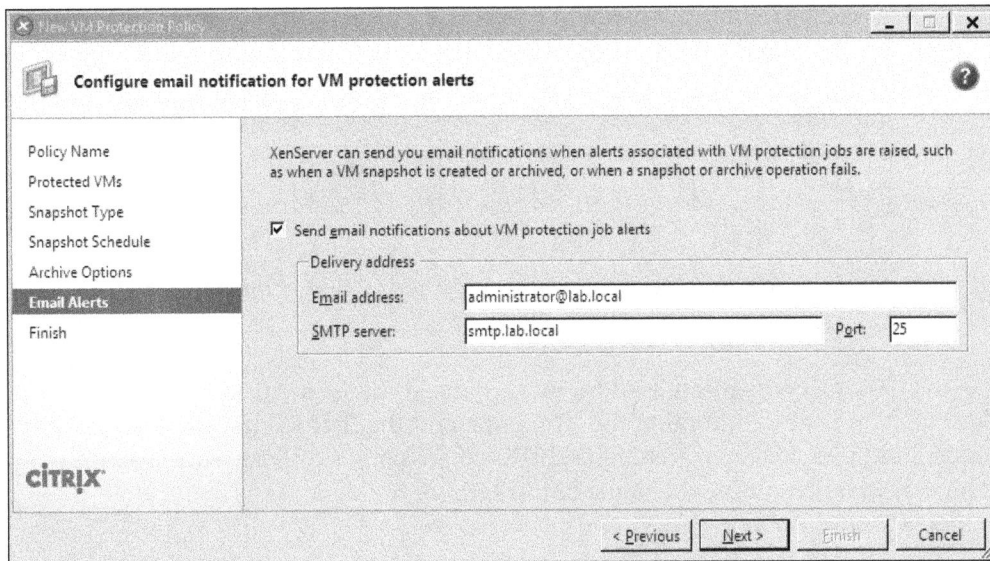

12. Review the configuration you have set and click on **Finish** to create the new policy. Note that you can instruct XenServer to run the job at the end of the creation process by clicking on **Run the new VM protection job when I click Finish** – this setting is disabled by default. In our example, we have set it to run the job at the end of the creation process.

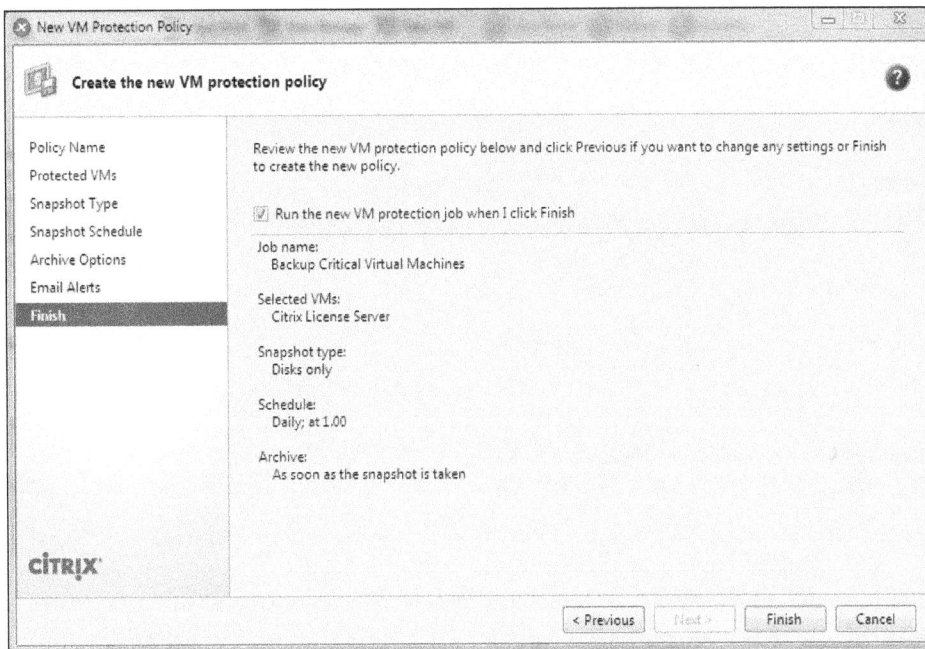

XenServer will execute the snapshot of the `Citrix_License_Server` virtual machine and will archive it on the path we have specified earlier:

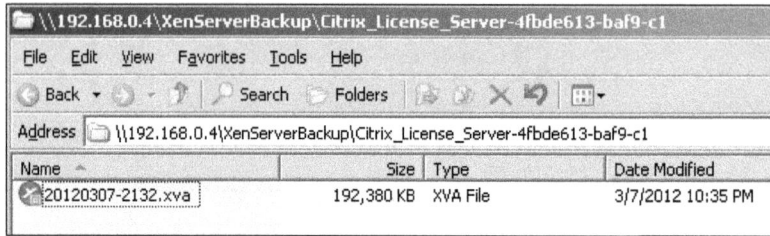

Note the naming convention used for storing the archived snapshot. The archive folder name is set by combining the VM name and the first 16 characters of the VM unique identifier. Thus the archived scheduled snapshots are named `YYYYMMDD-HHMM.xva`. In our example the name of the archive folder is `Citrix_License_Server-4fbde613-baf9-c1`.

`20120307-2132.xva` is the name of the snapshot related to Citrix License Server virtual machine that was created on **3/7/2012** at **10:35 PM**.

Managing VM protection policies

Once you have created your VM protection policies, you can access them for management using the **VM Protection Policies** page.

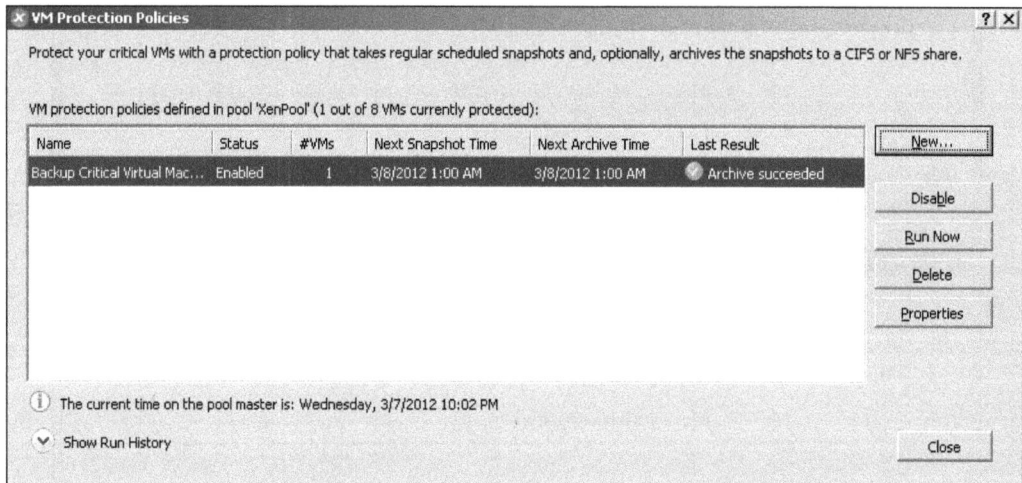

From here, you can enable, disable, or delete an existing policy. Also you can modify the settings for each policy you have deployed by clicking on the **Properties** button.

Furthermore, you can view details about historical events occurred for past jobs. To do this, click on **Show Run History**.

Assigning a VM to an existing VM protection policy

If you want to assign new virtual machines to an existing VM protection policy you can do this in a very simple manner by following the given procedure:

1. Select the virtual machine you want to protect with a VM protection policy.

2. Click on **VM | Assign to VM Protection Policy...**.

3. Select the VM protection policy you want to apply to the virtual machine.

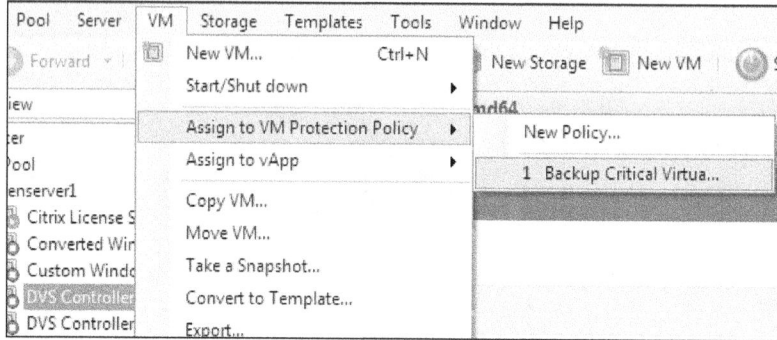

Recovering a virtual machine from snapshots

If you want to restore a virtual machine to a previous state for any reason, for example, because it is experiencing some issues, you can recover the VM from a scheduled snapshot or from an archived scheduled snapshot.

In the first case, you simply revert the VM to the specified snapshot.

To do this, follow the given procedure:

1. Select the virtual machine you want to revert to a previous state using a scheduled snapshot and click on the **Snapshots** tab.

2. Click on the **View** button and then on **Scheduled Snapshots** to show scheduled snapshots. By default, they are not shown on this tab.

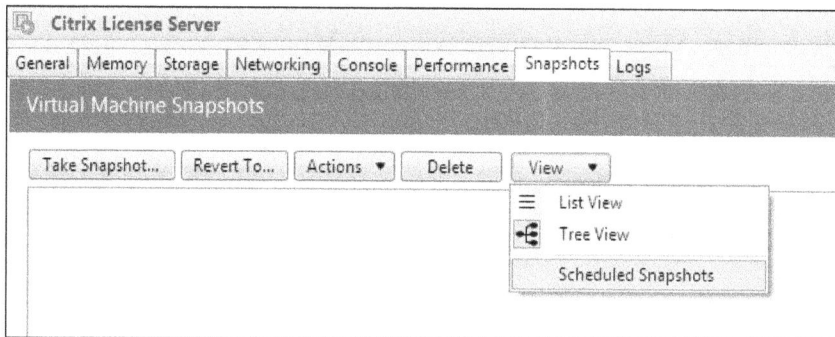

3. Select the scheduled snapshot you want to revert the VM to and then click on **Revert To**. You have the possibility to take a new snapshot of the current state of VM before reverting it to the scheduled snapshot. In our example, we don't want to save the current state of the VM before reverting.

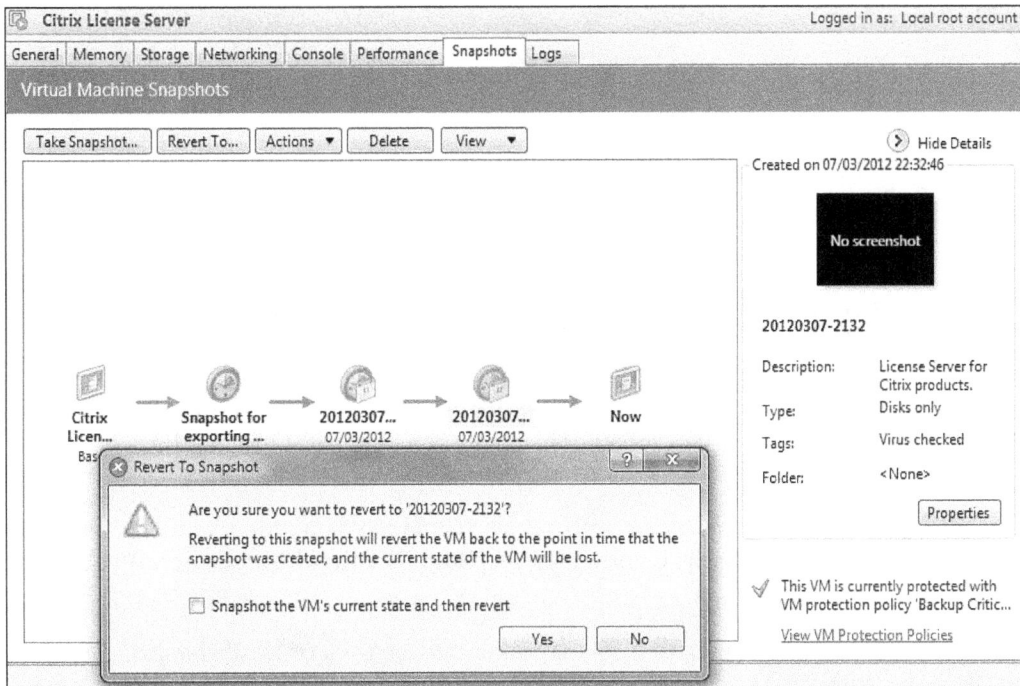

4. Click on **Yes** to revert the VM to the selected snapshot.

If you prefer to restore the VM from an archived scheduled snapshot, follow the given procedure:

1. From XenCenter, select your pool.

2. Right-click and select **Import...**.

3. Import the archive .xva file related to the archived snapshot. Refer to *Chapter 5, Managing Virtual Machines* for details about this operation.

4. Create a new virtual machine based on the archived snapshot template you have imported before using the New VM wizard.

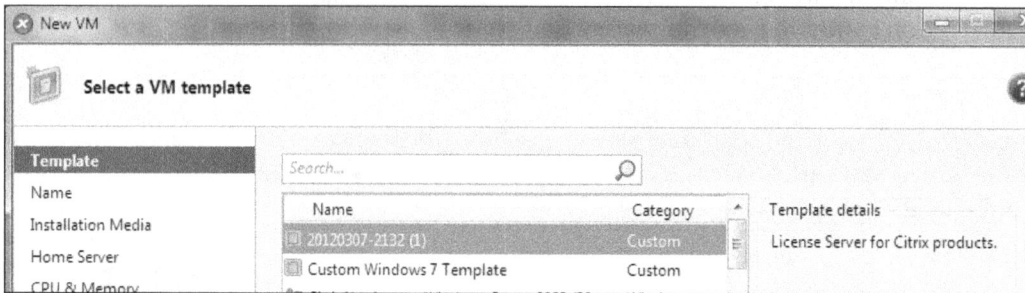

Overview of Workload Balancing

Workload Balancing (WLB) is a XenServer component, distributed as an `.xva` package by Citrix, that offers you reporting features about your virtual environment performances and usage. Also, Workload Balancing helps you in placing your virtual machines on the best possible hosts in the pool according to resource availability.

Since Workload Balancing (WLB) captures performance data, you use this component to generate reports, known as *Workload Balancing Reports*, about your virtualized environment.

These reports provide you with information about the pool or host's health, auditing, optimizations, and placement history. Also, you can monitor virtual machine resource usage history so that this can help you in compiling statistics and performing capacity planning.

When deployed to manage virtual machine workloads, Workload Balancing can:

- Balance virtual-machine workloads across hosts in a XenServer resource pool
- Determine the best host on which to start a virtual machine
- Determine the best host on which to resume a virtual machine that you powered off
- Determine the best host to move a virtual machine to when a host fails
- Determine the optimal server for each of the host's virtual machines when you put a host into or take a host out of Maintenance Mode.

As you can imagine, running virtual machines consume computing resources on the physical host such as CPU and memory. This reduces the host's available resources.

When Workload Balancing evaluates that the resources' utilization of virtual machines on a host are exceeding a performance threshold, it suggests that you move the VM to a host in the pool with available resources in order to balance workloads . This action is known as a *recommendation*.

Depending on your preference, Workload Balancing can accomplish these tasks automatically or prompt you to accept its rebalancing and placement recommendations.

Furthermore, if your hosts are configured with Wake-on-LAN enabled network cards, you can also configure Workload Balancing to power off hosts automatically at specific times of day, for example because you want to reduce power consumption at night.

You can configure Workload Balancing behavior in order to maximize your virtual machines performance or the number of virtual machines running on a host—in the latter case, you set Workload Balancing in order to achieve maximum *density* on a host. When you choose to maximize performances, Workload Balancing recommends placing virtual machines on hosts to ensure that maximum amount of resources are available for each running virtual machine. When you choose to maximize density, Workload Balancing's goal is to reduce the number of hosts powered on in the pool. To do this, it recommends placing virtual machines on as few hosts as possible.

Workload Balancing is available in Citrix XenServer Enterprise Edition or higher.

Installing Workload Balancing Virtual Appliance

In the overview, we have discovered that Workload Balancing is available as a virtual appliance packaged in the .xva format.

You can download Workload Balancing from the Citrix website: https://www.citrix.com/English/ss/downloads/ details.asp?downloadId=2313062&productId=683148#top.

In the next example, we will configure the Workload Balancing appliance in order to provide optimizations and recommendations for our XenServer pool.

To do this, we follow the given procedure:

1. First, import the Workload Balancing `.xva` package you have downloaded from the Citrix website using XenCenter if you haven't yet done this.

2. Power on the Workload Balancing virtual machine and click on the **Console** tab using XenCenter.

3. After startup, the Workload Balancing configuration wizard will start prompting you to enter and confirm a new root password for the virtual machine. It is best practice to use a strong password for security reasons.

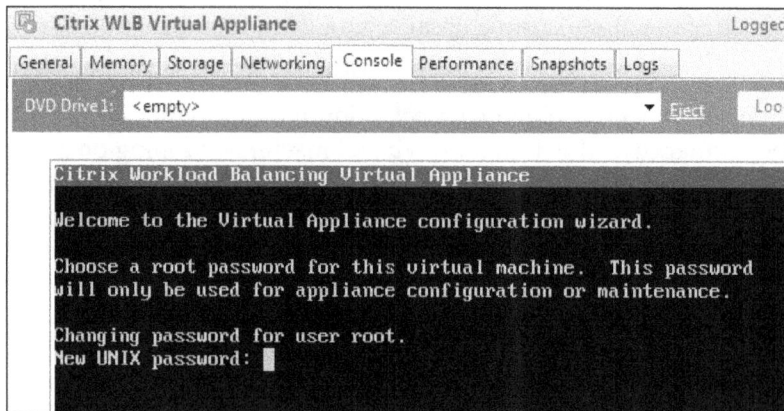

4. After you have set the password, enter the computer name you want to assign to the Workload Balancing Virtual Appliance. In our example, we will use `Citrix-WLB` as hostname.

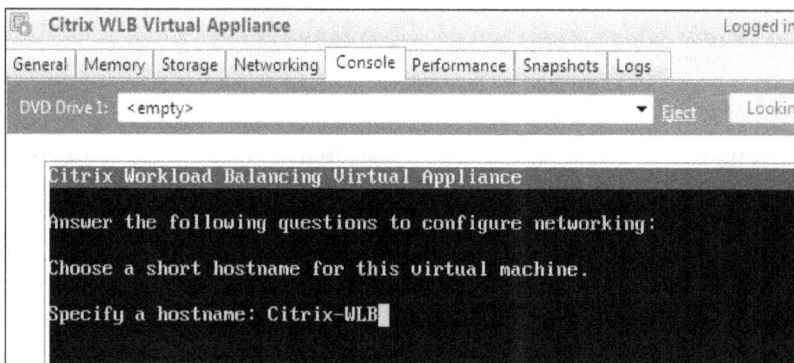

5. Enter the domain suffix for the virtual appliance. In our example, we use `lab.local`. Note that you have to create the FQDN record into your DNS if you want the pool to use an FQDN to connect to Workload Balancing.

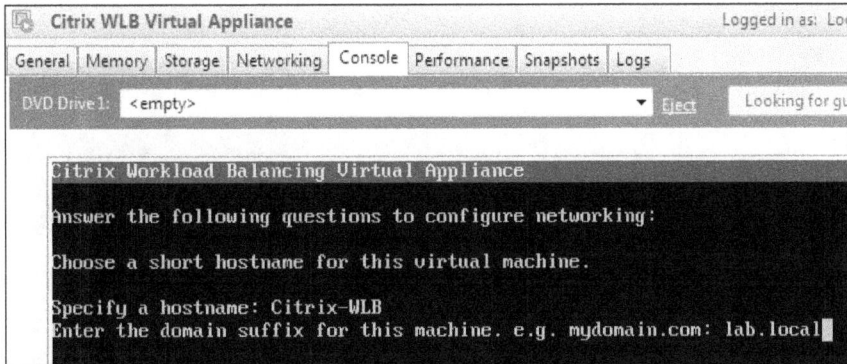

6. After you have set the domain suffix for the appliance, you need to specify if a DHCP server should be used to obtain the IP address automatically or if you prefer using a static IP address configuration. Best practice is to use a static configuration because if the IP address changes, it will break the connection between XenServer and Workload Balancing. In our example, we will use IP address `192.168.0.51/24`.

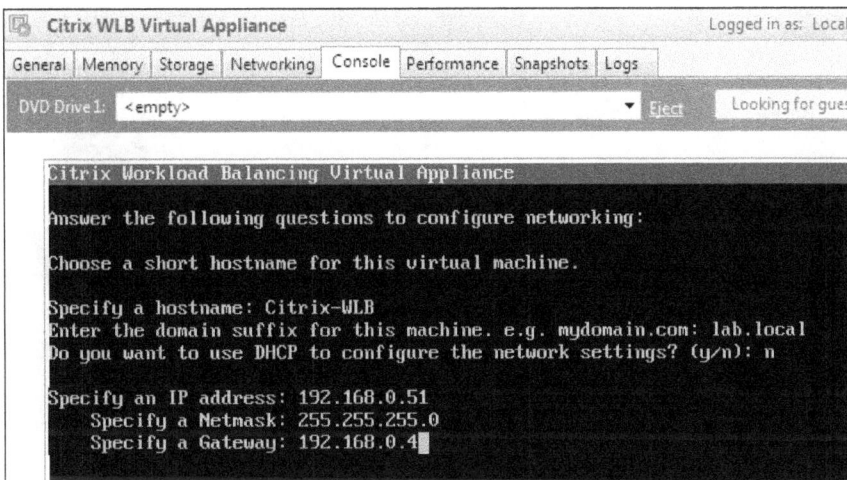

7. Confirm your network settings in order to proceed with the configuration. The wizard will start to configure the network interface.

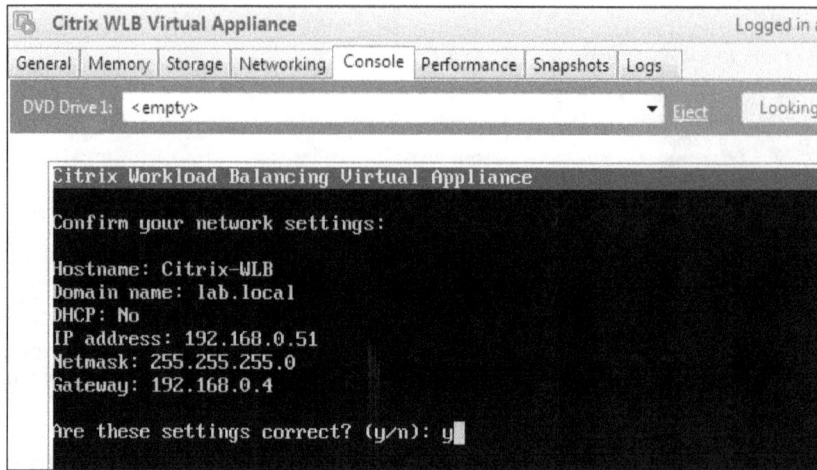

8. Once the network configuration has been done, the wizard asks you to create a username for the Workload Balancing database where data will be stored or to press *Enter* to use the default username (postgres) of the database account. Also, provide a strong password for the username. In our example, we will use the default username.

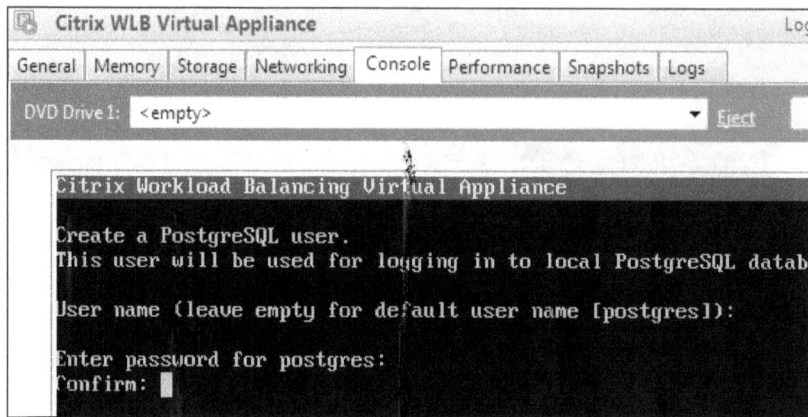

9. The configuration wizard will load database objects and after this enter a username and a strong password for the Workload Balancing server. This account will be used by XenServer to connect to Workload Balancing. The default username is wlbuser — in our example we will use the default username.

10. Enter the TCP port that the Workload Balancing appliance will use to communicate with the XenServer pool. By default, the Workload Balancing server uses port number `8012` and we use this in our environment.

> The port number cannot be set to `443` because Workload Balancing doesn't accept connections on this port.

11. After you have configured the port, the wizard will continue with the virtual appliance configuration saving it in the `/opt/citrix/wlb/wlb.conf` file and after the configuration finishes the connection information will be displayed. We will use this information to connect our XenServer pool to the Workload Balancing appliance.

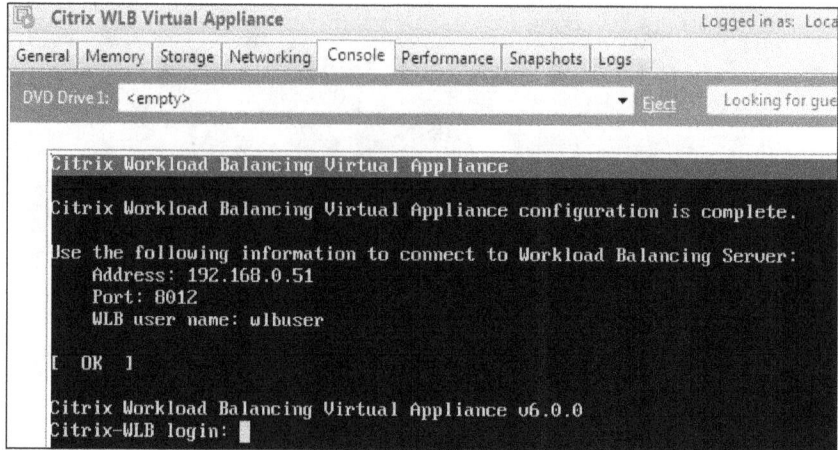

Now that the Workload Balancing appliance has been configured, we can proceed to connect it to the XenServer pool using XenCenter.

To connect the pool to the Workload Balancing, follow the given procedure:

1. Using XenCenter, select your XenServer pool and click on the **WLB** tab.

2. In the **WLB** tab, click on the **Connect** button – the **Connect to WLB Server** dialog box will be displayed.

3. In the **Server Address** box, type the IP address or FQDN of the Workload Balancing Virtual Appliance. In our example, we type `citrix-wlb.lab.local`. If you changed the Workload Balancing port during Workload Balancing Configuration, enter the port number in the **Port** box. XenServer uses this port to communicate with Workload Balancing.

4. In the **WLB Server Credentials** section, enter the username and password that the XenServer pool master will use to connect to the Workload Balancing Virtual Appliance.

    This must be the account you created during Workload Balancing Configuration. By default, the username for this account is `wlbuser`.

    WLB Server Credentials
    Enter the credentials XenServer will use to connect to the Workload Balancing server.

    User name: wlbuser

    Password: ********

5. In the **XenServer Credentials** section, enter the username and password for the pool you are configuring (typically the password for the pool master). Workload Balancing will use these credentials to connect to the hosts in the pool.

6. To use the credentials with which you are currently logged into XenServer, select the **Use the current XenCenter credentials** checkbox.

> If you have configured the Role Based Access Control (RBAC) feature for your pool, be sure this user has the *Pool Operator* role.

    XenServer Credentials
    Enter the credentials the Workload Balancing Server will use to connect to XenServer.

    User name: root

    Password: ********

    ☐ Use the current XenCenter credentials

7. After connecting the pool to the Workload Balancing Virtual Appliance, Workload Balancing automatically begins monitoring the pool with the default optimization settings. We will see later in this chapter how to modify the optimization settings.

Configuring Workload Balancing

After we have deployed the Workload Balancing Virtual Appliance and connected it to the XenServer pool, it is now time to discover how to manage it in order to determine the best host on which to run a virtual machine and to accept Workload Balancing optimization recommendations. In this section, we will also see how to perform performance analysis using reports.

When Workload Balancing is enabled and you start or migrate a virtual machine, XenCenter provides recommendations to help you determine the optimal physical host in the resource pool on which to start a virtual machine. This recommendation is indicated in XenCenter with *stars* beside the name of the physical host. These stars tell you what is the optimal XenServer host when starting or placing the virtual machine—a host with a rating of five stars is the optimal host where you can place the virtual machine, a host with no stars is the least optimal server where you can start the VM. Also, when the host cannot accept the VM for example because there are no available resources, the hostname is grayed out.

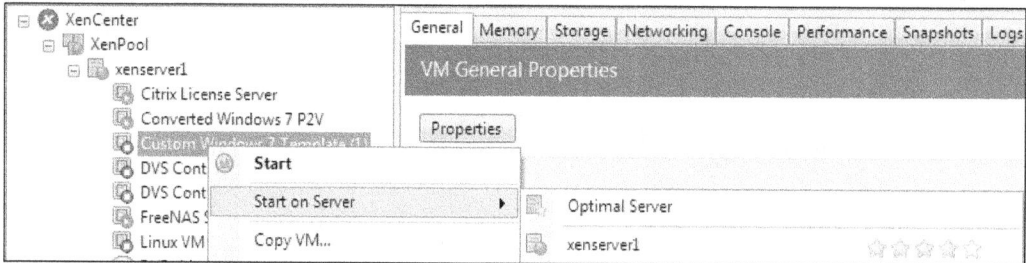

There are several factors Workload Balancing uses when determining the optimal host for a workload:

- The *amount of resources available* on each host in the pool
- The *optimization mode* you have configured
- The *amount and type of resources* used by the virtual machine

Recommendations for virtual machines are also displayed on the **WLB** tab of your XenServer pool. Here you can find out the new host candidate for hosting the VM based on the WLB suggestion and the reason Workload Balancing recommends you to move the VM. Furthermore, in this pane you can find recommendations about powering a particular host on or off.

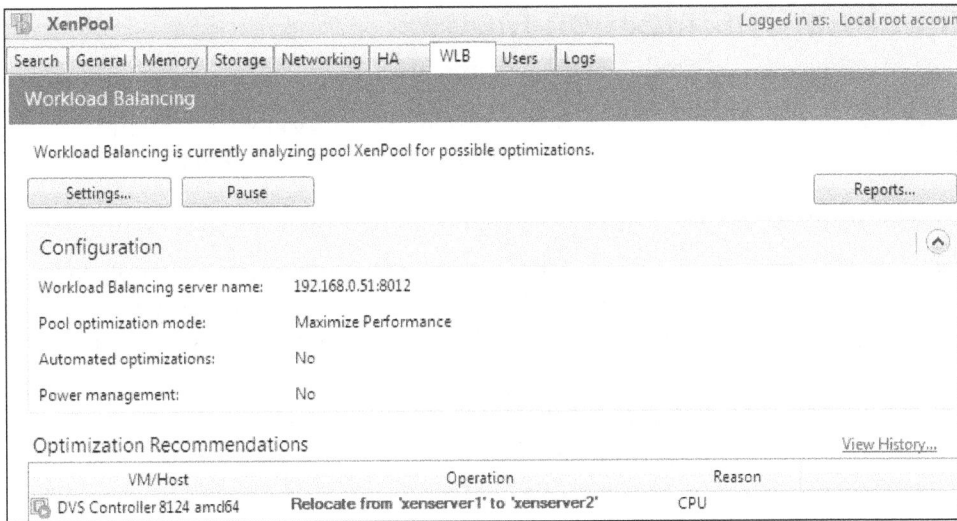

You can apply the recommendations provided by Workload Balancing by clicking on the **Apply Recommendation** button.

These optimization recommendations are based on the:

- **Optimization mode**: The mode that you have selected for the Workload Balancing
- **Performance metrics**: These are for resources such as CPU or memory
- **The role of the host in the resource pool**: A pool master is considered the last host to use for virtual machines placement and it is used only if there aren't other hosts available to host them

Managing Workload Balancing settings

After we have learned the main concepts related to Workload Balancing behavior, we can move on and see how to manage the WLB placement and optimizations settings.

In particular, you can also edit performance thresholds and Metric Weightings especially if WLB is not working according to your expectation.

> Always remember to review WLB thresholds in order to align them to your environment.

You can edit the Workload Balancing settings using XenCenter by clicking on the **WLB** tab and then on the **Settings** button.

Adjusting Optimization Mode

The first setting you can modify is the **Optimization Mode**.

As we have discovered before, this is the strategy that Workload Balancing is based on in order to make recommendations for rebalancing your virtual machines.

You can choose two different optimization modes:

- **Maximize Performance**: In this mode, Workload Balancing attempts to place virtual machines across all physical hosts in a resource pool. When a host reaches a high threshold, Workload Balancing will recommend optimizations.

- **Maximize Density**. In this mode, Workload Balancing attempts to minimize the number of physical hosts that must be powered-on for running virtual machines. Workload Balancing recommends consolidation optimizations when a virtual machine reaches the Low threshold.

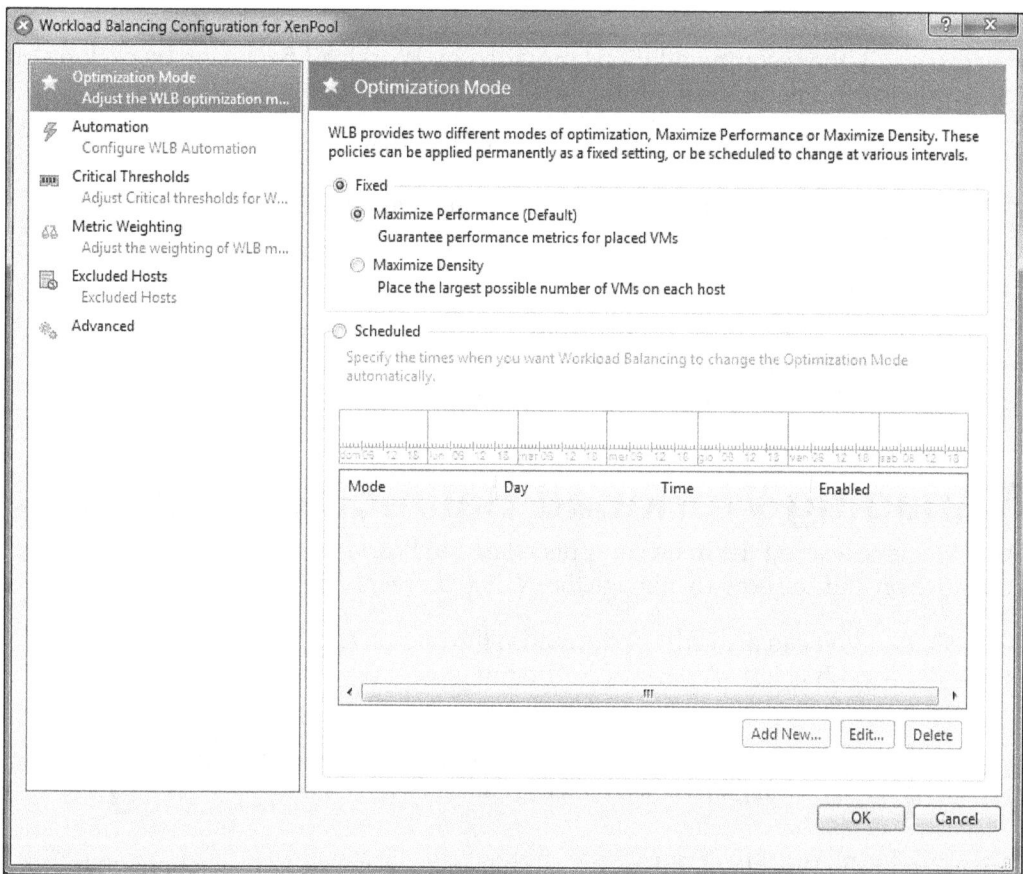

Also, you can instruct Workload Balancing to apply these optimization modes all of the time or according to a schedule you specify.

In this last case, you can select a different optimization mode depending on the time of day, for example, if you want to consolidate servers during the weekends when only virtual machines providing core services must be available. In the following example, we will set Maximize Density during the weekends, while we will set Maximize Performance during the weekdays when users are connected to your virtual environment.

To do this, follow the given procedure:

1. Choose **Scheduled** on the **Optimization Mode** page and click on **Add new...**.

2. Choose **Maximize Density** as optimization mode and instruct XenServer to start it on weekends:

3. XenServer will show you the new configuration which you have specified.

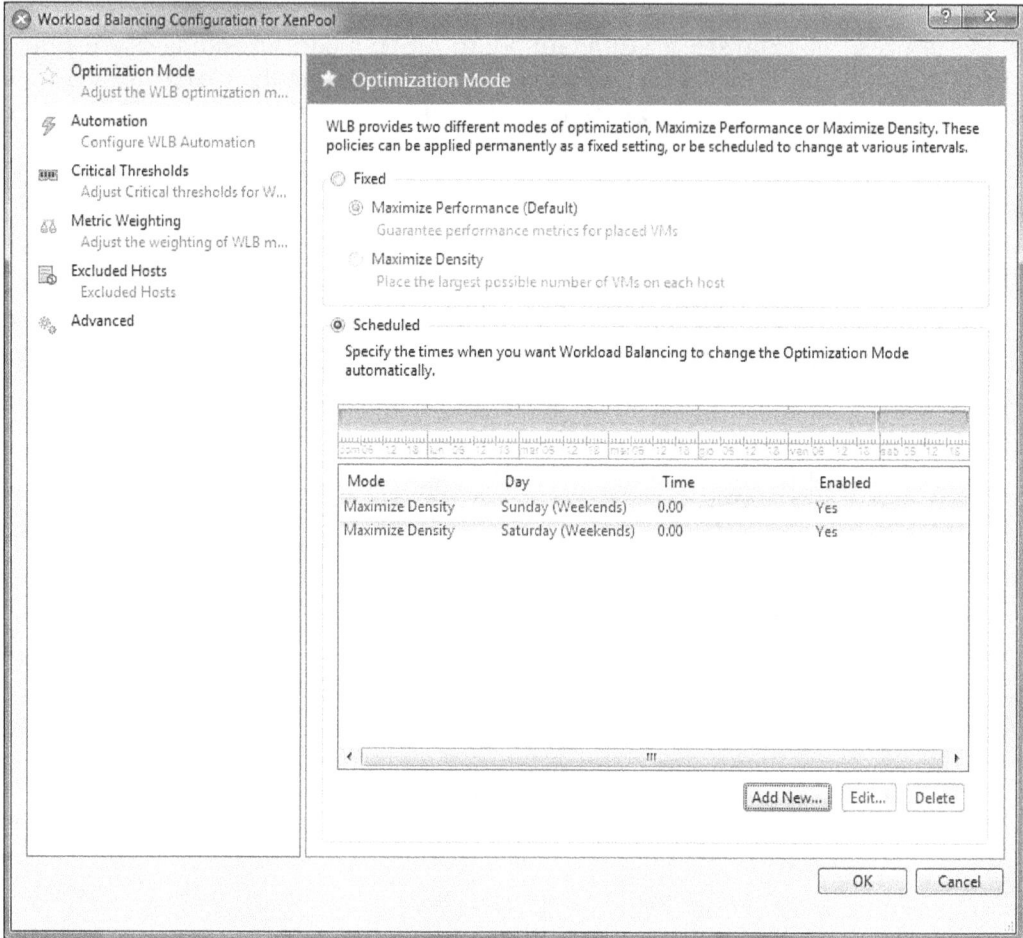

As you can see from the previous screenshot, XenCenter lets you add more than one entry for **Time** according to your needs when you use the **Scheduled** mode.

Adjusting Workload Balancing automation

In the **Automation** pane, you can configure Workload Balancing to apply recommendations automatically and configure power management, permitting XenServer to shut down or power-on physical hosts. This last setting is very useful when your virtual machines are not being used by users, for example, during the night.

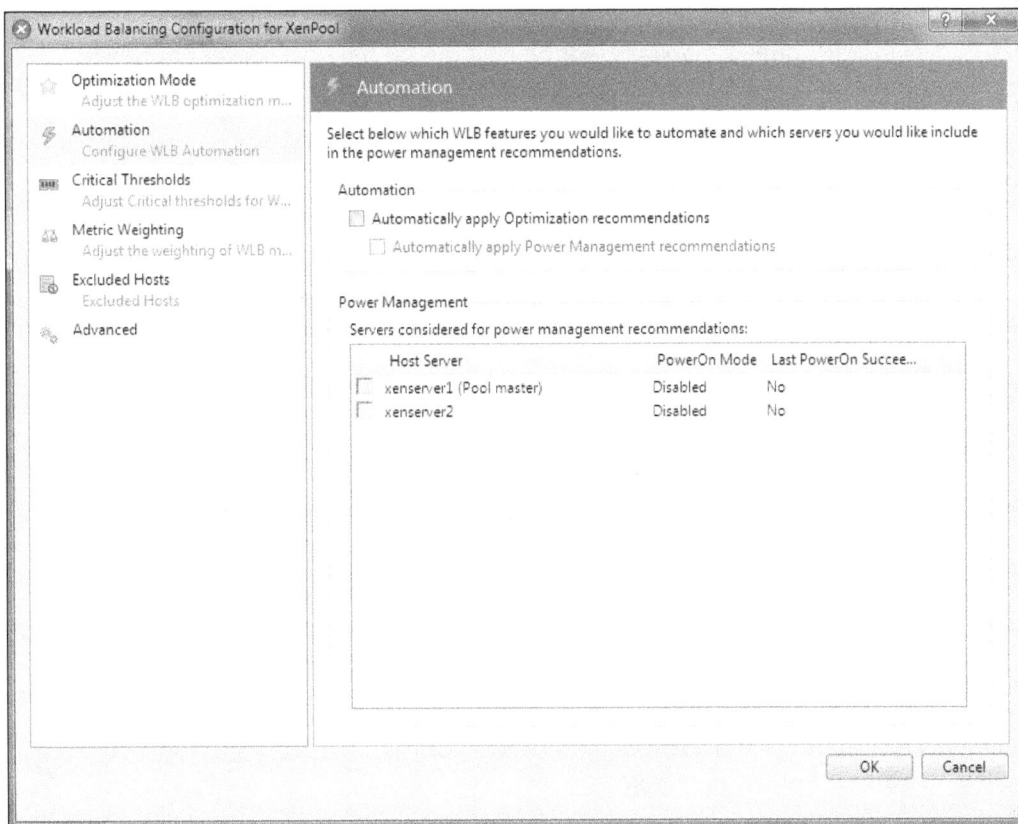

By default, Workload Balancing does not apply recommendations automatically. You must enable Automation if you want Workload Balancing to apply recommendations automatically; with the Automation feature enabled, WLB is sometimes referred to as running in *automated mode*.

If you do not, you must apply recommendations manually by clicking on **Apply Recommendations** on the **WLB** tab in XenCenter.

Note that Workload Balancing will not automatically apply recommendations to hosts or virtual machines if you have the High Availability feature enabled and these recommendations are in conflict with the High Availability settings, for example, if a pool will be out of resources by applying Workload Balancing optimization recommendations, XenCenter will prompt you whether or not you want to continue applying the recommendation. When Automation is enabled, Workload Balancing will not apply any power-management recommendations that exceed the number of host failures to tolerate in the High Availability plan.

If you want WLB to manage power management, you have to select the hosts WLB has to consider for power management by clicking on the host server checkbox, enable automation, and set **Maximum Density** as the optimization mode.

In order to successfully use this feature, remember that your hosts must satisfy the following requirements:

- The hardware for the host has remote power on/off capabilities: Wake-On-LAN enabled network card and Dell Remote Access Cards (DRAC) or Hewlett-Packard Integrated Lights-Out (iLO) must be installed and configured

- The Host Power On feature is configured for the host

> Refer to XenServer 6.0 Administrator's Guide available at
> `http://support.citrix.com/article/CTX130420`
> for further details about the Host Power On feature.

In the **Maximize Performance** mode, Workload Balancing automatically powers on hosts while improving host performance.

If Workload Balancing detects unused resources, it recommends powering off hosts and it designates a new host on which to place virtual machines before shutting down hosts with unused resources. The process of transferring VMs from one host to another is known as *filling*.

Changing Critical Thresholds and Metric Weightings

Workload Balancing continuously evaluates the resource metrics of physical hosts and VMs across the pool using *thresholds* and *weightings*.

Thresholds are values used by Workload Balancing to make an optimization or a recommendation. When a threshold for a host is exceeded, the Workload Balancing makes a recommendation after it has determined a destination host where you can relocate one or more VMs.

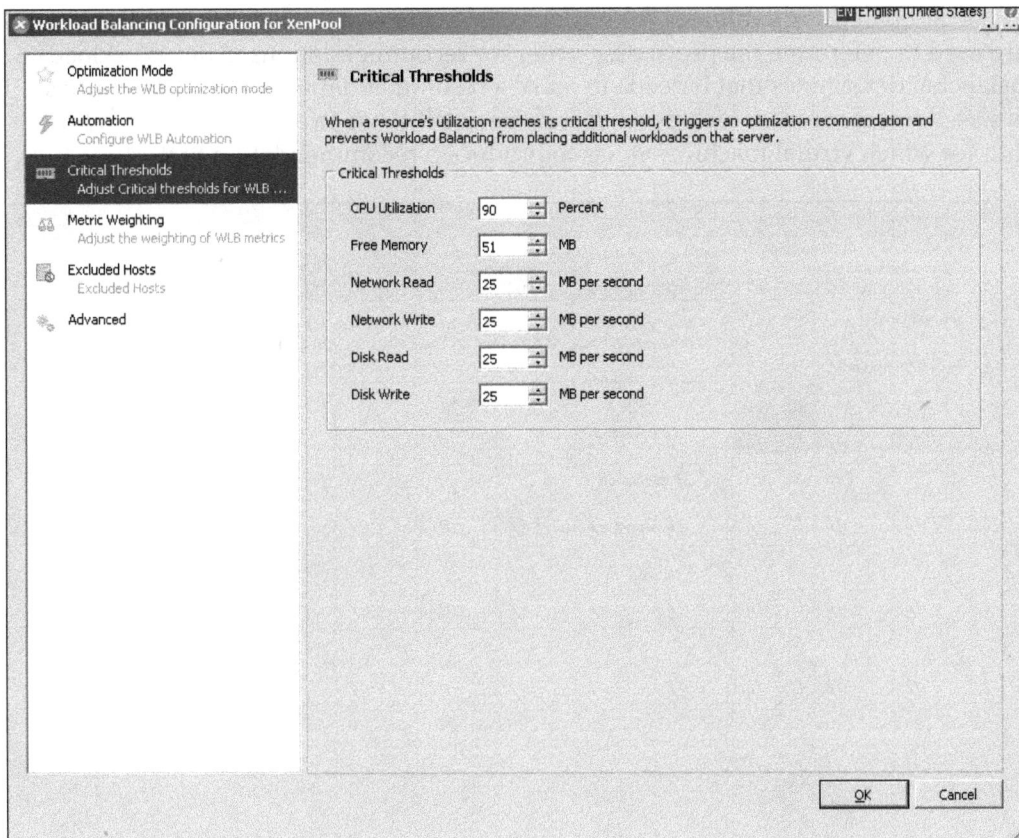

Workload Balancing has four levels of thresholds, namely *Critical*, *High*, *Medium*, and *Low*.

After you have set a new Critical threshold for a resource, Workload Balancing changes the other thresholds according to the newly set Critical threshold. This is because you can only modify the Critical threshold.

Workload Balancing evaluates resources usage using Metric Weightings—they are used to determine the processing order for recommendations. After Workload Balancing determines that it needs to make a recommendation, Metric Weightings are used to determine which performance issue WLB has to address first for a host and for which virtual machines it has to produce a recommendation first.

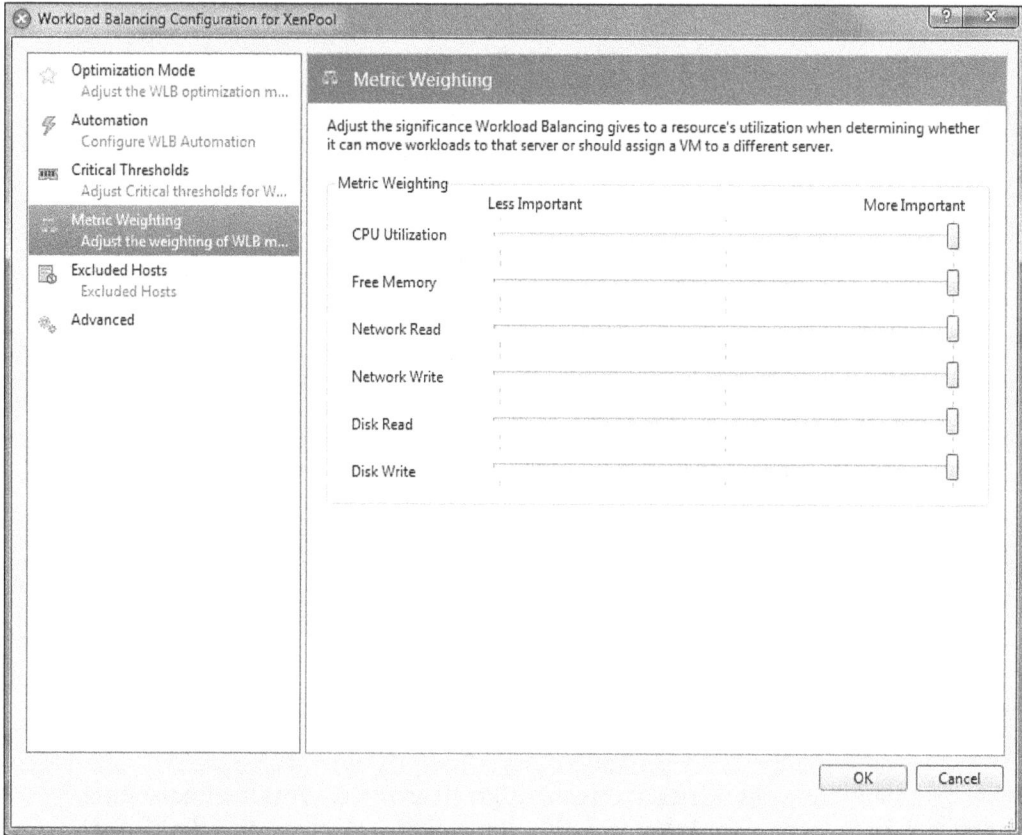

You can change the importance of each resource by moving the **Metric Weighting** slider to the right or to the left, setting the metric to **More Important** or **Less Important**.

If you configure all resources to be equally important, Workload Balancing addresses CPU utilization first and memory second, as these are typically the most constrained resources.

Excluding hosts from recommendations

When configuring Workload Balancing, you can specify that specific physical hosts are excluded from Workload Balancing optimization and placement recommendations.

For example, you are in situations where you have virtual machines that need to be placed on the same host. You can exclude a host from Workload Balancing by selecting it on the **Excluded Hosts** pane of the WLB settings:

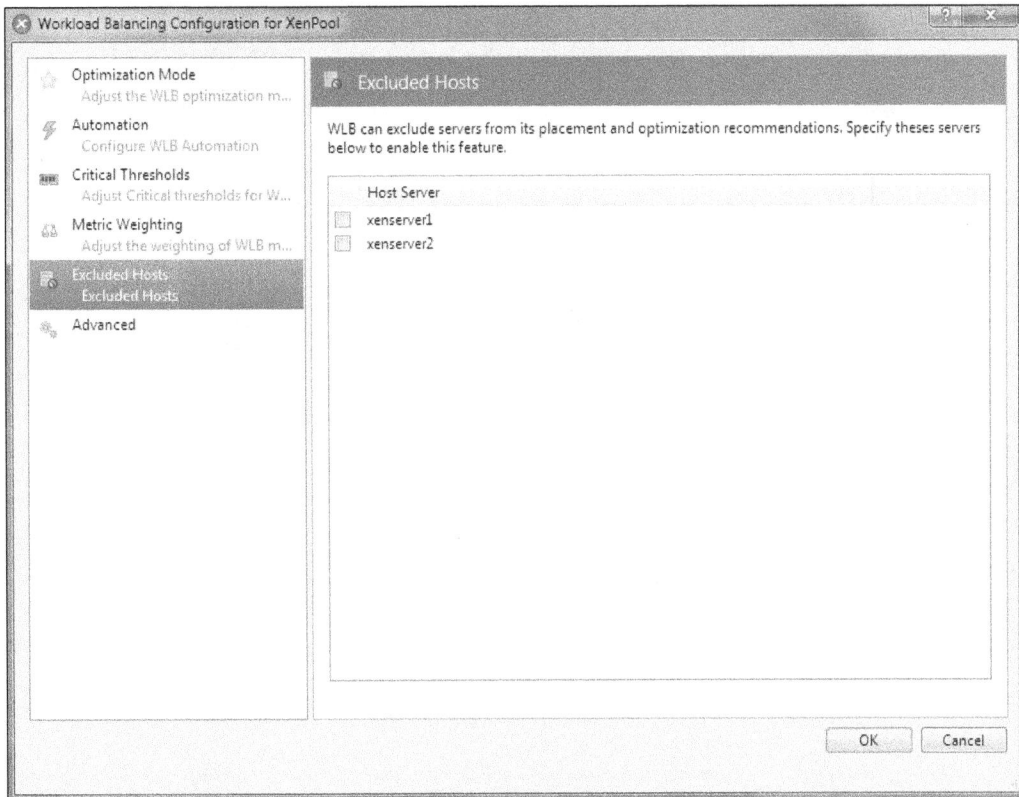

Controlling automated recommendations

You can control how Workload Balancing's recommendations are applied on the
Advanced page of the Workload Balancing settings dialog.

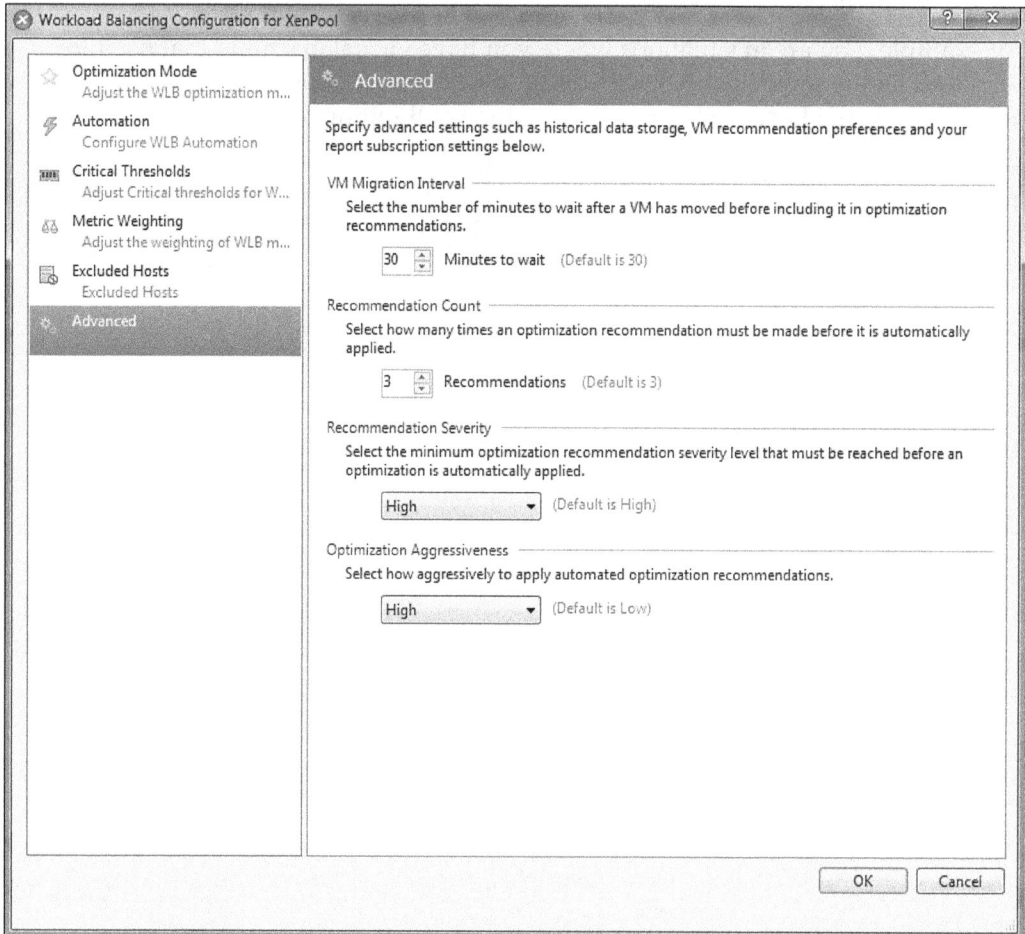

You can change the following settings:

- **VM Migration Interval**
- **Recommendation Count**
- **Recommendation Severity**
- **Optimization Aggressiveness**

With **VM Migration Interval**, you can specify the number of minutes Workload Balancing must wait after the last time a particular virtual machine was moved before generating another recommendation that includes that virtual machine.

When Workload Balancing is set in the automated mode, WLB does not accept the first recommendation it produces but waits until a host or VM continues to trigger that recommendation, before automatically applying a recommendation.

The number of times a recommendation must be made before Workload Balancing can automatically apply the recommendation is managed using the **Recommendation Count**.

Remember that Workload Balancing is set to be conservative by default. If you want to make WLB more aggressive, decrease the **Recommendation Count** value and raise the level of the **Optimization Aggressiveness** to a higher value — by default, it is set to low.

All optimization recommendations include a severity rating (Critical, High, Medium, and Low) that indicates the importance of the recommendation.

When you configure Workload Balancing to apply recommendations automatically, you can change the **Recommendation Severity** value setting the minimum severity level that should be associated with a recommendation before Workload Balancing automatically applies it.

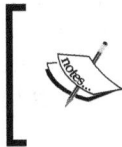

> You can find more details about Workload Balancing administration on the Citrix XenServer Workload Balancing Administrator's Guide available at `http://support.citrix.com/article/CTX127330`.

Monitoring performances with Workload Balancing

We have discovered that we can manage and automate virtual machine placement on the XenServer hosts belonging to our virtual environment according to the XenServer hosts' performance and resource availability.

With Workload Balancing, we can also monitor performance and virtual server health and perform capacity analysis using historical reports.

Workload Balancing lets you generate reports on three types of objects, namely, physical hosts, resource pools, and virtual machines.

> The pool should have been running Workload Balancing for a couple of hours or long enough to generate the type of data you want to display in the reports.
>
> You will find report images acquired by different XenServer pools in the *Generating reports* section.

Generating reports

Generating reports to display data collected by Workload Balancing during hosts and virtual machines usage is very simple.

This can be achieved following the given procedure in XenCenter:

1. From XenCenter, select your XenServer pool.

2. Click on **Pool | View Workload Reports...**.

   > You can also display the **Workload Reports** screen from the **WLB** tab by clicking on the **Reports** button.

3. Workload Reports will be displayed. Here you can select one of the available reports and display information about your environment. Also, you can limit the timeframe of your analysis by selecting a start and an end date. Depending on the report you select, you might need to specify a host in the **Host list** box.

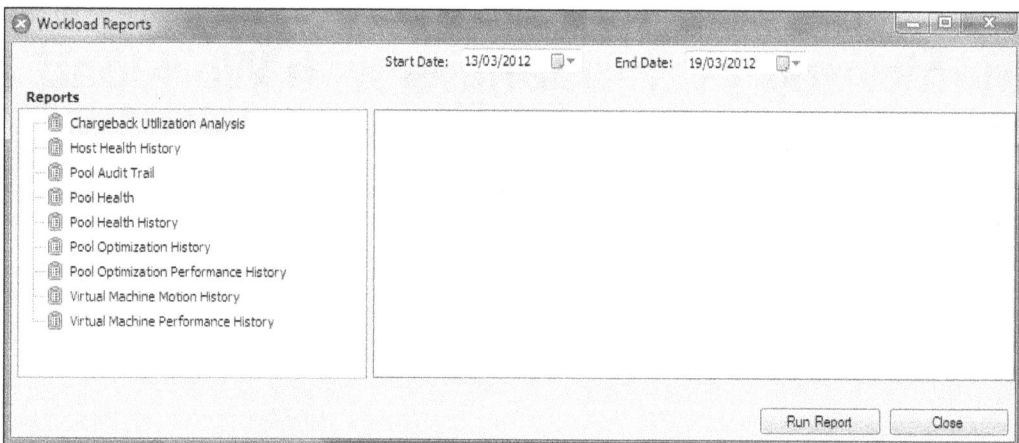

After generating a report, you can use the toolbar buttons in the report to navigate and perform certain tasks such as print or export to an *Acrobat PDF* or *Microsoft Excel* file.

You are asking yourself what reports are available. It is time to answer this question.

In Workload Balancing, you can use the following reports:

- Chargeback Utilization Analysis
- Host Health History
- Pool Optimization Performance History
- Pool Audit Trail
- Pool Health
- Pool Health History
- Pool Optimization History
- Virtual Machine Motion History
- Virtual Machine Performance History

Chargeback Utilization Analysis

The **Chargeback Utilization Analysis** report helps you to determine how much of a resource (such as a physical server) a specific department in your organization used. Specifically, the report shows information about all the virtual machines in your pool, including their availability and resource utilization.

This report is useful, for example, when you have to demonstrate virtual machine uptime or when you want to implement a billing solution according to resources usage if you are a solution provider offering private cloud services.

Host Health History

The **Host Health History** report displays the performance of resources (CPU, memory, network reads, and network writes) on a specific host in relation to threshold values.

In this report, you can notice that some colored lines (red, green, yellow) are displayed—these represent your threshold values. So you can use this report for insight into host performance when you are changing performance thresholds.

You can also display resource utilization as a daily or hourly average. This is useful when you want to perform analysis on specific hours of the day in order to find, for example, when your host is busiest. To view report data grouped by hour, expand **Click to view report data grouped by hour for the time period** under the **Host Health History** title bar.

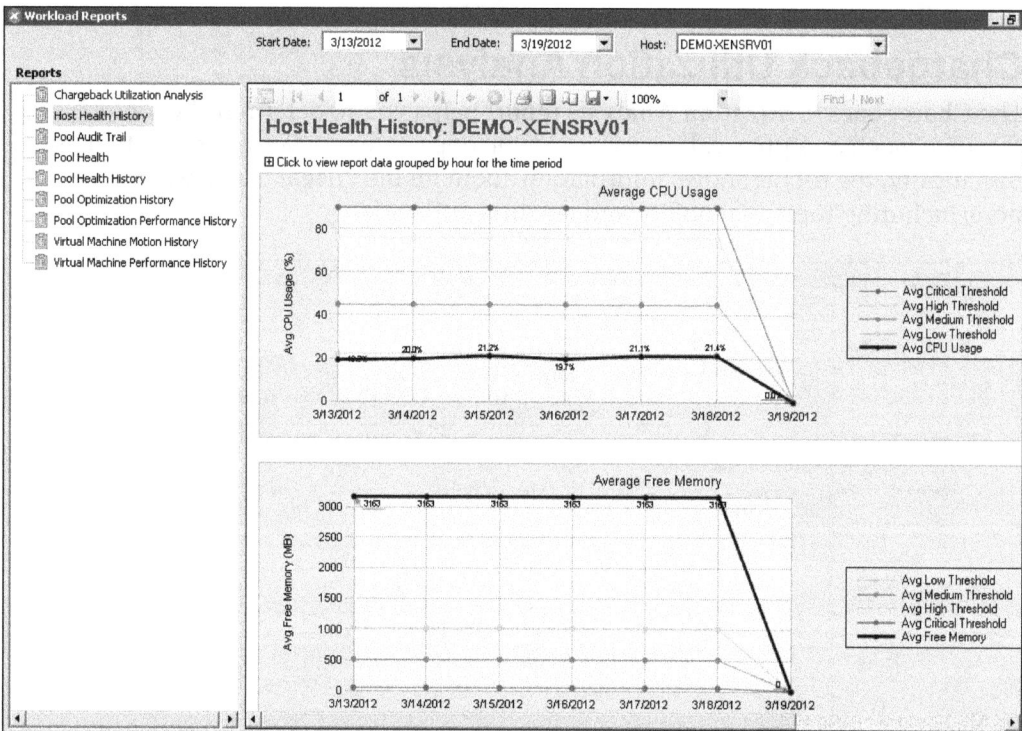

Pool Optimization Performance History

The **Pool Optimization Performance History** report displays optimization events.

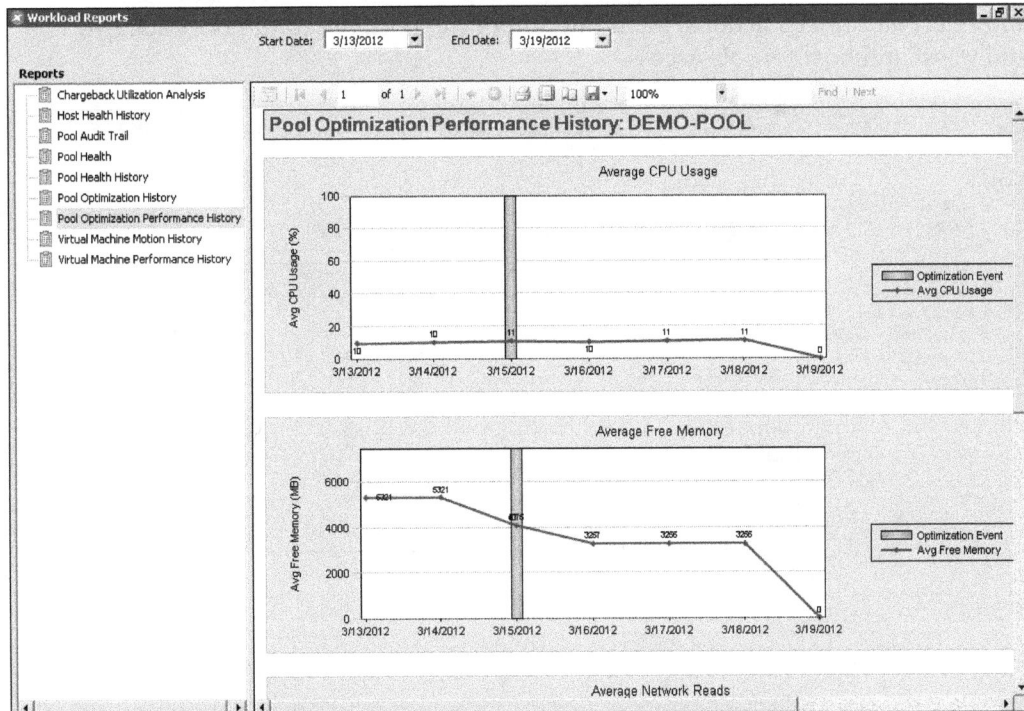

The dotted line represents the average usage across the pool on the period of days you have selected and a blue bar indicates the day on which an optimization occurred.

This report can help you determine if Workload Balancing is working successfully in your environment. You can use this report to discover the resource usage before Workload Balancing recommended optimizations.

In general, resource usage should decrease after an optimization event. If you do not see improved resource usage after an optimization, you should consider adjusting threshold values.

Pool Audit Trail

The **Pool Audit Trail** report displays the contents of the XenServer Audit Log, a XenServer feature designed to log attempts to perform unauthorized actions and select authorized actions, including import/export, host and pool backups, and guest and host console access.

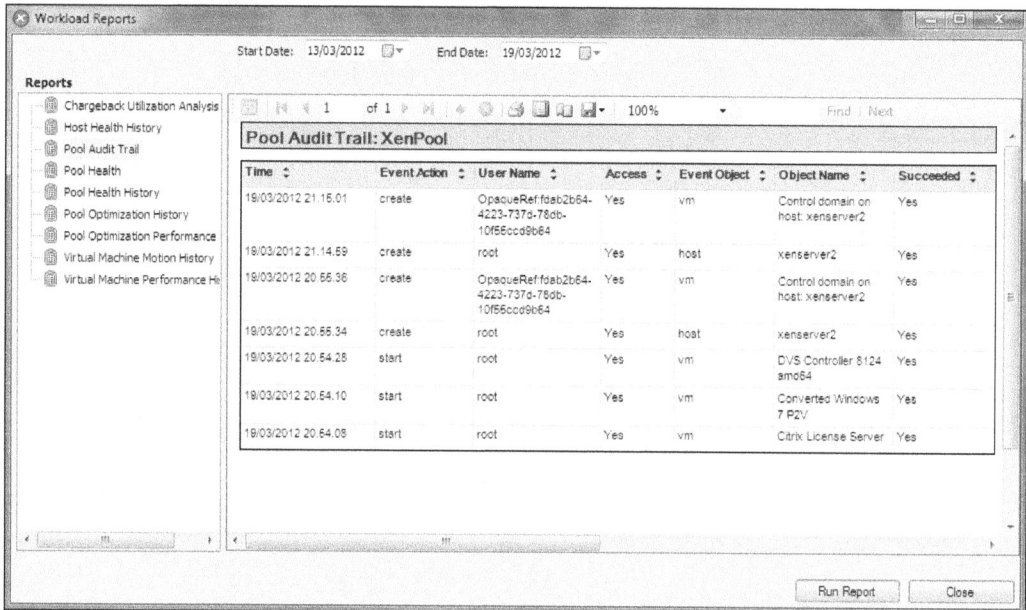

Note that the audit log only captures limited amounts of data for specific objects and actions.

> You can increase the detail by following the instructions in CTX130830 – Monitoring Additional XenServer Audit Log Events available at http://support.citrix.com/article/CTX130830.

Pool Health

The **Pool Health** report displays the percentage of time a resource pool and its hosts spent in four different threshold ranges, namely, Critical, High, Medium, and Low. You can use the Pool Health report to evaluate the effectiveness of your performance thresholds.

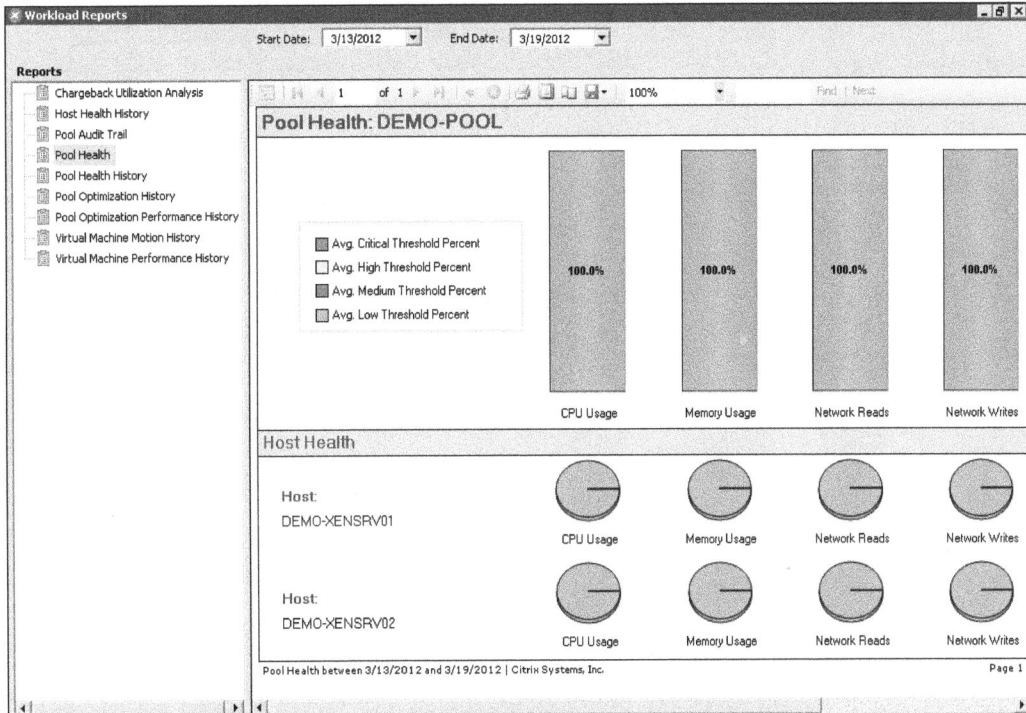

In this report, you should pay attention to **Avg. Medium Threshold Percent** of resources utilization. This is the optimum resource utilization regardless of the placement strategy you have set.

If you find that the majority of your report results are not in the **Avg. Medium Threshold Percent** range, you probably need to adjust the Critical threshold for this pool. If you do not have the thresholds adjusted to the correct level for your environment, the Workload Balancing optimization and placement recommendations might not be accurate.

Pool Health History

The **Pool Health History** report provides a line graph of resource utilization on all physical hosts in a pool over time. It lets you discover resource utilization trends.

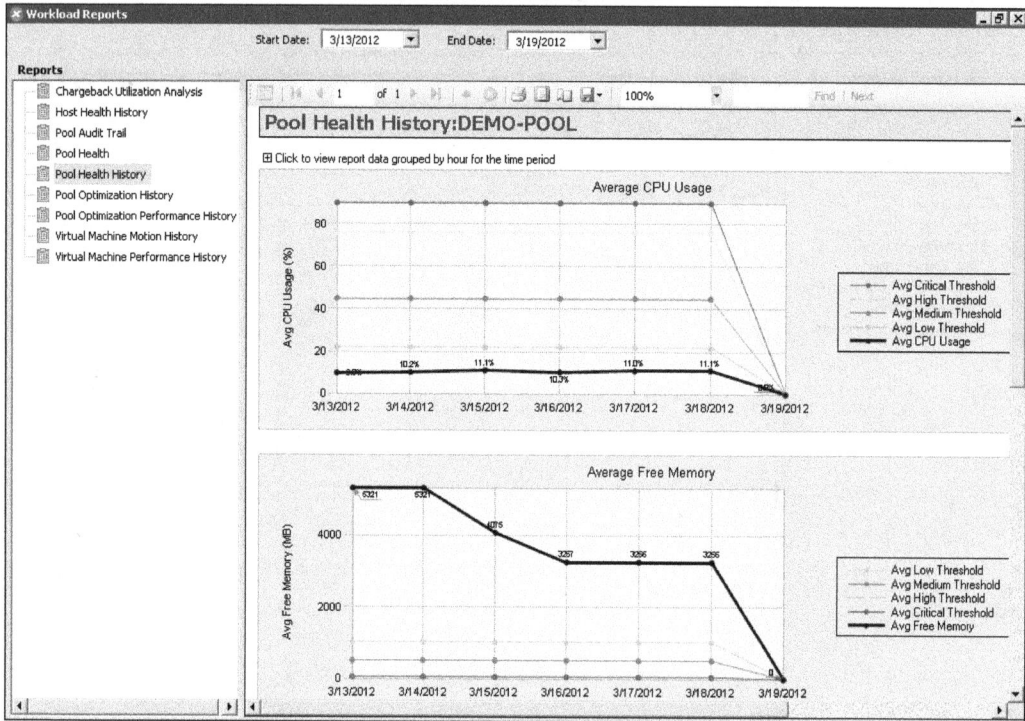

This report is quite similar to the Pool Health report but there is a difference – the Pool Health History report displays the average utilization for a resource on a specific date rather than the overall amount of time the resource spent in a threshold.

Pool Optimization History

The **Pool Optimization History** report provides chronological visibility into Workload Balancing optimization activity.

Optimization activity is summarized graphically and in a table. Drilling into a date field within the table displays detailed information for each pool optimization performed for that day.

> You can also generate a Pool Optimization History report from the **WLB** tab by clicking on the **View History** link.

Virtual Machine Motion History

The **Virtual Machine Motion History** report displays the number of times virtual machines migrated on a resource pool over a period of time.

Virtual Machine Performance History

The **Virtual Machine Performance History** report displays performance data, based on the amount of virtual resources allocated, related to a virtual machine located on a specific host for a period of time you specify.

Summary

In this chapter, we learned how to backup vital data about resources available in our XenServer environment. Also, we discovered how to protect virtual machines.

In the second half of the chapter, we introduced Workload Balancing concepts and management, and how to use reports to monitor our XenServer infrastructure.

Familiarize yourself with the concepts introduced in this chapter. Also, spend some time configuring and tuning Workload Balancing in order to have the best possible performance on your XenServer hosts.

A
Supported Guest Operating Systems and Virtual Machine Templates

Overview of supported guest virtual machines

In *Chapter 4, Creating Virtual Machines* we have learned how to create virtual machines in a XenServer virtual environment.

In the following table, you can find a list of operating systems that you can install in a virtual machine created in a XenServer environment.

The following table includes the values you can set for the minimum and maximum amount of memory and disk space you can set for each supported guest operating system:

Guest operating system	Minimum RAM	Maximum RAM	Disk space
Windows 7, Windows 7 SP1 (32-bit)	1 GB	4 GB	24 GB minimum, 40 GB or more recommended
Windows 7, Windows 7 SP1 (64-bit)	2 GB	128 GB	24 GB minimum, 40 GB or more recommended
Windows Server 2008 R2, Windows Server 2008 R2 SP1 (64-bit)	512 MB	128 GB	24 GB minimum, 40 GB or more recommended

Guest operating system	Minimum RAM	Maximum RAM	Disk space
Windows Server 2008, Windows Server 2008 SP2 (32-bit)	512 MB	64 GB	24 GB minimum, 40 GB or more recommended
Windows Server 2008, Windows Server 2008 SP2 (64-bit)	512 MB	128 GB	24 GB minimum, 40 GB or more recommended
Windows Server 2003, Windows Server 2003 SP1, SP2 (32-bit)	256 MB	64 GB	8 GB
Windows Server 2003, Windows Server 2003 SP1, SP2 (64-bit)	256 MB	128 GB	8 GB
Windows Vista, Windows Vista SP1, SP2 (32-bit)	1 GB	4 GB	24 GB
Windows XP SP3 (32-bit)	256 MB	4 GB	8 GB
CentOS 4.5, 4.6, 4.7, 4.8 (32-bit)	256 MB	16 GB	8 GB
CentOS 5.0, 5.1, 5.2, 5.3, 5.4, 5.5, 5.6 (32-/64-bit)	512 MB	16 GB	8 GB
Red Hat Enterprise Linux 4.5, 4.6, 4.7, 4.8 (32-bit)	256 MB	16 GB	8 GB
Red Hat Enterprise Linux 5.0, 5.1, 5.2, 5.3, 5.4, 5.5, 5.6 (32-/64-bit)	512 MB	16 GB	8 GB
Red Hat Enterprise Linux 6.0 (32-bit)	512 MB	8 GB	8 GB
Red Hat Enterprise Linux 6.0 (64-bit)	512 MB	32 GB	8 GB
SUSE Linux Enterprise Server 9 SP4 (32-bit)	256 MB	16 GB	8 GB
SUSE Linux Enterprise Server 10 SP1, SLES 10 SP2, SLES 10 SP3, SLES 10 SP4 (32-bit)	512 MB	16 GB	8 GB

Guest operating system	Minimum RAM	Maximum RAM	Disk space
SUSE Linux Enterprise Server 10 SP1, SLES 10 SP2, SLES 10 SP3, SLES 10 SP4 (64-bit)	512 MB	128 GB	8 GB
SUSE Linux Enterprise Server 11, SLES 11 SP1 (32-bit)	512 MB	16 GB	8 GB
SUSE Linux Enterprise Server 11 SP1, SLES 11 SP1 (64-bit)	512 MB	128 GB	8 GB
Oracle Enterprise Linux 5.0, 5.1, 5.2, 5.3, 5.4, 5.5, 5.6 (32-bit)	512 MB	64 GB	8 GB
Oracle Enterprise Linux 5.0, 5.1, 5.2, 5.3, 5.4, 5.5, 5.6 (64-bit)	512 MB	128 GB	8 GB
Oracle Enterprise Linux 6.0 (32-bit)	512 MB	8 GB	8 GB
Oracle Enterprise Linux 6.0 (64-bit)	512 MB	32 GB	8 GB
Debian Lenny 5.0 (32-bit)	128 MB	32 GB	8 GB
Debian Squeeze 6.0 (32-/64-bit)	128 MB	32 GB	8 GB
Ubuntu 10.04 (32-bit)	128 MB	512 MB	8 GB
Ubuntu 10.04 (64-bit)	128 MB	32 GB	8 GB

Virtual machine templates

In *Chapter 4, Creating Virtual Machines* we have discovered that we can create guest virtual machines starting from a template.

In the following table, you can find the templates XenServer offers you in order to create virtual machines based on Windows and Linux operating systems.

Also, you can find some notes for Linux distributions that help you in the installation phase.

Template Name	Notes
Windows 7 (32-bit)	
Windows 7 (64-bit)	
Windows Server 2003 (32-bit)	

Template Name	Notes
Windows Server 2003 (64-bit)	
Windows Server 2008 (32-bit)	
Windows Server 2008 (64-bit)	
Windows Server 2008 R2 (64-bit)	
Windows Vista (32-bit)	The Enterprise edition is supported.
Windows XP SP3 (32-bit)	Service Packs 1 and 2 are not supported.
Debian Lenny 5.0 (32-bit)	The standard Debian Lenny 5.0 DVD images are not compatible with XenServer. For details on how to obtain a suitable DVD image, see the Debian Lenny article available at `http://community.citrix.com/display/xs/Debian+Lenny`. To properly mount the XenServer Tools CD on a Debian guest, you must pass `-o exec` along with the other options on the VM.
Debian Squeeze 6.0 (32-/64-bit)	To install Debian Squeeze 6.0, you need to use the `multiarch.iso` from the official Debian mirror which can be found at `http://www.debian.org/devel/debian-installer`. To properly mount the XenServer Tools CD on a Debian guest, you must pass `-o exec` along with the other options on the VM.
Red Hat Enterprise Linux 4.5, 4.6, 4.7, 4.8 (32-bit)	Requires installing XenServer Tools after installing RHEL to apply the Citrix RHEL 4.8 kernel.
Red Hat Enterprise Linux 5.0, 5.1, 5.2, 5.3, 5.4, 5.5, 5.6 (32-/64-bit)	Use the 5.4 or later kernel.
Red Hat Enterprise Linux 6.0 (32-/64-bit)	You cannot install Red Hat Enterprise Linux using a physical CD media.
SUSE Linux Enterprise Server 9 SP4 32-bit	Installation supported only by network repository.
SUSE Linux Enterprise Server 10 SP1, SLES 10 SP2,SLES 10 SP4 (32-/64-bit)	
SUSE Linux Enterprise Server 10 SP3 (32-bit)	
SUSE Linux Enterprise Server 10 SP3 (64-bit)	Supported only if upgrading from SLES 10 SP2.

Template Name	Notes
SUSE Linux Enterprise Server 11, SLES 11 SP1(32-/64-bit)	
CentOS 4.5, 4.6, 4.7, 4.8 (32-bit)	Ensure that the operating system is using the RHEL 5.4 or later kernel.
CentOS 5.0, 5.1, 5.2, 5.3, 5.4, 5.5, 5.6 (32-/64-bit)	Ensure that the operating system is using the RHEL 5.4 or later kernel.
Oracle Enterprise Linux 5.0, 5.1, 5.2, 5.3, 5.4, 5.5, 5.6 (32-/64-bit)	With OEL 5.6 64-bit, the Unbreakable Enterprise Kernel does not support the Xen platform.
Oracle Enterprise Linux 6.0 (32-/64-bit)	You cannot install Red Hat Enterprise Linux using a physical CD media.
Ubuntu 10.04 (32-/64-bit)	Installation supported only by network repository.
	To create Ubuntu 10.04 VMs with multiple vCPUs, update the guest kernel to `2.6.32-32 #64`. For details on this issue, see the Citrix Knowledge Base article CTX129472 available at `http://support.citrix.com/article/CTX129472`.

You can find more details about supported Linux distributions in the Citrix XenServer 6.0 Virtual Machine Installation Guide available at `http://support.citrix.com/article/CTX130422`.

B
Applying Updates and Hotfixes

After the release of a XenServer version, Citrix occasionally makes available updates and hotfixes.

Hotfixes are released in order to fix bugs or issues that you experience while using the product.

Updates are similar to a service pack because they contain a set of hotfixes and also offer improvements to the initial release.

Public hotfixes and updates are made available for download from the Citrix Knowledge Center.

> The Citrix Knowledge Center is available at http://support.citrix.com.

When you plan to install a hotfix or an update, remember to follow the information and instructions that come with each update file. This is important because Citrix usually provides recommendations, requirements, and post-update operations that you need to satisfy and accomplish in order to complete the hotfix or update installation successfully.

> It is a best practice to not automatically apply each hotfix released by Citrix. Install only those that solve specific issues you are experiencing in your environment.

Hotfixes and updates can often be applied with minimal service interruption by using the **Install Update wizard** available in XenCenter or by using the xe CLI. Usually, the faster mode to apply a hotfix or update is using XenCenter.

Before you update XenServer hosts, take a note of the following recommendations:

- Take a backup of the state of the pool or the host before starting with the update process.

- Empty the CD/DVD drives of any VMs you plan to suspend.

- It is best to update all hosts in a pool within a short period. Running a pool that includes updated and non-updated hosts is not supported by Citrix.

- Start to update the pool master.

- Reboot any hosts that you plan to update to ensure that the hosts are healthy and the configurations correct.

> The reboot action is not required if you use XenCenter for installing updates or hotfixes because the Install Update wizard will reboot each host automatically before applying the update file.

- Disable the High Availability feature if it is in place.

- Log on to XenServer hosts using the local root account, or a user account that is a member of the Pool Administrator role, if you have configured Role Based Access Control.

Applying a hotfix or update using XenCenter

After we have introduced the main concepts, in the following example we will discover how to apply a hotfix using XenCenter to a XenServer host:

1. Download the update file related to the hotfix you want to apply, from the Citrix Knowledge Center to a known location on a computer running XenCenter. Usually the update is provided as a zipped archive, so extract it before you proceed. In this example we install hotfix XS60E001.

2. After you have extracted the archive file, you can notice that a folder containing two files, `.xsupdate` and `.BZ2`, has been created. The file `.xsupdate` is the file related to the update. The file `.BZ2` is the file containing the source code used for compiling the update, and is provided by Citrix in order to respect the open source license agreement:

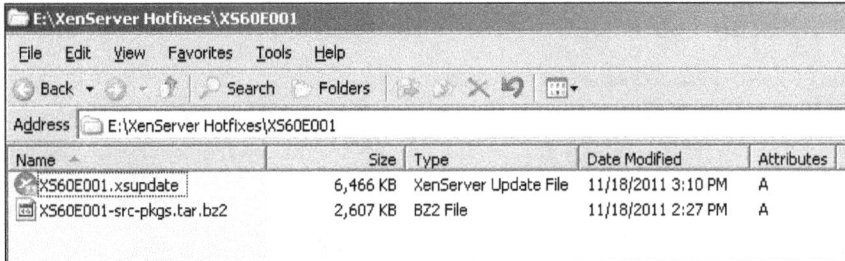

3. Shut down or suspend any virtual machine that is running if you don't want to allow XenCenter to automatically migrate it to another host before applying the hotfix.

4. Click on **Tools | Install New Update** in order to open the **Install Update** wizard:

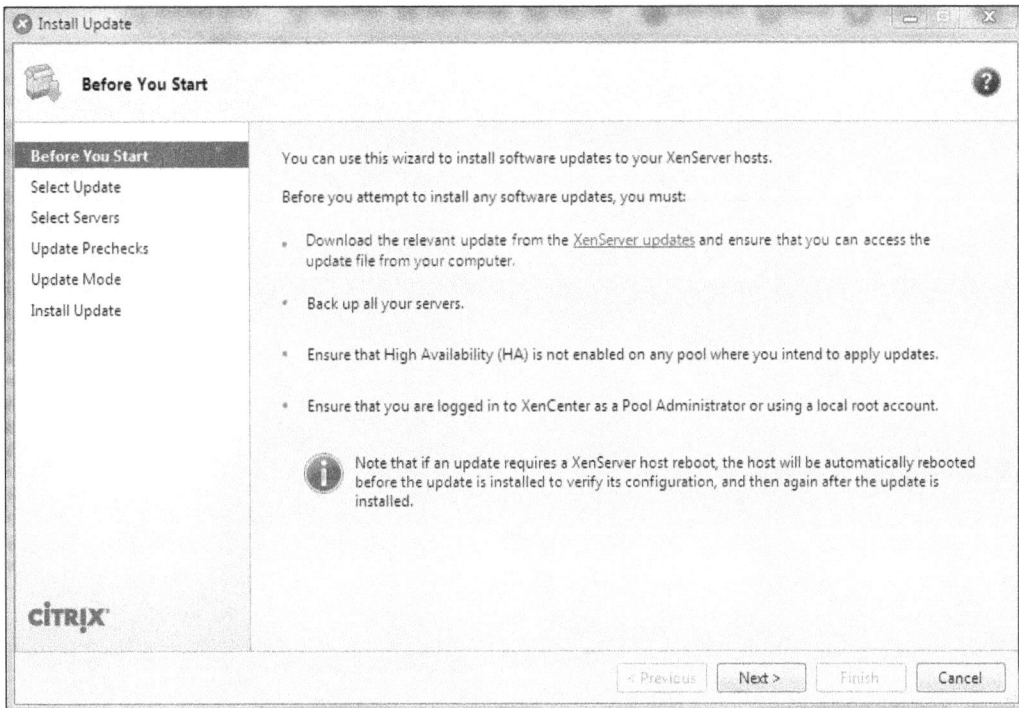

3. Click **Next** to proceed.

4. In the **Choose an existing update to install or upload a new one** dialog, click on **Add,** and then browse to and select the hotfix file that you have downloaded. Once the update file has been added, click on **Next** to continue as shown in the following screenshot:

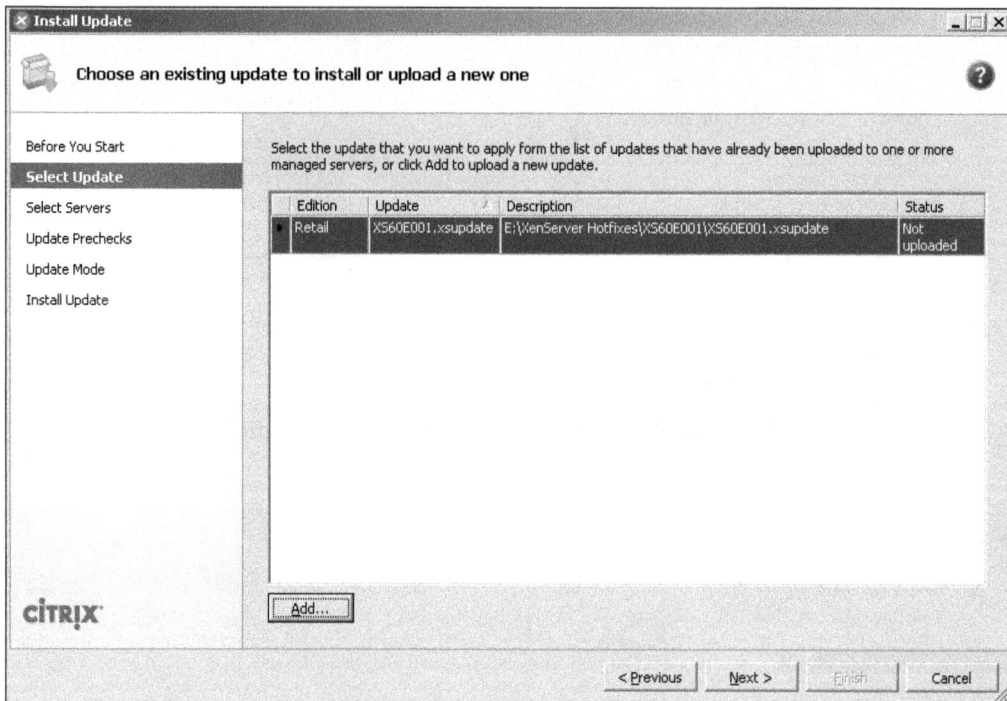

5. Select the servers or the pool that you wish to update and click on **Next**. In this example, for the moment we update only the pool master `xenserver1`.

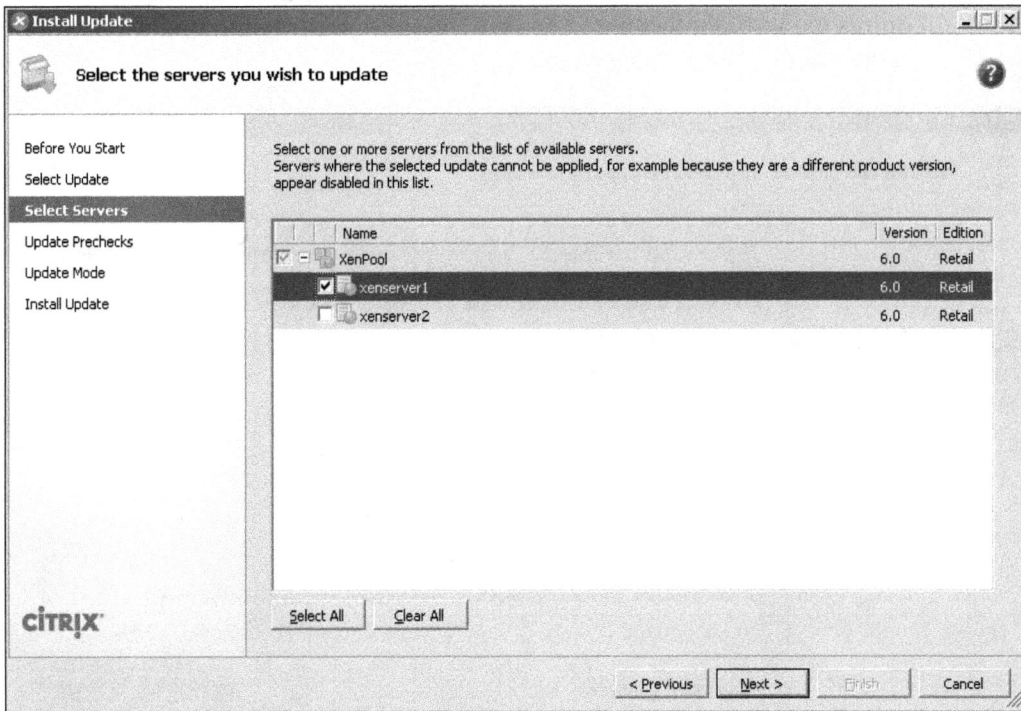

6. Follow the recommendations to resolve any update pre-checks that have failed. In this example, two pre-checks fail because the virtual machine `FreeNAS Server` is not suspended or powered-off, and the update wizard requires the virtual machine to be shut down to perform the update because it cannot be migrated to another host.

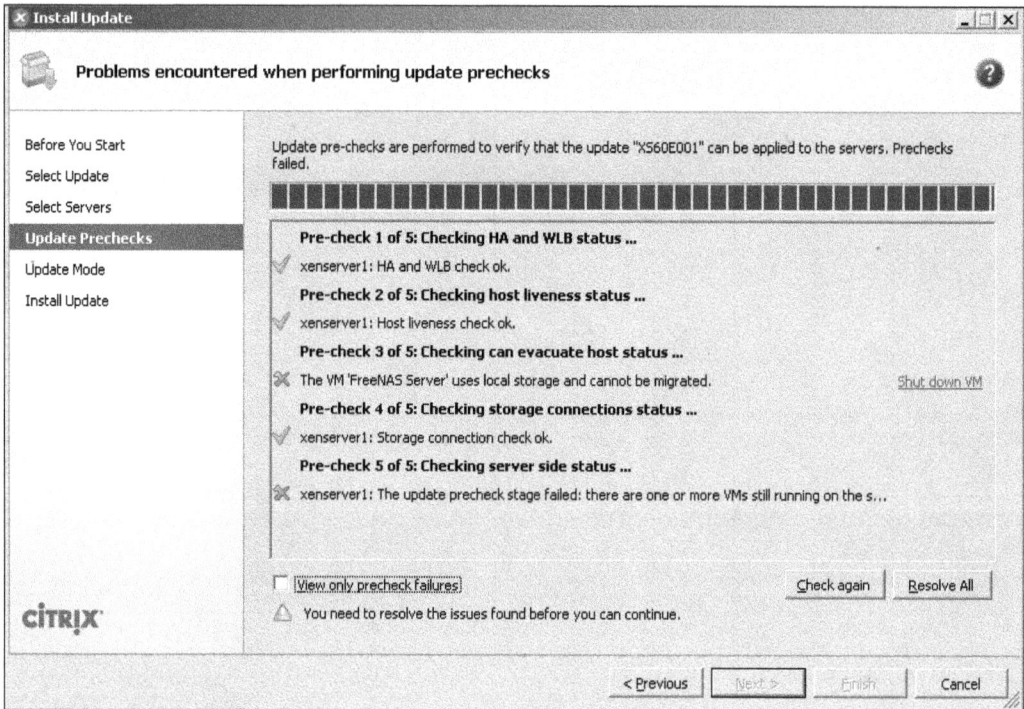

7. If you would like XenCenter to automatically resolve all failed pre-checks, click on **Resolve All**. After all pre-checks have been resolved, click on **Next** to continue as shown in the following screenshot:

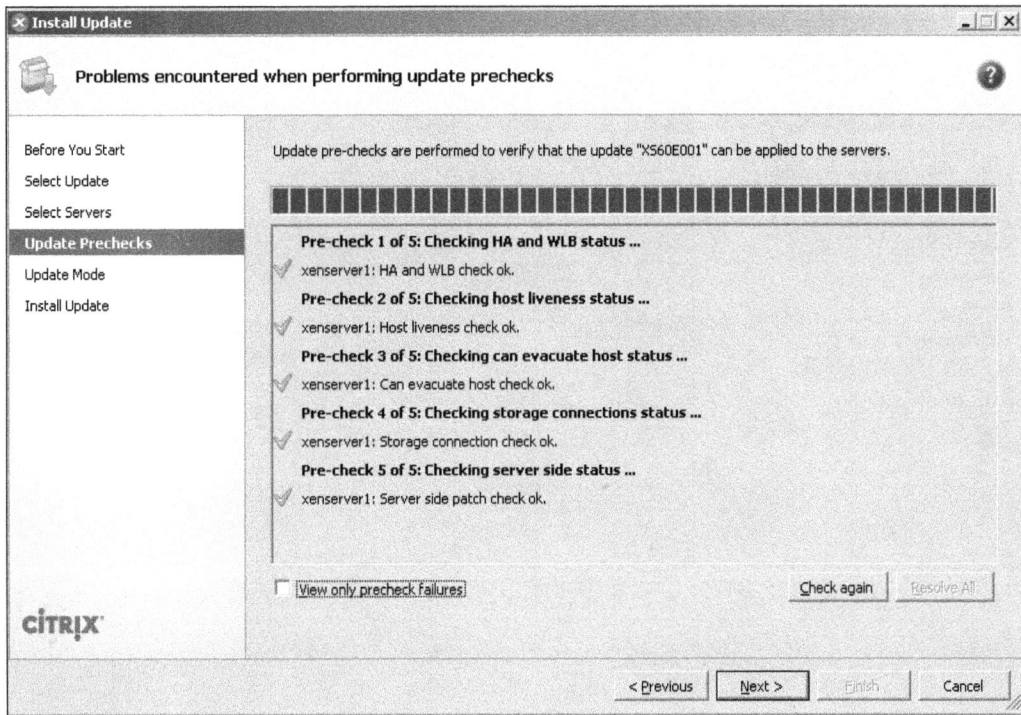

8. Choose between the *automatic* or *manual* update mode. If you choose automatic, XenCenter will perform any post-update actions that may be required, such as rebooting hosts. If you choose manual, you will need to perform the actions manually. The post-update actions required are listed in the **Post-update tasks to be performed** textbox. You can save the actions to a file for future reference.

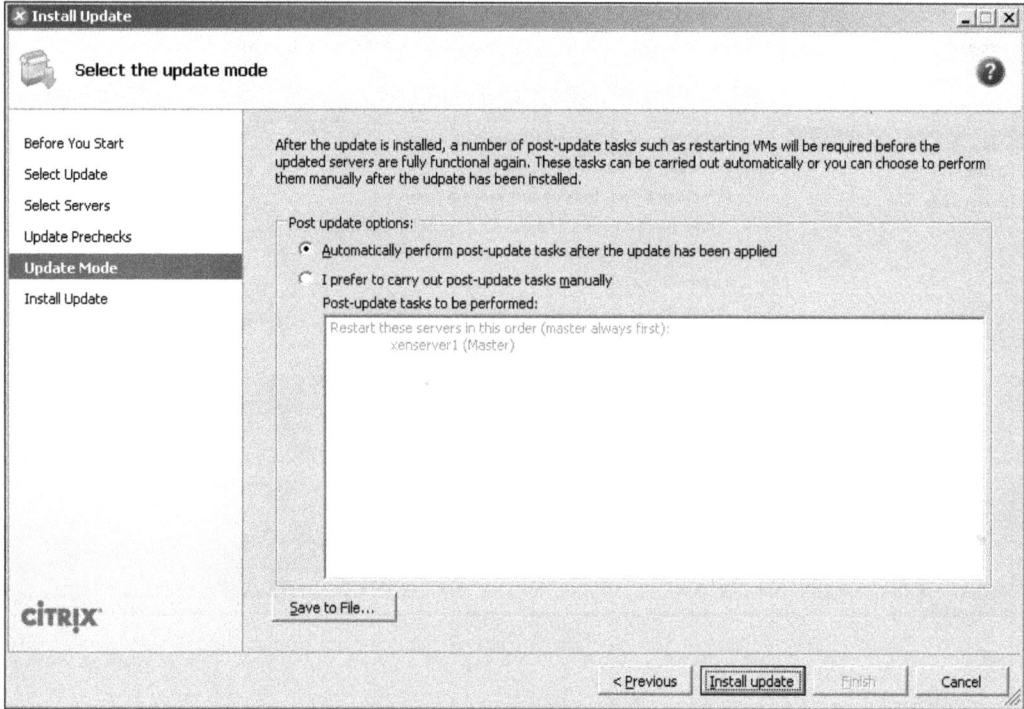

9. Click on **Install update** to proceed with the installation. During the update process, the **Install Update** wizard shows the progress of the update, displaying the major operations that XenCenter performs while updating each host in the pool.

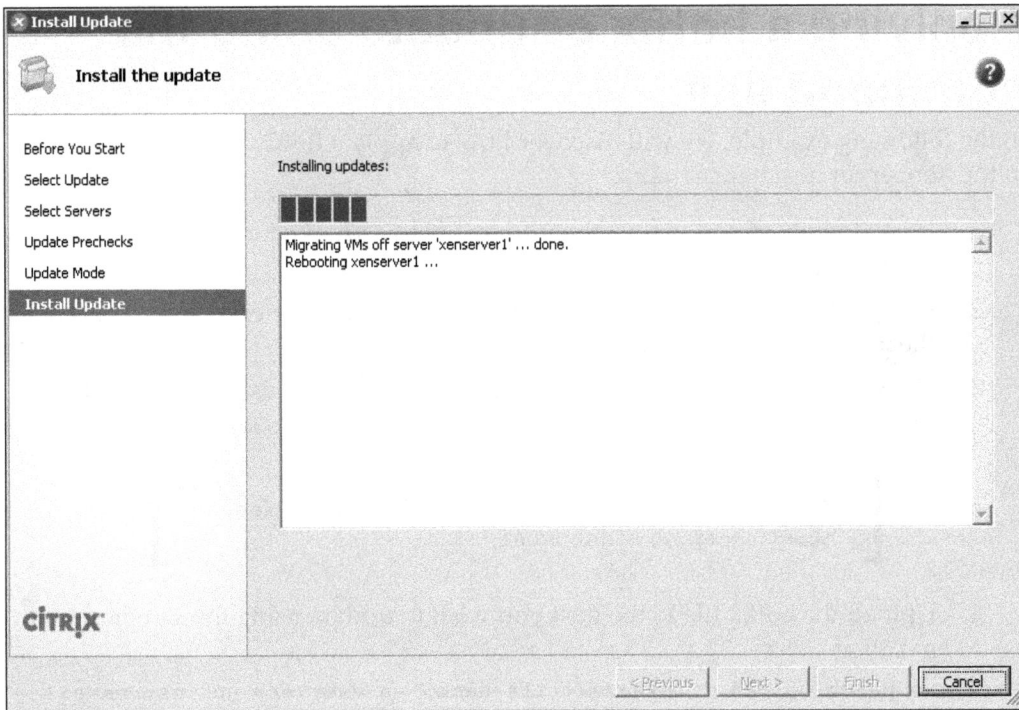

Note that while the pool master is being updated, XenCenter will temporarily lose connection with the pool.

1. Once the update is finished, click on **Finish** to close the **Install Update** wizard.

2. If you have chosen to manually perform post-update actions, perform them in order to complete the update process.

Applying a hotfix or update using the command line

In the following example, we will discover how to apply a hotfix using the xe CLI to the XenServer host `xenserver2`:

1. First, download and extract the update file to a known location on your computer.

2. If High Availability is enabled on the pool, disable it by executing the `xe` command `pool-ha-disable`.

3. Copy the update file to a folder on the XenServer host, using a tool such as `WinSCP`. In this example we copy the file to the path `/home/`.

> You can download the WinSCP tool available at `http://winscp.net`.

4. Upload the hotfix file to the host you wish to update using the `xe` command `patch upload`:

```
xe patch-upload file-name=<file-name> -s <server> -u <username>
-pw <password>
```

where:

- The `file-name` parameter is the path where you have uploaded the hotfix file

- The `server` parameter is the name or IP address of the host where you want to apply the hotfix

- The `username` parameter is the name of the user account that XenServer will use to upload the file

- The `password` parameter is the password related to the user account that you will use to upload the file

In our example, we execute the following command:

```
xe patch-upload file-name=/home/XS60E001.xsupdate -s 192.168.0.2
-u root -pw xenserver
```

XenServer assigns the hotfix file a unique identifier (UUID). We use this UUID for installing the hotfix. In our example, the uuid is 95ac709c-e408-423f-8d22-84b8134a149e.

> As we have seen using XenCenter, if XenServer detects any errors or preparatory steps that have not been taken it informs you. So, follow any guidance before continuing with the update.

5. Now, start the update process using the xe command patch-apply:

   ```
   xe patch-apply host-uuid=<host-uuid> uuid=<hotfix-uuid>
   ```

   where:

   ° The host-uuid parameter is the unique identifier of the XenServer host that you are updating

   ° The uuid parameter is the unique identifier of the hotfix that you have uploaded previously

   In our example, we execute the following command:

   ```
   xe patch-apply host-uuid=5b344339-620c-42f2-b0d1-1b6ad5ec8802
   uuid=95ac709c-e408-423f-8d22-84b8134a149e
   ```

6. After you have applied the hotfix, you can verify that the update has been successfully applied by using the xe command patch-list. If the update has been successful, the hosts (SRO) field contains the host UUID:

```
  xenserver2                                                          Logged in as:  Local root a

 Search │ General │ Memory │ Storage │ Networking │ NICs │ Console │ Performance │ Users │ Logs

 xenserver2 server console


 [root@xenserver2 ~]# xe patch-upload file-name=/home/XS60E001.xsupdate -s 192.16
 8.0.2 -u root -pw xenserver
 95ac709c-e408-423f-8d22-84b8134a149e
 [root@xenserver2 ~]#
```

The command patch-list also informs you about the post-update tasks that you have to perform. The after-apply-guidance (SRO) field in this example instructs you to restart the host.

7. After you have completed the update process, enable again the High Availability feature on your pool with the xe command pool-ha-enable.

Index

DMC 176-178
Dynamic Memory Control. *See* DMC

E

edition parameter 34
editions, XenServer
Citrix XenServer 8
Citrix XenServer Advanced Edition 8
Citrix XenServer Enterprise Edition 8
Citrix XenServer Platinum Edition 8
Enable multipathing on this server check-
box 109
entity 38
Excluded Hosts pane 309

F

FC
about 69
Arbitrated loop (FC-AL) 70
Point-to-Point (FC-P2P) 70
Switched fabric (FC-SW) 70
fencing 236
Fibre Channel. *See* FC

H

HA
about 235
configuring 238
host failures to tolerate concept 236
network heartbeat mechanism 236
overview 235-237
requirement 237
restart priorities, setting 237, 238
storage heartbeat mechanism 236
ha-always-run parameter 245
HA configuration
about 238
Attempt to start next VM after option 241
enabling, xe command line used 244-247
enabling, XenCenter used 239-244
HA Restart Priority option 240
host, managing 248
host, rebooting 248, 249
host, shutting down 248, 249

protected VM, shutting down 250
Start Order option 241
virtual machines, managing 248
Hardware Virtual Machine. *See* HVM
HA Restart Priority option 240
HBA 68
heartbeat-sr-uuids parameter 245
heterogeneous XenServer resource pool
creating 19, 20
High Availability. *See* HA
Home Server page 154
host
managing, HA used 248
Host Bus Adapter. *See* HBA
host-emergency-ha-disable command 249
host failures to tolerate concept 236
Host Health History report 314
Host list box 312
host-uuid parameter 27, 34, 104, 337
hotfix
applying, command line 336, 338
applying, XenCenter used 328-335
HVM 115

I

IETF 69
Import or Export button 167
initial network configuration
about 187, 188
XenServer Pools 188, 189
Install from ISO library or DVD drive
option 120
Install from URL option 121
Install Update wizard 328, 334
Internet Engineering Task Force. *See* IETF
Internet Small Computer System Interface.
See iSCSI
IQNs 82
iSCSI
about 70
hardware initiator 71
software initiator 70
iSCSI Qualified Names. *See* IQNs
iSCSI targets 82

K

key
  activation key 28
  Ctrl key 62
  Tab key 130
  private key 155

L

license-server-address parameter 34
license-server-port parameter 34
Log button 161
Logical Unit Number. *See* LUN
Logical Volume Manager. *See* LVM
LUN 67
LVM 66

M

Maintenance Mode 25
Manage vApps dialog box 167
Maximize Performance mode 306
memory, virtual machine
  DMC 176-178
  managing 179-184
  overview 174-176
mount command 66
multipathing
  about 107, 108
  enabling 109
  enabling, pre-action 108

N

name-label parameter 245
NAS 68
Network File System. *See* NFS
network heartbeat mechanism 236
network types
  about 190
  bonded network 189
  cross-server private network 189
  cross-server private network, conditions
    190
  external network 189
  single-server private network 189

network uuid parameter 209
new-name-description parameter 255
new-name-label parameter 130
new pool master host
  designating 21
New Storage Repository wizard 92
NFS 69
NFS VHD Storage Repository
  configuring 79
NIC bonding 209

O

Off-line Coalesce tool 263
Open Virtual Appliance. *See* OVA
Open vSwitch 214
optimization mode
  about 302
  maximize density 302
  Maximize Performance type 302
optimization recommendations
  Optimization mode 301
  performance metrics 301
Organizationally Unique Identifier (OUI)
    69
OVA 143

P

P2V 116
password parameters 15
pbd-create command 104
PBDs 74
permissions
  Accept WLB Placement Recommendations
    57
  Apply WLB Optimization
    Recommendations 57
  Assign/modify roles 53
  Cancel own tasks 57
  Cancel task of any user 54
  Configure, Initialize, Enable, Disable
    WLB 57
  Connect to pool and read all pool
    metadata 58
  Create/dismiss alerts 54
  Display WLB Configuration 57
  Generate WLB Reports 57

[PACKT] enterprise
professional expertise distilled
PUBLISHING

Thank you for buying
Citrix XenServer 6.0 Administration
Essential Guide

About Packt Publishing

Packt, pronounced 'packed', published its first book "Mastering phpMyAdmin for Effective MySQL Management" in April 2004 and subsequently continued to specialize in publishing highly focused books on specific technologies and solutions.

Our books and publications share the experiences of your fellow IT professionals in adapting and customizing today's systems, applications, and frameworks. Our solution based books give you the knowledge and power to customize the software and technologies you're using to get the job done. Packt books are more specific and less general than the IT books you have seen in the past. Our unique business model allows us to bring you more focused information, giving you more of what you need to know, and less of what you don't.

Packt is a modern, yet unique publishing company, which focuses on producing quality, cutting-edge books for communities of developers, administrators, and newbies alike. For more information, please visit our website: www.packtpub.com.

About Packt Enterprise

In 2010, Packt launched two new brands, Packt Enterprise and Packt Open Source, in order to continue its focus on specialization. This book is part of the Packt Enterprise brand, home to books published on enterprise software – software created by major vendors, including (but not limited to) IBM, Microsoft and Oracle, often for use in other corporations. Its titles will offer information relevant to a range of users of this software, including administrators, developers, architects, and end users.

Writing for Packt

We welcome all inquiries from people who are interested in authoring. Book proposals should be sent to author@packtpub.com. If your book idea is still at an early stage and you would like to discuss it first before writing a formal book proposal, contact us; one of our commissioning editors will get in touch with you.

We're not just looking for published authors; if you have strong technical skills but no writing experience, our experienced editors can help you develop a writing career, or simply get some additional reward for your expertise.

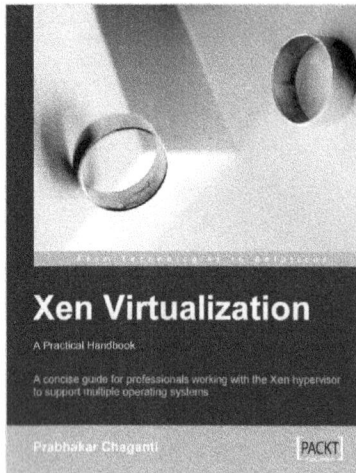

Xen Virtualization

ISBN: 978-1-84719-248-6   Paperback: 148 pages

A concise guide for professionals working with the Xen hypervisor to support multiple operating systems

1. Installing and configuring Xen

2. Managing and administering Xen servers and virtual machines

3. Setting up networking, storage, and encryption

4. Backup and migration

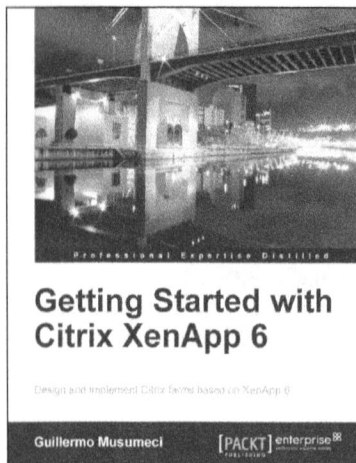

Getting Started with Citrix XenApp 6

ISBN: 978-1-84968-128-5   Paperback: 444 pages

Design and implement Citrix farms based on XenApp 6

1. Use Citrix management tools to publish applications and resources on client devices with this book and eBook

2. Deploy and optimize XenApp 6 on Citrix XenServer, VMware ESX, and Microsoft Hyper-V virtual machines and physical servers

3. Understand new features included in XenApp 6 and review Citrix farms terminology and concepts

Please check **www.PacktPub.com** for information on our titles

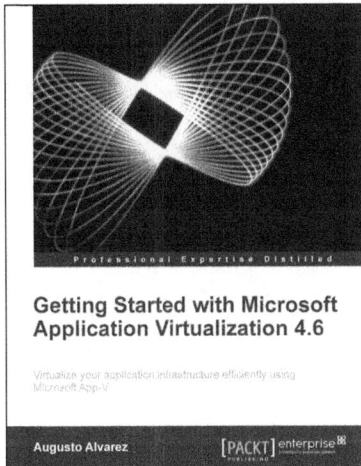

Getting Started with Microsoft Application Virtualization 4.6

ISBN: 978-1-84968-126-1   Paperback: 308 pages

Virtualize your application infrastructure efficiently using Microsoft App-V

1. Publish, deploy, and manage your virtual applications with App-V

2. Understand how Microsoft App-V can fit into your company

3. Guidelines for planning and designing an App-V environment

4. Step-by-step explanations to plan and implement the virtualization of your application infrastructure

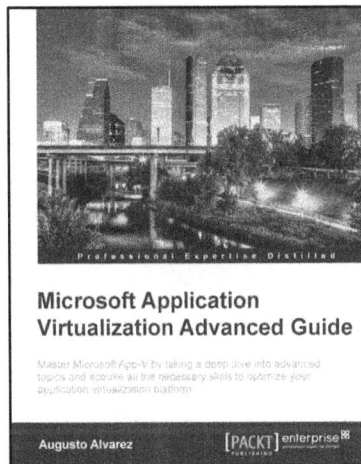

Microsoft Application Virtualization Advanced Guide

ISBN: 978-1-84968-448-4   Paperback: 474 pages

Master Microsoft App-V by taking a deep dive into advanced topics and acquire all the necessary skills to optimize your application virtualization platform

1. Understand advanced topics in App-V; identify some rarely known components and options available in the platform

2. Acquire advanced guidelines on how to troubleshoot App-V installations, sequencing, and application deployments

3. Virtualize server applications by using the upcoming platform Server App-V

Please check **www.PacktPub.com** for information on our titles

9 781849 686167